DOSTOEVSKY
and ROMANTIC REALISM

A STUDY OF DOSTOEVSKY
IN RELATION TO BALZAC, DICKENS,
AND GOGOL

DONALD FANGER

Phoenix Books

THE UNIVERSITY OF CHICAGO PRESS

CHICAGO & LONDON

ISBN: 0-226-23747-8

Library of Congress Catalog Card Number: 65-13841

The University of Chicago Press, Chicago

Phoenix Edition 1967

Second Impression 1974

Printed in the United States of America

TO MY PARENTS

Preface

LABELS — even the most happily chosen — are approximations, useful only if they are recognized as such and successful to the degree that they can suggest the complexities of the things they stand for. Since we cannot do without them, we can only keep trying to refine and sharpen. The label that this book proposes has been used before, but only as a casual paradox: as every schoolboy knows, there was, in the nineteenth century, first romanticism and then realism. Balzac was a realist, Dickens was a realist, Gogol turned realist as he matured, and Dostoevsky was, in his own words, "a realist in a higher sense." The quarrels that have multiplied over these propositions in recent years show the need for more exact terms — and a closer look at the history of the novel makes it clear that a whole stage in its nineteenth-century development, which up to now has been uneasily called romanticism or realism, is really marked by a fusion of the two.

"Romantic realism," in short, is not a paradox and can be made to seem one only by forgetting the historical relation between the terms — the fact that nineteenth-century realism evolved out of romanticism. The hybrid term thus indicates a particular stage of that evolution. But it would hardly be worth using if that were all it did: "early realism" might do as well. What I try to show in this book is that the work of four great writers — Balzac, Dickens, Gogol, and Dostoevsky — can be understood better in terms of this concept than of any other, that with its help we can see in them not "deviationists" from a familiar canon, but exemplars in their own right of a particular attitude toward the art of fiction, a broadly shared rationale and body of technique. In this light, the very elements they borrowed from the Gothic novel, the boulevard novel, the penny-dreadful, and the roman-feuilleton cease to appear the crudities they were once taken to be and become, instead, characteristics of a contemporary world that romantic realism deliberately and seriously re-created to interpret. Each of these writers, in his conscious concern to render the concrete life of a given time and place, was a realist, but each pursued this concern through a highly and openly personal vision. Dostoevsky proclaimed as much when he called his method "fantastic realism," Dickens when he spoke in the preface to *Bleak House* of having "dwelt purposely upon the romantic side of familiar things," Balzac when he characterized a whole aspect of his work with the statement, "Everything there is myth and figure." (Gogol, the most elusive of them all, never spoke clearly about his art or seemed sure what he was up to in the best of it; yet the visionary quality is extreme on almost every page of his work.)

It is fashionable now to seek the visionary and the mythmaker in every writer, yet the fact remains that these were the visionaries and mythmakers of the novel par excellence. Their common theme, in its newness and formlessness, required them to be: vision was necessary to encompass it, myth to give it order. That theme, at its most general, is the great modern city — Paris, London, Petersburg — whose transformation was going on before their eyes, signaling the end of "nature" and the "natural life," and the beginning of "modernity." They built their myths by returning to it obsessively, in a variety of essays, from a variety of angles, their obsessive concern being with the character of this new urban life, with what happened to the traditional staples of human nature when placed in an unnatural setting and subjected to pressures, many of them new in kind and all of them new in degree. The results — strangeness, alienation, crime, *as matters of fact* — explain much of the common technical inventory: a carefully fostered sense of mystery (atmosphere), of grotesquerie, a penchant for stark contrasts, for the improbable, the sensational, the dramatic. Technique and theme, in short, go hand in hand, and both are directly connected with urban social history. We need a study of that connection, but it would make a book in itself, and until such may be undertaken with the thoroughness it deserves, I have felt simple acknowledgment to be better than facile generalization. Romantic realism was an organic expression of its milieu, literary and historical; and a single study may indicate its ramifications, but hardly explore them all.

This book, then, is about a kind of fiction that was developed separately by Balzac, Dickens, and Gogol and that culminated in the obviously different but obviously related writing of Dostoevsky. The very differences that we shall remark among the first three clarify much in the work of their great inheritor, whose achievement in turn lends perspective to theirs. Because so much has already been written about Balzac and Dickens, I have treated them in chapters that are analytic surveys, designed to get at what is, for my purposes, the heart of their method. Gogol, anomalous in any context, stands out in the present one by being considered only as the writer of a cycle of short stories, his Petersburg tales: formally, he fits the scheme of the book only tangentially, but his credentials for inclusion are so substantial nonetheless that to exclude him on these grounds would be to exalt the ideal of tidiness out of all proportion. The chapters on Dostoevsky are, by contrast, more detailed and numerous — not because our criticism has neglected him, but because its angles of approach have been in general limited. So it has seemed necessary, on the one hand, to argue his place in the tradition of romantic realism at greater length and, on the other, to buttress the argument with sizeable extracts from some of his hitherto untranslated work: thus the relative emphasis of the title, "Dostoevsky and Romantic Realism."

For patient guidance, philosophy, and friendship before and during the writing of this study, I stand in grateful debt to the late and much-missed Renato Poggioli and to Harry Levin: without their precept and example it is no exaggeration to say that this book would probably never have been undertaken. To Mark Schorer, who first helped me to think more seriously and more clearly about the novel, thanks of the same order are due and here rendered. E. J. Brown and Juan López-Morillas read the manuscript and made valuable suggestions for its improvement, as did Grigory Abramovich Byaly of Leningrad University.

I should also like to express my appreciation to Brown University, whose General Faculty Research Reserve Fund helped generously in the preparation of this volume for publication. My thanks also to the editors of the *Slavic Review* for permission to reprint

Chapter 5, which appeared in abbreviated form in the September 1963 issue.

The greater the debt, the more difficult the acknowledgment. To my wife, then, an inadequate word of appreciation will have to do for her numberless gifts of aid, comfort, cheer, and perspective when all were wanting.

D. F.

Providence, Rhode Island

Contents

NOTE ON TRANSLITERATION AND TRANSLATION

Transliteration from Russian into English presents a constant series of dilemmas: one system will help the reader unfamiliar with Russian to approximate a correct pronunciation, but never without some violence to Cyrillic orthography; another will make it easy to reconstruct the original word or name in its Cyrillic form — but frequently at the price of strangeness to the reader who has only English, and sometimes at the price of utter phonetic paralysis. On the theory that the reader who already knows Russian will have no trouble identifying the original form of any transliterated matter, I have in the pages that follow opted for the nonspecialist system used by D. S. Mirsky in his *History of Russian Literature,* the sole exception being made for Dostoevsky (to whom Mirsky would give another *y*). Transliterated words in parentheses or brackets are given in the nominative form.

All translations, except as indicated, are my own; for the sake of easy reference, however, Dostoevsky's titles have been left in Constance Garnett's familiar renderings.

I

THE ROMANTIC REALISTS

And everywhere there is connexion, everywhere there is illustration: no single event, no single literature, is adequately comprehended except in relation to other events, to other literatures.

Matthew Arnold, "On the Modern Element in Literature"

1

Realism, Pure and Romantic

FEW literary terms have suggested more and signaled less than "realism." Originally a philosophical concept supporting the existence of platonic categories; later a casual neologism invented to characterize Rembrandt's refusal to idealize his subjects; in the mid-nineteenth century the rallying cry of a group of French novelists, which paradoxically outlived their novels and their method; in Soviet Russia a strange and constricting orthodoxy — the word persists, and with it the conviction that, if taken out of the hands of dogmatists and sectarians, it may still best describe a special kind of representation of a special artistic vision. Thus in a book significantly entitled *L'Epoque réaliste,* the writer is nonetheless moved to observe that the word realist does have a meaning when applied to Rabelais or Molière, Le Sage or Rétif de la Bretonne, Balzac or Flaubert, the Goncourts or Maupassant — from which he concludes that literary history is duty-bound to seek out the most general sense of the word and to compare "this essential realism with that of an age that claimed, not without injustice, to hold a monopoly on it." [1]

Realism, that is to say, may be considered in two ways: as a discrete *mode,* existing since antiquity, or as the product of a more recent historical *moment,* to be explained solely within the confines of its literary history. The present attempt partakes of both. In seeking to establish the nature of a kind of bedrock fictional realism, it seeks a norm by which to characterize the numerous varieties and offshoots that literary history may catalogue — and notably the one that may be labeled "romantic." But it is oriented, ultimately, toward the realism (or realisms) of the nineteenth century in Europe, because it is only then that the mode became dominant in both senses of the word, as a fully developed *way* of writing and as a fashion before which all others bowed. The sketch that follows, then, while eschewing any strict historical tracing, aims at catching the subsisting mode of modern realism in the intersection of two searchlights, the one based in the mid-nineteenth century and the other in classical poetics.

Classical times, with the exception of Petronius' fragmentary *Satyricon,* have left us no body of realistic fiction, and yet the starting point of the evolution of realism must be sought in antiquity because classical poetics bequeathed to posterity something perhaps more important even than a body of work: a way of thinking about literary art, a hierarchy of forms, styles, and values. Epic and tragedy ranked at the top of the list, since both treated of the destinies of men on that borderline where human greatness and divinity confronted one another. For such subjects of basic human concern the grand style was prescribed, where the majesty of the action was matched by the beauty of words; where — as Sidney observed of all poetry — nothing is false because nothing is affirmed; and where the illusion produced was justified by its intensity and not at all by its referential precision. Toward the other end of the scale, comedy, a far less consequential literary genre, could concern itself with low (everyday) subjects and render them in the low (colloquial, referential, even scurrilous) style.[2] The basic work of comedy was and is an irreverent look at what society agrees to regard as reality, the deflation of all kinds of idealistic pretensions by confronting them with all that our Anglo-American culture means by "the facts of life." Thus realism first evolved as a tendency of the comic, because only in this area could its own tendencies be legitimized. For a long time it would not lose the marks of this inheritance; indeed, it can be argued that it never has.

Well into the eighteenth century, accordingly, while serious, problematic, or tragic subjects were generally reserved for elegant treatment in one of the elevated genres, the old "low" subjects were relegated not only to the comparative indignity of popular prose, but to the bastard genre of fiction, to picaresque tales where the language might be racy, the characters and their depiction crude, the matter composed of adventures and excursions. In these tales the hero is generally lowborn; his adventures, though often rendered in convincingly realistic detail, are full of practical jokes and disguises (those conventional props of comic intrigue); and his attitude is most often one of irreverence toward all the sanctities.

Even works that did most to dignify realistic fiction, *Don Quixote* and, two centuries later, *Tom Jones,* developed their realism within the comic tradition, departing from colloquial language only to mock the loftier diction of other genres, symbolizing the new place of knight errantry and epic heroes by a crazy old man and a good-natured, passive bastard. It is not without significance that Richardson found the latter work to be "coarse-titled," or that many readers of the time found its realistic depiction of English life low and immoral. In fact, this inheritance in the line of low subjects extends through the nineteenth century, where in France the self-proclaimed *réalistes* of the 1850s placed it in the center of that campaign of self-advertisement which did so much to confuse the meaning of the word.

In a series of manifestos by Champfleury, Duranty, and others, they called for the de-poetization of fiction, for the painting of the unvarnished truth of the world around them; but the restricting implications of these calls were the only ones their fiction actually realized. One such implication, of course, is that the unvarnished truth is to be sought in those areas of social life that society has contrived to gloss over in the first place. Another is the peculiarly narrow construction they placed on the notion of the world around them. The resulting emphasis is identical; it is suggested by the habitual association of *réaliste* with *bohème,* by the very title of Murger's *Scènes de la vie de Bohème*. In this earlier phase, the public and the critics, turning to the novels of the group, no longer found the ordinary fictional heroes and heroines, but bohemians and grisettes; they found, seasoned with reassuring stretches of poetic platitudes and sentimental passages, titillatingly risqué pictures. They could find virtue in the author's sincerity and spice in the "low" side of the work.[3] Even when the scene shifted from Parisian low life to small-town mores, the focus was the same. Courbet, around whose painting the doctrine of realism crystallized even before Champfleury adapted it to fiction, outraged accepted notions of the spirituality of art by seeking "le vulgaire et le moderne," in paintings like *The Interment at Ornans,* where death and religion serve only as a pretext for a minutely exact rendering of the grotesque aspects of his fellow citizens. Champfleury defended this descent of the painter to the level of his subjects: "Is it the painter's fault if material interests and the pettiness of provincial life sink their claws into these faces, extinguish the eyes, line the forehead, make the mouth stupid? That's the way the bourgeois are." [4] Here as elsewhere the novelty that seemed so absolute was only relative. It gave the appearance of revealing a new truth because it treated an area currently disdained by artists and writers — or, rather, it treated this area in a new way. What had been the province of comedy, of satire or of the picaresque, was now receiving a more equivocal treatment — in Champfleury's words, "serious and convinced, ironic and brutal." [5] The first two adjectives represent the new element; the second two, the comic inheritance with which it was merged. The mixture, like that of the sublime and the grotesque which Hugo championed in his *Préface de Cromwell,* was claimed as the only one fit to render modernity. The point to observe here is, amid the journalistic and fictional work of the *réalistes,* their fidelity to the traditional province of comedy and, even as they sought to transform its treatment, their persistent attraction toward its means — irony and caricature.

For such a range of subjects, realism inherited a similar range of styles; and in this case the classical decorum specifying them is only a recognition of the axiom which says that the means for any task must be commensurate with it. In the *Satyricon,* Trimalchio's feast might have been rendered in less colloquial language and still qualify as comedy — but it could not have been otherwise rendered without the sacrifice of its realism. Once legitimize the accurate description of a vulgar scene and you require the use either of the language its participants would have spoken or of a language that does not do violence to its objects; that is, a diction for dialogue that is "the real language of ordinary men" and a diction for narration that is concrete and plain. The language of realism seeks to present the object with maximum clarity and a minimum of emotional or stylistic deformation. Its task, in Conrad's words, "is to make you hear, to make you feel — it is, before all, to make you *see*. That — and no more, and it is everything." [6]

according to Ruskin ie reading of human attributes into nature

To make primary the reader's ability to see accurately, the realistic writer must avoid what one may call the pathetic fallacy, if that term be broadened to include human beings and human situations as well: that is to say, he must extract emotion from his narrative and not simply pour it in. A lyrical effect, by this standard, is not ruled out, but it must be made consonant with what comes before and after — it must appear as something other than the illusion-shattering intervention of the novelist's own ego. For while the visionary picture of the world may include prosaic details, the matter-of-fact picture may not include poetic elements without "debunking" them, without reverting completely to the comic tradition, as Cervantes and Fielding both do for purposes of parody.

Thus, in a realistic novel, lyrical material has to be attributed or attributable to a character — a procedure that keeps it under narrative control, keeps it *judged,* as all the material of a novel is implicitly judged by its author. It is the rendering of objects in their essential quiddity that is the goal of the realistic method. And this raises a semantic problem, for whereas the concern of earlier writers of nonrealistic fiction was "not primarily . . . with the correspondence of words to things, but rather with the extrinsic beauties which could be bestowed upon description and action by the use of rhetoric," [7] the realist had to seek just that correspondence of words to things. Small wonder that in the nineteenth century the opponents of realism objected to the dethroning of stylistic beauty, as they understood it, and to the introduction of terms that serious literature had excluded as vulgarisms or technical barbarisms. A new criterion of beauty, appropriate to the realistic mode, was a long time in forming. Croce put it succinctly in finding the beautiful in art to be that which is perfectly expressive.

But the function of anything is definable only in terms of the strategy or conception it serves. What is the fundamental conception, the aesthetic strategy, of realism? The usual beginning is to skirt tautology in defining realism as the artistic method that aims at "the faithful and complete rendition of reality" — with reality identified by "a kind of Benthamite doctrine that the most real is that which is experienced by the greatest number." [8] The reference to Bentham (it might as well have been to Comte, so far as nineteenth-century realism is concerned), though useful for indicating the metaphysical and popular biases of realism, seems gratuitous and misleading. It may be more to the point to observe with Edouard Maynial that realism has historically been "a literature of opposition," and not only in the last century.[9] Like any latecomer among literary techniques, it has had to define itself against the guiding strategies and etiquettes of more established conventions. And it has had, willy-nilly, to seek its "reality" in one of two ways: either by going outside the boundaries of "higher" art for its subjects (say the Bohemia of the French *réalistes*) or by invading those boundaries and discovering within them a truth that other treatments had ignored or concealed.

Both ways reveal the mark of the comic inheritance, the second more fundamentally because the contrast of appearance with reality has been a prime comic function since Aristophanes. The process, which forms the plots of most of the great novels of the nineteenth century, might be summed up in the juxtaposition of two of their titles — *Great Expectations* and *Lost Illusions*. It is recorded as well in the life histories of most of the important realists. Thus Harry Levin has observed that every realist may be seen as "a reformed idealist, whose commentary is to be deduced from the ideals he has lived down." [10] To this one might add the contention that almost every great realist has been a great ironist, deflating with more seriousness and more regret than his purely comic counterparts the more hallowed social beliefs. The place of irony in the work of Stendhal, Flaubert, Maupassant, Tolstoy, and others is obvious enough. Similarly, Tolstoy's favorite ironic device, which Victor Shklovsky has called "making-strange" (*ostranenie*), may be seen as a time-honored comic device turned to new uses. More or less mutedly, and with more or less qualification, Stendhal's repeated reaction to the testing of some great expectation — "Quoi! n'est-ce que cela?" — might stand as emblematic of the ubiquitous theme of lost illusions. The prototype in the field of the comic novel is of course *Don Quixote*; with the comedy gone and the irony alone remaining, he reappears travestied as Emma Bovary, who seeks vainly, in the prototype of the realistic novel, to establish the truth of the romances of her time in the provincial world around her.

Flaubert's novel and the other nineteenth-century examples cited suggest a further hallmark of realism in their concern with contemporaneity. Comedy, in its realistic tendency, had always worked with the familiar detail of contemporary mores; it has even been suggested that, as opposed to the idealizing and abstracting tendencies of tragedy, such a concern is a prerequisite of the genre.[11] For all its revolutionary implications, it is a short step for realism to move on in this direction to a concern with the representative minutiae of a given place and time, as a means of representing a particular social reality in its uniqueness. The title pages of nineteenth-century realism's typical productions illustrate this, from Balzac's *L'Envers de l'histoire contemporaine* through Stendhal's *Le Rouge et le noir: Chronique du XIXe siècle* to Trollope's *The Way We Live Now.* And in so doing they emphasize the crucial role of society in the realistic novel — no longer a norm against which to measure individual comic aberrations, but a subject calling in its own right for investigation; not only a milieu, but an aspect of character, so that a twentieth-century novelist, Lawrence, could speak with profound relevance to the problems of his art of the double nature of every character, his "individual being" and its antagonist, his "social being." [12]

What made this concern with current history revolutionary was the seriousness with which it was undertaken, a seriousness founded on the assumption that the classical faith in universal truths was untenable without the anticlassical embodiment of these generalities in specific and persuasive forms, in exhaustively recreated times and places. In these representations, the typical might be found: but it would be locally typical, and the type would have to be not simply identified, but discovered. Typicality, that is, could lie not on the surface, but only at the heart of a living character or situation.[13]

The seriousness of this belief meant taking the character as well as the milieu seriously, and here the break with comic tradition is most evident. Comedy found types in the unrelieved presence of certain traits; realism would embed these traits in a total personality to give them a new context and a new individual perspective. A name — from *Moll Flanders* through *Anna Karenina* — is a favorite device for entitling a realistic novel: it suggests a unique phenomenon, an unrepeatable individual. The sort of typicality that may be disengaged from such entities is the opposite of mechanical; it tends rather toward the symbolic, and it marks, as Thibaudet argues, the summit of realist achievement. Realism, he contends, takes on the value of art only when its details are significant to the point of resonating with suggestion: "A realistic work attains its perfect artistic level when, from its intense truth, we pass naturally and necessarily to a great symbolic intuition," and it is precisely this symbolic value that distinguishes great, or epic, realism from *le réalisme anecdotique.*[14] This is to suggest that the comment, the significance of the work, must be implicit in the material chosen. It explains, for example, Tolstoy's answer to charges of prolixity in *Anna Karenina:* "If I wanted to express in words all that I meant to say with the novel, I would have to write the same novel I wrote, from the beginning." [15] What is paramount is the illusion of life, and it gains in intensity when the hand of the arranger is invisible, when, in Baudelaire's phrase, the writer presents "things as they are, or rather, as they would be, supposing that he did not exist." [16]

In such an abstractly defined realism, then, there is a hermetic quality, and it attaches to the total import of the work. The work yields its significance only to the attentive reader whose understanding of the problems involved — in the widest sense — allows him to disengage it. "The writer," Madame de Staël wrote, "forms his public"; so does a group of writers working in roughly the same direction. When, in the nineteenth century, critics reacted to works of realism as gratuitous vulgarity, or sensuality, or simply as compilations of "useless" detail, they were often merely expressing their own bafflement before a new convention. But behind the bafflement lay a question that "le réalisme anecdotique," if not "le grand réalisme," seemed to beg, and this was whether realism did in fact have any relation to art.

The question can arise, of course, in the presence of a second-rate production in any genre — but not quite with the same force. A poem is judged by the degree to which it satisfies the general standards of poetry, and there can be no other criterion of its worth. But a realistic novel of the second order may have little to distinguish it from reportage — and yet be defended on the grounds of its reportorial accuracy and importance. This is what the early *réalistes* did, but if they were right in seeing realism as a polemic weapon, a kind of literary puritanism or fundamentalism, they nonetheless failed to understand that, while it shows its greatest legitimacy as a means, it displays its greatest limitations when taken as an end. All this is succinctly formulated by Maupassant, in a statement that goes far toward characterizing the "purely" realistic mode in its highest nineteenth-century form:

In short, if yesterday's novelist chose to tell about the crises of life, its heightened spiritual and emotional states, the novelist of today writes the history of the heart, the soul and the mind in their normal state. To produce the effect he seeks, that is, the feeling of simple reality, and to bring out the artistic lesson he would draw from it, that is, the revelation of what contemporary man really is to him, he will have to employ facts of a constant and unimpeachable veracity. . . . The achievement of such a goal [*faire vrai* — the untranslatable opposite of "make believe"] consists, then, in giving the complete illusion of the real, following the ordinary logic of facts, and not in transcribing them slavishly in the pell-mell of their occurrence.[17]

Here Maupassant is suggesting that *any* sphere of life may serve the realistic novelist; and the emphasis accorded normal psychological states, in its turn, serves to focus attention on what is most common in common experience — not for its own sake, but for the sake of the closer knowledge it may provide of contemporary man. What is demanded is an imaginative synthesis of the facts of life in a particular society at a particular moment, in which imaginative selection of "facts of a constant and unimpeachable veracity" is the means, but the synthesis itself is the end, "the complete illusion of the real." The banishment of plot in the sense of complicated intrigue, hinted in the opening sentence, is underscored in the last by the reference to the ordinary logic of facts — which is, however, distinguished from the kind of stenography by which some earlier French protorealists avoided the problems and the higher dignity of art.[18] This, the ordinary logic of facts, has always to be made manifest beneath their simple sequence; and the manifestation, for the novelist, is always dictated by "the lesson he would draw from it."

If the main lines of this discussion so far are correct, many of the traditional confusions surrounding "realism" become explicable. As in the case of romanticism, we have with realism the problem of a term that arose *ad hoc,* partly as a polemic device around which a disparate group of literary malcontents slowly rallied, partly as a term of opprobrium thrown by literary reactionaries at a trend they feared. First of all, then, the word was a catchword, a publicity slogan — which, like so many, was taken into usage before it had much of a meaning.[19] But it has had another existence as well, in which it designates not a school but a mode of writing, a level of style proper to a certain lowness of subject, a style that might inform occasional passages in works of quite alien conception to produce a salutary contrast or perhaps underline a pathetic situation. (Amid the ruins of his grandeur, King Lear's "Pray you undo this button" might stand as an example.) But when the mode comes to dictate the form of a complete work, new confusions arise: even then, from among the three main variables in our scheme — style, subject, and conception — only one or two might be present. Thus *Les Misérables* qualifies for the realistic label by its subject, but only occasionally by its style and only equivocally in its conception.

The possibilities of mixture suggest a need to qualify the term, and it is to give these qualifications a sense that a "pure" conception of realism has been attempted here. If it fits most readily the works of novelists past the middle of the last century, it may remind us of the more problematic first half of the century, the period of confusion between neoclassic and romantic canons, in which realism first flowered. The next chapters will consider Balzac, Dickens, and Gogol, whose work constitutes a separate episode in the development of realism. This episode I have called romantic realism, a concept that requires some explanation in its own right.

If pure realism as it developed in the second half of the nineteenth century largely represented a reaction against the romantic credo and style, the qualified realism of the first half of the century was born precisely from that romanticism and shared many of its impulses. Georges Pellissier, in a book devoted to one side of this story, stressed the basic ways in which romanticism was what we would call realistic. "If," he argued, "one were to say that romanticism's role was to substitute the particular for the general and the characteristic for the beautiful, such a definition would mark its realistic tendency without lessening its fundamental opposition to neoclassical rationalism." [20] Literary terminology in the France of the 1820s tended to bear this out in making the words *romantisme* and *réalisme* practically interchangeable in the press of the day.[21] Nor was this only a French phenomenon. Wordsworth's concentration on "the real language of men," his care to individuate, to present his objects with scrupulous accuracy, tended in the same direction, though with a proviso that characterizes much of the romantic concern with particularity: "Objects," he wrote in 1816, "derive their influence not from properties inherent in them, not from what they are actually in themselves, but from such as are bestowed upon them by the minds of those who are conversant with or affected by those objects." [22]

In this cardinal romantic tenet of the bestowing power of the imagination lies the center of romantic realism. The Flaubertian notion of the realist's duty to efface all possible signs of his presence in the narration is a later one, which accords well with the *parti pris* of disillusionment and the consequent ironic tendency to let the characters damn themselves, so to speak, out of their own mouths. But if Flaubert and his contemporaries were "reformed idealists," Balzac and Dickens were still unreformed idealists, inclined to see the world, for all its detail, in terms of one or more primary colors, in terms of energy, will, passion, or sentiment. They would base themselves in observed or observable reality, claiming it as warrant for the extravagances of the stories they used. Balzac even notes in one of his most wildly melodramatic and sensational novels how the reality behind the daily *faits divers* can embarrass the novelist by its unlikely richness, thus laying on him the obligation "not to spoil reality by imposing a false dramatic form on it — especially when reality has taken the trouble to imitate fiction [de devenir romanesque]." The reality of social life, he goes on, "especially in Paris," is such that it is constantly outstripping "the imagination of inventors." In short, "the boldness of reality rises to combinations so implausible or indecent that they are forbidden to art unless the writer soften them, prune them, expurgate them." [23] A key word here is "especially," with its implications that a reality less colorful might call for an imaginative reconstruction that the contemporary scene renders unnecessary. How far Balzac intended the implication is irrelevant: what is of central importance is the conclusion that reality is to be portrayed as romanesque and that, accordingly, the embryonic conventions of such a portrayal are to be canonized.

The contrast with the romantic novel par excellence is significant. Where George Sand, for example, finds the possibilities life offers insufficient to the demands of her imagination, Balzac finds them more than sufficient. It is a finding in which Dickens and Dostoevsky concur. Facts — the raw material of the realist or "historian of mores" — leap to the eye already fraught with dramatic implications, Balzac seems to say, leaving to the novelist only the perennial problem of imposing on them a formal unity. And yet Balzac himself — to continue using him as an exemplar of romantic realism — acknowledged that such a program is incomplete. A critic may be a formalist; a novelist cannot. Within the mythos, or story, are myths in the modern sense of thematic complexes belonging more to ontology than to fictional architecture, conveying, in the definition of Philip Wheelwright, "that haunting awareness of transcendental forces peering through the cracks of the visible universe." [24] Each of these transcendental forces will be represented by a myth, as its workings disclose a characteristic pattern of action; and to the extent that the novelist, in the bulk of his work, attempts to see life steadily and see it whole, these myths will unite to form the outlines of a unity — a mythology.

That this word may be taken in vain is being proved by critics almost daily. Yet its use in characterizing romantic realism is doubly appropriate. On the one hand, it points to an aspect of the specifically romantic heritage, in the sense that the whole romantic movement (in the words of Harry Levin) "may be considered as a mythopoeic revival." [25] On the other, it signals the turning of that heritage toward the peculiarly modern world, in an attempt to interpret it. The mythologies constructed by the romantic realists (who are the mythopoets of the novel) thus unite what is most personal in their art with what is most objective. They serve to give shape and color and cohesion to fictional worlds, but not only to fictional ones: their realism enters in the fidelity of description that made their myths tenable and relevant for their times. They are, that is, local interpretations at the same time that they are general ones: the Paris and London and Petersburg evoked for us are Balzacian and Dickensian and Dostoevskian, but they are also evocations of the life of carefully specified historical junctures. Albert Béguin's formulation of this double tendency cannot be bettered: "A fictional society, when it is the work of a great artist, arises at the point where two different projections meet: the projection into the imaginary of a real world which the novelist has recorded to the best of his ability; and the projection into reality of a personal myth, expressing his self-knowledge, his knowledge of fate, his notion of the material and spiritual forces whose field is the human being." [26] In the light of this statement, much of the apparent paradox in referring to romantic realism disappears, and the crucial element that may make one of two equally good reporters a great novelist is underscored. That the novelist does his best to record the real world is assumed; but his recording is shaped by his vision of that world, and his vision is inevitably a function of his autobiography — as personal and as inimitable. This shaping aspect of realistic creation is guided by what Maupassant calls "the lesson the novelist would draw from it"; Béguin calls it "the projection into reality of a personal myth." The common ground here is important; but the differences in emphasis are perhaps even more so, and these differences are signaled by the verbs in both statements. In having the writer *extract* a moral from the material he presents, Maupassant is emphasizing the primacy of the presented material itself; in seeing the writer as one who *projects* a personal vision on to the reality he has evoked, Béguin is, if not making the vision primary, at least suggesting a parity of importance, in which the vision may never be so completely effaced in the finished narrative as Maupassant and the "pure" realists would have it.

From the vision is born the myth. "All that we saw," Blake tells the angel in *The Marriage of Heaven and Hell,* "was owing to your metaphysics." Similarly, all that Balzac and Dickens record is owing to their vision — not simply selected by it, as Maupassant would prescribe, but presented in terms of it. The result, in the broadest terms, is a principled deformation of reality: its familiar contours are presented to us, but in a new, manipulated light. Gide once criticized Tolstoy for "head-on illumination" and the absence of "shadow" in his great novels. His own advice: "First study the source of the light; all the shadows depend on that. Every form rests on and finds support in its shadow. . . . Dickens and Dostoevsky are past masters at this. The light that illuminates their characters is almost never diffuse." [27]

This metaphor of lighting, which independently attracted two such sensitive critics (and Henry James's name might be added to the list), is doubly suggestive. It calls attention to something that goes beyond "point of view." In emphasizing the importance of shadows, of the deliberately unilluminated portions of the picture presented, it reminds us of the constant presence of mystery in romantic realism on a whole series of levels — from a metaphysical one (here belongs Wheelwright's notion of transcendental forces looming over the visible world), to a purely technical one, where we recognize the penchant for masks, devious intrigues, and sensational plots. And, in its emphasis on highlighting, it points to a practice affecting the rendition of characters and situations, which I shall call heightening.

By heightening is meant intensification of the original datum (whatever it may be), a tendency to extremes. It is such intensification in the presentation of character that led Baudelaire to observe that even the concièrges in Balzac are endowed with genius — a remark to which Balzac himself supplied the gloss when he wrote, "Distributed equally, human vitality produces fools, or universal mediocrity; unequally distributed, it engenders those anomalies to which one gives the name of genius — and which, if they were visible, would seem deformities." [28] One may note in passing the explicitly romantic concern with genius here; and note, too, the failure to appreciate its rationale in Zola's reproach to Balzac for thus manipulating his scales: "What almost always produced a feeling of strain in Balzac's novels is the magnification of his heroes; he can't make them too huge: his powerful fists know how to create only giants." [29] For the enlargement to which Zola objects is, to Balzac, only a concentration of energy or vitality — what he calls *la force humaine*. The predilection for such concentration may reflect that thirst for strong emotion by which Stendhal defined his era;[30] but it has wider functions as well. By heightening character, by adding passion (in Balzac's phrase) *as an element* to characters who would in all other respects appear unexceptional, the romantic realists could and did claim that they were underlining the typical as much as the idiosyncratic in them. Besides putting into relief whatever is unique in an individual, that is, this sort of characterization in emotional italics might transcend the purely individual in the direction where myth and symbol intersect. In such a way George Lukacs explains Balzac's heightening of character: "What he did was to depict the typical characters of his time, while enlarging them to dimensions so gigantic . . . [that they] can never pertain to single human beings, only to social forces." [31]

If individual characters are depicted, each at the top of his bent, it follows that the works in which they meet will be dominated by the principle of contrast, from the inevitable shock of opposites. There is an obvious danger of crudity in such a technique, as there is of caricature in such an approach to character. Both suggest the simplified, dramatic world of the popular novel, with its sharp antinomies of rich and poor, heroic and villainous. And, of course, the romantic realists were among the last great novelists to command a wide popular audience; driven by financial need, courted by the large-circulation periodicals, their work channeled into a form that serial publication could accommodate, they skirted the melodrama and sensationalism that lesser talents were producing out of the same play with extremities and contrasts. One thinks of Wilkie Collins and Charles Reade in England. Sue and Dumas *père* in France, and a host of indiscriminate imitators in Russia and elsewhere. It was, in fact, one of the signal achievements of romantic realism that it took precisely these elements of the popular novel and drama and made them yield unsuspected potentialities.

The ballast for this achievement is the thoroughness of the realism on which it is built; however extreme the romantic or mythopoetic presentation of character and situation may be, the counters that are to be patterned, the raw materials, are drawn from reality, and with a maturity and an eye for significance that the more purely popular novelists could not evince. Thus, in the presentation of character, romantic realism would tend to accept what later became a canon for the "classical" realists: that, in contrast to Aristotle's dictum that men are to be distinguished in terms of their moral goodness or badness, what really constitutes our common humanity is the irrational mixture of both in us. What the romantic realists retained, however, was an Aristotelian concern with the moral components of the mixture, so that the microcosm of an individual soul will typically reveal the same laws of contrast at work. We have a world of blacks and whites, where the greys on examination turn out to be only subtler twinings of the same two basic threads. The conferring vision, that is, sees each man's struggle, however obscure, in the light of the ultimate contest between good and evil; and it dramatizes this framework by incarnating the opposed principles through the introduction of purely good characters (most often women and children) and, more important, of characters clearly identified as diabolic surrogates. The former tend often to be sentimentalized portraits; they tend almost always to be victims, beatified by Christian passivity and resignation. The latter are active, aggressive, predatory; and they tend to appear suprahuman, surrounded with a demonic aura and seemingly possessed of at least quasi-demonic powers. They are, literally, evil geniuses. One remembers Vautrin, Fagin, Svidrigailov — and behind them a whole tradition of romantic Satanism.

These paired and opposing forces suggest the predominance in romantic realism of a Manichean world view, in which human beings and human societies become a battleground. If character is heightened in part to emphasize the moment of the conflict, that conflict itself will naturally enough be presented with analogous emphases. To complement heightening of character, we find, then, a heightening of pace and situation, of drama.

Speaking of drama in its basic sense, Francis Fergusson finds it "an art which eventuates in words, but which in its own essence is at once more primitive, more subtle and more direct than either word or concept." [32] Put another way, the fugitive dramatic essence might be found to reside in a strong confrontation of opposing forces. But drama is a form as well as an essence; the distinction is important when the term is being adapted to fiction, for the novelist may make his work dramatic in either of the two senses. He may, with Flaubert, make the generic conventions of drama his goal, seeking to achieve a narration that as nearly as possible implies no narrator, so that the reader may seem to apprehend the action directly, as in a theater. Or the novelist may, with Balzac and Dickens, accept the impure narrative bias of the traditional novel and exploit all the prerogatives of the choral narrator, using them to intensify the portent of already dramatic stories.

To do this is to accept the dangers, and the possibilities, of melodrama. Indeed, the former imply the latter, as T. S. Eliot recognized when he wrote, "You cannot define Drama and Melodrama so that they shall be reciprocally exclusive; great drama has something melodramatic in it, and the best melodrama partakes of the greatness of drama." [33] This may only suggest that crudities — large, simple categories of action and import — have a validity of their own; but it is a great deal. In relation to romantic realism, the question once more is the degree to which it charges elements of popular appeal with new meaning. For melodrama is, as one of its historians concludes, "tragédie populaire." [34] Simplified and sensational, seeking effect often at the cost of any probability, it arose as an offshoot of the sentimental drama of the end of the eighteenth century. It worked with heroes and villains; it emphasized coincidence and mystery for their own sake. It lacked a rationale for these, which romantic realism was to find, most notably in its myth of the modern city. For terror and pity is substituted the no less vigorous cathartic of thrills and the pathetic. But here — in an era of social change, when the audience for literature was changing, along with traditional values — a certain rationale could be claimed, since the pathetic served ultimately to maintain the worth of the "commoner" against the aristocratic conception of life. When the *Grand Dictionnaire universel du XIXe siècle* declares that "the pathetic rarely can have a dangerous effect in works of the imagination, or fail to move on behalf of an object that is interesting, agreeable and morally good," it is recommending an essentially democratic literary instrument, and it underlines the invidious nature of the recommendation by quoting Lamartine: "The sublime wearies, the beautiful deceives, only the pathetic is unfailing in art." [35]

In the evolution of the form, one of its historians sees "melodrama becoming conscious of its powers and of its literary dignity" only with the publication of Hugo's *Préface de Cromwell.*[36] The terms of Hugo's manifesto do throw light on the further development of melodrama by proclaiming a new cluster of artistic values

— or, rather, a cluster of artistic values newly connected. At the center is the romantic rediscovery of the notion of the grotesque. Balzac, Dickens, Gogol, Dostoevsky — each would make a somewhat different use of it, but all would employ it under the double aspect Hugo indicated in remarking that, "on the one hand, it creates the deformed and the horrible, on the other the comic." It remains only to add that "the deformed and the horrible" is newly enfranchised as a carrier of the pathetic (as Hugo implies in his references to Shakespeare and in his praise of it "as a means of contrast"), and to observe that Hugo's dichotomy may in fact inhere simultaneously in one and the same character or event. The grotesque, that is, becomes an instrument for yoking literary values that had hitherto been considered antithetical, to produce something in the nature of a *frisson nouveau.* If the philosophical end product of this conjunction is to be found in the writings of Kierkegaard and some of his followers, it is artistically prefigured, with so much else, in Shakespeare. Thus in a persuasive discussion of the problem in relation to *King Lear,* G. Wilson Knight observes, "Much that is always regarded as essentially pathetic is not far from comedy." [37] The relevance of this observation to Baron Hulot, to Miss Havisham, to Akaky Akakievich or Fyodor Karamazov, needs no underlining.

Thus we are brought once more to an area where the traditional province of the comic shades off into something like its opposite. Just as my earlier discussion suggested that realism, largely through the use of irony, continues to bear the marks of a comic inheritance adapted to new ends, so it might be hypothesized here that romantic realism reveals a parallel adaptation of comic techniques, largely through the use of the grotesque. It will be argued that this process reaches its apogee in Dostoevsky, where the grotesque is pushed into areas that skirt comedy to end in tragedy, while Dickens exploits the comic more directly (though seldom without tragic overtones). As for Balzac, who chose to call his monument *La Comédie humaine,* his awareness of the problem is expressed in the preface to *Splendeurs et misères des courtisanes,* where he joins the chorus of romantic deniers that traditional comedy is possible in the nineteenth century.[38] The texture of French life, he finds, is growing constantly flatter; even nuances are disappearing. "The only strongly marked mores and the only possible comedy are to be found among thieves, prostitutes, and convicts; the only energy is to be found in these beings separated from society. Present-day literature lacks contrasts, and contrasts are not possible without [social] differences." And a little further on, where he is speaking of these "beings separated from society," Balzac stresses again that "no one has dared to take up *the profound drama* of these existences." [39] In undertaking to fill the gap in this most sensational of his mature works, he furnished an ideal demonstration of the fusion of the comic and the pathetic under the aegis of that transformed melodrama which occupies so central a place in the tradition of romantic realism. And he did it, significantly, in a novel that he himself called "an essentially Parisian work" — significantly, because the possibilities of poetry, as of comedy, had been generally denied to the larger urban setting, at once the precondition, the product, and the symbol of modern life. "Sur les pavés poudreux d'un bruyant carrefour / Les poétiques fleurs n'ont jamais vu le jour," Chénier had written;[40] but little more than a half century later they had appeared, as *Les Fleurs du mal.* In this case, however, the work of poetry had been prepared by the achievements of prose.

The romantic realists — notably Balzac, Dickens, and Gogol — were the first fully to realize the potentialities of the metropolis as a subject of fiction. In the city, they found an ideal nexus for all the attributes of their work that have so far been discussed. In a sense, it is even possible to see their achievement as having been to give romanticism a fresh lease on life by providing a new field of operation for some of its favorite themes and methods. Thus, romanticism had made much of the outlaw, the noble criminal, of whom the first claimed ancestor was Milton's Satan and the first nineteenth-century exemplars the rash of Byronic heroes. What romantic realism did, while preserving both the type and its mythical aura, was to renew its appeal and deepen its relevance to contemporary life by discovering a milieu that would give it support and substantiation.

Hitherto these heroes had infested lonely forests or exotic seas. They were escaping — and helping their audiences to escape — the ennui of everyday contemporary life, which all sensitive souls hastened to agree was trite, monotonous, colorless. The first wave of romantic heroes was a wave of expatriates — the Childe Harolds, the Renés, the Alekos, *die Räuber*. In Nature — which seems to have meant all that was unarranged by the hand or mind of man — romanticism pursued its defining endeavor: "In the face of growing factual obstacles, to achieve, to retain, or to justify that illusional view of the universe and of human life which is produced by an imaginative fusion of the familiar and the strange, the known and the unknown, the real and the ideal, the finite and the infinite, the material and the spiritual, the natural and the supernatural." [41] For such a quest the city was assumed to be inherently unsuited, since it embodied all that civilization meant in the way of unnatural restraint, familiarity, routine. Then, gradually, came the discovery that the city itself was, to an exhilarating degree, terra incognita, and that, to the properly armed investigator, it could offer all the wonder of the strange in the familiar which might be desired. One of Gautier's *Jeunes-France* puts the case forcefully to a friend: "Oh, my friend!" he cries, "one must be mad indeed to venture afield in hopes of finding poetry. Poetry is no more in one place than in another; it is in us." Those who go seeking inspiration in every corner of the earth, he says, fail to see that they have everything they need around them, within twenty-five miles of Paris. "How many magnificent poems unfold from the garret down to the porter's lodge, which will find neither their Homer nor their Byron! How many humble hearts are consumed in silence, and extinguished without their flame having ever shone outside! How many tears have flowed that no one has wiped away! How many passions, how many dramas that no one will ever know!" He turns to the room in which they are standing to comment that, calm and bourgeois as it is, it has perhaps seen as many "domestic tragedies" and "interior dramas" as the theater shows in a year — and he imagines the stories of love, death, jealousy, and joy that must have been enacted here. The conclusion: "Poetry is everywhere: this room is as poetic as the bay of Bahia or any locale reputedly poetic." [42]

Gautier's enthusiastic spokesman is proposing that a thirst for strong emotions can be satisfied artistically without the external trappings of exoticism, even in a single bourgeois room. When he tells his friend that the secret corners of his room somehow fit and reflect him uniquely, he is expressing a notion of which others were to make much: the notion that his living quarters are nothing less than a symbolic revelation of an individual's inmost being. One recalls the harmony that Balzac establishes between the Maison Vauquer and its dowdy mistress; or Krook's cluttered room in *Bleak House,* in which he explodes from spontaneous combustion; or the furniture of Sobakevich in *Dead Souls,* which seems to cry out, "I, too, am Sobakevich"; or the religious symbolism in the number of windows in the rooms of Raskolnikov and Sonia in *Crime and Punishment.* The passage from Gautier, of course, contains this only in embryo, but it illustrates the genesis of such ideas in the period when an outré romanticism was transferring some of its ideals to a realistic method.

The room, however, despite Xavier de Maistre's tour de force in his *Voyage autour de ma chambre,* is too limiting an area to found a work on. "All human life in several square feet!" Gautier's speaker exclaims, but he is talking about the stages of life — birth, marriage, death — about its range and quality, not its form. The social component is missing. One contemporary of Gautier's, Jules Janin, supplies this by a widening of perspective. For the novelist in search of an organizational framework offering a multitude of secrets and an atmospheric unity, he finds that the peculiar organization of the city may offer "something more curious than the pyramids of Egypt, the Kremlin, or the glaciers of Switzerland, something more astonishing than all the marvels that one goes to see at such cost in money and fatigue — a great Parisian building, in a crowded quarter, tenanted from the basement right up to the roof." To satisfy a taste for picturesque scenes sharply contrasted, Janin goes on to sketch the possibilities of what a Russian critic has called "romantic urbanism." [43] Taking a typical Parisian building in cross-section, he catalogues the gradations between extreme luxury on the second floor and extreme poverty in the garrets. He evokes merchants, clerks, solicitors, and the crowds of their clients up to the middle of the building. Then the population becomes denser: the "narrow and active bourgeoisie" — symbolized oddly by "a woman working, a child crying, and a canary singing" — represents the boundary line of well-being. Beyond it and above them are the dismal and narrow rooms where an artisan may live, or a grisette, dreaming of castles in Spain. "And, if there is anything higher yet — a pallet, some straw, tears, prisons of Venetian lead [the roofs] in summer, ice in winter, a lifelong suffering. And not a glimmer there of the candles on the first floor, not even the smell of the kitchens, not the sound of songs, not the movement of the courtyard; the only spectacle is that of overflowing haylofts . . . an insulting abundance that seems to have been put there expressly to emphasize what a distance separates an unhappy man from a fine horse." [44] In the novel from which this passage is taken, *La Confession,* Janin does go part of the way toward exploiting such a framework for a version of the picaresque, but once again the quarters are cramped, the juxtapositions mechanical, the result less promising than the idea.

In the pursuit of a usable microcosm, the next step outward would be a vision of the city itself. The task had been assayed already in the decade preceding the French Revolution by Louis-Sébastien Mercier who, while claiming to have made in the four volumes of his *Tableau de Paris* "neither an inventory nor a catalogue," nevertheless did announce: "I have pursued my investigations among all classes of citizens, and have not disdained the objects which are farthest from haughty opulence, the better to establish through these contrasts the moral physiognomy of this huge capital." [45] Mercier's immediate successor in the opening years of the new century was Victor-Joseph Jouy, who wrote as a journalist and was renowned in his time as the French Addison. Under the pen name of *L'Hermite de la Chaussée d'Antin,* he set out to catalogue the "difference of mores and habits which makes each section of Paris a sort of nation apart" and to seize, in the sum of his observations, "the general character of Parisians and the particular physiognomy of this great city." [46] What Jouy — the first of the nineteenth-century *physiologistes* who were so instrumental in discovering the modern city for literature — missed, however, was a unifying principle: in the last analysis, he could offer only himself. His task, as he saw it, was to observe the extremities between which there was no communication in the ordinary course of things and "to let each know what is being said and done among the others; to point out the vices, the faults, the foolishnesses, the very virtues that distinguish them; to establish between them, *in my disquisitions,* a central point of communication." [47]

A unifying principle for the diversity of quarters, of classes, of individuals is unnecessary not only for the journalist, but for the writer of short stories, since the separation of countless urban existences offers him less a problem than an inexhaustible resource. Thus it is that Janin's cry of excitement over the conjunction of romance and reality, quoted above, finds echoes throughout the nineteenth century. The perennially hardy Sherlock Holmes puts it cogently to Dr. Watson at the beginning of "A Case of Identity":

> "My dear fellow," said Sherlock Holmes, as we sat on either side of the fire in his lodgings at Baker Street, "life is infinitely stranger than anything which the mind of man could invent. We would not dare to conceive the things which are really mere commonplaces of existence. If we could fly out of that window hand in hand, hover over this great city, gently remove the roofs, and peep in at the queer things which are going on, the strange coincidences, the plannings, the cross-purposes, the wonderful chains of events, working through generations, and leading to the most *outré* results, it would make all fiction, with its conventionalities and foreseen conclusions, most stale and unprofitable."
>
> "And yet, I am not convinced of it," I answered. "The cases which come to light in the papers are, as a rule, bald enough, and vulgar enough. We have in our police reports realism pushed to its extreme limits, and yet the result is . . . neither fascinating nor artistic."
>
> "A certain selection and discretion must be used in producing a realistic effect," remarked Holmes. "This is wanting in the police report, where more stress is laid perhaps upon the platitudes of the magistrate than upon the details, which to an observer contain the vital essence of the whole matter. Depend upon it, there is nothing so unnatural as the commonplace."

The argument here is not new; but its terms are relevant to the problem under discussion. The first lies in the notion that the separate atoms making up the city are connected by "strange coincidences," "plannings," "cross-purposes," "wonderful chains of events," all suggestive of a network of subterranean relations that significantly most often come to light in the offices of the police.

The atomism, then, is only ostensible, and it is partial at best; the real connections are clandestine, and they are known to the urban *pícaro* — himself a romantic, often a disguised figure — and to the police, who just as often may be confused with him in a world of double-dealing and masks beneath masks. Indeed, where high society forces a mask of convention on its citizens, its antithesis forces on *its* citizens the equally effective mask of anonymity. This truly fantastic situation makes the city resemble, in Balzac's phrase, the forests of North America, inhabited by tribes of Mohicans, keen to all the hidden pathways and partially covered trails that traverse it. The images may vary; Balzac himself used many, as did all the portrayers of the romantic reality of the city. What emerges from them — and what is important here — is that ultimate means of enforcing a unity on the whole atomistic scene by the characteristic romantic device of mythifying it, of seeing it as an organism. Balzac begins an early work, *Ferragus,* by observing, "There are certain streets in Paris as dishonored as a man guilty of infamy can be; there are noble streets, streets simply honest, streets about whose morality the public has not yet formed an opinion." Pursuing this line, he tells us, "At noon everything is alive, chimneys smoke, the monster eats; then he roars, then his thousand paws move." And, in a significant indication of the moment when the city as an organism is most fully itself, he apostrophizes: "But oh, Paris, whoever has not admired your somber vistas, your vistas of light, your deep and silent culs-de-sac; whoever has not heard your murmurings between midnight and two in the morning — such a one still knows nothing of your true poetry, or of your great and bizarre contrasts." For the initiated, "Paris is a living being." [48]

The words and the city here happen to be Balzac's, but the theme and the treatment are typical for the London of Dickens or the Petersburg of Gogol and Dostoevsky. The city has not only an atmosphere, but a soul; one might say not only that it has a character, but that it is one. And it is generally true for all the writers mentioned that the city reveals its true character least in the clear sunlight of midday. That is its official face, bland and deceptive. It takes the simulated night of fog and storm or the actual hours of darkness to awaken the creature. (Significantly, Wordsworth, a romantic hater of cities, is moved by its dormant unity at the crucial hour of dawn, when the nocturnal organism has not yet yielded place to its diurnal specter "and all that mighty heart is lying still.")

Ferragus is, Balzac tells us in his preface, the story of thirteen men joined in a secret society, profoundly devoted to each other, bold enough to run the greatest risks, strong enough to place themselves above all laws, utterly fearless ("trembling neither before the prince, nor the hangman, nor innocence itself") — "criminals no doubt, but certainly remarkable for some of the qualities that make great men. Finally, so that nothing should be lacking to the somber and mysterious poetry of their story, all have remained unknown, though all have realized the most bizarre ideas which the fantastic power falsely attributed to the Manfreds, Fausts, and Melmoths might suggest to the imagination." [49] Once more, this work, for all its imperfections of outrance and perhaps because of them, may serve as a paradigm of the more mature productions of romantic realism. The bewildering changes of identity between outlaws and respectable citizens, like those between police agents and their quarry; the fantastic powers translated from the realm of the supernatural to that of the everyday; all these suggest the romantic concerns that were to be legitimated anew in the urban setting.

The young Baudelaire, in proclaiming the "heroism of modern life" (by which he meant urban life) eleven years before he published *Les Fleurs du mal,* was generous in his acknowledgment of the work of his predecessor. Parisian life, he found, was rich in poetic subjects ("The marvelous envelops and saturates us like the atmosphere"), in examples of a modern beauty and heroism, and more than worthy to stand with the exemplars of tradition. "For the heroes of the Iliad," he concludes, "cannot hold a candle to you, O Vautrin, O Rastignac, O Birotteau . . . and you, O Honoré de Balzac, you, the most heroic, and the most singular, the most romantic, and the most poetic of all the characters you ever created!" [50]

Between the very form of a novel and that of a great city, an affinity exists.[51] Having recognized some of the ways in which the city is the perfect ground for all the tendencies of romantic realism, its products now call for closer and less schematic attention, beginning with those of Balzac.

2

Balzac: The Heightening of Substance

Poetry has been sublime; prose has no other resource than the real, but the real is terrible enough as it is to be able to vie with lyricism.

Splendeurs et misères des courtisanes

Modern myths are still less understood than the ancient ones, although we are devoured by myths. Myths press in on us from all directions.

La Vielle fille

IN 1832 at the end of his anonymously published *Echantillons de causerie française,* Balzac poses the problem, "Is nature, literally copied, beautiful in itself?" and goes on, in a phrase that strikingly prefigures Baudelaire's paean to the heroism of modern life, "We go to the Exposition to see the work of painters, and pay no attention to the creatures who are swarming in the streets of Paris, poetic in quite a different way, beautiful in misery, beautiful in expression, sublime creations, but in rags." His conclusion: "Today we hesitate between idealization and the literal transcription of facts, men, and events. Choose." [1] An analogous choice has remained to confront his critics, some of whom have chosen to see his work under the rubric of *La Recherche de l'absolu,* while others have found its essence in the exposing of *L'Envers de l'histoire contemporaine.* Thus the triumphantly literal-minded *Studies in Balzac's Realism* of Dargan on one side and, on the other, Albert Béguin's suggestive *Balzac visionnaire.* What is perhaps more significant than the existence of such rival camps is the way in which one of the nineteenth century's finest critical intelligences mirrors the split internally, so to speak. "Balzac is, in fact, a novelist and a savant, an inventor and an observer; a naturalist who knows equally well the laws by which ideas and visible beings are generated," Baudelaire writes on one page of *L'Art romantique;* and on another, "I have frequently been astonished that the great glory of Balzac was to pass for an observer; it always seemed to me that his chief merit was being a visionary, and a passionate visionary." [2]

It is as if Balzac's critics took his injunction — "Choose" — as being directed at them rather than at artists in general — an understandable situation, but one rendered ironic by his own avoidance of the choice. To be sure, in his work we find "the literal transcription of facts" to such a degree that a recent social historian of France could conclude, "Reading Balzac's novels, one can follow not only the appearance of new social types, but also the movement of manners [*moeurs*] and ideas from 1789 to 1848," and adds, "All the observable reality of his time, gathered with the rudimentary means then available, passed into the novels of Balzac." [3] But one notes that Balzac's setting down of facts is seldom merely literal, in the sense that the solidity of the recorded world is sufficient as a justifying achievement. There is always behind each fact — each character or event — a larger significance, carefully indicated. Facts become symbols, revealing through the events of the temporal world a transcendent sphere of causes and effects. This explains the aura surrounding so many Balzacian characters, and the resonance by which the import of events is amplified throughout his pages.

CREATION OF A UNIVERSE

It is in this sense that Balzac may be said to have created a fictional universe, not just a world. In attempting to "compete with the Civil Registry" in reproducing the pattern and texture of his world, he was taking on the role of a demiurge and the responsibility of providing laws to govern its internal movement. As long as he was dedicated only to the drawing of scenes, he might have declined the responsibility; from the moment that he united his scenes into cycles, and his cycles into the total design of a *Comédie humaine,* he could not. For the design allows objectivity of a new and special sort, in which the independent concreteness of a thing in all its detail renders it no less expressive of a personal vision; the vision has determined its place in a whole network of relations and given the reader a double (if not a multiple) perspective on it. We may recall Balzac's words, quoted in the last chapter, about the unlikely crossings and conjunctions of individual fates in the city — bearing in mind that it is only such a pattern, quite above and beyond individual characters and destinies, that forms the luminous identity of his suprareal Paris. We may recall also the observation of Henry James: "Wherever in his novels Paris is not directly presented she is even more vividly implied." [4] Paris is thus the main theater and the key myth in Balzac's larger mythology, and the very inclusiveness of that mythology suggests how various must be the specific roles of the city.

There is, first of all, the realistic Paris of Balzac. On this level we must note his faithful precision in matters of geography, the fruits of his early journalistic sketches in the manner of Jouy, the *physiologistes,* and Monnier, of his wanderings to indulge what he once called "la gastronomie de l'oeil." The revolutionary implications of his geographical exactness were not lost on his contemporaries, constituting as they do a fundamental stratum of his realism. Gautier noted that, before Balzac, the characters of fiction did not eat, drink, have lodgings or an account at the tailor's, but rather moved "in an abstract milieu like that of tragedy." [5] Balzac, by situating his characters topographically, situated them socially as well. The fact that Daniel d'Arthez lives on the squalid Rue des Quatre Vents characterizes his position in society quite as much as Rastignac's move to the little bachelor apartment on Rue d'Artois characterizes his.

To geographical realism must be added a historical realism, disputable in some of its details, but noteworthy in its total achievement. Balzac may have slighted the process of industrialization in favor of the more dramatic chicanery of financial speculation; this, in an era when money was scarce and fiduciary transactions insufficiently regulated, is at worst a relative inaccuracy of emphasis, and not of perception.[6] What he did do was to incorporate into literature for the first time the romantic appreciation of the historic particularity of times and places as applied to the present. His subtlety is apparent in such laments as the one quoted earlier, where he takes note of the leveling of mores within a single decade and specifies some of its indices. In the careers of Birotteau, Nucingen, David Séchard, Lucien Chardon de Rubempré, and a hundred others, he portrayed the form and pressure of his time, observable in their ideal concentration in the life of the capital; and in this sense he is indeed "the creator of the modern world." But this very historical realism, though rooted in a dense, constructed reality, tends to flower in the regions of myth — in part from the fact, in Lukacs' formulation, "that he radically thinks through to the end the necessities of social reality, beyond their normal limits, beyond even their feasibility." [7] In part, also, the sources of the myth are to be sought in the temperament of its creator; for present purposes, it is important only to remark how naturally the transition from reality to myth is effected. Speaking of the acquisitive inhabitants of Paris, Balzac writes: "What power destroys them? Passion. Every passion, in Paris, can be subsumed by two terms: gold and pleasure." Here speaks the realist, charting the main currents of his time. But the terms in which he pursues his point relate more to metaphysics than to history: everyone "exceeds his powers," wears himself out "in a thousand spurts of creative will." [8] We sense the guiding parable of *La Peau de chagrin*. Behind the temporal pattern is the timeless one; behind the realistic Paris, the mythological one.

"City of contrasts, homeland of mud, of dung and of marvels, of merit and of mediocrities, of opulence and misery, of charlatanism and celebrities, of luxury and destitution, of virtues and vices, of morality and depravity," the city that Balzac evokes in his poem in prose, *Paris en 1831*, is almost a sketch for the myth it shows in process of formation.[9] With its facile contrasts and paradoxes, it is akin to inventory, and there is no suggestion that its contrasting disparities are united by anything more than the city limits. By 1833 the essential ingredient has been added, and we find him speaking (in the preface to the first edition of *Eugénie Grandet*) of "the poetry in the atmosphere of Paris";[10] the following year, the myth has been born. Paris is still "essentially . . . the city of contrasts," [11] but it has an internal unity: "Paris is a living thing." [12] It is, literally, protean: it will appear as a shark-infested ocean, a savage-infested forest, even as the inferno itself. It is — or it compels — a way of life, and its own shifting aspects have their counterparts in the Parisians, "a people terrible to behold," who display "not faces but masks . . . all stamped with the ineradicable signs of a breathless greediness." [13] Balzac notes "the almost infernal hue of Parisian faces," explaining, "it is not only in jest that Paris has been called a hell." [14]

The everyday appearance of Paris thus masks its real character; correspondingly, its people are masked — metaphorically, as in Madame de Beauséant's scene of stoical triumph in *Le Père Goriot* and, literally, as in the several metamorphoses of Vautrin. At work are the tyrannical conventions of social life, on the one hand, and the more sensational conventions of melodrama, on the other. But melodrama should not be taken here as necessarily implying denigration. It belongs to life itself, as Balzac liked to point out by appealing to the evidence of daily journalism; and it has, too, an artistic rationale when deliberately and maturely handled. Balzac states the crux of the matter in his preface to the first edition of *Le Cabinet des antiques,* where he replies to charges of falsifying life by conceding that real life tends to be either too dramatic or insufficiently literary: "Life will often seem implausible, just as literary truth cannot be the truth of nature" (*Le vrai souvent ne serait pas vraisemblable, de même que le vrai littéraire ne saurait être le vrai de la nature*).[15] The determinants of literary truth, as Balzac makes clear elsewhere, will vary from one writer to another, inhering in the way individual genius will show an affinity for certain subjects, which will themselves suggest the means appropriate to their rendition.[16] The writer who finds life often implausible cannot be expected to eschew altogether the depiction of scenes that exceed conventional notions of a "normality" he has already denied — particularly when he believes that "great works of art . . . live on through the passion that is in them." [17] His artistic credo will furnish, instead, a double imperative for setting into relief, often melodramatically, the new, "truer" reality he has perceived.

Baudelaire was among the first to recognize the extent and the artistic legitimacy of this side of Balzac's work. In a single brilliant paragraph, casually inserted into a discussion of Gautier, he calls Balzac's works "as profoundly colored as dreams." All of Balzac's characters he finds possessed of genius, compact of will, "more eager for life, more active and wily in struggle, more patient in misfortune, more gluttonous in enjoyment, more angelic in devotion" than their counterparts in real life. Moreover, without once using the words "type" and "typical," he fixes the crucial incarnation of dominant character traits so habitual to Balzac by noting that in painting his figures "he blackened their shadows and brightened their light areas" — and he explains the need for such simplifying emphases in character, as well as for the frequent melodramatic emphasis in action, by observing, "His prodigious appetite for detail, which comes from an excessive ambition to see everything, to divine everything . . . obliged him to mark the main lines more sharply in order to preserve the perspective of the whole." Finally, by referring to "the actors of his *Comédie,*" he stresses Balzac's own underlining of the essentially dramatic pattern of his work.[18]

"The narrator is everything," Balzac observed early in his career: "He is a historian; he has his theater; his profound logic, which moves his characters; his painter's palette and his observer's magnifying-glass." [19] The key clauses here are the two central ones. They justify Harry Levin's observation that Balzac's characters "do not step out of his books and into our lives, like some of the memorable characters in fiction. Rather it is we who remain detached, while they become increasingly involved in the trammels of circumstance." [20] Intricacy, denied to Balzac's characters in the psychological sense, is granted to the working out of their fates — a conception that accords, not accidentally, with Aristotle's awarding to action the primary role in tragedy. Such a view, indeed, is inherent in Balzac's concern with the fusion of individual and type: behind each individual one senses the legions of his *semblables* — whose likeness is not and could not be one of temperament so much as one of fate. For Balzac's characters are above all destinies, whose incarnation in no way limits their general significance.

The concept of destiny here figures in a double sense: it signifies the trajectory of a given life or career, and, in the larger sense, it is the stern necessity that shapes the separate careers of certain men. "An author should scorn turning his story — when that story is true — into a kind of jack-in-the-box," Balzac wrote, and even his frequent invocation of coincidence does not betray this principled disdain.[21] In fact, the absence of surprises even in his melodramatic works is one of the most striking features of his writing; he never teases the reader's concern. He makes him the spectator of an irrevocable progress toward a prefigured end: future and past merge into a single entity that dwarfs and colors whatever is strictly present in his novels.

This tendency of his fiction to slight present time is of central importance to the nature of Balzac's art, and it functions on a number of levels. Maurice Bardèche credits its adoption in Balzac's early work to the example of Scott, quoting the passage from *Waverly* in which Scott compares the progress of a story to the increasing momentum of a stone bounding down a hillside, and finding the analogous formula in the early Balzacian habit of preparing his action through a long exposition, as in *La Duchesse de Langeais,* after which he releases the rolling-stone action by the simple declaration: "From this point on, the facts tell everything. Here, then, are the facts." [22] The utility of such an observation is limited only by the critic's tendency to divorce consideration of Balzac's technique from consideration of the nature of the world it creates. The special quality of Balzac's characters and the peculiar resonance of his scenes are often the result of exactly this combination, whereby actions are closely flanked by their determinants in the past on the one side and by harbingers of the future on the other. One does not witness an experience simply from the point of view of the character undergoing it so often as from the point of view of its position in the continuum of that character's total fate. The ways in which Balzac achieves this effect are various, but the most common is the way of narrative comment. "In seeing himself feted and envied, the poet found his self-assurance," he tells us at one point in *Illusions perdues:* "He was the Lucien de Rubempré who shone for several months in literature and in the artistic world" — and already the earlier somber intimations of failure are ratified. From here on, Lucien's triumphs, as we witness them, are invested with a pathos entirely free from any factitious impatience to know where they will end; and the immediacy of his experience, as we share it, takes on the cast of retrospection; we do not know the future in detail, but it has an air of *déjà vu*. The narrator is thus not only omniscient about the present, but prescient as well. It is more than the crudity of an earlier convention that keeps him from a Flaubertian effacement behind the story: it is the imperative of an entirely different kind of fiction. For Balzac as narrator is more than the creator of a self-sufficient artistic entity. "What is the storyteller's talent," he had asked, "if not the sum of all talents? It comprehends logical deduction with its rigor, the drama with its mobility, the very essence of the lyrical with its inner ecstasy." [23] And more than that, the teller of tales is a demiurge: "To write the *Itinéraire de Paris à Jérusalem* is to share in the human glory of an age; but to compel belief in the life of René or Clarissa Harlowe — is that not to usurp the powers of God?" [24]

If characters are destinies in Balzac's world, they are destinies in the social, not the psychological sense. This explains the striking dearth of children in his work: for the historian of psychological destinies, childhood is the necessary starting point, as Proust, Balzac's great inheritor, was to show most exhaustively. But the mythographer of Paris worked on the basis of different axioms. "In a great city," he wrote, "life is never young except by accident." [25] Life as a whole, moreover, has its developmental stages: the *Scenes of Private Life* are designed "to represent human life in its early awakening, and growing to blossom"; the *Scenes of Provincial Life* "are intended to represent that phase of human life in which passions, calculations, and ideas take the place of sensations. . . . Finally, life has darkened in maturing. In the *Scenes of Parisian Life* the questions broaden. Existence there is painted in large strokes; it comes gradually there to the age that borders on decrepitude. A capital was the only possible frame for these pictures of a critical epoch, where infirmities afflict men's hearts no less than their bodies." [26]

The catalogue that follows, detailing the nature of Parisian life, is not least remarkable for sounding so much like the philosophy of Vautrin, minus his passion:

> Here genuine feelings are the exception; they are broken by the play of interests, crushed between the wheels of this mechanical world. Virtue is slandered here; innocence is sold here. Passions have given way to ruinous tastes and vices; everything is sublimated, is analyzed, bought and sold. It is a bazaar where everything has its price, and the calculations are made in broad daylight without shame. Humanity has only two forms, the deceiver and the deceived. . . . The death of grandparents is awaited: the honest man is the fool; generous ideas are means to an end; religion is adjudged

a necessity of government; integrity becomes a pose; everything is exploited and retailed; ridicule is a means of advertising oneself and opening doors: the young men are a hundred years old, and insult old age.[27]

In the light of such a vision it would seem not inappropriate to conceive Balzac's entire work under the title he proposed for an unwritten one: *La Pathologie de la vie sociale.* Indeed, the article just cited goes on to refer to "this society which is corrupt *because* it is eminently civilized." [28]

The two great appetites of this society, as Balzac repeatedly proclaimed, were for money and pleasure; since it consisted only of the deceivers and the deceived, it follows that the indulgence of these appetites must be reserved to the former and must be pursued according to the unwritten but nonetheless powerful rules of the game. These rules cover the pursuit of money, and as a prime example we have the Baron Nucingen. They cover love ("Love in Paris in no way resembles love elsewhere") and give us, among others, Nucingen's wife, Delphine, née Goriot. They neglect the keystone of a healthy society, the family ("We have destroyed the family," Balzac announces in *La Cousine Bette*), and give us the harrowing stories of *Les Parents pauvres.* So powerful are the rules in their operation that few question them or are aware of their existence as anything remarkable. This is truly, in Poulet's word, a world of determinance. And we have Balzac's own word that anyone aware of the rules must embrace them in all their evil ramifications, yield to them passively or exist outside society, opposed to it. To this last possibility are dedicated the two cardinal Balzacian myths of the prostitute and the criminal.

When Balzac states that the disappearance of nuance in the mores of his time increasingly leaves only those outside the law — prostitutes and thieves — as fitting subjects for his drama, he is exaggerating, but tellingly. Both groups, beyond serving as pretexts for sensationalism, are comments on the society on which they prey. Regarding the first, it is clear that, despite his statement in the *Avant-Propos* ("I consider the Family and not the Individual as the true social unit"), his own doubts of the compatibility of love and marriage were fundamental. In any case, the nature of the Balzacian universe requires that love — *l'amour passion* — must be untrammeled, for passion is "that divine emanation, superior to the virtue which man has contrived for the preservation of his societies";[29] but at the same time, "passion is excess, is evil." [30] Nor is it this imperative alone that gives importance to the role of the courtesan in Balzac. There is also the fact that these creatures, deprived of all the protection of the laws of society, represent an almost endless variety of possible destinies; they are surrendered more than any others to the dictates of "chance — the greatest novelist in the world." And, because their position in society renders this surrender a conscious one, they acquire in the eyes of the novelist a pathos, as well as an excitement, which is rare in other characters. The courtesan can be heartless as Valérie Marneffe; but she can also be the embodiment of love — one of love's saints, in fact, like Esther. Finally, the courtesan affords the novelist a unique point of view and a focus for all the complex interrelationships of his enormous *comédie,* for her relations with a variety of men become a way of judging them, as well as of bringing them into an odd sort of community (this function is grimly parodied in the situation of "the five fathers of the Marneffe church" in *La Cousine Bette*). The aura surrounding Balzac's courtesans, then, is only a reflection of the fact that, without them, love in his world would not be "that force which drives everything and transfigures the real." [31]

The case of the criminal is analagous. In one of his youthful exercises in *la littérature marchande,* Balzac notes: "Thieves form a special class in society: they contribute to the functioning of the social order; they are the oil on its wheels." Here is the sociological sanction for dealing with an outlaw class. But there is a romantic one as well:

A thief is a rare man. He is nature's spoiled child. She has heaped on him all sorts of perfections: an imperturbable sang-froid, unfailing daring, the art of seizing the occasion . . . nimbleness, courage, a good constitution, piercing eyes, agile hands, a happy and expressive face. All these advantages are nothing special for a thief — yet they already form the sum of talents of a Hannibal, a Catiline, a Marius, a Caesar.

Is it not necessary for the thief, in addition, to know men — their character and their passions? — for him to lie smoothly, foresee events, judge the future, have a fine and quick mind? — for him to have a lively understanding, to be a good actor and mime? — for him to be able to seize the tone and manners of the various classes of society, ape the clerk, the banker, the general, know their habits, and clothe himself at need in the toga of the police prefect or the yellow trousers of the policeman? Finally — most difficult and wonderful of all, advantage which gives the Homers, Ariostos, tragic authors and comic poets their renown — must he not have imagination — brilliant, divine imagination? Must he not be perpetually inventing new plots? For him to be booed means to go to the galleys.[32]

And Balzac is speaking here not of the exceptional but of the averagely successful thief. By the time he comes to write *Le Père Goriot,* the exceptional qualities will remain, but they will attach to a supremely symbolic figure — "the Cromwell of the galleys," Jacques Collin, alias Cheat-Death, alias Vautrin, who will represent as well the romantic progeny of Milton's Satan.

In Balzac's phrase, Vautrin serves, "by his horrible influence," as something of a vertebral column joining *Le Père Goriot* to *Illusions perdues,* and *Illusions perdues* to *Splendeurs et misères des courtisanes.*[33] In so doing he connects the quintessential Balzacian drama, via a sort of epic hiatus, to the quintessential Balzacian melodrama — works that furnish in shifting combinations a conspectus of some of the main ingredients of the Balzacian universe.

LE PÈRE GORIOT

Le Père Goriot, published in 1835, represents a crucial stage in the development of Balzac's work. Here his mythology in its double sense — as idea and as form — may be seen to crystallize. His technical mastery is secure, and that enabling device of the *Comédie humaine,* the *retour des personnages,* is first put to work here. The city, society, and money are first fully invoked in the central roles they will henceforth fill — the Parcae of the Balzacian world. *Le Père Goriot* is nothing less than the cornerstone of the vast edifice to whose completion he gave the remaining decade and a half of his life. By any standards it is an intricately plotted, highly compressed book, and just because it is so, the need — remarked by Henry James and many others — to take Balzac in bulk, rather than in small doses, is in large measure obviated. For there is in this book a bulk of matter that its physical slenderness belies. What makes this possible is a consistency of heightening (not unlike that of Shakespeare, to whose Lear Goriot offers a conscious parallel) which creates a total atmosphere of myth, a decorum akin to that of poetic drama — and it inheres not in the speeches but in the particular character of the narration, one might almost say of the narrator.

The distinction is of some importance; while a narrative always implies a narrator, in the way that a chair implies a chairmaker, the implication may be fostered or weakened, as the literary strategy requires. Balzac's beginning, with its present-tense immediacy and its total objectivity, seems to promise an uncompromising realism: "Madame Vauquer, née de Conflans, is an elderly woman who, for the last forty years, has kept a family boardinghouse in the Rue Neuve-Sainte-Geneviève between the Latin Quarter and the Faubourg Saint-Marceau." Yet a dozen lines later, we find our attention distracted by the narrator's assurances that, however overworked the word "drama" may be, "it must be used here; not that this story is dramatic in the true sense of the word, but by the time it is finished some tears may perhaps have been shed — *intra muros* and *extra.*" The author steps forward as stage manager, reminding us that the drama exists, already finished; what we are to see are the workings-out of several interrelated destinies toward an end already known, if not yet revealed. The time perspective is indicated; the geographical one, dependent as it is on "local color," is similarly announced in the rhetorical question, "Will it [the novel] be understood outside Paris?" and the response, "One may doubt it." The voice assuring us that "this drama is neither fiction nor romance" gives repeated evidence of a concern with its proper reception. Erich Auerbach has brilliantly analyzed the description that follows of the boardinghouse and its mistress, showing how "the motif of the unity of a milieu has taken hold of [Balzac] so powerfully that the things and the persons composing a milieu often acquire . . . a sort of second significance which, though different from that which reason can comprehend, is far more essential — a significance which can best be defined by the adjective demonic," so that "every milieu becomes a moral and physical atmosphere." [34] What is perhaps of equal interest is the author's preparation of the reader for such multiple significances. In this case, Balzac informs us, "The Rue Neuve-Sainte-Geneviève especially is like a bronze frame, the only one befitting this story, for which the mind must be prepared by gloomy colors and heavy thoughts."[35] To the interior lighting corresponds an exterior one, and these monitory emphases on the emotional tone of the story, as on its significance, have the important function of reminding the reader of his role as spectator: they are invitations to see, understand, and judge, rather than to participate in the action.

This preparation of the reader's intelligence is a constant feature in Balzac. "Nothing could be more dismal than the sight of this sitting-room" (23), he writes in introducing the famous catalogue of the interior of the Maison Vauquer, in which the personality of place fuses with that of its mistress; and one wonders whether, in view of what follows, this is not supererogatory. The same technique, however, has wider functions. Besides underlining a given aspect of the physical scene, as above — or even of the spiritual one, as when Balzac refers to the lodgers as "these narrow minds" — it can on occasion furnish an orientation obtainable in no other way. Rastignac, well into his education by now, resolves "to open two parallel lines of attack on success, to lean on knowledge and on love, to be a learned jurist and a man of fashion." "He was still very much a child!" Balzac comments: "These two lines are asymptotes, which can never meet" (105). In editorializing, Balzac limits the reader's freedom of judgment by guiding it; yet this is no simple didacticism. What keeps it from being that is one's overriding awareness that the world in which the action takes place is, though an interpretation of reality, so complete a one that it must have its own laws, its own iron necessities. Made constantly aware that he is witnessing *un passé déjà accompli,* the reader cannot resent the historian's underlining of critical junctures.

The narrator, then, is the chorus to the drama he presents. Like the chorus in Greek tragedy, he announces the exigencies of Fate, the limits of possibility. As chorus, too, he may color present action by invoking — like the shadow it casts before — the future. In the Balzacian world, where things have their destinies as well as men, we see futurity hanging over them. Balzac completes the description of the wretchedness of the Vauquer furniture by noting: "If it is not yet filthy, it is spotted; if it has neither holes nor tatters, it is going to fall into pieces from decay" (25). The same is true even of secondary characters: when Rastignac goes to the Marquis d'Ajuda-Pinto to reclaim his cousin's letters, Balzac tells us of the marquis: "He seemed to wish to talk to Eugene, to question him about the ball or about the Viscountess, or perhaps to confess to him that he was already in despair about his marriage, as he was later known to be" (289). And when he describes Anastasie, brilliant in her diamonds, he takes care to add in passing: "She was wearing them for the last time" (291).

If the future represents one form of potentiality, there are others as well, which the narrator as chorus will emphasize. Sometimes this emphasis comes by way of analogy, as when the conventions of graphic art are invoked to ratify the disposition of the novelist's figures. Thus, among the lodgers of Madame Vauquer, Balzac notices in singling out Goriot for attention that on him "a painter, like the teller of this story, would have made all the light of his picture fall" (35). Again: "Victorine was like one of those naive paintings of the Middle Ages in which all accessories are neglected by the artist, who has reserved the magic of his calm and proud brush for the face, yellow in tone, but in which heaven seems to be reflected with its golden tones" (215). But there are other sorts of potentialities, which depend more strictly on the force of the subjunctive: "If the excitement of a ball had reflected its rosy tints in that pale face; if the ease of an elegant life had filled out and colored those cheeks, already slightly hollow; if love had lit up those sad eyes, Victorine could have rivaled the loveliest girls" (31).

From such comparisons of what is with what might be, it is only a short step to the use of metaphor and symbol. Thus, describing the boardinghouse, Balzac underlines in passing a symbol that will come to dominate a whole aspect of his story; having mentioned a statue of the God of Love, he notes that in its peeling and scaly surface "those fond of symbols might perhaps discover an allegory of Parisian love" (22). Paris itself appears in two main metaphorical guises, each suggestive of a side of its mythical character. The first is contrasted with the Paris of *comme il faut* and stresses the wonder and the variety that the metropolis contains: "But Paris is a veritable ocean. Throw in the plummet, you will never know its depth. Survey it, describe it? Whatever care you take in surveying and describing it, however numerous and curious the explorers of this sea may be, there will always be a virgin realm, an unknown cavern, flowers, pearls, monsters, something unheard of, overlooked by the literary divers" (30–31). Midway through the book, the metaphor is taken up again; the money received from his mother and sisters leaves Rastignac "free for fifteen months to sail the Parisian ocean and devote himself to the woman trade, or to fishing fortune from it" (111). The other metaphor is Vautrin's, and it will serve as a base for the multifarious intrigues of *Splendeurs et misères des courtisanes* (as well as for Dumas' later *Les Mohicans de Paris*):

> Paris, you see, is like a forest in the New World where a score of savage tribes operate — the Illinois, the Hurons, who live on the proceeds offered by the different social classes. You are a hunter of millions; to capture them you employ snares, limed twigs, decoys. There are several ways of hunting. Some hunt dowries . . . some fish for consciences, others sell their clients bound hand and foot. The man who comes back with his gamebag well stocked is hailed, feted, received into good society. (137)

The speaker of these lines, it should be noted, is himself the choicest example of symbolic heightening in the novel; partly for this reason, partly because of his thematic connections with later books, discussion of him is deferred for separate treatment. What we may notice meanwhile, in completing this survey of the special functions of the narrator as chorus, is the way he manages to present character itself as symbol. It is not a question of Balzac's identifying Goriot as "this Christ of Paternity" or of his having Bianchon find on him the identifying marks of "an Eternal Father." Such allusions, among which we might include the marks of Judas on Mademoiselle Michonneau, suggest an erratic religious light playing about the action, underlining the fateful nature of the ethical issues — but finally applying only to the action itself. In the process of characterization, they are only metaphors, casually invoked and casually dropped. More important by far is the way Balzac makes each of his characters symbolize a whole army of his fellows and explain them, or be explained by them. Here it is customary to invoke the parallel Balzac set forth in his preface between the varieties of social man and the species of the animal kingdom: "The differences between a soldier, a worker, an administrator, a lawyer, an idler, a scholar, a statesman, a trader, a sailor, a poet, a poor man, a priest, are, although more difficult to seize, as considerable as those which distinguish the wolf, the lion, the ass, the vulture, the shark, the seal, the lamb, etc." [36]

Certainly the invocation is justified. Madame Vauquer, Balzac says in introducing her, "resembles all *women who have had their troubles.*" Poiret, the only comic character in the book, is classified with elaborate care: only after "the great family of simpletons" has been surveyed does he emerge as "a bureaucratic ninny," and the traits of his species explain his part in the betrayal of Vautrin. "Such natures are almost all alike" — this is the Balzacian axiom. Proclaiming it in his characterization of Goriot, however, he adds by way of explanation: "At the heart of almost all of them you find a sublime sentiment" (113). With such a remark, we are at the point where sociological classification merges with a more personal one; we are reminded that Balzac's principal characters hold a dual citizenship, in the historical Paris and in the mythical, Balzacian one. Thus Delphine's anxiety to be received by Madame de Beauséant is explained by the former, by her being a parvenue. But when, deploying against Rastignac "all the resources of feminine diplomacy as practiced in Paris," she is nevertheless pictured as sincere, the explanation derives rather from the myth: "Women are always true, even in the midst of their greatest hypocrisies, because they are yielding to some natural sentiment" (184).

Behind each figure rise the legions of the class he represents. Rastignac is introduced as "one of those young men accustomed to work by poverty" (27). His reaction to the snubs of Madame de Restaud is explained not in terms of his individual psychology, but of his class's: "When a young man of his age is treated with scorn, he flares up, flies into a rage, and shakes his fist at all society; he seeks revenge, but at the same time doubts himself" (103–104). Even his self-divisions are typical. Thus in speaking of them, Balzac can refer to "all the instincts, good and bad, of the two or three men that make up a young Parisian" (184). In such ways, the narrator is not only guide but philosopher, pointing through and beyond the characters he presents to the main lines of a world that they incarnate and interpret, but one that he interprets also. To Rastignac's dawning awareness of the nature of Parisian society, the narrator adds his own ratification: "He saw the world as it is — laws and moral judgments powerless among the rich — and saw in success the *ultima ratio mundi*" (104). Ultimately, this freedom of narrative comment welds together the realistic and the melodramatic planes of the work by its modulations between emotional coloring and documentary objectivity, between harbingers of futurity and disclosures of potentiality, between symbolic presentation and passages of rationalization. The result is a richness of narrative texture that can accommodate in a single paragraph the flat summary, "In his heart of hearts [Rastignac] had surrendered completely to Vautrin," and the lurid but not artistically unjustified picture of the result, "Desperation lent him new beauty, and he shone with all the fires of the hell he carried within him" (202). But such suppleness could not be the work of the narrator as chorus alone; it is made possible as well by the skill of the narrator as architect, by the unremitting pace of his narrative and the multiple tensions resulting from contrasting variations on a few key themes. It is the passion in great works that gives them life, Balzac had said; but he also knew the value of structure and "the first law of literature . . . the necessity for contrasts." [37]

Contrast had been a central principle in Balzac's writing from his earliest pseudonymous productions, and his use of it shows constant efforts at refinement.[38] A whole school of writing — to which he himself inclined for a while — had, at the height of the romantic period, enshrined the crudest kind of contrast as the basis for its productions; the character of this *école frénétique* is strongly enough suggested by the title of Jules Janin's parodistic *L'Ane mort et la femme guillotinée*. No novel, of course, is without its internal contrasts — but they may be implicit and ironic or explicit and intentionally emphasized. The second of these two manners was more common in the romantic period and followed naturally from that penchant for the depiction of strong feelings which the eclectic Balzac most notably shared with his contemporaries. Passionate people produce passionate contrasts. Further, the very act of definition always emphasizes the contrast of the area defined with the areas adjacent to it — and Balzac, as the great definer of social types, by underlining their salient characteristics also underlined their sharpest differences. Despite his periodic protests about the leveling of mores in French society, Paris remained for him always "the home of contrasts." As he was consistent in proclaiming, "In

Paris, extremes meet through the passions. Vice is perpetually joining the rich man to the poor there, and the great to the humble." [39] So it is not surprising to find *Le Père Goriot,* one of Balzac's most carefully constructed books, built around this "first law of literature," in both the architecture of its scenes and that of its themes.

The scenes in the novel number some twenty-four, taking "scene" roughly in its theatrical usage, to designate directly presented actions, diversely located. Their succession is characterized by a regular alternation between scenes in the boardinghouse and those outside it. Thus, at the end of the lengthy exposition (marked by the sentence, "Such was the general situation in the boardinghouse at the end of November 1819"), the first scene is that of the ball chez Madame de Beauséant, presented through Rastignac's retrospective musing on his return and contrasted strikingly with the poverty of the two scenes that follow: Rastignac's discovering Goriot in the act of twisting his silver service, and the boarders during a typical day. The next two scenes take Rastignac to the aristocratic houses of Mesdames de Restaud and de Beauséant, between which Balzac underlines the contrast: "He had seen the luxury which a Mademoiselle Goriot was bound to love, the gilding, the expensive objects prominently displayed, the unintelligent luxury of the newly rich, the squandering of the kept woman. This fascinating picture was suddenly eclipsed by the imposing Beauséant mansion" (104). Right after this, his return to the boardinghouse produces an important effect: "The transition was too abrupt, the contrast too complete, not to develop in him an ambition beyond measure." Two scenes at the boardinghouse follow, with documents and exposition interpolated, and Rastignac once more visits the Beauséant house, where he meets Delphine — only to be struck, on his return home, by an even crueler contrast. Visiting Goriot for the first time in his room, Eugene "could not repress a start of astonishment in seeing the awful hole the father lived in, after having admired the finery of his daughter" (156).

As contrasting scenes of squalor and luxury continue to alternate, Rastignac's reactions become more pronounced, his attraction to the fashionable world more passionate, his revulsion to poverty more instinctive and physical. When, on the heels of Vautrin's arrest, he is led to the luxurious new bachelor apartment that Delphine and her father have arranged for him, "this last contrast between what he saw now and what he had just seen made his overwrought nerves give way" (242). Moreover, as the book draws to a close, the scenes become shorter, until the effect produced by this acceleration becomes almost one of montage. The climax comes when Rastignac has hurried home from the sumptuous ball of his retiring tutor in strategy to the squalid deathbed of his tutor in sentimental generosity; and here the narrator is again at pains to underline what is already dramatically evident. With the fruitless visits to Goriot's two daughters, the scene shifts for the last time to the Vauquer establishment, and from there to the cemetery of Père-Lachaise, where the fidelity of Rastignac is set in relief against the callousness of the daughters, represented by the empty carriages, marked with the Restaud and Nucingen arms, which join the funeral procession.

The alternation of scenes is thus calculated to sustain the maximum dramatic effect in the recurring contrasts of atmosphere. But scenic structure is only the scaffolding of a novel; well managed, it facilitates the full orchestration of key themes. Bardèche has noted of the early Balzac that, even before he had any experience to guide him, he showed a vivid sense of the illumination his characters might be made to lend each other. We see this same sense, now highly developed, at work from the beginning of *Le Père Goriot*. So in the preliminary canvass of Madame Vauquer's lodgers, he sets apart Rastignac and Victorine: "Two figures there formed a striking contrast with the mass of boarders and habitués" (31). Beyond this initial contrast, of course, Rastignac and Victorine take their places in a continuum representing varieties of child-parent relationships, a continuum that is itself only one of several sets of themes with contrasting variations. These themes may be grouped according to Rastignac's climactic awareness of "the three great expressions of society: Obedience, Struggle, and Revolt; the Family, the World, and Vautrin" (285).

The primacy of the family is sufficiently indicated by the title of the book; it is that basic element of society which represents the social ties of uncorrupted nature and so serves as a barometer, measuring the degree of social corruption in terms of its corrosion of family ties. It is no accident that "this obscure but dreadful Parisian tragedy" reveals parallels to *King Lear:*

"Oh! well, yes, their father," replied the Viscountess, "a father, a good father who, they say, gave each of them five or six hundred thousand francs to secure their happiness by marrying them well, and kept only eight or ten thousand livres of income for himself, two homes where he would be adored and made much of. Inside of two years his sons-in-law had banished him from their society as if he were the lowest of outcasts." (98)

Perhaps even more strongly than in *King Lear,* pathos is produced by temporal contrast: each character's past is invoked to lend illumination and pathos to the present. Thus when Goriot first appears in the exposition, it is in 1813 — six years before the main action of the book takes place — and the successive stages of his ascent, floor by floor, to cheaper rooms in the boardinghouse reveal the ebbing of his fortune; and the ebbing of his fortune is made to symbolize his fading prospect of family happiness. Already in the beginning the dominant connection is underlined between the themes of family and money: Goriot, still relatively affluent, unpacks his silver service, which recalls to him "the solemnities of his domestic life" (37). Ardently devoted to his wife (whose nature, characteristically, "contrasted sharply with his" and who might, had she lived, have cultivated "that inert nature"), on her death we are told how he transferred all his affection to his two daughters, "who, at first, fully satisfied all his emotional demands" (114). The brief period of past happiness is recalled more than once at moments of extreme tension; it colors the whole tragedy of Goriot and gives it its pathos.

If Goriot represents the indulgent father wounded by the neglect of his daughters, a contrasting picture is offered in the situation of Victorine Taillefer, whose father is insensible alike to the deathbed entreaties of his wife on the girl's behalf and to the eloquent pleas for recognition from Victorine herself. And both of these situations, which Balzac identifies as essentially Parisian, form a further contrast with that of Rastignac and his family in the provinces. This, significantly, is pictured immediately on the heels of the recital of Goriot's history, as Rastignac has pieced it together from his inquiries. The Rastignac family is shown as harmonious, unified, and affectionate; his mother and sisters are generously ready to scrape together the money he requests — and he, on his part, receives the money with a noteworthy consciousness of its value to them. This awareness of others sets him apart from the Goriot daughters, even as he himself is perceiving the outward similarity of their situations: "Your mother has broken up her jewels!" he says to himself. "Your aunt has doubtless wept as she sold some of her keepsakes! What right have you to condemn Anastasie? Out of egoism, you have just done for your future what she did for her lover! Of the two of you, who is the better?" And Balzac adds, "He experienced that noble secret remorse, whose merit is rarely appreciated by men when they judge their fellows but which often makes the angels of heaven absolve the criminal condemned by earthly justice" (118).

Three sets of parents and children, then: Goriot, Taillefer, Rastignac, whose fates are all connected and serve as commentaries on one another. Two loveless women between whom Rastignac hesitates: Delphine de Nucingen and Victorine Taillefer. And a corresponding series of spiritual relationships: Rastignac, more than either of Goriot's real children, stands to him as a son and is so called. "Papa Vautrin," as he calls himself, similarly stands to Rastignac as a would-be spiritual father (Rastignac senior being, for all practical purposes, out of the picture), and goes so far as to offer to make him his heir: "If I have no children . . . I'll will you my fortune!" (189). Vautrin further boasts the largest possible spiritual family, in the midst of a society where the rule tends to be every man for himself. "Is there one of you," he asks the startled lodgers, "who can say, as I can, that he has ten thousand brothers ready to do anything for him?" (233).

The conclusion to which all these examples tend is that genuine family ties are impossible in Paris. It is implicit in Balzac's description of the scene in which the Duchesse de Langeais summarizes the history of Goriot and his family situation: "Tears glistened in Eugene's eyes. He had recently felt renewed by the pure and holy influence of family affection, was still under the spell of youthful beliefs, and this was only his first day on the battlefield of Parisian civilization" (98). The whole adverbial tendency of this statement is toward a future in which Rastignac's familial susceptibilities will be less tender, as his membership in Parisian civilization becomes less tentative, more conscious and more willed. For society is struggle, in which the sole consideration, and the most important weapon, is money. Whatever the goal of the struggle — power or love — money comes to be the *sine qua non.* In the course of the novel, this theme encroaches gradually on the others, but it is present from the first. When the lodgers are introduced, we are told how much rent each pays. The unfolding of Goriot's tragedy — and of his daughters' — is a demonstration of the pathetic hollowness of the Parisian equation of love and money. Rastignac's own imperative need to realize a fortune is ascribed to his desire to settle a dowry on the sisters he loves, who are made to sacrifice what little they have as a sort of down payment. His abortive pact with the devil, Vautrin, turns on the question of money, is sealed with his acceptance of a loan, and has in view the fortune Victorine will inherit when her brother is murdered. Vautrin himself is betrayed for money. Goriot, even in death, is pursued by the money question in the arrangement of his pauper's funeral — "in an age," as Balzac notes ironically, "where religion is not rich enough to pray gratis" (321). And the pathos of the closing scene in the cemetery includes the significant detail of Rastignac's having to borrow twenty sous from the menial Christophe in order to tip the gravediggers.

The larger tragedy of the book, centering on Rastignac, has to do with the nature of Parisian society where, as Rastignac soon concludes, "success is virtue." That society is twice analyzed in the book — by Madame de Beauséant and by Vautrin. The former explains the power of fashionable women, and the ways of exploiting them, in which the cardinal rule is the concealment of all true emotions, on pain of losing all.[40] Her concluding summary is that the world is "an assembly of fools and knaves," and her concluding advice is, "Take care that you belong to neither class" (103). In resolving to follow this advice, Rastignac decides to pursue two simultaneous paths, to be a "learned jurist" and "a man of fashion" (105). But Balzac is quick to comment on the impossibility of such a course, and Rastignac's gradual abandonment of his studies follows shortly. Madame de Beauséant's picture of society is true, but her suggestion that it is possible to avoid joining one of its two camps is wishful thinking. The analysis given by Vautrin is more terrifying precisely because it is so completely without sentimentality. "He has told me bluntly," Rastignac muses, "what Madame de Beauséant was telling me in more polished fashion" (140). In Vautrin's analysis, the emphasis is on money: "Do you know what you need, the way you're going? A million, and at once" (129). But Vautrin goes beyond money, as he goes beyond sentiment and beyond morality; his arguments rest on the belief that "there are no principles; there are only events" (138). Therefore he can speak "with the superiority of a man who, after examining the state of things here below, has seen that there are only two choices: either a stupid obedience or revolt" (129). His arguments impress Rastignac, who muses afterwards: "This brigand has told me more about virtue than I ever learned before from men or books." Yet he ends his meditations with a characteristic evasion: "Hell! My head is swimming. I don't want to think about anything; the heart is a good guide" (141). Only at the end of the book will the choice he has made be declared. The final contrast is between that "last tear of his youth" which he buries with Goriot and his "first act of challenge to society" in going to dine with Madame de Nucingen. He has chosen to follow, if not join, the party of revolt, whose legendary spokesman now calls for attention.

VAUTRIN

Vautrin is the "vertebral column" of this book no less than of the series that includes it: he is the principal carrier of mystery, the most flamboyant figure of melodrama, the most consistent embodiment of religious themes; he is the most complex symbol and perhaps the most complex character; certainly he is the Balzacian character par excellence, compact of energy, will, and passion to the point of transcendence; at once the rebel and revolt itself. It is not for nothing that we find his name taken as a common noun in Balzac's startling series, "the Family, the World, and Vautrin." He is, in short, the most striking guide to the various levels of the Balzacian universe, for he exists on every one of them.

Vautrin is introduced, in the exposition, as "the man of forty," a figure of transition between the two young lodgers "carried away by the whirlwinds of Parisian life" and the others, "those old men indifferent to everything that didn't touch them directly" (32, 34);

he is the only figure in his prime. We learn that he is amiable, but that this amiability serves to fend off any intimacy; that he is affluent and ready to lend money; that he is an expert locksmith; that he dyes his sideburns; that he returns late each night with the aid of a master key. All this suggests either the criminal or the policeman (and it is well to remember, as Vautrin's own final "incarnation" will show, that in the popular novel of Balzac's time the two were often interchangeable).[41] There is nothing to contradict either possibility in the hints that we are dealing with an extraordinary nature, tending toward omniscience, if not omnipotence: "He knew everything, moreover: ships, the sea, France, foreign countries, business, men, events, laws, great houses, and prisons. . . . His eye, like that of a stern judge, seemed to penetrate to the heart of all questions, to probe all consciences, to divine all feelings" (33). One may, it is true, doubt the judgment of a narrator who finds evidence of "an imperturbable sang-froid which bespoke a man who would not hesitate to commit a crime to get out of a dubious position" in the way in which the man spat; and one notices what seems a crude heightening in the reference to the "fearful depth" of his character. The closing observation, however, tends to be more matter-of-fact: "Often a burst of invective worthy of Juvenal, by which he seemed to delight in scoffing at laws, in scourging high society and proving its inconsistency, suggested that he held some grudge against the social system, and that he had in his background some carefully buried secret" (34).

Oddly enough, in this book, where he functions most consistently *as a character* beneath all the symbolic trappings and melodramatic heightening, the personal reasons for this attitude are not given in any fullness. We learn from Inspector Gondureau that Vautrin first ran afoul of the law in a manner that made his conviction "something that brought him no end of honor in his own set. . . . He agreed to take another man's crime upon himself, a forgery committed by a handsome young man of whom he was very fond, a young Italian, a bit of a gambler, who later entered military service, where his record has been spotless" (193). But already the hints of homosexuality are sufficiently telling in the passing reference to the young Italian's beauty, as in the sole slip that Vautrin makes in the course of the book, when he exclaims to the handsome

Rastignac: "I'm fond of you, as sure as my name is Cheat — (good God!) — Vautrin" (127). Gondureau says flatly that Vautrin does not like women, and Vautrin himself tends to confirm this in offering to make Rastignac his heir "if I have no children — which is likely, since I'm not anxious to plant slips of myself here" (189). "Is that being a friend to a man?" he goes on: "But I'm fond of you. I have a passion for devoting myself to another. I've done it before. . . . Well, for me — and I know life inside out — there exists only one true sentiment, friendship between man and man. Pierre and Jaffier, there you have my passion" (189–190). When he has put Rastignac into a drunken sleep, he moves him so that he may sleep comfortably and "kisses him warmly on the forehead" (212); and it is difficult not to see in his words when captured — " 'Goodbye, Eugene,' he said in a gentle and sad voice that contrasted strikingly with the rough tone of his earlier speeches" — the "sad sweetness of loves that might have been" (234).[42]

Vautrin's personal relations with Rastignac on this level are all relations *manquées,* doomed by the student's strength of will and cut short by his own summary removal from the scene. Nor is this, in any case, their most significant level. Vautrin gives few indications (beyond paying fifteen extra francs a month for a gloria at dessert) of being primarily a sensualist. His campaign of seduction is waged with consummate artistry, but on a larger field. His homosexuality does not obviously affect his actions; it serves to complete his outlawry — since all the other criminals in Balzac have more socially acceptable sexual ties — rather than to define it. Vautrin's attempted seductions are, first of all, more general temptations; whatever else there may be is deferred: "You're wondering, why this devotion? Well, I'll tell you sometime; I'll whisper it sweetly into your ear" (189). Thus Balzac refers to him more than once as, simply, "the tempter" or "this fierce logician"; the latter is particularly significant because the temptations that Vautrin strews in Rastignac's path have in view (literally, at least) nothing more personal than an ideological change of allegiance. Balzac's emphasis on "the seductive arguments which he had sown in the heart of the student" finds its counterpart in the scene where Vautrin offers him financial aid but refuses to press the advantage to secure Rastignac's assent to his proposition regarding Victorine:

"But listen!" he says, "I have my delicacy, like any other man. Don't make up your mind now. You're a little off balance, you have debts. I don't want it to be passion or desperation that decides you to come over to me, but reason" (187).

Nonetheless, Vautrin's speeches are a striking combination of social analysis and arguments *ad hominem*. If his analysis of "the present state of your social disorder" coincides largely with Balzac's, it is still an interested one, and the longest exposition of it, in Vautrin's first tête-à-tête with Rastignac, ends with a proposition from which he stands to gain 200,000 francs. The second one — when he lends Rastignac the 3,500 francs — shows a similar progress from an insistence on seeing "the world as it is" to a display of personal temptations: "Ah! if you wanted to become my pupil, I would make you achieve all your ambitions. You would not form a desire but what it would be instantly satisfied — anything you might wish: honors, wealth, women" (188). Always the point of view remains the same: "I am taking the inventory of your desires in order to put the question to you" (130). The result is that Rastignac accepts the lessons without accepting the tutelage; he will not compromise his freedom of action; nor will he abandon the residue of sentimentality, the vestiges of those qualities that Madame de Beauséant praises in him ("You have seemed to me to be kind and noble, unspoiled and open, in this world where such qualities are so rare") at the very moment of his decision to abandon them.

"What kind of a man are you, then?" Rastignac asks Vautrin. The answers are various. "I am what you call an artist," he says at one point — and one recalls Balzac's view of the artist as a usurper of God's attributes in Vautrin's homage to Cellini, from whose memoirs, he says, "I have learned to imitate Providence, which kills us at random, and to love the beautiful wherever it may be found" (128). In engineering the death of young Taillefer, Vautrin is as good as his word, and Balzac himself takes every opportunity to suggest, somewhat melodramatically, Vautrin's possession of providential powers. His magnetic eyes are forever casting "glances by which this man seemed to penetrate the best-hidden secrets of the heart" (105); he is forever divining the thoughts of those around him; and at the moment at table when Bianchon alludes, too late, to the treachery of Vautrin's betrayer, "His magnetic glance fell like a ray of sunlight on Mademoiselle Michonneau, and this spurt of will made her legs buckle" (229).

Behind the exercise of these powers, and behind Vautrin's very conception of providence, we find his conviction that there are no principles, only events; we move in a sphere beyond good and evil, the sphere of the superman. "I do not accuse the rich in favor of the people," he tells Rastignac; "man is the same at the top, at the bottom, in the middle. For every million head of this human cattle, there are ten sharp fellows who put themselves above everything, even laws; I am one of them. You, if you are a superior man, go straight ahead with your head high" (134–135). As for him, "When I have resolved on something, God alone is strong enough to stop me" (211). One recalls Balzac's statement about criminals' possessing many of the qualities that make great men. Vautrin, on one side, is the apotheosis of this romantic view. He is related in passing to Juvenal, Diogenes, Cromwell, Don Quixote, the Pierre of *Venice Preserved,* Cellini, and Rousseau ("whose pupil I am proud to be"). He boasts that he has never betrayed anyone, that his devotion to his friends and comrades is unwavering, as theirs to him; he operates a sort of welfare scheme for convicts, in which he shows himself strikingly more honest with money than any of the respectable characters in the book. That all these marks of the romantic tradition of the outlaw have their origin in the romantic interpretation of Milton's Satan is of particular significance because of the numerous ways in which Balzac deliberately invokes an identification of Vautrin with his legendary exemplar. Vautrin the man is aggrandized to include the tradition at its fullest, and undergoes in the process an assumption to religious heights.

In elevating Vautrin to the level of religious mythology, Balzac does not cease to betray a divided attitude toward him, but the divisions are here appropriately magnified. On the positive side there is the fact that the initials of Vautrin's given name, Jacques Collin, are those of Jesus Christ; and what might seem farfetched in itself is bolstered by his sobriquet, Cheat-Death, as well as by the story of his sacrificial suffering in taking on himself the crime of another. These hints, of course, are in the final analysis ironic. In a letter answering criticisms of this character, Balzac took pains to emphasize the biblical portrayal of Satan as the most beautiful of the angels, and though Vautrin is hardly presented as being physically beautiful, he has a clearly Satanic grandeur that derives from the Balzacian equation of evil with excess and passion.[43] We see this in his being called constantly tempter and demon; in his emblem of revolt, carried to such extremity; in his continually smiling "diabolically" and manifesting his "infernal genius." One may even find an echo of Milton's "Better to reign in hell than serve in heaven" in Vautrin's "Everything or nothing! That is my motto" (162). His campaign against Rastignac is put into this perspective by Balzac in speaking of "the seductive arguments which he had sown in the heart of the student to corrupt him" (181). And the hints in his own speech are progressively less veiled. Thus, referring to those who practice honesty and altruism, he speculates sardonically on "the wry faces of these fine people if God should play us the bad joke of staying away from the last judgment" (134). More pointedly, he tells Rastignac, "You would be a fine catch for the devil," tempts him with promises of wealth and power, and predicts that "in a few days you will be ours" (188). Thus it is that when Rastignac momentarily yields, he is presented as "made even more beautiful by his despair, and shining with all the fires of the hell in his heart" (202). Similarly Vautrin, at the moment of his arrest, becomes "an infernal poem, expressing all human emotions except one — repentance. His look was that of the fallen archangel who desires eternal war" (232).

It is true that Balzac calls him in this book "typical of a whole degenerate nation, of a people savage and logical, brutal and supple" (232), but the proof of this, and the sense of its horror, is unstressed. It could hardly be otherwise when the whole context of the novel renders Vautrin's countercharge so persuasive: "There is less infamy in the brands on our shoulders than in your hearts, you flabby members of a rotting society: the best among you wouldn't resist me" (232). Twelve years later, Balzac was to write that Vautrin represented "corruption, prison, social evil in all its horror," and to add, surprisingly, that there was "nothing gigantic about him"! [44] But by then Vautrin had reappeared in a new avatar. In the daylight world of Parisian society, his corruption could hardly eclipse that of society; in the later works, the focus is on the nocturnal underworld itself, and Vautrin is rejudged against the background of his own subsociety, where the flamboyance of the action puts all the characters on the same scale. In *Le Père Goriot,* by contrast, Vautrin, while playing an important part in the action, lends it a new dimension by his very outrance. In the extremity of his antisocial persuasion, he carries the social analysis of the book to a pitch attainable in no other way; and in so doing, he justifies the terror as Goriot does the pity of tragedy. This is perhaps more than a conventional character might be able to do. Balzac, at least, declines any such attempt and, by keeping biographical details to a bare minimum and heightening the transcendental aspects of Vautrin, makes him a presence almost more than a personage. In the later books he remains this, but the perspective changes: the dimension he lends to *Le Père Goriot* becomes the scale of the whole presented world as we move from mixed drama to pure melodrama, from a recognition of the ubiquity of masks to a view of the world behind them.

"Each work must have its own form," Balzac had written; "otherwise contrasts disappear, and monotony would inevitably arise." [45] Accordingly, the next variation on the theme of the young provincial's initiation into Parisian life takes on an epic rather than a dramatic tone. Unlike *Le Père Goriot,* whose focus is on the peeling walls of the Maison Vauquer and the circumjacent world of society, *Illusions perdues* begins with a broader perspective. The metropolis, the whole world of the earlier novel, is here only a part of a larger world, and where in the earlier book it is explored, here we see it in process of *discovery*. For this reason, the atmosphere of youth and hope can never, up to the very end, be quite extinguished. In Paris, Lucien's education follows the line of Rastignac's: he too discovers that money is "the key to every enigma"; he too is pressed to choose between the path of slow honorable work à la d'Arthez and "literary warfare" with its quick returns and self-betrayals; he too comes to see (in Balzac's favorite phrase) things as they are. His failure, however, is the result of a weakness of will, which contrasts strongly with Rastignac's determination; it is a feminine trait and completes the early emphasis on the feminine delicacy of his features. Where Paris challenges Rastignac, it seduces Lucien, whose progress is from one protector to another until he departs the city with money for which his mistress' maid has turned streetwalker. Finding only further failure and more guilt in Angoulême, he turns despairingly back toward Paris, looking for a remembered roadside pool in which to drown himself. He will not use the Charente because his body would be discovered — he prefers a body of stagnant water with a symbolically mirrorlike surface: "Anyone with the courage to fill his pockets with stones must find an inevitable death there, and never be found." [46] At this point, preparatory to the arrival on the scene of Vautrin disguised as the abbé Carlos Herrera, the symbolic hints begin to converge. "Reason as well as despair," Balzac points out, "made Lucien want to kill himself — the two suicides from which a man may return" (1047). D'Arthez had prophesied of Lucien some time before, "He would willingly sign a pact with the demon tomorrow, if that pact gave him a glamorous and easy life for a few years" (911–912). Now the demon appears — *diabolus ex machina* — and finds Lucien dressed like a bridegroom, with a bouquet in his hand. Carlos resembles, Balzac comments, "a hunter who, after long and fruitless searching, finds his quarry" (1048).

From the opening gesture of this meeting, when Carlos offers Lucien a cigar "in a seductive sort of way, accompanied by glances full of charity," what follows is a parody of a seduction, for all its fateful implications not without its moments of high comedy: " '*Santa Virgen del Pilar!* You are an atheist,' cried the priest, putting his arm around Lucien with a maternal solicitude. 'Well, here's one of those curiosities I promised myself to observe in Paris. In Spain we don't believe in atheists' " (1049). The end point of these blandishments is a demand and a promise: "Obey me as a wife obeys her husband, as a child obeys its mother, and I guarantee that in less than three years you will be the Marquis de Rubempré, marry one of the noblest daughters of the Faubourg Saint-Germain, and take your place one day on the benches of the Peerage" (1064). When Lucien yields ("Father, I am yours"), he is accomplishing a symbolic death and rebirth that Balzac is at pains to underline. "This young man," Vautrin says of the reborn Lucien, "no longer has anything in common with the poet who just died. I have fished you out, I have given you life again, and your relation to me is that of the creature to its creator, of the body to the soul, of the Afreet to the genie in fairy stories" (1064). And Lucien, Balzac writes, is like the sailor of some Arab tale, "who, trying to drown himself in mid-ocean, lands instead in some undersea country and there becomes king" (1054).

In *Le Père Goriot* the most consistent image for Paris was that of an ocean; these "undersea countries" from the Arabian Nights are, in *Splendeurs et misères,* the no less legendary Parisian underworld. It was necessary, Balzac said, to paint this world in order to complete the inventory of the *Comédie humaine;* but the world with which this "essentially Parisian work" deals is more than a missing piece in the jigsaw picture of society. It is a connecting link for all the pieces, and its actors, by being outside the respectable hierarchy, are free to enter into relations with all of its levels — indeed they exist to do so. The role of the courtesan in this has already been mentioned above and here finds its fullest illustration, as the title alone indicates. But beyond the necessity for treating the spheres that his general design urged, there were more particular reasons why the underworld should have a special appeal for Balzac. One, already noted, is his conviction that the leveling of mores he saw taking place after the July Monarchy left outlaws as the increasingly exceptional carriers of colòr and drama in the nineteenth century (to the thieves and prostitutes might be added the figure of the dandy, on the evidence of Balzac's own exploitation of that figure); and Balzac's genius, as he emphasized through Félix Davin, inclined to the creation of a world where everything radiates drama.[47]

Another reason, related to the first, is more literary in nature and concerns the indelible impression that an early reading of Cooper had left on Balzac. "Oh!" he wrote Ratier in 1830, "to live the life of a Mohican! . . . Oh! how I have understood the savage! Oh! how admirably I have comprehended corsairs, adventurers, lives of opposition." [48] The image of Paris as a Cooperesque forest had appeared in *Le Père Goriot,* in Vautrin's characterization of Parisian society, but it remained in the background. In *Splendeurs et misères* it becomes central. Describing the maneuvers of the spies and counterspies, Balzac demonstrates how "that poetry of terror which the stratagems of enemy tribes at war impart to the forests of America (and which Cooper has so well described) became attached to the smallest details of Parisian life." [49] Not only the excitement he found in the American author, but the mythical quality as well could be transposed to his own work. Finally, a certain change in the great reading public on whom Balzac was so dependent may have played its part in his new attention to Paris as underworld. Serial publication of novels had become canonized; the formal conventions of such serialized novels had become stricter; and, in a reversion to *bas romantisme,* sensationalism was the order of the day. To such a view Balzac himself lends credence in writing to Madame Hanska, in the spring of 1843 while working on this book: "I'm turning out pure Sue." [50]

Whatever the relative weight of all these considerations, their combined effect issues in the melodramatic depiction of a nocturnal world of masks and disguises. Truly we have passed with the resurrected Lucien from one world — the daylight, realistic world of *Illusions perdues* — to another. When Lucien himself reappears in the opening scene of *Splendeurs et misères* he is, in fact, no longer the Lucien of the earlier book, but a mask among the other masks at the opera ball. At the ball he is widely remarked, and in reporting this Balzac is significantly careful to note that "youth and beauty could mask profound abysses in him," just as the Rubempré title now masks the apothecary's son (27). When Vautrin appears beside Rastignac at the ball, his somber voice sends shivers down his spine, "for it was no longer disguised" (44) — and when he removes his mask it is only to reveal another: "The devil has allowed you to change yourself completely, except for your eyes, which no one could forget," Rastignac tells him (45). From this point on, disguises proliferate at a dizzying pace. The prostitute Esther becomes for a time, touchingly and genuinely, an angel, only to fall again. A false Esther appears to aid in the bilking of Nucingen — who himself makes ludicrous efforts to disguise his age. Jacqueline Collin enters the scene disguised as the exotic Asie and is metamorphosed into Madame de Saint-Estève, Madame Nourisson, a hawker, and two grandes dames before she leaves it. Putting aside the stolen persona of Carlos Herrera, Vautrin himself turns up as one William Barker and again as an *officier de paix.* Peyrade, among other disguises, is Samuel Johnson; Contenson is his valet;

Corentin is a financial bureaucrat. Even the Rue de Langlade wears a disguise that it throws off only at night: "Passing by during the day, one cannot imagine what all these streets become at night; they are alive with bizarre beings that belong to no world" (46).

However exaggerated, this dwelling on mystery has its rationale, which connects it with the more realistic parts of Balzac's work. Noting that such an interest is a part of the romantic outlook, Curtius notes as well the particular ways in which Balzac assimilated it to all his thought, to the point where "every mystery is life, and every life is mystery." [51] Vautrin provides the relevant gloss on these words when he tells Lucien: "There are two Histories: the official, lying history which is taught in the schools, history *ad usum delphini;* and a secret history, where you find the real causes of events — a scandalous history." [52] And, even more pointedly: "We are all the slaves of something, some vice, some necessity, but observe the supreme law — secrecy." [53]

These statements help to explain the particular character of the melodrama of *Splendeurs et misères;* the first is the axiom, the second its corollary — and in the second, the key word is "all." It is the simple concentration of vices that gives this book its lurid atmosphere, a concentration so unrelieved that even the rare virtues that do appear are surrounded and finally strangled by vice (as Esther's love for Lucien or Peyrade's daughter's trusting innocence), or else appear as the pathetic outgrowths of vice in all its passionate excess. (The prime example of this last is the humanizing grief that racks Vautrin on Lucien's death.) But the prime mover of all the separate secret histories is, ultimately, the fact of Vautrin's homosexuality.

Paradoxically, Vautrin's strange passions, which serve on the one hand to make him the most complete outlaw in Balzac, serve as well in this book to humanize him. "This truly diabolical man," as Balzac never tires of calling him, is nonetheless "attached to humanity through love." [54] A whole side of Vautrin's usurpation of the role of providence, hitherto depicted chiefly in metaphysical terms, is now made personal: he takes vicarious pleasure in Lucien's worldly triumphs and sees in him "a handsome, young, noble Jacques Collin, arriving at the post of ambassador." Vautrin has, Balzac says, "realized the German superstition of the Double by a phenomenon of moral paternity which will be understandable to those women who have loved truly in their time, who have felt their souls pass into that of the loved one, who have lived in his life, noble or infamous, happy or unhappy, obscure or glorious." [55] Proof of this appears in Vautrin's speeches to Lucien, where the occasional intrusion of the lover's accent is all the more poignant for its restraint; and there is no reason to doubt the truth of his cry when Lucien has hanged himself, "Monsieur! Monsieur! At this moment my life, beauty, my conscience, all my strength are being buried!" (612). Drained of these, the old tempter disappears; in his place, operating with all the old skills but few of the old motives, appears a new chief of the secret police, a new defender of society (the only one it deserves, as Georges Limbour remarks). "We were the game, now we will be the hunters, that is all," he explains; but it is not all.

For the implications of Vautrin's homosexuality, at the last as at the first, have involved many fates besides his own. The original meeting with Lucien on the road outside Angoulême occurs because Vautrin is hurrying back to Paris to find his "tante," Calvi. The ensuing relationship determines Esther's temporary beatitude and premature death. ("I have never ceased to detest her," Vautrin says [115]; and Lucien, knowing this, recognizes in Vautrin's returning Esther to him "a devotion which he alone was in a position to appreciate" [86].) From the involvement of Esther comes the involvement of Nucingen, with the grotesque comedy of his old man's passions and his ludicrous dialect. Ultimately the cause of Esther's suicide, he is brought into the plot in order to secure Lucien the million he needs to marry Clotilde de Grandlieu. Clotilde and the aristocratic world she represents are the final goal of all this intermediate scheming; and though unattained under the original plan, she and her circle turn out toward the end of the book to be at the center of the intrigues that tie their fates directly with those of Vautrin and his protégé Calvi. Thus is the unity of Balzac's Paris proved by the secret version of history, "where you find the real causes of events — a scandalous history."

The unity of tone comes similarly from this angle of vision. The details may be, as Balzac claims in his preface, profoundly true, but the manner of the narration is hardly realistic — except, perhaps, for the painstaking exposition of judicial processes and prison topography in the third book and for the subtleties of the protracted interrogation of Vautrin and Lucien. In general, bald melodrama rules. Where heightening had in the earlier works been selective, here it is uniform. Rastignac does not, in the opening scene, simply feel Vautrin's hand on his arm cautioning him to silence: it is *"an iron hand* which squeezed his arm to charge him with *eternal silence."* Nothing exists but in superlatives: Lucien is one of the most beautiful men in Paris, as Esther is the most beautiful woman; Vautrin is the strongest and wiliest of strategists; Nucingen is the richest financier. Unwonted things are constantly happening. The prostitute becomes an angel. The banker, who has known "natural love, sham and self-regarding love, conventional love and vain love; *amour-goût,* decent and conjugal love, eccentric love" — everything but genuine love — finds himself at the age of sixty-six disastrously enamored of "one of those women unique in a whole generation . . . the sublime Esther" (106). Vautrin, "that somber minister whom God must only use for the wreaking of his vengeance," becomes a guardian of society. The list of extravagances is almost endless.

"No one has dared to take up the profound drama of these existences; the censorship will no longer have them in the theater," Balzac says in his preface, and the emphasis is rightly on theatricality, on the primacy of effect over cause, motive, and probability.[56] The technique, in short, is roughly that of the roman-feuilleton, which Sue and Dumas were exploiting with such success at the time. Balzac at the end of his preface tends to admit the resemblance to his competitors while deploring its commercial necessity; but he suggests too that, in the total perspective of his work, this novel will find both its justification and its compensation. And so it does. In the final analysis, *Splendeurs et misères* takes its place among Balzac's most characteristic works, by representing some of the chief ingredients that the novelist employed in other proportions elsewhere. Let us be clear, however, about the limits of such a generalization. My concern has not been with Balzac as Novelist or with the *Comédie humaine* as a whole: these subjects would involve a quantity of texts and a range of qualification much vaster than any single chapter could encompass. The aim here has been to consider three Balzac novels, not because they are more "typical" than any three others, but because they are arguably more central to his work. Paris was the heart of Balzac's France and became the heart of the para-France he created. A poetry of Paris had existed before him, but a myth of Paris was largely his creation. All that has traditionally been said about his realism, his attention to the importance of things, his awareness of social institutions, the disillusioning tendency of his work, remains true. But if realism usually leaves its characters (and readers) with their illusions shattered against the hard and chaotic facts of life, Balzac's does not: for in his novels of Paris, where things and institutions take on a symbolic dimension, disillusion itself takes its place in a larger illusional scheme. We are led in the end not to see life as common sense has always known it, but rather to share the vision of a superior truth, as far above common sense as it is above common illusion. Paris is a sea full of subterranean marvels, a forest full of unseen predators — anything but a common place.

The vision that makes it so is romantic; the writing that carries the vision must be called romantic realism. In discussing Vautrin, emphasis was laid primarily on the method of presentation, on the ways he is aggrandized by legendary association — but no reader will overlook the enormous part he plays in Balzac's analysis of Parisian society. The romantic conception serves the realist's plan as Vidocq, Vautrin's real-life model, could not have done. This genius of disguise unmasks society; this "ferocious logician" alone is sufficiently cynical to lay bare the cynicism of a whole social order. And when, in a final spasm of melodrama, his lurid world falls to pieces, he emerges from the wreckage looking more like Vidocq than Vautrin — reformed, a good citizen, placing his talents (but not his genius — that clearly is gone) at the service of law and order. And this, Balzac tells us, happened in about 1830, when the July Monarchy ushered in that era of bourgeois colorlessness which he himself lamented and his successors unceasingly attacked.

Balzac is the first of the romantic realists, the first to investigate the fact and the poetry "of that gulf, that sea, that wave forever in motion, call it the world, the century, Paris, London, or Petersburg, as you will." [57] In this as in much else he was prophetic: by the time of his death romantic realism had discovered both London and Petersburg.

3

Dickens: Realism, Subjunctive and Indicative

> Dickens was a mythologist rather than a novelist; he was the last of the great mythologists, and perhaps the greatest.
>
> G. K. Chesterton, *Charles Dickens*

> Sadly as Dickens was led astray, now and then, by his melodramatic impulses, [imaginative vision] is none the less one of his greatest qualities; in the best moments, it enables him to give tragic significance to the commonplace, and all through his finer work it helps to produce what one may call a romantic realism.
>
> George Gissing, *Charles Dickens*

THE very rise of romantic realism, as I have suggested, is traceable to the romantic impulse to see, and to present, the new urban life of the nineteenth century at once in its truth and in its strangeness. Romantic realism would open up new areas of life to serious art and show what the properly attuned vision could find in them — what Dickens called "the poetry of fact." [1] Vision thus was central, and the writer neither could nor would practice that self-effacement before his creation which a later generation, able to take his achievement for granted, was to advocate. Although he swore by the truth of what he wrote, he remained defiantly aware that that truth would be denied by many, equipped with common sense but not with the artist's apprehension of what lay beneath the surface of things. Where a whole public sees red, the artist sees blue, Balzac had said. And Dickens is on record with a similar claim: "What is exaggeration to one class of minds and perceptions, is plain truth to another. That which is commonly called a long-sight, perceives in a prospect innumerable features and bearings non-existent to a short-sighted person. I sometimes ask myself whether there may occasionally be a difference of this kind between some writers and some readers; whether it is *always* the writer who colours highly, or whether it is now and then the reader whose eye for colour is a little dull?"[2] From such an assumption, the need for the novelist to take on the role of guide follows naturally enough. He will write in a kind of emotional italics to force his reader to an apprehension of the drama and the significance being revealed to him in what may initially seem the most prosaic of scenes. The contours of the admissibly real will predominate in his work, but not necessarily the conventional colors.

ATMOSPHERE AND MYTH

Whenever the narrative persona is present, whether in exposition or in interstitial comment, the romantic realist pursues his task, in Balzac's term, of preparing the reader's intelligence — now by somber colors, now by dazzling ones. That is, he is a constant manipulator of atmosphere. Rarely is a scene presented without a surrounding aura of a particular cast and density. Dickens is a master of this, and his mastery is seen to best effect in the openings of his novels and in the closing chords of his chapters. The fog at the beginning of *Bleak House,* the Mediterranean sun at the opening of *Little Dorrit,* the Thames at twilight in *Our Mutual Friend,* are well enough known: they are all literally atmospheric, as well as symbolic, and may remind us of the frequency with which Dickens exploits the weather. Sometimes this atmosphere serves to reflect the psychology of the participants in a scene, as does the sunshine that attends the setting-out from London of Little Nell and her grandfather:

> It was the beginning of a day in June, the deep blue sky unsullied by a cloud, and teeming with brilliant light. The streets were as yet nearly free from passengers; the houses and shops were closed; and the healthy air of morning fell like breath from angels on the sleeping town.
>
> The old man and the child passed on through the glad silence, elate with hope and pleasure. . . . Every object was bright and fresh: nothing reminded them, otherwise than by contrast, of the monotony and constraint

they had left behind. Church towers and steeples, frowning and dark at other times, now shone in the sun; each humble nook and corner rejoiced in light; and the sky, dimmed only by excessive distance, shed its placid smile on everything beneath. (*The Old Curiosity Shop,* ch. 12)

At other times, however, it will reflect rather the attitude toward the scene that the narrator seeks to impose:

The mud lay thick upon the stones: and a black mist hung over the streets; the rain fell sluggishly down: and everything felt cold and clammy to the touch. *It seemed just the night when it befitted such a being as the Jew to be abroad.* As he glided stealthily along, creeping behind the shelter of the walls and doorways, the hideous old man seemed like some loathsome reptile, engendered in the slime and darkness through which he moved; crawling forth, by night, in search of some rich offal for a meal. (*Oliver Twist,* ch. 19; my italics)

What is most striking — and one of the badges of his artistry — is the infrequency with which Dickens uses atmosphere to wring an emotional response from the reader beyond what the facts of the scene might justify. Atmosphere seldom wars with conception, and where an effect miscarries the fault is usually in the strategy, rather than in the execution. The aura is almost always an artistically logical emanation.

Atmosphere may inform a scene, emanate from a place, or surround a character. In the last-named case, it will serve to mark a quasi-mythical individual and to underline his largely mythical significance. Thus in Balzac's Parisian works, over and above the carriers of social evil, looms Vautrin, with his Satanic aureole never for long concealed. Dickens, too, will make the same curious distinction between the pathetically insignificant representatives of the evil system — Merdle, Podsnap, Veneering, Casby — and the intense, larger-than-life incarnations of the Devil himself. It was Chesterton who noticed that Dickens "certainly created a personal devil in every one of his books." [3] It would be truer to say that there is diabolism in every one of his books, but a devil only in some of them. When he appears, he is the real thing, clearly labeled. In *Oliver Twist* he is Fagin, of course, "the old gentleman," whom we first meet toasting-fork in hand, with his perpetually evil leer, "slowly instilling into . . . [Oliver's] soul the poison which he hoped would blacken it, and change its hue forever" (ch. 18). He meditates "with his face wrinkled into an expression of villainy perfectly demoniacal"; and when Sikes's dog growls at him, Sikes abuses the animal, "Don't you know the devil when he's got a great-coat on?" (ch. 19). And, as with Balzac, the lighting is always carefully adjusted when he is on stage:

> Oliver looked up; the Jew, pointing to the candle, motioned him to light it. He did so; and, as he placed the candlestick upon the table, saw that the Jew was gazing fixedly at him, with lowering and contracted brows from the dark end of the room.
>
> "Take heed, Oliver! take heed!" said the old man, shaking his right hand before him in a warning manner. "He's a rough man, and thinks nothing of blood when his own is up. Whatever falls out, say nothing; and do what he bids you. Mind!" Placing a strong emphasis on the last word, he suffered his features gradually to resolve themselves into a ghastly grin; and nodding his head, left the room. (ch. 20)

Rigaud-Blandois in *Little Dorrit* is another such explicit devil, as Dickens illustrates with a crude pun in the first words he utters. Shivering in his dark prison cell, cut off from the warmth of the sun that floods Marseilles, Rigaud growls: "To the devil with this Brigand of a Sun that never shines in here!" (I.1). He has a "diabolical persistency" in him (II.7) and inspires aversion in the innocent: in the jailer's little daughter at the beginning of the book, in Pet Gowan and Little Dorrit later on. And — always a sure test — Gowan's dog, like Sikes's, growls his instinctive hostility. Of course there is a great difference between the devil at the beginning of Dickens' career and the devil toward the end of it, and the difference marks the evolution of the whole Dickensian mythology. Fagin is a central figure, romantically grotesque, romantically satanic; objectively, it is hard to see how he is more socially evil than the Bumbles, who are horrific enough in the harm they do. But mythologically, there is an aggressive menace in this man who does not leave tracks when he walks, this active seducer of innocence, that makes him represent all the danger in the world (or in the city) to lonely goodness. Blandois, by contrast, is a marginal figure, a shabby devil who gives himself airs, able to repel but not to attract, oddly ineffectual; he is a mere shell of his old self, as if his traditional powers for spreading confusion had passed to the Merdles and the Barnacles, to the whole oppressive machinery of finance and government.

It may well be that Fagin is a much more successful devil because he is a much more professional criminal; also, perhaps, because he is so happily incarnated. The merry old gentleman, after all, wields a considerable attraction and, in his final agonies, can call forth just enough human sympathy to gladden the justice-seeking heart of the reader of this melodrama without robbing him of the pleasure that is his virtue's due. One is inclined, by contrast, only to feel relieved of a nuisance when Blandois dies. It seems a negligent gesture of the novelist's that rids us of him, as indeed it seemed a negligent gesture which brought him forth to skulk and posture almost irrelevantly through the action of the book. The difference may be, finally, that the devil, the villain, and the criminal — three different sorts of figures, belonging, respectively, to mythology, melodrama and realism — converge to form the figure of Fagin (as they did, in different proportions, to form Vautrin), while Blandois has only a mythological aura and an off-stage villainy, but nothing at all of realism in his makeup or in his role. Interestingly enough, in his preface to the third edition (1841) of *Oliver Twist,* Dickens expresses his fear that "there are in the world some insensible and callous natures that do become, at last, utterly and irredeemably bad." But the words apply to Sikes, not to Fagin. Dickens' method, it has been observed, is to make his black characters — by which I would designate devils and villains — probable "by greying them not with virtues but with humor." [4] That is, the devices appropriate to one or another convention surround and justify characters in these categories, while the simple criminal represents an evil unsanctified by any tradition on which Dickens draws.

The contrast with Balzac in this regard could not be greater. In his preface to the third edition of *Oliver Twist,* Dickens notes how many romantic thieves he had read of — "seductive fellows (amiable for the most part), faultless in dress, plump in pocket, choice in horseflesh, bold in bearing, faultless in gallantry, great at a song, a bottle, a pack of cards or dice-box, and fit companions for the bravest." The models he seems to have in mind are of the order of

Gay's Macheath — eighteenth-century gentleman-criminals, anachronisms by his time, and gifted with few of the workaday talents that Balzac was to exalt in recreating a more suitable capitalistic myth. The "miserable reality," he goes on, he had met only in Hogarth. "It appeared to me that to draw a knot of such associates in crime as really do exist; to paint them in all their deformity, in all their wretchedness, in all the squalid poverty of their lives; to show them as they really are, for ever skulking uneasily through the dirtiest paths of life, with the great, black, ghastly gallows closing up their prospect, turn them where they may; it appeared to me that to do this, would be to attempt a something which was greatly needed, and which would be a service to society." This sort of simple badness concerned him constantly as a citizen: "Why is a notorious Thief and Ruffian ever left at large?" [5] It concerned him also as a writer, as the remark quoted above about "irredeemably bad" natures indicates; but it did not significantly concern him as a mythologist. In the first place, Dickens' cast of mind was neither intellectual nor political; being so little drawn to ideas himself, he could hardly have created a "ferocious logician" (as did Balzac and Dostoevsky) to stand against society on principle. His own opposition to Victorian society is constantly evidenced in his books, but it is not shared by his characters and he entrusts it to no fictive spokesman. All this is because his was fundamentally a loyal opposition, and here he is most typically the nineteenth-century Englishman. As Harry Levin suggests, the limitations of range and depth that the Victorian novel shows by comparison with the French or the Russian may ultimately reflect the greater stability of English institutions, untroubled by revolution in the recent past and not seriously liable to it in the near future.[6]

Devils and villains, then — if not thieves — pass from popular mythology into that of Dickens and mark the climate of one of its moral poles; at the other we find, as might be expected, angels. Rose Maylie in *Oliver Twist* is one, "in the lovely bloom and springtime of womanhood; at that age, when, if ever angels be for God's good purposes enthroned in mortal forms, they may be, without impiety, supposed to abide in such as hers (29). Esther Summerson in *Bleak House* is another, as is, to a supreme degree, Little Dorrit. Dickens' work in this respect amplifies Balzac's observation,

"Women have this in common with angels: that suffering beings belong to them." [7]

Dickens has frequently been criticized for this angelism of his, for the inhuman way certain Dickensian young women, exempted from the play of his humor, shrug off provocation, weariness, and all invitations to a selfhood rooted in something besides abnegation. Such criticism of their conception includes naturally a criticism of the atmosphere that accompanies them, the choirs of angels in the offing, the softening in the very tone and cadence of the language that creates them. Humphry House and others have suggested that our impatience with such devices might be tempered by a realization of the attitudes — especially the attitudes toward children — against which Dickens was writing; that is, the extreme callousness of society required an extremely pathetic image to move it to awareness. This is an important enough argument, but an even more basic one would contend that a mythology using devils can hardly be criticized for using angels as well. In any case, the point remains that it is not the fact of angelic characters that is a weakness, but rather their general inferiority to the devils. Beneath the deformation and grotesquerie of the Dickensian devils, their humanity is perceptible: they are frankly labeled monsters of wrong-doing, and it is this admission of their monstrosity that lets them function as Dickens would have them function. Similarly, his *triumphantly* good characters are exactly those whose goodness is based, as with Mr. Pickwick, on a monstrous innocence or, as with Mr. Micawber, on an equally monstrous improvidence — and seen, as both of them are, in a light no less benevolent for being comic. It may be, by contrast, exactly his failure to allow for the corresponding monstrosity of his angels that makes them so scarcely tolerable.

By manipulation of externally imposed atmosphere, by creating those careful harmonies of a character with his surroundings, of an indoor scene with its lighting and a landscape with the weather and time of day — by all such techniques of emotional underscoring, Dickens manages to involve his reader in "a world that is strikingly, appallingly relevant to our world." [8] It is, in fact, our world transfigured by vision, sometimes comically, sometimes pathetically. The *objects* are all real and minutely observed. It is only their functions, their relations, that are different. Circumstantial realism, realism of topography, physical ambience, dress, custom, is present, but tinged romantically with the sense of strangeness and wonder that is Dickens' own contribution to fiction and to the varieties of romantic realism. A letter written in 1859 is a central document:

It does not seem to me to be enough to say of any description that it is the exact truth. The exact truth must be there; but the merit or art in the narrator, is the manner of stating the truth. As to which thing in literature, it always seems to me that there is a world to be done. And in these times, when the tendency is to be frightfully literal and catalogue-like — to make the thing, in short, a sort of sum in reduction that any miserable creature can do in that way — I have an idea (really founded on the love of what I profess), that the very holding of popular literature through a kind of popular dark age, may depend on such fanciful treatment.[9]

The statement, with its uneasy overtones of attacking a straw man, is predictable in its hostility not just to unnamed exponents of an inferior realism, but to the very possibilities of the tendency; its key expressions are "popular literature" and "fanciful treatment." Six years earlier, the latter had been stressed in the author's preface to *Bleak House,* where he declared that he had "purposely dwelt upon the romantic side of familiar things." And, at the very beginning of the decade, Dickens' manifesto in the first number of *Household Words* had rung variations on the same two themes:

No mere utilitarian spirit, no iron binding of the mind to grim realities, will give a harsh tone to our Household Words . . . We would tenderly cherish that light of Fancy which is inherent in the human breast. . . . To show to all, that in all familiar things, even in those which are repellent on the surface, there is Romance enough, if we will but find it out — to teach the hardest workers at this whirling wheel of toil that their lot is not necessarily a moody, brutal fact excluded from the sympathies and graces of imagination; to bring the greater and lesser, in a degree, together upon that wide field and mutually dispose them to a better acquaintance and a kindlier understanding — is one main object of our Household Words.[10]

The "light of Fancy," it would seem, is to discover, or be fed by, the romance that is sufficient in all familiar things; and imagination — which may or may not be a different thing from fancy — is a faculty productive of sympathies and graces, in the purest romantic tradition, a softener of "brutal fact."

In the light of these declarations and of all the textual evidence in Dickens that anticipates and supports them, one wonders why Gissing should have thought it odd that Dickens seemed "to make more allusions throughout his work to the *Arabian Nights* than to any other book or author," and one can only agree with him that this continuing interest is "a circumstance illustrative of that habit of mind which led him to discover infinite romance in the obscurer life of London." [11] That this affinity (not to speak of influence) with the tone and manner of the *Arabian Nights* was based on personal acquaintance, we know. The book, along with the *Tales of the Genii,* was part of the childhood reading that formed the mature writer; and in the early planning of *Master Humphrey's Clock* Dickens even projected a series of Arabian Nights tales by Gog and Magog, the Giants in the Guildhall.[12] No less than Balzac, Dickens might have spoken of his work as "les Mille et une Nuits de l'Occident."

The tales of the *Arabian Nights* suggest vision and magic; they might suggest, farfetchedly but not implausibly, that conquering of death which was Scheherezade's motive and achievement in telling them. And they certainly raise again the question of popular literature, to which we have seen Dickens refer in the 1859 letter quoted above. The preface to *Household Words* approaches the subject from a different angle, stressing not just the appeal to a popular audience, but the consolatory nature of that appeal ("to teach the hardest workers at this whirling wheel of toil that their lot is not necessarily a moody, brutal fact").[13] Here, too, one may see an indirect reflection of one kind of romanticism, didactically expressed. That is the humanitarian strain, embodying the same concern with poor people and with the insulted and injured that motivated Dostoevsky in his early period, touched Gogol before him, and Balzac as well. Its artistic expression will be considered later; its expression as a creed must concern us here, for it is another mark of a distinction to be made between the products of romantic realism and those of the later, stricter school. The *locus classicus* for a discussion of this question is undoubtedly in the correspondence of Flaubert and George Sand, and the broadest points of disagreement, like the shifting terms of the discussion itself, have a relevance that goes beyond the borders of France. The ideal of an art oblivious to questions of its putative effect on the everyday sympathies of readers is stated succinctly by Flaubert, in a defense of his own work:

> I don't create "desolation" wantonly, believe me, but I can't change my eyes! As for my "lack of convictions," alas, I am suffocated with convictions. I am bursting with anger and suppressed indignation. But in line with my ideal of art, I believe that one must not show his own convictions, and that the artist should no more appear in his work than God appears in nature. The man is nothing, the work—everything! This discipline, which may arise from a false point of view, is nevertheless not easy to observe. And for me, at least, it is a kind of permanent sacrifice that I make to good taste. It would be quite pleasant for me to say what I think and to comfort Mr. Gustave Flaubert with phrases; but what is the importance of the gentleman in question? [14]

Flaubert seeks beauty above all; George Sand indicates a different priority of values. In the letter that elicited the passage here quoted, she compares the effect of her work and that of her friend's:

> What will we do? It is certain that you are going to create *desolation,* and I—*consolation.* I don't know what governs our destinies; you watch them pass; you criticize them; you abstain literarily from judging them; you confine yourself to painting them while hiding your personal feeling with great care, on principle. Nevertheless, one sees it through your story, and you make the people who read you sadder. As for me, I would render them less unhappy.[15]

The most striking point of difference is in the last-mentioned guiding desire, a desire so clearly irrelevant to what Flaubert *knew* of himself and his capabilities that his own tormenting preoccupations leave no room for its consideration. Such a criterion—at least until the time of Henry James—seems peculiarly French: for all their differences, it puts Balzac with Flaubert. And clearly it sets Dickens and the early Dostoevsky apart, putting them in the company of George Sand—whom the Englishman echoes almost literally and whom the Russian will idolize up to the end of his life.[16] The later Tolstoy, writing as that rare bird, a cosmopolitan dogmatist and puritan, will make much the same observation in his *What Is Art?* Speaking of that art which knows "the true ideal of our time," he notes: "On the one hand, the best works of art of our time convey feelings impelling to the unity and brotherhood of men (such are the works of Dickens, Hugo, Dostoevsky . . .); on the other hand, they aspire to the transmission of those feelings which are peculiar not alone to people of the highest [social] strata, but such as might unite all people without exception." [17]

This striking difference in tendency between the work of Dickens and that of Balzac involves many others. It is true that they shared the themes of the city, the criminal, money and worldly success, angelic selflessness and demonic rebellion; that they treated these themes by consistent use of devices of "heightening," symbolism, and atmosphere is equally true. And however dubious Henry James's observation that "as individuals they strongly resemble each other," few readers would dispute his claim for their parity: "In intensity of imaginative power, the power of evoking visible objects and figures, seeing them themselves with the force of hallucination and making others see them all but just as vividly, there is little to choose between them; they have no rivals but each other and Shakespeare." [18] Yet Dickens' treatment of the common themes differs markedly from that of his illustrious contemporary, whose works he seems to have been aware of, but not to have read. And not only is the mixture of romantic and realistic elements likely to be different in any novel of Dickens' as compared with any novel of Balzac's, but the nature of both elements is likely to be equally different. To say this much is to say that their mythologies contrast radically — a contrast that may be explored, first of all, in Dickens' treatment of the city.

REPRESENTING LONDON

Balzac had begun his career with a series of conventional, romantically melodramatic novels and only discovered Paris, literarily speaking, when he was about thirty; Dickens, on the other hand, discovered London at the very beginning of his career, so that where *Paris en 1831* or *La Fille aux yeux d'or* represents a reorientation of work already undertaken, *Sketches by Boz*, appearing in the middle of the same decade, marks the beginning of a direction to which its author would remain true throughout his career. "Never had been known such absorbing interest in the commonplace," Gissing remarks of these sketches, unintentionally echoing the literary style of Miss Toppit. The remark is borne out by the emphasis of the full title: *Sketches by Boz, Illustrative of Every-Day*

Life and Every-Day People. Leaving aside the section called "Tales" — which Dickens himself later singled out as "crude and ill-considered, and bearing obvious marks of haste and inexperience" — one finds the largest section to be that headed with a word of which Balzac was particularly fond: "Scenes." Here are "The Streets — Morning" and "The Streets — Night" at the beginning and, at the end, "Gin-Shops," "The Pawnbroker's Shop," "Criminal Courts," and "A Visit to Newgate." London, like Balzac's Paris, is proclaimed to be in its glory only at night — but the irony of that glory and its invidious comparison with domestic snugness not only mark a difference in national values, but prefigure one of the most constant Dickensian themes.[19] Here are no brilliant scenes of fashionable people, but rather, with a suitably lesser intensity, something already close to "the cold, wet, shelterless midnight streets of London" to which Oliver Twist will come. But Oliver will move in a world whose picturesqueness carries the ballast of constant moral preoccupation. In this first book, the picturesque tends rather to be a sufficient value in itself, and the city is seen not as a unity or a society so much as a collection of picturesque neighborhoods; again and again the adjectives "lively," "interesting," and "amusing" occur. What they indicate is not only the occasional nature of these pieces but, as Sylvère Monod has pointed out, a basic indecision on Dickens' part about the attitude he should take toward his material.[20]

This uncertainty extends, much of the time, to the people he presents — are they ludicrous? contemptible? pitiable? — and to the milieu itself. It appears notably in the chapter on "Shabby-Genteel People" and vitiates a promising opening, in which Dickens notes the existence of "certain descriptions of people who, oddly enough, appear to appertain exclusively to the metropolis. You meet them, every day, in the streets of London, but no one ever encounters them elsewhere; they seem indigenous to the soil, and to belong as exclusively to London as its own smoke, or the dingy bricks and mortar." Here, broached with pity if not with sympathy, is a theme that more than one of the novels will refine, until a Frederick Dorrit can appear invested with sympathy and explained by the workings of the social machine of which he forms a part. Similar are the attitudes toward officialdom ("Dismissing from our minds, therefore, all . . . feeling of awe . . . we enter at once into the parliament building, and upon our subject" — "A Parliamentary Sketch"), the compassion for prostitutes ("The Pawnbroker's Shop") and for children ("A Visit to Newgate").

But perhaps most notable of all is that uniting of close observation with imagination which was to become a Dickensian hallmark. Central in this respect is the chapter called "Meditations in Monmouth Street." As a good *physiologiste* of London, Dickens begins by explaining (with some archness) in what general ways "the inhabitants of Monmouth Street are a distinct class." But the meditations the street provokes are the heart of the sketch, and they are, characteristically, meditations accessible only to a keen observer. They allow him to animate the inanimate, to invest things with life, and imaginatively to practice the invention of the ideal wearer for any given garment. The way objects have of taking on a life of their own, conferred in the beginning only conditionally by an observing eye, is striking and typical. Thus he speaks at first of liking to look at clothes in secondhand store windows, to speculate on the former owner of a "deceased coat" or "dead pair of trousers," but it is not long before the ex-post-facto animation, begun as a manner of speaking, has turned literally into a runaway — before "whole rows of coats have started from their pegs, and buttoned up, of their own accord, round the waists of imaginary wearers; lines of trousers have jumped down to meet them; waistcoats have almost burst with anxiety to put themselves on; and half an acre of shoes have suddenly found feet to fit them, and gone stumping down the street." If it be objected that these lines show more imagination than observation, the passage that follows will redress the balance. Outside one shop window Dickens sees a few suits of clothes "which it immediately struck us must at different periods have all belonged to . . . the same individual." Runaway fancy will this time be curbed: "The idea seemed a fantastic one, and we looked at the clothes again, with a firm determination not to be easily led away." The controlling, knowing eye must ratify the idea, and it does. "There was the man's whole life written as legibly on those clothes, as if we had his autobiography engrossed on parchment before us." The first paragraph of the long demonstration that follows deserves to be quoted in full:

The first was a patched and much-soiled skeleton suit; one of those straight blue cloth cases in which small boys used to be confined before belts and tunics had come in, and old notions had gone out: an ingenious contrivance for displaying the full symmetry of a boy's figure, by fastening him into a very tight jacket, with an ornamental row of buttons over each shoulder, and then buttoning his trousers over it, so as to give his legs the appearance of being hooked on, just under the armpits. This was the boy's dress. It had belonged to a town boy, we could see; there was a shortness about the legs and arms of the suit, and a bagging at the knees, peculiar to the rising youth of London streets. A small day-school he had been at evidently. If it had been a regular boys' school they wouldn't have let him play on the floor so much, and rub his knees so white. He had an indulgent mother too, and plenty of halfpence, as the numerous smears of some sticky substance about the pockets, and just below the chin, which even the salesman's skill could not succeed in disguising, sufficiently betokened. They were decent people, but not overburdened with riches, or he would not have so far outgrown the suit when he passed into those corduroys with the round jacket; in which he went to a boys' school, however, learned to write — and in ink of pretty tolerable blackness, too, if the place where he used to wipe his pen might be taken as evidence.

The key phrase as Dickens goes on with this circumstantial biography is "we saw, or fancied we saw — it makes no difference which." Throughout all of the mature work, sight and vision will be thus combined.

With the exception of such bravura pieces, the *Sketches* are of interest only as they foreshadow the later work. In "The Pawnbroker's Shop" the forerunner of Bill Sikes's Nancy appears — and also of the prostitute who will pause so dramatically to speak with Little Dorrit on the pre-dawn streets: "There is something in the glimpse she has just caught of her young neighbor, and in the sight of the little trinkets she has offered in pawn, that seems to have awakened in this woman's mind some slumbering recollection, and to have changed, for an instant, her whole demeanor." Fagin's sufferings before his execution are foreshadowed in the dream sequence of the condemned convict in "A Visit to Newgate." And the sinister side of that urban anonymity which so attracts Oliver Twist at first is already spelled out in "Thoughts About People," which begins by observing: "It is strange with how little notice, good, bad or indifferent, a man may live and die in London. He awakens no sympathy in the breast of any single person; his existence is a matter of interest to no one save himself; he cannot be said to be forgotten when he dies, for no one remembered him when he was alive."

The *Sketches* signal the literary discovery of the city and the themes peculiar to it, and also Dickens' groping for a manner and an attitude appropriate to their treatment. If they lack any serious pursuit of individual fates, they will furnish, in compensation, a source for a good part of the auxiliary population in the novels. Much in *Oliver Twist* will grow out of them, as will the major change in the portrayal of this milieu: When a noncomic hero — and most particularly a child — is set into it, the urban milieu takes on new hues, a more consistent atmosphere, and becomes the mazy ground of alienation and corruption.

This ground had been literarily prepared in the previous decade by one of Dickens' favorite writers, Thomas De Quincey. Speaking of his nightly wanderings in the city, he recalls "such knotty problems of alleys, alleys without soundings, such enigmatical entries, and such sphinx's riddles of streets without obvious outlets or thoroughfares as must baffle the audacity of porters, and confound the intellects of hackney coachmen," and concludes: "I could almost have believed, at times, that I must be the first discoverer of some of these *terrae incognitae*." This daedalean London may be the discovery, but it is not the product, of De Quincey and after him Dickens. It existed, as a fact of stone and brick and mud, and it is more likely that a romantically stylized view of the city would have softened these features, for they seem to have been more amenable to understatement than to exaggeration. Similarly, it is De Quincey's actual search for his friend, the young prostitute Ann, that he reports and on which his anguished imagination feeds: "If she lived, doubtless we must have been sometimes in search of each other, at the very same moment, through the mighty labyrinths of London; perhaps even within a few feet of each other — a barrier no wider, in a London street, often amounting in the end to a separation for eternity!" [21]

It is just this quality of the city that Oliver Twist seeks: "London! — that great large place! — nobody — not even Mr. Bumble — could ever find him there!" (ch. 8). However, the quality that spelled tragedy for De Quincey and seems to spell safety for Oliver is illusory. The mighty labyrinths of London are the same, but the anonymity they offer is not absolute; and detection by the devil who rules them seems both easy and inevitable. So Oliver, after his first rescue by Mr. Brownlow, walks to the bookstall, "little dreaming that he was within so very short a distance of the merry old gentleman." Attacked by Sikes and Nancy, he is dragged off uttering unintelligible cries, and Dickens comments: "It was of little moment, indeed, whether they were intelligible or not; for there was nobody to care for them, had they been ever so plain" (ch. 15). The indifference of London is its chief moral quality in *Oliver Twist,* and if it has a unity it is the paradoxical unity of a bustling chaos of undifferentiated people and things. Goodness, once threatened by the city, can only hope to survive in flight to the unspoiled country, and it is there indeed that Oliver finds refuge and haven. There is no question of a Balzacian conquest of the city; it is the heart of darkness, and evasion seems to offer the only hope of a place in the sun.

That such an evasion could not long content Dickens is not surprising, and when he comes to face the problem foursquare, in *The Old Curiosity Shop,* he arrives not yet at a new solution, but at least at a rejection of the old one. Here the city, in its economic inhumanity, is as dark a place as in *Oliver Twist,* albeit presented in somewhat different terms, and it impels its victims, as before, to flee to the quasi-divine purity of the country, which is repeatedly identified with the remote springs of childhood, innocence, and peace. If this appears simply to take up the standard romantic theme of escape from the present to the past, and from the city to the countryside, it does so, as J. Hillis Miller has shown, only to demonstrate how impossible such an escape has become, for the journey to the country is now explicitly equated with the journey toward death.[22]

Writers like Alain have seen Dickens' London as built up like coral, from the cumulative force of descriptions of individuals, each one bearing his domicile, his neighborhood, and his class to the common edifice: "Wherever Dickens evokes a character, he establishes forever a cell of London, which does not cease to grow as one discovers its inhabitants; the impression of nature is in such a case so strong that one cannot reject these beings: one has to follow them."[23] With its implication that there is no central, all-embracing whole, the image is apt enough, but only for the novels of the early and middle periods. The later group of *Bleak House, Little Dorrit,* and *Our Mutual Friend* — these last three novels to be published in the *Pickwick* form, in nineteen monthly installments — deal with the city quite differently, just as they deal with plot quite differently. The increased incidence of complicated intrigue in these works is usually ascribed, and with some justice, to the influence of Wilkie Collins. But another reason, more relevant to an evolving treatment of the city, is offered by Humphry House: Dickens "was intending to use these novels as a vehicle of more concentrated sociological argument."[24] In these novels, that is, London achieves a unity it has never had before. It is still not an organism, as Paris had been for Balzac, and it is nowhere personified. On the other hand, in all three books a network of symbols, representing an actual network of social ties, connects the various characters and the classes they represent; Tom All-Alone's is related to Chesney Wold, and The Six Jolly Fellowship-Porters to the house in Portland Square, in much the same way that the Rue Neuve Sainte-Geneviève is to the Hotel Beauséant.

In these books London takes on its full significance as capital, as the head and symbol of national life; and this significance is underlined by the repeated warnings of national disaster which present policy may bring about. The explicit warning is sounded in *Bleak House* in the meditation on the death of Krook, the grotesque self-styled "Lord Chancellor":

> The Lord Chancellor of that Court, true to his title in his last act, has died the death of all Lord Chancellors in all Courts, and of all authorities in all places under all names soever, where false pretenses are made, and where injustice is done. Call the death by any name Your Highness will, attribute it to whom you will, or say it might have been prevented how you will, it is the same death eternally — inborn, inbred, engendered in the corrupt humours of the vicious body itself, and that only — Spontaneous Combustion, and none other of all the deaths that can be died. (ch. 32)

Similarly in *Little Dorrit,* Amy's "desolate idea of Covent Garden, as having all those arches in it, where the miserable children in rags among whom she had just now passed, like young rats, slunk and hid, fed on offal, huddled together for warmth, and were hunted about" leads to the parenthetical warning, "look to the rats, young and old, all ye Barnacles, for before God they are eating away our foundations, and will bring the roofs on our heads!" (I.14). And in *Our Mutual Friend,* the London dust heaps lead Dickens, describing their enormity, to exclaim: "My lords and gentlemen and honorable boards, when you in the course of your dust-shovelling and cinder-raking have piled up a mountain of pretentious failure, you must off with your honourable coats for the removal of it, and fall to the work with the power of all the queen's horses and all the queen's men, or it will come rushing down and bury us alive" (III.8).

To the characters in these novels, institutional society is a central, very real fact, and the most farfetched connections between individuals and classes not only operate but come eventually to light. No longer do we meet those citizens of the metropolis who, as Dickens says in *Martin Chuzzlewit,* "shooting arrows over houses as their daily business, never know on whom they fall." [25] The shooters and the shot meet in these books — nor are the shots so random. Jo the crossing-sweeper will meet Lady Dedlock and leave the mark of his contagion on Esther Summerson; Casby, the hypocritical patriarch, will visit the people he exploits in Bleeding Heart Yard and be unmasked before them; the unambitious daughter of a Thames scavenger will marry a pre-Shavian man-about-town. The workings of Chancery will unite the characters in *Bleak House;* as will the combined forces of the Circumlocution Office and the Marshalsea and the Merdle-dominated stock market in *Little Dorrit;* as will money — money as inheritance and money as shares — in *Our Mutual Friend* (see the opening of book I, ch. 10). Each of these novels will involve detective work, not simply to unravel the mysteries of plot but, more importantly, to lay bare the subterranean network of social relationships.

The city here is variously evoked. The symbolic juxtaposition of two extremes may do it, as in the memorably ironic evocation of Christian charity at the end of chapter 19 of *Bleak House.* The outcast Jo is sitting on Blackfriars Bridge with his scraps of dinner, looking up at the great cross of St. Paul's, and Dickens comments: "From the boy's face one might suppose that sacred emblem to be, in his eyes, the crowning confusion of the great, confused city; so golden, so high up, so far out of his reach." The whole of this closing paragraph gives a chordlike resonance to the chapter ending, and this is frequent in these novels; but even more frequent is the reversal of perspective, so that we are not looking up from but rather down on "the great, confused city." The night characteristically provides this kind of overview: "Midnight had come upon the crowded city. The palace, the night-cellar, the jail, the madhouse: the chambers of birth and death, of health and sickness: the rigid face of the corpse and the calm sleep of the child: midnight was upon them all" (*Oliver Twist,* ch. 46). Midnight, a kind of cosmic fact, suspending the city's usual animation and, for once, encompassing its chaos, here bespeaks that "higher" unity which Dickens was forever evoking to contrast with the world he showed. Within that world, a similar unifying role is played by great inanimate things — fog, dust, the river, blocks of buildings. The fog, which in the frequently cited overture to *Bleak House* symbolizes the nature and ubiquitousness of legal entanglements, operates this way, as it does at the opening of book III of *Our Mutual Friend,* where the heart of darkness is the heart of the city, and in the "foggy sea" the great dome of St. Paul's "seems to die hard."

The same symbolic, unifying overview occurs elsewhere in *Our Mutual Friend,* shot through with the dust-equals-money motif that is central in the book, and in *Little Dorrit* a prime example shows how religion and the rise of capitalism have turned the city into a desert (I.3). Such passages produce their powerful effect by doing many things at once: they generalize aspects of urban life; they merge the animate and the inanimate, subordinating both to a single moral point of view; they show man mastering nature with noxious results and nature taking revenge. From Ludgate Hill, Arthur Clennam sees "ten thousand representative houses . . . frowning heavily on the streets," "miles of close wells and pits of houses, where the inhabitants gasped for air." And "through the heart of the town a deadly sewer ebbed and flowed, in the place of a fine fresh river."

The river, in its own right, plays a great role in the Dickensian myth of London, nowhere greater than in *Our Mutual Friend,* where it provides a similar unifying overview at the end of chapter

3: "Thus, like the tides on which it had been borne to the knowledge of men, the Harmon Murder — as it came to be popularly called — went up and down, and ebbed and flowed, now in the town, now in the country, now among palaces, now among hovels, now among lords and ladies and gentlefolks, now among labourers and hammerers and ballast-heavers, until at last, after a long interval of slack water, it got out to sea and drifted away." The river is many things: life and continuity and, most of all, mystery. The successive inmates of the Marshalsea are "a turbid living river" to Little Dorrit who watches them pass before her and out again into the world (I.7). To Clennam in the same book it is oblivion: "And he thought — who has not thought for a moment, sometimes? — that it might be better to flow away monotonously like the river, and to compound for its insensibility to happiness with its insensibility to pain" (I.17). "We are all sailing away to sea," Dickens writes Maria Beadnell Winter in 1855, apropos of his enthusiastic recollection of his youthful infatuation with her, "and have a pleasure in thinking of the river we are upon, when it was very narrow and little." [26] But where he concentrates on the retrospect, Lizzie Hexam turns to the prospect, standing "on the river's brink unable to see into the vast blank misery of a life suspected, and fallen away from by good and bad, but knowing that it [the great black river] lay there dim before her, stretching away to the great ocean, Death." [27] The fascination of the river as a symbol in this last novel has been well analyzed by Monroe Engel and A. O. J. Cockshut, and there can be little doubt of the deliberateness of its role as such.[28] Dickens' admirer, Dostoevsky, will make a similar, though less extended, use of the Neva in his Petersburg novels. Precisely because of this deliberateness, however, care must be exercised in preserving critically the balance Dickens preserved artistically — the balance, that is, between the romantic-symbolic view of the river and the realistic-topographic one. For the Dickens signature is to be found exactly, and only, in their conjunction. When Mortimer Lightwood and Eugene Wrayburn leave the Veneerings to answer Jesse Hexam's note, we follow their carriage "down by the Monument, and by the Tower, and by the Docks; down by Ratcliffe, and by Rotherhithe; down by where accumulated scum of humanity seemed to be washed from higher grounds, like so much moral sewage, and to be pausing until its own weight forced it over the bank and sunk it in the river." When they arrive, Mortimer remarks, "This is a confoundedly out-of-the-way place" (*Our Mutual Friend,* I.3) — and reminds us that the riverbanks, and even the water between them, are not only a symbol, but also a neighborhood of London.

Sections of the metropolis, as soon as they are recognized as neighborhoods, become emblematic in a literal, sociological way; their names become a kind of shorthand. So Dickens can state, in the preface to the third edition of *Oliver Twist:* "Nor did I doubt that there lay festering in Saint Giles's as good materials towards the truth as any flaunting in Saint James's." It is not, of course, a matter of truth alone with Dickens: the truth of everyday places and things will contain "romance" as well. The sinister atmosphere of Saffron Hill in *Oliver Twist* has already been noted, and it is chiefly to such aspects of the early work that Gissing refers when he finds that "London as a place of squalid mystery and terror, of the grimly grotesque, of labyrinthine obscurity and lurid fascination, is Dickens's own; he taught people a certain way of regarding the huge city." [29] These epithets apply in fact to certain neighborhoods only. In the depiction of others, the Dickensian vision will produce satire rather than melodrama. Thus the description of Harley Street, Cavendish Square, in *Little Dorrit,* where "like unexceptionable Society, the opposing rows of houses . . . were very grim with one another. Indeed, the mansions and their inhabitants were so much alike in that respect, that the people were often to be found drawn up on opposite sides of dinner-tables, in the shade of their own loftiness, staring at the other side of the way with the dulness of the houses" (I.10). Balzac had noted how dwellings reflect their inhabitants; Dickens carries the process further, sometimes, as here, to a satirical identification of the two — sometimes, as in the case of Krook's room in *Bleak House,* ringing a grotesque variation on the technique. With Krook, once the identification of man with milieu has been made, a bizarre irony caps it: not, as we would expect, the littered room, but the man himself is destroyed by spontaneous combustion.

In the Dickens world, men increasingly take on the qualities of their surroundings, and vice versa. In the first chapter of *Little*

Dorrit, Rigaud "gurgle[s] in his throat" and "some lock gurgled in *its* throat immediately afterwards." Mr. Merdle, on the other hand, true to the suggestion of a pun in his name, "ooze[s] sluggishly and moodily around his drawing room." Mrs. Merdle's famous bosom is a jewel stand. In *Our Mutual Friend,* at a village fair, we meet desperate baked goods and sly vegetables: "Some despairing gingerbread that had been vainly trying to dispose of itself all over the country, and had cast a quantity of dust upon its head in mortification, again appealed to the public from an infirm booth. So did a heap of nuts, long long exiled from Barcelona, and yet speaking English so indifferently as to call fourteen of themselves a pint" (IV.6). As if in revenge, the Covent Garden drunkards in the same book flaunt their ontological allegiance to neighborhood: "Such stale vapid rejected cabbage-leaf and cabbage-stalk dress, such squashed pulp of humanity, are open to the day nowhere else" (IV.9).

More significantly, a character may appear to be grotesquely in transition from animate to inanimate: Silas Wegg is introduced as "a knotty man, and a close-grained, with a face carved out of very hard material, that had just as much play of expression as a watchman's rattle. When he laughed, certain jerks occurred in it, and the rattle sprung. Sooth to say, he was so wooden a man that he seemed to have taken his wooden leg naturally, and rather suggested to the fanciful observer, that he might be expected — if his development received no untimely check — to be completely set up with a pair of wooden legs in about six months" (I.5). This device, widely employed by Dickens, is of course a traditional comic one, whose rationale Bergson's theory of laughter accommodates better than some others; the point is openly acknowledged in the passage above by the mention of a fanciful observer. But the fanciful observer in these books does not confine his fancy to producing purely comic effects. It enters as well into the very fabric of the narration and constitutes one of the indices of the quality of hallucination that observers from Taine on have remarked in the Dickensian vision. To take another minor but typical instance, the counterpart of the process at work on Wegg is shown a few pages later at work on a tavern: "The wood forming the chimney-pieces, beams, partitions, floors, and doors, of the Six Jolly Fellowship-Porters, seemed in its old age fraught with confused memories of its youth. In many places it had become gnarled and riven, according to the manner of old trees; knots started out of it; and here and there it seemed to twist itself into some likeness of boughs. In this state of second childhood, it had an air of being in its own way garrulous about its early life" (I.6). In this kind of writing, comic and supra-comic by turns, Dickens has no rival but Gogol. Both in this regard point toward surrealism, though both are too deliberate and too conscious in their abandonment to vision to sustain full comparison with later writers whose situation may have its roots in the nineteenth century, but whose response to it is peculiarly contemporary. A surrealist might approve of the way houses cogitate in Dickens ("Many years ago [the Clennam house] had it in its mind to slide down sideways"), the way furniture "hides," or the way a churchyard seems to have taken laudanum. But a nearer connection may be with that folklore, real and spurious, on which Dickens' child's imagination fed.[30] And the very sharpness of his eye may call forth the compensating intensity of imaginative transformation, as if in resistance not only to all the ugliness that met that eye, but to the process Frazer noted, whereby "the army of spirits, once so near, has been receding farther and farther from us, banished by the magic wand of science from hearth and home." [31]

A conveniently central text for this discussion — especially as it touches on the portrayal of the city — has been found by two recent critics, though differently interpreted by each.[32] It occurs in chapter 9 of *Martin Chuzzlewit* ("Town and Todgers's"). Both the singularity and the typicality of Todgers' boardinghouse and the neighborhood around it are stressed at the opening of the chapter:

> Surely there never was, in any other borough, city, or hamlet in the world, such a singular sort of place as Todgers's. And surely London, to judge from that part of it which hemmed Todgers's round, and hustled it, and crushed it, and stuck its brick-and-mortar elbows into it, and kept the air from it, and stood perpetually between it and the light, was worthy of Todgers's, and qualified to be on terms of close relationship and alliance with hundreds and thousands of the odd family to which Todgers's belonged.

Todgers' does not represent the city as such, for it is a victim of the city; but exactly for this reason the building's suffering merges with that of the human victims of London life, and a perspective broader than the merely picturesque or comic is opened. The view from the roof carries the perspective further and sharpens it; here what has seemed only confusion threatens to turn into a revolution of the inhuman against the human:

After the first glance, there were slight features in the midst of this crowd of objects, which sprung out from the mass without any reason, as it were, and took hold of the attention whether the spectator would or no. Thus, the revolving chimney-pots on one great stack of buildings seemed to be turning gravely to each other every now and then, and whispering the result of their separate observation of what was going on below. Others, of a crook-backed shape, appeared to be maliciously holding themselves askew, that they might shut the prospect out and baffle Todgers's. The man who was mending a pen at an upper window over the way, became of paramount importance in the scene, and made a blank in it, ridiculously disproportionate in its extent, when he retired. The gambols of a piece of cloth upon the dyer's pole had far more interest for the moment than all the changing motion of the crowd. Yet even while the looker-on felt angry with himself for this, and wondered how it was, the tumult swelled into a roar; the hosts of objects seemed to thicken and expand a hundredfold; and after gazing round him, quite scared, he turned into Todgers's again, much more rapidly than he came out.

Here indeed we see demonic possession and "a world undergoing a gruesome spiritual transformation." [33] Or at the least we see the shadow of such a transformation cast before the event itself, the threat being kept from actuality by "seemed" and "appeared," which restrain the passing of simile into metaphor. The "as if" formula, so constant in Dickens' writing, functions continually in this way, permitting him to render imagistically all the radical alienation going on in his world and, at the same time, offering an equivocal escape from that grim contemplation in the admission of the figurative character of the image.[34] One may notice, moreover, a counterpart in the way in which the good characters are continually being threatened and continually saved: the threats are too real to be conjured away, and the escapes seem increasingly miraculous and doubtful. So Arthur Clennam and Little Dorrit, after their marriage, "went quietly down into the roaring streets, inseparable and blessed; and, as they passed along in sunshine and in shade, the noisy and the eager, and the arrogant and the froward and the vain, fretted and chafed, and made their usual uproar" (II.34).

So, too, Eugene Wrayburn and Lizzie Hexam will marry at the end of *Our Mutual Friend* and go on, not into assured happiness after all their trials, but into possibility only.

The transforming vision and the escape both testify to the faculty that David Copperfield claims and that his creator possesses supremely: the ability to see the world in adult terms but with a child's vision. The child's delight in naming things is likewise evident — not only in the odd, playful rightness of the dozens of Dickensian surnames (Pecksniff, Cheeryble, Noggs, Boffin), but in the additional proliferation of nicknames, which serve within each book to connect and reconnect the characters in subtler relationships.[35] Similarly, the child's vision reflects the child's demands. (There is, of course, nothing derogatory intended in this formulation. "Child's" is not a synonym of "childish"; rather, it links Dickens most directly to the English romantic tradition.[36]) Where the adult observer in Dickens most often sees in London chaos and alienation — and latterly the unifying action of inhuman forces, economic and political — the child's eye opposes to its embroidery of grotesque terrors the redeeming examples of elementary virtues, simply exercised — kindness, love, good humor, fortitude — the family virtues. Each book will contain them somewhere among all the complications. They are the lines of such true community as is found in the novels, and it is on them that Dickens sets up his community with "his best friend," as he himself put it at the outset of his career — "the Public." Twenty years later (in the year of *Madame Bovary*) he was still declaring himself to his readers "deeply sensible of the affection and confidence that have grown up between us." [37] It has often been remarked that the Dickens world — which is virtually to say the Dickensian metropolis — is strikingly incomplete by comparison with Balzac's Paris or Dostoevsky's Petersburg, lacking as it does any major place for ideas or art, for serious politics or adult sexual experience. Yet this, too, is a double result of the peculiar nature of the Dickensian community. Both aspects are made clear in a letter to Forster of 15 August 1856, written from Paris:

I have always a fine feeling of the honest state into which we have got, when some smooth gentleman says to me or to some one else when I am by, how odd it is that the hero of an English book is always uninteresting—

too good—not natural, &c. I am continually hearing this of Scott from English people here, who pass their lives with Balzac and Sand. But O my smooth friend, what a shining impostor you must think yourself and what an ass you must think me, when you suppose that by putting a brazen face upon it you can blot out of my knowledge the fact that this same unnatural young gentlemen (if to be decent is to be necessarily unnatural), whom you meet in those other books and in mine, *must be* presented to you in that unnatural aspect by reason of your morality, and is not to have, I will not say any of the indecencies you like, but even any of the experiences, trials, perplexities, and confusions inseparable from the making or unmaking of all men! [38]

On the one hand, the public is blamed for the prudery of its tastes, to offend which would be to violate "the affection and confidence that have grown up between us." On the other — albeit parenthetically — the writer himself stands out for "decency," from which it fairly follows that, though the absence of the experience inseparable from the making or unmaking of all men leaves his novels incomplete, it does not distort their basic truth; a writer committed to a more skeptical or more complex view of decency could not have made such a statement without drastically impeaching his whole literary performance.

Dickens, therefore, was not entirely reluctant about keeping his realism within the hedges of Victorian respectability. While defending the presentation of low life in *Oliver Twist* ("I will not, for these fastidious readers, abate one hole in the Dodger's coat, or one scrap of curl-paper in the girls' dishevelled hair," he says in the preface), he nevertheless gave a proud assurance — which he was later to parody as Podsnappery — that he had "banished from the lips of the lowest character . . . any expression that could by possibility offend." He went beyond this position, it is true — but even in that last major novel, where Podsnappery makes its dismayingly hilarious appearance and takes the full brunt of his scorn, the same impossible goodness that was once incarnated in Oliver Twist appears again in Lizzie Hexam, speaking the same improbably pure English; and the pride that goes before an unconvincing fall in the person of Bella Wilfer leaves this "boofer lady" as the rightful reward of the palely good, long-suffering John Harmon. Part of the answer lies in the observation of R. C. Churchill that, though Dickens could be critical of his age when he saw the need for social reform, "the things that did not arouse either his righteous indignation or his sense of the ridiculous slipped through his guard unobserved"; he accepted the sentimentality and vulgarity of the age because "he was an important part, himself, of that sentimentality and vulgarity." [39] But it is important to recognize, too, that the sentimentality — vulgarity is another, and cloudier, matter — is not simply a gratuitous intrusion: it is an intrinsic part of the myth. Decency is an aspect of goodness; goodness, pure and simple, must be shown in the novels because it is one of the chief missions of art to display and inculcate it. If this flies in the face of "realism" — which is only one school among many — then so much the worse for realism. Ruskin states in extreme terms the case for a notion of art that Dickens served quite faithfully: "All healthy and helpful literature sets simple bars between right and wrong; assumes the possibility, in men and women, of having healthy minds in healthy bodies, and loses no time in the diagnosis of fever or dyspepsia in either; least of all in the particular kind of fever which signifies the ungoverned excess of any appetite or passion." [40]

How, then, strike the balance of Dickens' realism?

FANTASTIC FIDELITY

The usual difficulties in applying a term such as "realism" are compounded with Dickens. He himself offers little help in the form of the kind of literary discussion so natural to Balzac and Dostoevsky; his letters are as singularly free of conscious theorizing as his friendships were of intellectual companionship. He did, to be sure, begin introducing new material into major English fiction as early as *Sketches by Boz* and *Oliver Twist* — and averring the truth of his presentation in the prefaces. "It is useless," he says of Nancy in the preface to *Oliver Twist,* "to discuss whether the conduct and character of the girl seems natural or unnatural, probable or improbable, right or wrong. IT IS TRUE." Only a few years earlier, Balzac had used virtually the same phrase to make a similar statement at the outset of *Le Père Goriot:* "After having read about the secret misfortunes of old Goriot, you will dine with relish, blaming the author for your insensibility, taxing him with exaggeration, accusing him of poeticizing. Ah! but be assured: this drama is neither a fiction nor a romance. *All is true.*" [41] But both pleas are disingenuous, Dickens' the more so since, like most of his prefatory remarks, it is a defense after the fact against otherwise unanswerable criticisms of his performance.

More to the point have been those critical examinations that seek the special meaning of truth in the Dickensian novel by attending to the Dickensian form itself. The most cogent and influential of these is probably W. C. Phillips' work on the so-called sensation novel,[42] in which simple likelihood is rejected as any sort of index to truth. What the fantastic aggregate life of the city provides, what the newspapers chronicle daily, what the observer may see with his own eyes not frequently but even once, is truth in the absolute sense and therefore usable by the novelist, no matter how it may strike his readers. Wilkie Collins, an influence on Dickens, is usually quoted in this regard, as is Charles Reade, the third member of the putative Dickensian school of sensationalism. At the beginning of *Basil,* Collins wrote: "I have not thought it either politic or necessary, while adhering to realities, to adhere to everyday realities only." Reade put the matter even more strikingly in his *Autobiography of a Thief:* "I feign probabilities; I record improbabilities. The former are conjectures, the latter truths." [43]

There is no question but that these statements are applicable to Dickens, though it would be dangerous to go beyond them in trying to explain his method by reference to the words and works of his friends. The talents involved are too disparate. More significant is the fact that, in Dickens' prefaces and letters, the two most frequently recurring themes are probability and unity.[44] Except for the explosion of Krook, Dickens is not much drawn to freak accidents — not even so much as we might expect of a man caught, as he was in 1865, in a train accident that left him in a coach hanging precariously over a viaduct, miraculously unharmed. The sort of unlikelihood that struck him rather more was coincidence. "On the coincidences, resemblances and surprises of life Dickens liked especially to dwell," Forster reports, "and few things moved his fancy so pleasantly. The world, he would say, was so much smaller than we thought it; we were all so connected by fate without knowing it; people supposed to be far apart were so constantly elbowing each other; and tomorrow bore so close a resemblance to nothing half so much as to yesterday." [45] A characteristic passage in *Little*

Dorrit, among many others, bears this out: "Strange," Dickens comments, "if the little sick-room fire were in effect a beacon fire, summoning some one, and that the most unlikely some one in the world, to the spot that *must* be come to." Generalizing the point, he asks rhetorically: "Which of the vast multitude of travellers, under the sun and the stars, climbing the dusty hills and toiling along the weary plains, journeying by land and journeying by sea, coming and going so strangely, to meet and to act and react on one another, which of the host may, with no suspicion of the journey's end, be travelling surely hither?" (I.15).

For all the differences of their work, Dickens' use of coincidence here parallels Balzac's, and with the same rationale, as set forth by Lukacs. Why, Lukacs asks, would the most brilliant medico-pathological explanation of why Antony lost his voice just before he was due to make his oration over Caesar's body be unable to keep such a thing from seeming merely a grotesque accident, and why, by contrast, do not "the rough-hewn, scarcely motivated accidents" in the catastrophe of *Romeo and Juliet* appear as mere chance?

> For no other reason, of course, than that the necessity which nullifies chance consists of an intricate framework of causal connections and because only the aggregate necessity of an entire trend of developments constitutes a *poetic* necessity. Romeo's and Juliet's love *must* end in tragedy and only this necessity nullifies the accidental character of all the happenings which are the immediate causes that bring about, stage by stage, this inevitable development of the plot. It is of secondary importance whether such happenings taken by themselves, are motivated or not, and if the former, to what extent. One happening is not more a matter of chance than another and the poet has a perfect right to choose, among several equally accidental occurrences, the one he regards as best suited to his purpose. Balzac makes sovereign use of this freedom, and so did Shakespeare.[46]

As with Balzac, too, the identification of this freedom as the *poet's* freedom is apropos in placing, by implication, the primary emphasis on the shaping vision and not just on the selecting one—on the mythographic and not just on the "realistic." That the debased mythology of melodrama played a significant role in his work has been sufficiently remarked; what is to be further noted is the way Dickens, in defending the melodramatic mode of characterization early in his career, seems to found his defense on the double ground of everyday reality *and* fictional convention (read, poetic freedom). He finds it strange "that what we call the world, which is so very credulous in what professes to be true, is most incredulous in what professes to be imaginary; and that while every day in real life it will allow in one man no blemishes, and in another no virtues, it will seldom admit a very strongly-marked character, either good or bad, in a fictitious narrative, to be within the limits of probability." [47] The tension persists between the literal fact of real life and the literary fact of fictitious narrative: Dickens himself was to characterize the relation of the second to the first as "fantastic fidelity." [48]

Fidelity of a kind is not and never has been seriously in question in considerations of Dickens' realism. Humphry House, Monroe Engel, and others have shown the degree of Dickens' concern with the society around him, and none of the charges that he lacked a philosophy, a theory, or an intellectual grasp of politics can lessen the fact of that continually growing concern. But realism is not a matter of concern alone: it is also a matter of the way that concern is conveyed. It is not part of the design of this chapter to attempt an enumeration of the varieties of Dickensian style, but since that job has never been done as fully as it should be, something must be said about its nature as it touches on the problems of his realism. For, lapses aside, Dickens was an astonishing stylist, and in the service of his own vision found the *mot juste* with a frequency that might be the envy of more deliberate searchers. Unlike Balzac, he was intoxicated with words, and the effect of reading him is often a re-creation of that intoxication. Detail with him is never neutral. Instead of any attempted self-effacement in rendering a scene, we find the opposite: a continual presence, not necessarily in terms of overt comment, but always implied in the very selection and bias of the words. Speaking of the painter's art, Dickens said that it should not so much render objects in their naked otherness, as "inform" them "with mind and sentiment." [49] Mind and sentiment similarly inform his prose and often move it up to the very borders of poetry. His lapses into blank verse have received their share of attention. Less noticed, perhaps, has been the frequency with which not only poetic rhythms and diction appear in his prose, but even the humbler mainstays of assonance and alliteration, so that a question like the following (from his preface to the third edition of *Oliver Twist*) contains its answer in the texture of the language: "The cold, wet, shelterless midnight streets of London; the foul and frowsy dens, where vice is closely packed and lacks the room to turn; the haunts of hunger and disease, the shabby rags that scarcely hold together: where are the attractions of these things?" The "attractions," as in most poetry, are in the imposition of form, order, and structure through style. The accumulation of four heavily accented adjectives to a single noun in the opening phrase sets the theme; alliteration then comes into conspicuous play ("*f*oul and *f*rowsy," "*h*aunts of *h*unger," "*th*ese *th*ings"), as does assonance ("f*ou*l and fr*ow*sy," "p*ack*ed and l*ack*s," "sh*a*bby r*a*gs," "attr*a*ctions"). The same thing may be observed in many of the quotations used in this chapter; careful patterns of sound, subtle manipulations of rhythm are ubiquitous, and by their very conspicuousness add a dimension to the matter of his prose that is absent from writing we usually think of as realistic in manner. Dickens himself admitted his unfortunate tendency to fall into blank verse at times; but this is the other side of the coin and has yet to be sufficiently recognized.

The effect is sometimes lyrical, occasionally bathetic. It tends to be absent — and the realism most nearly pure — when the narration is conducted by a character, as in *David Copperfield* and, most notably, in *Great Expectations*. In these works the first-person narration is essentially only an extension of that monologue by which so many Dickensian characters exist and which, in juxtaposition with other monologues, produces dialogue in the novels. Dickens is on record with a belief that the story should be carried on by the actors themselves — and so it is, in a way that carries his novel form a good way toward the purely theatrical. This point has escaped few of his commentators, beginning with contemporaries, and would call for no comment here if the contrast with Dostoevsky were not in prospect and did not suggest an important qualification. For the Dostoevskian novel places a similar premium on dialogue, makes it primary, to produce what one Soviet critic has termed the "polyphonic novel."[50] In such a novel, the argument runs, dialogue predominates over exposition, reversing the more usual, "homophonic" practice by which a single point of view dominates all the presented material and dialogue appears only as illustration of what has already been established respecting character and situation. The polyphonic novel is thus the most "objective" possible and the closest possible approximation to theatrical practice — because, as in the theater, conflicts appear in all their complex immediacy, unmediated and unresolved by any external agency. This point will be developed in its place; it is raised here because it gives us a basis for qualifying Dickens' theatricality (and objectivity) by reminding us that his novels are, in the last analysis, homophonic. The extent to which narrative exposition is restricted (and it is restricted particularly in the earlier works) is matched by a correspondingly greater intensity and personality of tone when it does appear; and while this does not usually detract from the independence of the characters, it does bind them to a single context and hold them in a single light.

Partially in speech, all the same, and generally outside it, the tendency of style is either toward the prerealism of the comic or the suprarealism of the satiric — the second growing in importance toward the end of Dickens' career, as is evident in the set pieces on the Circumlocution Office in *Little Dorrit* and the parvenu households of the Veneerings and Podsnaps in *Our Mutual Friend*. If, as has been argued earlier, the historical achievement of realism was in large part a promotion of the traditionally comic to a new seriousness, a major point of their intersection deserves comment. Chesterton saw it clearly when he observed that Dickens "could only get to the most solemn emotions adequately if he got to them through the grotesque." [51] He never explains what he means by grotesque, but we have indications enough of what it meant to Dickens.

Thus in *Nicholas Nickleby* he seems to adhere to the traditional interpretation of the grotesque as equivalent to the bizarrely amusing. In chapter 8, describing the starving children, he notes: "And yet this scene, painful as it was, had its grotesque features, which, in a less interested observer than Nicholas, might have provided a smile." The character of Quilp, as that of Fagin in the preceding book, would seem to illustrate such a conception. By the time of *The Old Curiosity Shop* a more serious attitude toward the grotesque appears to be forming. In the preface to the First Cheap Edition (1848), he states: "In writing the book, I had it always in my fancy to surround the lonely figure of the child with grotesque and wild but not impossible companions, and to gather about her innocent face and pure intentions, associates as strange and uncongenial as the grim objects that are about her bed when her history is first foreshadowed." In this series of paired adjectives, grotesque seems equated simply with strange — neither implying nor necessarily excluding a comic perception. And, in fact, as Miller has noted, these novels together with *Barnaby Rudge* strike one most with their "multitude of grotesque characters, who are altogether unique, each vivid and distinct, each living as the perpetual re-enactment of his own peculiar idiosyncrasies." [52] Each, in his individuality, is an achievement of style — of the narrative style that describes him and of the style of speaking that is distinctively his own. These characters do not change and do not — as the characters of more realistic fiction would do — reveal themselves in their differing responses to different situations; but one reason for this, surely, is their function as accessories, diversions or foils to the main character in each story. It is not until he comes to write *Great Expectations* that Dickens will take a thoroughly serious view of the grotesque — and with it a great step toward a controlling realism. Reference is not to a character, but to "the grotesque tragicomic conception" that, Dickens said, "first encouraged me." [53] The conception is that of the concealed connection of Pip's rise in the world with Magwitch the convict. And if in the execution, "tragicomic" becomes something closer to patheti-comic, the combination is no less significant, for it is no less central. Into this scheme a grotesque character like Miss Havisham fits well; deranged and bizarre, like many of the earlier characters, she has none of their vitality, and when Pip describes her, the impression of painful reality clearly outweighs any amusement:

> Saving for the one weird smile at first, I should have felt almost sure that Miss Havisham's face could not smile. It had dropped into a watchful and brooding expression—most likely when all the things about her had become transfixed—and it looked as if nothing could ever lift it up again. Her chest had dropped, so that she stooped; and her voice had dropped, so that she spoke low, and with a dead lull upon her; altogether, she had the appearance of having dropped, body and soul, within and without, under the weight of a crushing blow. (ch. 8)

The same might be said for the first appearance of Frederick Dorrit. The description is stylized in a similarly comic way — and yet the final, grotesque impression is suffused as much with pity as with amusement:

He was dirtily and meanly dressed in a threadbare coat, once blue, reaching to his ankles and buttoned to his chin, where it vanished in the pale ghost of a velvet collar. A piece of red cloth with which that phantom had been stiffened in its lifetime was now laid bare, and poked itself up, at the back of the old man's neck, into a confusion of gray hair and rusty stock and buckle, which altogether nearly poked his hat off. A greasy hat it was, and a napless; impending over his eyes, cracked and crumpled at the brim, and with a wisp of pocket-handkerchief dangling out below it. His trousers were so long and loose, and his shoes so clumsy and large, that he shuffled like an elephant; though how much of this was gait, and how much trailing cloth and leather, no one could have told. Under one arm he carried a limp and worn-out case, containing some wind instrument; in the same hand he had a pennyworth of snuff in a little packet of whitey-brown paper, from which he slowly comforted his poor old blue nose, with a lengthened-out pinch. (I.8)

If Dickens rarely presents a protagonist who can himself be called grotesque, this is due in large part to the nature of his constant myth, which deals with the attempts of an alienated, *good* individual to find a place in society.[54] The necessity of pure goodness — a goodness often stiflingly conventional in the portrayal — precludes quirks at the same time that it calls for them as foils, and it sets up a descending series, whereby the unnatural purity of the good finds compensation in the motley grotesque of the secondary characters and whereby they, in turn, maintain their reality "because they are so carefully linked to a world of commonplace affairs," shown with "marvellous fidelity." [55] The Dickens world, in all its physical concreteness, is fully and faithfully realistic — and for all his flights of fancy, he preserves an Antaeus-like relation to it.

There is perhaps another reason for Dickens' refusal to let the grotesque touch his exemplary characters; it springs from "one of the chief conditions of his genius" — as Henry James found it — "not to see beneath the surface of things." It has been argued by Dorothy Van Ghent that the tendency of objects in the Dickensian world to take on human attributes and vice versa serves actually to psychologize the novels in an unconventional way, by *objectify-*

ing psychological states, so that even if his novels are all surface, they include much that does not ordinarily reside there. Yet, even granting this, one has to agree with James that "he has added nothing to our understanding of human character." "He is a master of but two alternatives," James commented: "he reconciles us to what is commonplace, and he reconciles us to what is odd. . . . The value of the latter service is incontestable. . . . But what is the condition of the truly great novelist? For him there are no alternatives, for him there are no oddities, for him there is nothing outside of humanity." [56] Seen from such a lofty standpoint, the grotesques of Dickens reveal the chief limitation in their conception; it is, on the positive side, the same limitation that Humphry House has seen in Dickens' portrayal of vice, that it is never done in such a way as to tempt or compel a reader to recognize its symptoms or even its possibility in himself.[57] For Dickens there *are* oddities.

James is right, but unfair. He is trying Dickens by rules the older writer never accepted, convicting him of failure to realize intentions that never were his. One might as fairly criticize James for having created no Pickwick and no Sairey Gamp. It would seem, on the other hand, both reasonable and just to investigate the extent of a realism Dickens was continually proclaiming and as continually qualifying, in his statements and in his fiction. In discovering London and in appropriating the discovery to his own particular genius, he served the novel generously — including that stricter and narrower realism that appeared during his time and after. One may always be sure that the observed detail is true, however fanciful the rendering, just as one may be increasingly sure that Dickens' *concerns* are an immediate response to the form and pressure of his time. His closest self-avowed disciple proclaimed, with the knowledge that comes of artistic kinship, the importance of his gift of "knowing exactly how to be unerringly true whilst entertaining your reader with every freak . . . that imagination and humour can conceive at their freest and wildest." [58]

If realistic writers are reformed idealists, Dickens must finally be considered an idealist whose whole progress is toward disillusion and whose most striking constant is his resistance to it; both the progress and the resistance are observable in the genius of his stylistic presentation. In approaching Dostoevsky, who drew on Dickens as on Balzac, we must consider a writer who is utterly without the Dickensian Victorian ballast and who, sharing many elements of Dickens' vision and using many of the same techniques, realizes their extremer potentialities, leaving behind "normalcy," community, and proportion to confront yet another city and to produce yet another grotesque rendition of the complexity of everyday life and everyday people.

4

Gogol: The Apotheosis of the Grotesque

> For isn't everything in the world arranged with wondrous whimsicality? The gay can in an instant turn into the sad, if one stand and contemplate it overlong, and then God knows what odd notions may not stray into your head.
>
> *Dead Souls,* ch. 3

> Where is our life? Where are we with all our contemporary passions and singularities? If only we saw some reflection of it in our melodrama! But our melodrama lies, in the most unscrupulous fashion . . . A most incomprehensible phenomenon: what surrounds us daily, what is inseparable from us, what is usual, only a deep, great, unusual talent can notice.
>
> "Petersburg Notes for 1836"

MORE elusive perhaps than any other great writer of his century, Nikolai Gogol demands inclusion here — both because his work offers a brilliant and highly original combination of the elements of romanticism and realism; and because his pioneering achievements in romantic realism led the young Dostoevsky to the themes, and in large measure the language, of his early work. This last fact is vital to an understanding of Dostoevsky and has been a commonplace in Russia for over a century, though not in the West.

Moreover, to call Gogol a romantic realist may be the best way to redress a historical injustice, in which civic-minded Russian critics, taking one side of his work for the whole, proclaimed him a realist; while others (notably the symbolists) took only the other side and so claimed him as one of themselves. There are historical reasons for this, of course, and it would not matter so much if the quarrel were over different stages or even items of his work. But it is not. The quarrel includes his early stories, collected as *Evenings on a Farm near Dikanka* and *Mirgorod,* and centers on his novel, *Dead Souls,* along with the stories traditionally known as the Petersburg tales.

The early stories need not concern us; they are his most clearly and unabashedly romantic works, full of Ukrainian local color, popular legends, warriors, and demons. "Old-World Landowners," it is true, looks like an affectionate farewell to the genre, and the story of the two Ivans points toward *Dead Souls* with its inverse romanticism. Yet none of these stories is really concerned with contemporary life, and none can be called a product of its author's experience. *Dead Souls* is a more complicated affair. Gogol's contemporaries generally took it as an exposé of provincial life and the serfowning system, and as the first great exemplar of the realistic prose novel in Russian (Pushkin's verse-novel, *Eugene Onegin,* preceded it by a decade). Why they should have taken it as an exposé is a question for the cultural historian; the answer seems to be that nothing so fiercely negative had been written about that area of Russian life and, since all Russian liberals knew that it deserved attacking, they assumed that this attack on human rascality and vulgarity must be aimed at the system — as it would have been if any of them had written it. As for the book's exemplifying realism, neither the times nor the nature of Gogol's own genius supports such a contention. Russian realism, as we see it in Goncharov, Turgenev, and Tolstoy, was born in the decade after *Dead Souls* (1842), and its practitioners rejected more of Gogol than they took. With its lyrical digressions and its manifesto-like claim for the legitimacy of showing "all those things that an indifferent eye fails to notice — all the stupendous, terrible slime of trivia in which our lives are mired," Gogol's picaresque novel may qualify as romantic realism; but it qualifies as a sport, belonging in point of technique as much to the European eighteenth century as to the Russian nineteenth, and treating an area of life that Gogol barely knew at first hand.

More fruitful for this discussion are his Petersburg tales. Born of the writer's own intimate experience, they show him turning his attention from the Ukraine and the past to Russia and the present. More clearly than *Dead Souls,* they illustrate the originality of his manner, and more immediately than *Dead Souls* they prefigure the early tales of Dostoevsky, whose alleged acknowledgment of his generation's debt to one of them has been endlessly quoted: "We all came out from under Gogol's 'Overcoat.' "[1] Once more, the city provides a main theme; and if stylistically Gogol may be said to begin where Dickens leaves off, he may also, in his evocation of the metropolis, be said to begin where Balzac leaves off.

Not, however, in any direct sense. Gogol did read Dickens, at least once, but that was already near the end of his urban period, when any Dickensian "influence" must have been corroborative, rather than productive — the recognition of a kindred artistic soul, a congenial but distant cousin.[2] For a Balzacian influence, the circumstantial evidence is rather more impressive. The argument, briefly, is that at the beginning of the thirties, translations of the early Balzac — the Balzac of *Ferragus* with its romantic evocations of the city's strange unity — strengthened the vogue that translations of Jouy had enjoyed, together with the flood of "physiological sketches" of Petersburg and Moscow he had inspired.[3] To the extent that these works were an important part of the literary ambience that the suggestible young Gogol absorbed, they may profitably be noticed in considering his own work: if they suggested anything to the young writer, it was most likely a direction to explore, a theme and an approach — just as the themes for *The Inspector General* and *Dead Souls* are said to have been given him by Pushkin. They showed how the city might be explored with the eye of a realist and evoked with the tools of a romantic; but in the matter of stylization of the city, there were examples to be found closer at hand, examples that reflected the historical uniqueness of the Russian capital. While Gogol was working and reworking his Petersburg tales, in the same years that Balzac and Dickens were showing their publics unsuspected sides of Paris and London, Pushkin was publishing his *The Bronze Horseman* (1833) and *The Queen of Spades* (1834). There was already forming a separate and, over the years, a more long-lived myth of Petersburg — which deserves a preliminary word.

Pushkin, it has been claimed with justice, "is in the same measure the creator of the *image* of Petersburg as Peter the Great was the builder of the city itself." [4] To be sure, the century since the founding of the city had seen its share of literary celebration of Peter's work. But this celebration consisted mainly of hymns or odes to the "Palmyra of the North," the "new Rome," exalting alike the abstract imperial idea and the concrete, classical symmetry of the imperial capital, with its imposing palaces, avenues, and embankments — thus, within the limitations of the neoclassic canon, Lomonosov, Derzhavin, and a host of their inferiors. As late as 1818, Prince Vyazemsky was writing in Russian alexandrines: "I see the city of Peter, wondrous and majestic, / By the will of the Tsar erected from the marshes, / The inherited monument of his mighty glory, / Already a hundredfold embellished by his descendants. . . . / Art here waged everywhere a battle with nature / And everywhere blazoned its triumph." [5]

Pushkin also sang the praises of this beauty of line and stone, most notably in the introduction to *The Bronze Horseman,* in the passage beginning: "I love thee, masterpiece of Peter — I love thine aspect, graceful and severe, Neva's mighty stream, her granite banks, stiff lace of iron fences." [6] But what he did, moved by the disastrous flood of 1824, was to go on to show the tragic price of Peter's achievement, the uncertainty of that triumph of art over nature which Vyazemsky had sung before him. So to the hymn of praise in his introduction, he adds a narrative (the poem is subtitled "A Petersburg Tale") in which a humble civil servant without a surname loses his fiancée, his reason, and his life to the mania, hymned by Vyazemsky, that had for reasons of state founded a city in such constant danger of the elements. The tragic note has been discovered; the grandeur of the city — as idea and as reality — is upheld; but in its very origin a hubris is recognized whose price, paid once by the thousands of workmen who perished in the first construction, continues to devolve on succeeding generations. Against the abstract grandeur is posed the concrete loss of humble lives; against the public achievement, the private sacrifice. Thus the image of the city is doubled: no longer passively heroic, it has become active, and an antagonist as well.

If the outlines of a myth of Petersburg are laid down in *The*

Bronze Horseman, a coloring or a tonality for that myth is supplied in *The Queen of Spades.* There are, strikingly, no descriptions of the city, nor does everyday life — what the Russians call *byt* — occupy much of a place in the tale. Rather, this Hoffmannesque story of a Russified German with Napoleonic ambitions enriches the myth of Petersburg through its atmosphere — a constant, equivocal mixing of the soberly realistic with the apparently fantastic. Dostoevsky was later to call Pushkin's Hermann "a colossal figure, an extraordinary, completely Petersburg type," and the city itself "the most fantastic in the world." The claim is evidently based on certain suppositions about the nature of the city that are extraliterary, but no less forceful for being so. At the heart of the myth of Petersburg is the image of an unreal city, an image countenanced historically by the fact of the city's founding as an arbitrary act of will (thus, again, Dostoevsky's designation of it as "the most abstract and intentional city in the world") and countenanced physically, so to speak, by the peculiar Petersburg situation and climate. This peculiarity has been remarked countless times, but perhaps most memorably by Custine:

The slow melting of the tints of twilight, which appeared to perpetuate the day in struggling against an ever-increasing gloom, communicated to all nature a mysterious movement; the low lands of the city, with their structures a little raised above the banks of the Neva, seemed to oscillate betwixt the sky and the water, which gave the impression of their being about to vanish in the void. . . . That little spot of earth which seemed to detach itself from the water and to tremble upon it like the froth of an inundation, those small, dark, irregular points scarcely observable beneath the white of the sky and the white of the river, could they form the capital of a vast empire?—or rather, was it not all an optical illusion, a phantasmagoria? . . . The whole scene was beautiful;—scarcely any movement, but a solemn calm, a vague inspiration. All the sounds and bustle of ordinary life were interrupted; man had disappeared, the earth remained in the possession of the supernatural powers. There are in these remains of day, these unequal and dying lights of a boreal night, mysteries which I know not how to define, but which explain to me the mythology of the North.[7]

The same note is repeated by Gogol:

When via the Admiralty Boulevard I reached the pier in front of which two jasper urns gleam, when the Neva opened before me, when the rosy color of the sky smoked from the Vyborg side as an azure mist and the structures of the Petersburg side were enveloped in an almost lilac color which hid their homely exterior, when the churches, all their protuberances hidden by the monochrome covering of the mist, seemed to be sketched or pasted on a rosy material, and in this lilac-azure haze there shone only the spire of the Petropavlovsk belfry, reflected in the infinite mirror of the Neva —it seemed to me as if I were not in Petersburg; it seemed to me as if I had crossed into some other city, where I had already been, where I knew everything, and where there was what there is not in Petersburg.[8]

The fantastic atmosphere of the city was a fact. The shiftings between the prosaic and the fantastic in *The Queen of Spades* had, without Pushkin's needing to stress the fact, been in consonance with the setting. It remained only to make explicit what Pushkin had left implicit, to evoke the city directly, projecting onto the various levels of its life this same interpenetration of the real and the phantom, the probable and the improbable, the exalted and the mundane, the tragic and the comic. This accomplishment was Gogol's, in his cycle of Petersburg tales.

GOGOL'S CITY

Our ultimate warrant for considering Gogol's Petersburg tales as a whole is in the tales themselves, but their interconnection was first suggested by Gogol himself — with his usual indirection. On November 28, 1836, he wrote Pogodin that his previous works, his tales, were "poor excerpts of those phenomena of which my head was full and from which was to be created one day a full picture." [9] If the only "full picture" he left posterity is *Dead Souls,* he evidently contemplated others, among them a picture of Petersburg. The tales can be considered his sketches for this, and their unity — not complete, but not inconsiderable either — was first made manifest in 1843, when Gogol brought them together to form the third volume of his collected works. The stories here assembled and disposed by theme (rather than by chronology) had been written, and in some cases rewritten, over the course of the preceding decade: "The Nevsky Prospect," "The Nose," "The Portrait," "The Overcoat," "The Carriage," "Notes of a Madman," and "Rome." The available evidence, moreover, suggests that Gogol worked on these stories chiefly in two periods, 1833–1835 and 1841–1842, and in both cases over the whole group of them. Aside from "The Carriage," which will not be considered here, the unifying element is the urban one; and if we require further proof of Gogol's direct concern with Petersburg as a theme, we may find it in two pieces of his from the mid-thirties, uncollected in his lifetime and hitherto untranslated; they cast considerable light on the "full picture" that these stories combine to suggest.

The first — and slighter — dates from the end of 1833 and is the twenty-four-year-old writer's lyrical salutation to the new year. "Mysterious, ineffable 1834!" he writes from Petersburg: "Where shall I mark thee with great works? Amid this heap of houses thrown one on top of another, of roaring streets, of seething commercialism — this ugly heap of fashions, parades, civil servants, wild northern nights, glitter and low colorlessness? Or in my beautiful, ancient, chosen [*obetovanny*] Kiev, wreathed with populous gardens, girdled by my southern, beautiful, wonderful sky, by ravishing nights, where the hill is bestrewn with bushes, as though with its own harmonious precipices, and washing it my clean and swift one, my Dnieper?" [10] Written at a time when Gogol had already won recognition as the author of *Evenings on a Farm near Dikanka* and when he was already at work on the Petersburg tales, this fragment, understandably, remained unpublished during his lifetime. What it lacks in restraint and finish, however, it makes up for by the explicitness of the attitude it conveys — an attitude of revulsion toward Petersburg, the obverse of which is a romantic nostalgia for the quiet and harmony of the Ukrainian capital (a longing, incidentally, that Gogol was finally to satisfy not in Kiev but in Rome). It is almost as if the young writer, who had been working that year on *Taras Bulba* and others of the pieces for *Mirgorod,* were loath to make the impending transition from these characteristically romantic themes to the more realistic ones that the city was revealing to him. One should not, of course, make a manifesto of a hastily jotted *cri de coeur.* Yet one has to notice what a leading place the items of this indictment of Petersburg assume in the stories themselves: the chaos, the power of money, the bureaucracy, the juxtaposition of fashionable glitter and "low colorlessness." They are all there, for instance, in the opening paragraph of "The Nevsky Prospect."

More circumstantial are the remarks in an article entitled "Petersburg Notes for 1836," published in Pushkin's journal, "The Contemporary." Petersburg, "already a punctilious German," is first compared with Moscow, "still up to now a Russian beard":

How old Moscow has spread out and broadened! How uncombed she is! How the dandy Petersburg has pulled himself together, how he has snapped to! Before him are mirrors on all sides: there is the Neva, there the Gulf of Finland. He has no dearth of places to observe himself. As soon as he notices a piece of down or fluff on him, that same minute, off with it with a flick. Moscow is an old stay-at-home . . . Petersburg—a sprightly fellow, never sits at home, is always dressed and sauntering on the border, preening before Europe, which he sees but does not hear.

All Petersburg is in motion, from the cellars to the garret; from midnight he starts to bake French breads, which on the morrow will be devoured by a German people, and all through the night now one of his eyes is shining, now the other; Moscow is all asleep at night, and on the morrow, after crossing herself and bowing in all four directions, drives out to the market with *kalachi* [a fancy white bread]. . . . *Moscow is necessary for Russia; Russia is necessary for Petersburg.*[11]

Considered by itself, Petersburg proves elusive:

It is difficult to catch the general expression of Petersburg. There is something akin to a European-American colony: just as little basic nationality and just as much foreign admixture which has still not merged into a compact mass. There are as many different nations in it as there are different strata of societies. These societies are completely separate: aristocrats, working civil servants, artisans, Englishmen, Germans, merchants—all make up completely separate circles, which rarely merge, rather living and making merry unseen by the others.

And each of these classes, if one looks closer, is composed of a multitude of other little circles, also not amalgamated with each other. For example, take the civil servants. The young assistants of office chiefs [*stolonachalniki*] make up their own circle, into which a department chief will not sink for anything. . . . In a word, it is as if an enormous diligence arrived at an inn, in which each passenger had been sitting all the way muffled up and went into the common hall only because there was no other place.[12]

The city thus has no unity or community of its own: and in this it resembles Dickens' fragmented London more than Balzac's organic Paris. But Gogol's treatment of it in his tales bears an interesting relation to both Balzac and Dickens. The corollary of Dickens' attitude toward the city — that because its essence is ungraspable, a writer who takes it as his subject can only keep adding new areas of its life with each work — applies equally to Gogol and makes clear the inevitability of his own series of "excerpts." There is, however, one difference, and here enters the affinity with Balzac: by an odd dialectic, the city that has no positive unity turns out, on examination, to have a negative one. The city, that is, which has no "general expression" to be caught, may be defined precisely in terms of its elusiveness, and the city that lacks a heart becomes a creature of heartlessness. The qualities uniting Balzac's characters into a community — will, energy, passion — strike the observer of Gogol's Petersburg by their absence, and Balzac's love for Paris finds its counterpart in Gogol's hatred of Petersburg.

It will be obvious that such an attitude implies the presence of strongly held positive values. To perceive the negative image, one must believe in the possibility, constantly betrayed, of a positive one. Otherwise we would not get the Gogolian play with perspective, and our view of Petersburg life would be that of Akaky Akakievich, Lieutenant Pirogov, the artist Piskaryov, and the rest. In Dickens, positive values appear in individuals, often in families, who constitute islands in the midst of the alien city; Gogol, by contrast, offers us no such visions of the ideal, not even approximations, within his city. Rather, these are reserved for "Rome," the excerpt from an unwritten novel with which Gogol closed the cycle of Petersburg tales in the third volume of his collected works. Here, opposed to Europe's "trivial luxury" and "fragmentation of thought," opposed to the whole nineteenth century, is presented a view of graciousness and unity, where "even poverty itself appeared in a certain bright guise, untroubled, unacquainted with torment and tears, carefree and picturesquely extending its hand." [13] The point is made explicitly: all this exists "in order to rouse the world, in order that *the dweller of the north,* as through a dream, might sometimes visualize this south, so that the dream of it might tear him out of his milieu of cold life, given over to pursuits that dry up the soul . . . so that, if only for once in his life, he might be a fine human being" (221; my italics). The prophetic tone of these remarks does not fully characterize the tales themselves, nor does it entirely explain them. But its appearance from time to time does offer an important clue to the interpretation of these often puzzling works.

Petersburg is represented in the stories in a variety of ways. There is, of course, the sort of direct characterization with which the first tale of the series opens:

> There is nothing finer than the Nevsky Prospect, at least not in Petersburg; for Petersburg it is everything. What doesn't it shine with, this street — the beauty of our capital! I know that not one of her pale and bureaucratic inhabitants would exchange the Nevsky Prospect for all the world. . . . Here is the only place where people show themselves not out of necessity, where they have not been driven by need and the mercantile interest that grips all Petersburg. It seems that a man met on the Nevsky Prospect is less an egoist than on Morskaya, Gorokhovaya, Liteinaya, Meshchanskaya, and other streets, where greed and self-interest and need are to be read on those who walk and those who fly in cabs or carriages. The Nevsky Prospect is the universal communications-line of Petersburg. . . . No directory or information bureau will furnish such correct information as the Nevsky Prospect. All-powerful Nevsky Prospect! The only diversion of a poor man out for a stroll in Petersburg! How clean are its sidewalks swept, and, my God, how many feet have left their marks on it! ("The Nevsky Prospect," 7–8)

What follows this double-edged encomium, laced with casual condemnation, is the sort of genre sketch represented in Dickens' first book by the pieces entitled "The Streets — Morning" and "The Streets — Evening." Here are the various classes who take their turn along the avenue in the course of a typical twenty-four hours. "What a rapid phantasmagoria passes over it in a single day!" the narrator exclaims, and the word is carefully chosen, for the afternoon crowd resembles but exceeds the fantastic Dickensian vision of the runaway clothes in Monmouth Street:

> You will meet here unique side whiskers, tucked with extraordinary and astonishing art under the cravat, velvety whiskers, satiny ones, ones black as sable or coal, but, alas, belonging to the Foreign Office alone. Providence has denied black side whiskers to the employees of other departments; they must, to their great annoyance, wear red ones. Here you will meet wonderful moustaches undepictable by any pen or brush; moustaches to which the better half of a lifetime has been devoted — the objects of long vigils, by day and by night, moustaches upon which have been poured the most ravishing scents and essences and which have been anointed with the most precious and rare sorts of pomades, moustaches which are wrapped up for the night in delicate vellum, moustaches which bespeak the most touching attachment on the part of their possessors and are envied by passers-by.

> Thousands of sorts of hats, dresses, multicolored kerchiefs, light ones, to which sometimes their owners will preserve an attachment for two whole days, dazzle everybody on the Nevsky Prospect. It looks as if a whole sea of butterflies has suddenly risen from flower stalks and is fluttering in a brilliant cloud above the black beetles of the male sex. Here you will meet waists such as you have never even dreamed of: little thin narrow waists no thicker than a bottleneck, on meeting which you will step deferentially aside, so as not to carelessly poke them with an impolite elbow; your heart is seized with apprehension and terror lest even from your careless breathing a most charming work of nature and art should somehow break in two. And what ladies' sleeves you will meet on the Nevsky Prospect! Oh, how lovely! They are a little like two balloons, so that the lady might suddenly rise in the air if her gentleman didn't support her; for a lady is as easily and pleasantly lifted in the air as a goblet of champagne to the lips. (10–11)

This visionary crescendo, in which synecdoche and hyperbole work together in the service of satire, subsides into a further synthetic catalogue of daytime sights, and then night appears — "that mysterious time when the lamps give to everything an alluring, wondrous light" (12). With night, the story proper begins.

It is a story of the deception of two young men — one is Piskaryov, a member of that class of people "which constitutes a rather strange phenomenon in our country and belongs among the citizens of Petersburg as much as a face we see in a dream belongs to the material world." He is an artist: "A strange phenomenon, is it not? A Petersburg artist! An artist in the land of the snows, an artist in the land of the Finns, where everything is wet, smooth, flat, pale, grey, misty" (14). The other is a smug officer. Each goes off to pursue a young woman he has seen on the avenue — the artist to find that the beauty he has taken for "a perfect Bianca of Perugino" is a prostitute and to kill himself out of despair at this identification of beauty and evil, the lieutenant to find that his anticipated easy conquest is the wife of a German artisan who thrashes him for his presumption. One tragedy, one comedy. Contrast is the guiding device here — contrast of what should be (Piskaryov's prostitute "should have been the priceless pearl, the whole world, the whole paradise, the whole wealth of an ardent husband") with what is ("But, alas! by some horrible whim of a fiendish spirit eager to destroy the harmony of life she had been hurled with laughter into his abyss" [20], and contrast of what is with what it appears to be. The Manichean nature of this world is underlined again in the closing expostulation:

> Oh, do not trust that Nevsky Prospect! . . . All is deceit, all is a dream, all is not what it seems. . . . It lies at all times, this Nevsky Prospect, but most of all when night settles on it in a thick mass and separates the white and pale yellow walls of houses, when the whole city turns into thunder and glitter, myriads of carriages come hurtling off the bridges, postillions shout and jog on the horses, and when the demon himself lights the lamps expressly in order to show everything in an unreal guise. (42–43)

Thus is the tone set for the cycle. In various embodiments, the themes touched on in this story will be recombined in the later ones, to create a pattern and from it an atmosphere that comes to characterize Gogol's Petersburg. The fantastic, held in check in the plot of this first story, running more freely and more ambiguously through the narration itself, will dominate the events of "The Nose" and of "The Portrait" (though with romantic-allegorical overtones); it will appear in the important epilogue to "The Overcoat"; and in the "Notes of a Madman" — the only first-person narrative of the series — it will be present with a psychological motivation, as if to underline the correspondence of the madman's vision to the vision conveyed in the other stories. (I speak here only of fantastic events or themes: the question of the fantastic as we get it through the narrative style is for the moment deferred.) Similarly, the devil, who lights the streetlamps along the Nevsky Prospect, appears incarnate in the typically romantic "Portrait," where, as before, he drives an artist to suicide, but this time through the lure of money; and if he is absent from the other stories, the themes of money and social rank — his agents — continue to play prominent parts, as do hallucination and madness. Even the quality the Russians call *poshlost,* that self-satisfied vulgarity for which Gogol had such a keen eye, comes increasingly to appear a phenomenon not simply comic but positively evil.

By the same token, direct characterization of Petersburg by the narrator runs from the opening and closing chords of "The Nevsky Prospect" through all the other stories. Leonid Grossman has called attention to the fact that, with the exception of the Nevsky, Gogol eschews the fashionable sections of the capital, traditionally celebrated in literature and art, to situate the action of his stories in shabby buildings and outlying sections.[14] Thus in the young artist's description of the suburb of Kolomna ("The Portrait"), a genre sketch concludes with mention of "the usual small fry": "It is," the narrator remarks with characteristic Gogolian imagery, "as difficult to name them as it is to reckon the multitude of insects that are bred in old vinegar" (112). Overviews of the Dickensian or Balzacian kind are rare, as might be expected from one who sees only an arbitrary and negative unity in the city, and when they do occur they are social, not topographical — concerned with the *quality* of life lived in Petersburg: thus the page-long sentence in "The Overcoat," ticking off in montage the various evening amusements of Petersburg's army of clerks, only to end, "in short, even at the time when everyone was seeking to be diverted, Akaky Akakievich did not give himself over to any diversion" (134). From these and other references to the city, what emerges is less a picture than an atmosphere, and one that is consistently negative. Literally, "it's the Petersburg climate that's to blame" for the dreary look of Akaky Akakievich at the beginning of "The Overcoat," just as at the end it is "thanks to the magnanimous assistance of the Petersburg climate [that] the disease progressed more rapidly than could have been expected" (154). I have already noted, apropos of the romantic hero of "The Nevsky Prospect," Gogol's sardonic exclamation, "an artist in the land of the Finns, where everything is wet, smooth, flat, pale, grey, misty." In the same passage, he goes on to broaden the point and, with it, the conception of atmosphere: "They [Petersburg artists] often nourish a genuine talent, and if only the fresh air of Italy were to blow on them, it would probably develop as freely, broadly, and brilliantly as a plant which is finally brought out of a room into the fresh air." But it is not only to artists that Petersburg is inimical: the poor clerks, Akaky Akakievich Bashmachkin and Aksenty Poprishchin, can cry with justice, "There is no place for me!"; and if the first, who has become so dehumanized that he takes home documents to copy for his own pleasure, can feel normal impulses only under the stimulation of acquiring a new coat, the latter, feeling them constantly, is driven to madness because no real dignity is available to him. Only the *poshlyaki,* the conventional and self-satisfied, the Lieutenant Pirogovs, the Major Kovalyovs, the chiefs of bureaus, and Important Personages can thrive in this atmosphere — and even they may be deceived by it into painful misadventures.

The city, then, is the hero, or antihero, of Gogol's cycle, and the city is less a geographical, political, or aesthetic unity than an atmosphere.[15] It was in this way that Gogol solved the problem posed in his "Petersburg Notes for 1836" ("It is difficult to catch the general expression of Petersburg"). The atmosphere is defined by means of incidents, which are extreme often to the point of improbability, and in terms of social groupings (these, and their synecdochic badges, are everywhere stressed). Elements of the earlier Ukrainian stories reappear here, transmuted. As Andrey Bely puts it: "The overthrown images of romanticism [*romantika*] turned, as it were, inside out, overflow [these] works of the second phase: they are shown in another circle, in another guise, in another era; and — head over heels, as if the soles of their feet were stuck to the soles of their romantic doubles; it is a matter of turning the double universe of Gogol around, so that the nadir becomes the zenith and the zenith the nadir, in order that the Cossack patriarch becomes a landowner from the petty gentry, evil spirits become the civil-servant class, though not of the Ukraine, but of the whole Russian empire, which means Petersburg." [16] What is more, foreign influences contribute to the creation of atmosphere, the stylization of this city. The early Balzac, as previously noted, may have contributed something; De Quincey's hallucinated London may have provided a stimulus for the young Gogol; as may Hoffmann, via Balzac, Janin, and the *école frénétique*. Even Washington Irving must be listed among conjectured influences.[17]

This question of romantic influences on Gogol has been studied from a variety of standpoints in a number of languages, and — as might be expected — the cumulative result forms at best only a provisional, short catalogue. The traditional case for Gogol as a realist is no less exasperating — and hardly less plausibly founded. Only the premise that "romantic" and "realistic" are mutually exclusive need be swept away for the historically transitional character of Gogol's work to stand out in relief. Insofar as such a unique writer may be usefully labeled, the label here must be romantic realism. And its main justification, apart from affinities with this or that school or writer, must be sought beyond theme in technique, in the peculiar Gogolian verbal texture — that "mosaic of words," as Rozanov called it[18] — which is the ultimate and basic carrier of his vision of Petersburg. For Gogol's Petersburg is, like Balzac's Paris, neither wholly subjective nor wholly objective, but rather the synthesis of a personal vision (Bely finds Gogol himself the hero of the Petersburg cycle, but that is only half the story) and sensitively observed social fact. This union of opposites, which parallels the Manichean contrasts of themes, is a constant feature of Gogol's technique, making the comic verge constantly on the tragic, the melodramatic on the mundane, the supernatural on the trivial. The hard core, the nexus of all these ambiguities, is the grotesque.

REALISM, ROMANTICISM, AND THE GROTESQUE

Philip Rahv has suggested as a crucial test of naturalism a given work's treatment of the relation of character to background, the naturalistic being defined as "that type of realism in which the individual is portrayed not merely as subordinate to his background but as wholly determined by it — that type of realism, in other words, in which the environment displaces its inhabitants in the role of hero." [19] Half a century ago, a similar observation had already been made about Gogol's work. "The collective always swallows the individual in Gogol's works," Vengerov wrote: "With the exception of the almost autobiographical studies about the torments of creation, Gogol does not even have heroes in the ordinary sense. The heroes of his works are always collective figures, some class, some estate, some slice of life. Even in Gogol's pieces on Little Russian life, which stand apart, not in the least satirical, and therefore quite free from social concerns, the mass all the same comes to the fore. In *Evenings on a Farm near Dikanka,* there is not one central personage, and the hero is the whole Little Russian folk-epic way of life." [20] In the case at hand — the Petersburg tales — a supraindividual entity, the city itself, is the hero: the environment, in Rahv's formula, displaces its inhabitants in the role of hero.[21] It does so, however, in an unusual way and with the obtrusive connivance of the narrator. Gogol, who once signed a work of his "0000," does more than subordinate his characters: he debases and frequently de-features them. With the exception of the two artists (Piskaryov in "The Nevsky Prospect" and Chartkov in "The Portrait"), both of them doomed to madness and suicide, Gogol's characters all incline toward facelessness, toward an identity only nominal. There was an intentional clue to this in his naming the 1835 volume that contained three of these tales *Arabesques,* and it was not lost on a contemporary reviewer: "Why are they Arabesques? In painting and sculpture, one calls arabesques those fantastic, patterned and capricious ornaments composed of flowers and figures. Arabesques were born in the East, and therefore no representations of animals or people, which the Koran forbids drawing, enter into them. In this respect, the title of the book is successfully chosen: in it, for the most part, one encounters figures without faces." [22]

So "The Nose" opens by introducing "the barber Ivan Yakovlevich, who lives on the Voznesensky Avenue (his surname is lost, and even on his sign — where there is depicted a gentleman with a lathered face and the legend, 'also lets blood' — nothing more is written)" (44). In the same story, Major Kovalyov awakes to find in the middle of his face, "instead of his nose . . . a completely smooth place!" (His nose, on the other hand, in the disguise of a general, looks, shouts, frowns, smiles, and is seen "hiding his face completely in his large stand-up collar and . . . praying with an expression of the utmost piety" [50].) Akaky Akakievich is introduced as "a clerk one could not call very remarkable: short of stature, somewhat pockmarked, somewhat reddish-haired, even somewhat blind-looking, balding in front, with wrinkles on both sides of his cheeks, and a face of the color that is called hemorrhoidal" (129) — a blurred collection of characteristics with considerably less individuality than the rather odd syntax that conveys them. "Well, look at yourself," Poprishchin's ("Notes of a Madman") chief tells him — and he might be speaking to the majority of Gogolian characters — "just think a minute, what are you? Why, you are a zero, nothing more" (178). Poprishchin's recurrent phrase — "Never mind, never mind [*nichego:* literally, "nothing"], silence" — is similarly emblematic. When Rozanov remarks that Gogol's characters "are made out of some sort of waxy mass of words," he echoes Gogol himself, who refers in "The Portrait" to a mother and daughter whose faces suggest "that they had danced themselves out at balls to such an extent that both had almost become wax figures."[23] These are all dead souls.

This impression is borne out by their actions, which, in the classic comic tradition, tend to be mechanical, determined by circumstances of employment or social rank, or else by some personal tic or mania. The stories of the two artists stand slightly apart; being more purely romantic, and quite free from any comic or quasi-comic treatment, their central action is less literally mechanical. Yet even here infernal obsession is the prime mover, and its gradual encroachment displaces the "real" world. In the others, this mechanistic quality is everywhere to be seen, in major and minor examples. Major Kovalyov, eternally rank-conscious, does not know how to approach his uniformed Nose. The poor petty civil servant Poprishchin, enamored of his chief's daughter, sees nothing beyond the world of rank closed to him, until the full onset of his madness makes him the King of Spain. Akaky Akakievich's life is a void until he acquires his new overcoat, and for that acquisition he undergoes great privations:

At first, the truth must be told, it was a little hard for him to get used to such limitations, but then the habit somehow took hold and everything went well; he even trained himself perfectly to go hungry evenings; but on the other hand he was nourished spiritually, carrying in his thoughts the eternal idea of his overcoat-to-be. From that time on, his very existence seemed to have become somehow fuller, as if he had married, as if some other person were with him, as if he were not alone but some pleasant female companion had agreed to travel the road of life with him — and this female companion was none other than the overcoat itself, with the thick padding and the indestructible lining. (142)

Not only are these people dominated by an *idée fixe;* they are caught in what might be called an *être fixe*. They have no range, either of perception or expression. Akaky Akakievich — thanks to the genius of Gogol — is practically a speaking mute, an unparalleled and untranslatable triumph of the inarticulate put into words and yet left miraculously intact, neither caricatured into nonsense nor reduced to simple ellipsis. As the narrator himself notes, "Akaky Akakievich . . . explained himself for the most part in prepositions, adverbs, and, finally, such particles as have absolutely no significance" (137). Thus his musings on the street, after the tailor Petrovich has told him his old overcoat is irreparable (the margin of defeat in any translation is considerable):

> Out on the street, Akaky Akakievich walked along as one in a dream. "What do you know?" he said to himself, "I really didn't even think that it could turn out, you know . . ." And then, after a short silence: "So there you are! Look how it finally turned out, and really, I couldn't ever have supposed that that's how it would be." After this another long silence ensued; then he said aloud: "So that's how it is! There's a really absolutely unexpected one for you, I mean . . . there's one you couldn't have . . . What a situation!" (139–140)

The Important Personage to whom Akaky Akakievich applies for help when his overcoat is stolen is no less absurd in this regard: "His customary conversation with inferiors reeked of strictness and consisted of just about three phrases: 'How dare you? Do you know whom you're talking to? Do you understand who it is that's standing before you?' " (152). The narrator goes on to suggest that "at heart he was a kind man," that "having received the rank of general, he had somehow got mixed up," and that, "if he happened to be with equals, he was still . . . a very decent man, in many respects even not a stupid man." The subtle adverbial oddness here is justified by the scene that immediately follows, where we see the Important Personage closeted with an old friend: "He and his friend had already long since talked over everything and had for a long time now been interlarding the conversation with drawn-out silences, merely patting each other lightly on the thigh occasionally and repeating 'So that's how it is, Ivan Abramovich!' — 'That's how it is, Stepan Varlamovich!' " (152–153). Their laconic exchange bears a suspicious resemblance to Akaky's own locutions.

The overcoat is more than a symbol, and more than the companion that Gogol calls it: it is a spiritual acquisition, the new personality of the poor clerk. This merging of the spiritual and the physical, the animate and the inanimate, is a law of Gogol's world, just as it is a law of Dickens'. But with Gogol it is more central, because the "normal" world in his work is not so much refracted as displaced; the difference is all the difference between conventional and "realized" metaphor. The Dickensian transformation is usually signaled by "as if" — a phrase seldom used by Gogol, who characteristically destroys such links with the world of common sense, just as he eschews the main Dickensian ballast of normality, the narrative tone and point of view with which a normal, right-minded reader might identify himself. Human beings are not so much characterized as usurped by their possessions and attributes. We have seen the inhuman parade of waists and whiskers down the Nevsky Prospect, and contemplated the near-ruin of Kovalyov through the loss of a nose that outfaces, outwits, and outshines him. Such examples are innumerable. Here, for instance, is the way the doctor is introduced in "The Nose": "The doctor was a fine figure of a man, had excellent pitch-black whiskers, a fresh, healthy wife, ate fresh apples in the morning and kept his mouth in extraordinary cleanliness, rinsing it every morning almost three quarters of an hour and polishing his teeth with five different kinds of brushes" (63). Small wonder that, when he leaves, we are told that "Kovalyov did not even notice his face, and in his profound insensibility saw only the cuffs of his white and snowy-clean shirt peeping out of the sleeves of his black frock coat" (64). Small wonder because clearly he has no face; he has succumbed to the danger Gogol cited in "The Portrait" — the danger of "turning into one of those strange creatures who turn up in such large numbers in our callous world . . . [who] seem to be walking stone coffins with a corpse inside instead of a heart" (102). Dickens has been called a surrealist before the fact; the title is more justly Gogol's.

In short, there are characters in Gogol's world, in the sense of dramatis personae, but there is little character in the sense of moral qualities. This grotesque presentation of human beings, with its affinities to the creations of Goya and Daumier, is matched by the grotesque character of the incidents themselves. A nose absconds; a poor civil servant eavesdrops on the conversation of two dogs and even reads their correspondence, while another, after mute sufferings that waver between the ridiculous and the pathetic, dies of a broken heart and returns to haunt his oppressor; the devil gazes out of a portrait and lights the lamps along the Nevsky Prospect. Where these incidents are unequivocally fantastic, they tend to be related to a romantic aesthetic either directly ("The Portrait") or satirically ("The Nose"); the humanitarian strain makes its appearance in "The Overcoat" and, oddly combined with an unglamorized depiction of the romantic theme of madness, in "Notes of a Madman." What makes generalization difficult here is the obvious way Gogol is making of each story a new experiment, addressing himself in each to new technical problems; and what compounds the difficulty is the complexity of Gogol's relation both to romanticism and to realism in this period. That he prepared the ground for later realistic fiction by legitimizing the depiction of vulgarity (*poshlost*) is doubtless; that, while invoking romantic themes, he attacked standard romantic treatment of them, partly by the use of this very vulgarity, is similarly true. Contemporaries saw this; as one noted, "The chief and most important quality of Gogol's talent is *fine observation* and strong comprehension of the poetry of reality. . . . In my opinion, the less poetic an object is in itself, the better it is for Gogol." [24] Much the same had been said by and about the romantic realists of the West, Balzac and Dickens — yet even Gogol's affinity with them must be qualified.

Like them, he was a mythographer of the city, evoking it through a highly personal vision, the chief element of which — as Andrey Bely pointed out — is terror and the chief theme, kinlessness and alienation.[25] But with Gogol, much more than with Balzac or Dickens, one feels that the vision is not chiefly directed *at* the city, that the artist in creating his world takes his material from the life of the city not to re-create that city in a new light, but to create a new universe that stands in a grotesque relation to the real city. The conventionally romantic element in such a transformation is absent because there is no heightening of the prosaic image: rather, there is a debasing of it. The conventionally realistic component of the transformation is similarly absent because there is no attempt to synthesize a new explanation of Petersburg life. Gogol's Petersburg period is a kind of *saison en enfer,* but one cannot even conclude from it that hell is a city much like any other. Hell is an atmosphere, a way of living, a nightmare, where the only horror is that, for the inhabitants, there is no horror. Gogol is giving us a city of the mind, deprived of grace, and superimposing it on the map and mores of Petersburg, where it stays because, in key spots, it fits. Aside from the numerous invocations of the devil, we know this is hell, not so much because it lacks beauty as because it lacks clarity. Its atmosphere is uncertain: all is illusion along the Nevsky

Prospect — but even away from that artery one cannot be sure. Balzac and Dickens, too, had preferred extreme situations and had not spurned improbability, defending it as often a surer way to truth than its opposite. But listen to the Gogolian narrator making a similar protestation at the end of "The Nose":

> That is the sort of story that happened in the northern capital of our far-flung state! Only now, on considering it all, we can see that there is a lot that is improbable in it. . . . And yet, in the face of all that, although, of course, one may admit this and that and the other, it is even — but then where doesn't one find all sorts of incongruities? — All the same, however, when you think it over a little, there really is something in all this. Say what you like, but such things do happen in the world — not often, but they do happen. (69–70)

The tone and effect are quite different, disconcerting and equivocal. What is one to make of it all? The narrator offers only conflicting, confusing clues. The grotesqueness of what is presented is matched by the grotesqueness of the presentation. So pursuit of the object leads us to pursuit of the vision, and pursuit of the vision leads us to the style. As André Malraux has observed in speaking of Goya, every artist of genius discovers his unique expression of the world through his style rather than his "vision," which is always subordinate to it.[26] For Gogol's style, Rozanov's "mosaic of words" is a particularly apt description, because the tension between the total presentation and the discrete elements composing it stands out everywhere as the fundamental mystery of his art.

Such is not the case with Dickens. When he opens *Bleak House* in that strikingly verbless way, from a point of view neither conventionally first-person nor conventionally third-person, the reader is saved from disorientation by the distinctness of the sensuous scene, by the familiar certainty of specified time, place, and institutions; and as he reads on, he finds, for all the stylistic vagaries, that the point of view remains constant throughout. He is never in doubt about the lighting: he knows when it is intended that he should laugh and when he should yield to sympathy. In the relatively straightforward narration of "The Nevsky Prospect," however, this is already not so true: "There is nothing finer than the Nevsky Prospect, at least not in Petersburg; for Petersburg, it is everything. What doesn't it shine with, this street — the beauty of our capital!

I know that not one of her pale and bureaucratic inhabitants would exchange the Nevsky Prospect for all the world." Who is this "I" that steps out to buttonhole the reader? His identity will remain doubtful — and so, we learn, does his logic, as in that passing rhapsody on ladies' sleeves: "They are a little like two balloons, so that the lady might suddenly rise in the air if her gentleman didn't support her; for a lady is as easily and pleasantly lifted in the air as a goblet of champagne to the lips." Like all the rest in this story, that "for" is not what it seems. Alogism peeps around the corners already, as does hyperbolism: "One man has an excellent cook, but, unfortunately, such a small mouth that he cannot possibly get down more than two little bites; another has a mouth as big as the General Headquarters arch, but, alas, he has to be content with some German dinner of potatoes" (42). In this keynote story, these qualities are kept in check; in the later ones, they come to dominate. Tragedy and farce, that is to say, are already here — yoked but not, as in the later work, fused.[27] Already present, too, is the narrative tendency so well observed by Vasily Gippius: "When from sketches of everyday scenes with a Ukrainian setting . . . Gogol turns to the Petersburg milieu, he tends to the representation of this milieu in a fantastic light: impressionistic images by the very approximateness of their outlines come near to caricature, whence it is not far to the fantastic; the style becomes nervously lyrical, and the third person in narration is constantly struggling with the first, with the role of the author who interrupts the narration with questions and exclamations." [28]

The manner and the matter of these stories thus have in common the theme of bewilderment. "The Portrait" and "The Nose" both end on a note of puzzlement ("And for a long time the people remained in perplexity, wondering whether they had really seen those uncanny eyes"). The dominant motif of "The Portrait" is the same ("He felt something inexplicable to himself"; "My God, what is this!"; "an inexplicable feeling remained in his soul").[29] Automatism born of bewilderment characterizes Akaky Akakievich. The first two sections of "The Nose" end similarly: "But here the incident is completely shrouded in fog and absolutely nothing is known of what happened next" (47). "The Overcoat" opens: "In the Department of . . . but it might be better not to say in which

Department" — three sentences later an event is reported "I don't remember in which town." And it is not simply that precision is sometimes disclaimed; the confusion becomes worse when it is promised. See, for example, the astonishing passage in "The Overcoat" about the naming of Akaky Akakievich that begins: "And the precise way this came about was as follows. Akaky Akakievich was born — unless my memory deceives me — on the night of the twenty-third of March" (130).

If what happened in any given case is so often unclear, the causes of things are no less so — *neizvestno pochemu* ("why is unknown") is the constant refrain. But the process of bewilderment does not stop when the unclear issue of unknown causes has been reported: the very reporting itself may be called into question, as at the end of "The Nose": "But what is strangest, what is most incomprehensible of all, is that authors can choose such subjects. I confess that is quite unfathomable, that is as if . . . no, no, I don't understand at all. In the first place, there's no use whatsoever to the motherland; in the second place . . . but in the second place, too, there's no use. I simply don't know what to make of it" (70). Just as the line is blurred between the animate and the inanimate, the real and the fantastic, the true and the false, so is the line blurred between the significant and the insignificant: the play with physical proportion is paralleled by a play with moral proportion.[30]

From this comes that crucial uncertainty of tone which has permitted some readers to see "The Overcoat" (for example) as a plea for brotherhood and social justice, others to see it simply as a grotesque comic *skaz,* or *récit,* and still others to see it as an oblique moral condemnation of the surrender of individuality to a soulless external world. The story offers grounds for all these emphases and for none of these conclusions — insofar as they would pretend to exclusiveness. The pathetic exclamation ("I am your brother!") echoes only in the imagination of a transient and unnamed character at the beginning; and while the passage on Akaky's death ensures that we shall never quite forget it, the consistent emphasis on the absurd throughout the rest of the story makes it clear that the narrator is least of all disposed to feel any brotherhood with his character. The result is that these opposing qualities which were mechanically juxtaposed in "The Nevsky Prospect" are, in the subsequent stories, joined directly in a peculiar tension — without destroying their separate identities and without reconciling them.[31] ("Not one story of Gogol's is so packed with the comic as 'Notes of a Madman,'" writes Gippius, "and yet this is a tragedy!"[32]) This tension is the defining mark of the grotesque.

Grotesque, of course, may mean other things as well. In the works of high romanticism (in Germany especially and, through the influence of Hoffmann, in France), the grotesque meant the fantastic, the supernatural, the diabolic, the causes or the effects of alienation and madness; in Gogol's work, one may see this in the Ukrainian stories pre-eminently — and one may trace its survival in the Petersburg tales, where these themes persist and where, it has been claimed, the devil himself is the hero.[33] Or the grotesque may be considered — perhaps in the tradition of the baroque, for Gogol's style has been called with justice "a whimsical baroque" — as residing in the play with proportion, an essentially comic manipulation of reality to construct a new and unreal world where any trifle can grow to colossal proportions.[34] In all its qualifications, however, the common element is the notion of some sort of monstrous deviation from accepted norms: where, then, are the norms in the Petersburg tales?

One answer has been provided by Cizevsky. Illustrating the constant hyperbolic base of Gogol's writing, he finds two main kinds of extreme comparison — those directed upward toward an ineffable beauty, on the one hand, and those directed downward toward the inexpressible baseness of vulgarity, on the other.[35] From this he concludes that Gogol created his "natural style" in order, "by an exaggeratedly disgusting, repulsive representation of everyday life in somber colors, to evoke in the reader that same longing for a higher, nonterrestrial world, which Gogol in his works of a romantic style (and in *Selected Passages*) tries to evoke by other means — by lyricism and enthusiasm."[36] (Here, in terms of the Gogolian treatment of the city, is the importance of "Rome" as a pendant to the tales of Petersburg.) Such an interpretation receives support from Gogol himself in his "After the Play" (*Teatralny razezd*), where he has the Second Amateur of Art declare: "But cannot the positive and the negative serve the same end? . . . In the hands of talent everything can serve as an instrument to the beautiful, if only it is guided by the high conception of serving the beautiful." [37]

Whether or not Gogol was so guided at the time he wrote his Petersburg tales,[38] whether or not his singular talent really heeded any high imperatives or simply gave form to the writer's own terrors, this declaration for the equality of the high and the low, the comic and the tragic, has all the force of a manifesto. For if the comic mode, via irony, led ultimately to nineteenth-century realism, this kind of grotesque comedy — by its very instability — may be seen as an early stage of the strange, tragic realism that Dostoevsky was to create. Especially in the early novels, Gogol's great successor would time and again take elements of the Gogolian grotesque and, by adding a new perspective, draw new power from the expectation of comedy that these grotesque elements raised. In this sense, Gogol's work is not only chronologically transitional to Dostoevsky's: it is a necessary preparation for it. And Dostoevsky's remark about how all later Russian fiction came out of Gogol's "Overcoat" is no less apt for being evidently apocryphal. Dostoevsky's image of Petersburg is unthinkable without the precedent of Gogol; so is his early style; so is his treatment of many key themes, among them that of the poor civil servant. However complex the relation of mainstream Russian realism to the prose of Gogol, there is another branch that goes directly from him to Dostoevsky and from Dostoevsky to the symbolists (who, fittingly, first rescued Gogol from his arbitrary designation as a realist).

Gogol was not, of course, the only formative influence on the young Dostoevsky, but he was a crucial one exactly because his work represented such a successful and original adaptation of disparate foreign trends to the Russian scene and the Russian language. To say this is not to suggest that Gogol transmitted certain specific "influences," but rather that he produced a particularly viable, particularly Russian, response to literary problems that existed in the West at the same time and for similar reasons. Thus there is, strictly speaking, no Western European counterpart to him, just as there is none to Dostoevsky. In Western Europe, romantic realism in its major manifestations led, by example and reaction, to that "normative" ironic realism of Flaubert and George Eliot. In Russia, Gogol's peculiar romantic realism led, by example and reaction, to the "fantastic realism," that "realism in a higher sense," of Dostoevsky, in which the comic ballast dropped away, the supernatural was rationalized, the essential ambiguity was given a philosophical basis, and the grotesque and absurd — against the background of fantastic Petersburg — took on an existential starkness, a dark beauty, and a new and indisputable tragedy.

II
THE INHERITOR: DOSTOEVSKY

5

The Most Fantastic City: Approaches to a Myth

Nineteenth-century Petersburg, in spite of all the fantastic coloring Dostoevsky imparted to its description, has not been depicted by anyone more exactly, more sharply, more palpably, or more truly.

Leonid Grossman

Dostoevsky is the direct inheritor of the romantic realists in the nineteenth century, and he is their evolutionary link with the twentieth. Critics as different as the theologian Berdyaev and the Marxist Pereverzev have agreed that he belongs to the present as much as to the past, that he alone among nineteenth-century novelists speaks to a peculiarly modern consciousness that he anticipated and in part created.[1] These arguments are by now commonplace; his spiritual discomforts are too plainly ours. Why is it that his myth — and it is an urban myth — can affect us so immediately? His Petersburg has at least as much strangeness about it as the Paris of Balzac, the London of Dickens, or the earlier Petersburg of Gogol; and the real city he wrote about is, moreover, even remoter from our own historical experience. Why, then, the difference in our perception of it?

One is tempted to answer that in his hands Petersburg turns out to be a city of the mind, all its concrete features drawn upward by a kind of osmosis into the metaphysical drama that is being played over it. But this is at best a half-truth. If, as has been claimed,[2] Dostoevsky's real hero is Everyman, there is nothing of the medieval abstraction about his theater; in the manner of the romantic realists, he grounds his metaphysical concerns with consummate care in the three-dimensional world. We know which way Raskolnikov turns when he leaves his apartment; we know which street he follows; we know the color of the pawnbroker's wallpaper. The tavern in which he plays cat and mouse (or mouse and cat) with Zametov, like the amusement park to which Svidrigailov resorts on the eve of his suicide, is not just the symbol for a state of mind, and there is a healthy if naive reminder of this in the printed literary excursions that even now guide enthusiastic pedestrians in the footsteps of one or another Dostoevskian hero through the streets of Leningrad. His city did have its pedestrian side.

The difference is not, then, that Dostoevsky's concerns led him to slight historical reality, or even that his concerns were less social than those of Balzac and Dickens; they were social, but they were otherwise motivated. They were unresponsive to the whole theme of ambition as Balzac and Dickens understood it, and so unresponsive to all the allure of "success." For this reason we miss in his novels much of what is most perishable in the work of his Western predecessors — the details of a Lucien's sartorial glamor, the ponderous Victorian furnishings of a Veneering, the *ideals* of the age in matters small and great. The success that rewards or eludes their characters is outside the field of Dostoevsky's attention; he gives us the world of failure. One recalls the early illustrations to the works of Balzac and Dickens, so saturated with romantic and Victorian fashion: they reflect the coloring of historical distance that the texts also convey. No such nostalgia surrounds the work of Dostoevsky (perhaps that is why he has had so few illustrators): the props are few and nondescript; there is no period quaintness. Even as we sympathize with Rastignac's chagrin at being seen to arrive at Madame de Restaud's on foot, we are reminded of the century that separates us from him; when Dostoevsky's characters chase around in *drozhkies* and *britzkas,* the familiar feverish pace so far outweighs the obsolete nature of the conveyance that it may hardly occur to us to notice the latter. What is true in these minor examples is true in larger ways, as we shall see later: Dostoevsky demands less effort of the historical imagination.

And yet he *was* a nineteenth-century novelist in ways that are more than accidental — and these ways are still insufficiently familiar to those who read him under the sign of *Weltliteratur*. We lack, in the English-speaking world, not simply a historical perspective that would place him back in the company of his Russian predecessors and contemporaries, and not simply the sort of historical testing undertaken for Dickens by Humphry House in *The Dickens World* or by Pradalié in *Balzac Historien:* we lack even the full corpus of his work. Such journalistic sketches as Balzac and Dickens elaborated for their urban myths have their Dostoevskian counterparts, but they have only very recently been translated and remain to be assessed. In short, before we talk about Dostoevsky's transcendence of his time and place, we should do well to investigate how he achieved that transcendence. The fact that he, too, makes the city the hero of his work only makes it more imperative to begin by examining his evocation of Petersburg, "the most fantastic city in the world" and the foundation of his myth. We need to see him on his own ground and in his own national tradition before trying to define his place in the European tradition and in its current of romantic realism.

Petersburg is the most obvious constant in Dostoevsky's work; it is the setting for his first novel as for his last but one, and it is not unlikely that, had he lived to finish his last one. Alyosha Karamazov's career as a great sinner would have also led him into its maelstrom.[3] Unlike the broken line of his political development, the image and function of the city in his art show a consistent growth, so that the recurrence of the urban theme becomes finally a measure by which his evolving mastery of technique, like the deepening of his concerns, may be gauged.

This growth is not lateral and cumulative in the manner of Balzac: there is no patient building of a single edifice, métier by métier and neighborhood by neighborhood. Such a thoroughness is not part of his design. His *curiosity* is not for the city itself—though his *sensitivity* is. His daughter explains in biographical terms what we might infer from the novels. Dostoevsky, she relates, loved to wander aimlessly around the city: "He would roam down the darkest and most remote streets of Petersburg. In the course of his walking he would converse with himself and gesticulate, so that passers-by would turn around to watch. Friends who ran into him considered him a madman." He would stop, "unexpectedly struck by the glance or smile of a stranger, which impressed itself on his brain." [4] He must have seen features of the urban landscape in the same way. What he brought away from these walks must have struck him almost in spite of himself because it answered a current preoccupation, met a mood, or simply obtruded in those intervals when the daydreamer's fantasy left his attention free. Throughout his work the city tends to be portrayed through (or in consonance with) the consciousness of his characters. His first protagonists are dreamers; so, differently but no less, are his later ones. This is one reason why his Petersburg, the physical place with all its spectral inhabitants, its buildings, canals, bridges, and streetlamps, seems so perpetually on the point of evanescence. "Perhaps," the narrator of *A Raw Youth* reflects, "all this is someone's dream, and there is not one real, true person here, nor one real action. Someone who is dreaming all this will suddenly wake up — and everything will suddenly disappear" (I.8.1).

Rather than a Balzacian development, then, we see in his treatment of the city over the years the same spiral movement that his novels describe,[5] widening less than ascending as he finds new significance in his theme. In this respect he is much closer to Dickens, whose vain quest for a positive unity in the city brought him from the shallow juxtapositions of *Nicholas Nickleby* to the deeper discoveries of *Bleak House* and *Little Dorrit.*

This is not to deny that his Petersburg is relatively complete. But its neighborhoods are not equally represented. His favorites are middle- and lower-class sections, such as the area around the Voznesensky Prospect (now Maiorov Prospect), full of lodging houses, narrow streets and alleys, with its Haymarket Square (Sennaya Ploshchad — now Ploshchad Mira, Peace Square), its several small churches, and at the northern end the great Cathedral of St. Isaac. It is to neighborhoods like these, little worlds in themselves, that he continually returns in the novels. The more fashionable districts, like the Liteiny, are hardly mentioned (the Epanchin house, in *The Idiot,* forms the single important exception); here lived members of the nobility and the wealthy bourgeoisie who tend, when they do appear in Dostoevsky's works, to do so either out of doors or on socially lower ground; and since even the ambitious Dostoevskian hero — in contrast to his Balzacian and Dickensian cousins — rarely aspires to join the ranks of his social betters, these neighborhoods are singularly uncharacterized when they figure in the stories. The Nevsky Prospect itself has a minor place — and probably not because Gogol had left such an indelible mark on its representation, for Dostoevsky always showed readiness to cope with the Gogolian inheritance directly, sometimes through parody and sometimes through open polemic. Rather, as one commentator suggests, "he probably did not feel on the Nevsky Prospect that fantastic element of prose which he so sharply observed and conveyed in the Haymarket, the canals, and the other landmarks of Petersburg." [6]

What is true of physical Petersburg is true of social Petersburg as well. It, too, is relatively complete — if we count minor figures and incidents. But the predominant emphasis is on the vulgar and often sordid "elements of prose." The image of the Northern Palmyra was not to survive the hegemony of poetry in Russian literature; its last singer was, significantly, the poet Pushkin, whose experiments in prose underlay the whole development of the Russian novel in the nineteenth century. The transition can be seen in his *Bronze Horseman,* subtitled "A Petersburg Tale," where the last hymn to the classical image of the city contrasts, in its lyricism, with the first notes of the new and tragic image in the narrative itself. It is the high point of Pushkin's hymn that Dostoevsky quotes in one of his notebooks: "I love thee, city of Peter's making," but only to comment, "Sorry, I don't love it," and to add, "Windows, godforsaken holes [*dyrya*] — and monuments." [7]

In the city's physical and social elements of prose Dostoevsky saw more than a hidden luminosity: he saw material for that "new word" which he would contribute to Russian literature. For he found, as no French or English writer could have found of his own, that Russian literature, in the hands of writers like Turgenev and Tolstoy, had been a "landowners' literature" (*pomeshchichya literatura*). And he found that "it has said all that it had to say (splendidly in Tolstoy). But this pre-eminently landowners' word was the last one. There was still no new word to replace the landowners'." [8] The implication is clear: the new word was Dostoevsky's, and the new social class he represented (in both meanings of the word) was the declassed gentry, the petty government officials, and the urban intelligentsia, struggling, helpless and without roots, to find their way in the chaos of the indifferent city.

All this suggests one important reason why questers after a picture of mid-century Petersburg have turned so seldom to Dostoevsky, despite his unflagging concern with it. His heroes are not only outside the dominant classes; they despise them. Their great expectations, like their lost illusions, are not social. Only the accessories to their stories are: the observed detail and the topical references, culled from the newspapers of the day. Grossman may be right in pointing out the authenticity of Dostoevsky's observation of city life, but the fact remains that observation is always ancillary to his more pressing concerns. The early works bear this out in one way, the later ones in another. But with the exception of his first book, the sentimental-philanthropic *Poor Folk,* it can be said that the authenticity Grossman praises performs one general function: it is the author's realistic ballast, his way of anchoring the feverish improbabilities of the action of his books in real life. The mundane detail of his city is the warrant for his extremities, but these very extremities — of situation, character, and behavior — inevitably color the picture of the city itself. Petersburg is established as the most real of real places in order that we may wonder at what strange things happen in it: it is, in fact, the condition of our perceiving the full force of the strangeness, the lever that forces the suspension of our disbelief. But once our wonder has been stimulated, the city itself becomes its object, and all that seemed most real a moment before may at any time begin to appear the sheerest fantasy. The dialectic process is the Dostoevskian hallmark: he himself called his method "fantastic realism."

Like Balzac and Dickens, Dostoevsky was a working journalist who did not, after an initial hesitation, see any contradiction between this sort of work and the writing of novels — quite the contrary — and his generally neglected journalism is of special interest for the study of his myth of the city. Here we can see him speaking more or less in his own person, groping his way in the early pieces toward an attitude and a theme. Both the form and the direction of the gropings were supplied by the events of his time.

The decade of the 1840s, which saw Dostoevsky's literary debut, also saw the rise of the quarrel between Slavophiles and Westerners, of which Petersburg became a center and a symbol. Comparisons with Moscow, on the order of Gogol's, proliferated on all levels. Herzen wrote his "Moscow and Petersburg," and Belinsky wrote his "Petersburg and Moscow." Conclusions about the nature of the contrast between the two cities tended to bear out Gogol's findings, but the tone was different, more matter-of-fact, fuller of social detail. He had found Moscow "a Russian beard," spread out and uncombed; Belinsky — who paid tribute to Gogol by ending his own piece with a long quotation from Gogol's — nevertheless proceeds differently. "Only walk an hour along the crooked and angular streets of Moscow," he writes, "and you will notice immediately that this is a city of patriarchal domesticity [*semeistvennost*]: the houses stand separate, almost every one has a spacious enough courtyard, overgrown with grass and surrounded with outbuildings." [9] Observation is replacing metaphor.

The trend was general.[10] And if new ideological emphases impelled Petersburg writers to explore the city, so too did the still influential example of French literature. The sensation of 1842 in Paris — and soon in Petersburg as well — was Eugène Sue's publication of *Les Mystères de Paris* in the *Journal des Débats;* its success among the Russian literati was so complete that Belinsky found himself agreeing with Bulgarin in its praise, and Russian editors hastened to commission imitations. E. Kovalevsky's *Petersburg by Day and Night* was written on order and appeared in the journal "Library for Reading" in 1845; the same year saw publication of Nekrasov's *Petersburg Corners,* Krestovsky's *Petersburg Slums,* Butkov's *Petersburg Summits* — and, standing somewhat apart, Dostoevsky's own *Poor Folk* followed in January 1846.

The significance of Sue's success, for present purposes, lay in the form of his work. Here was the first great example of the roman-feuilleton, marking equally the appearance of a new kind of novel and a new development of the feuilleton as a journalistic genre. The feuilleton had begun as a free-wheeling column in the newspapers, commenting in highly personal fashion on goings-on about town and most frequently containing a theatrical review; one may recall, as Dostoevsky was to do, the piece that first opened the doors of the journalistic world to Lucien de Rubempré. But by the second half of the 1830s it was changing: the "physiology" of the city was making itself felt in the feuilleton. The conjunction can be seen in Gogol's "Petersburg Notes," which has been quoted: its concluding section is taken up with a review of the Petersburg theater.

From the lowest level of transient journalism, then, the feuilleton was aspiring, in the hands of at least some writers, to greater dignity as a literary form. By the middle forties, some of the most talented and serious of the younger writers were practicing it, among them Sollogub, Grigoriev, Grigorovich, Pleshcheyev, Panayev, Turgenev, and Goncharov.[11] That the aspiration was still not universal in 1847, however, is evident from the complaint of the critic Ksefont Polevoy, that "in the conception of some writers and readers the feuilleton should be without fail a collection of city news, seasoned with agreeable little jokes" — instead of serving the interests "of the educated circle of society." [12]

All this explains the young Dostoevsky's trepidation at undertaking such work. Full of Schiller and romantic doctrine about the high calling of art, his ambition could tempt him to cheaper successes but not entirely blind him to their dangerous seduction. On the crest of his success with *Poor Folk* (which had not yet been published but was circulating in manuscript), he writes his brother on 16 November 1845: "Nekrasov . . . has undertaken 'The Banterer' [*Zuboskal*], a charming humorous almanac, for which I have written the announcement. This announcement has made a splash; for this is the first instance of such lightness and such humor in things of this sort. It has reminded me of the first feuilleton of Lucien de Rubempré." [13] One feels in his mention of Lucien chiefly the allure of sudden success, but Dostoevsky cannot have been entirely unaware of the further symbolism. Here is the central passage from his announcement:

Is it his [The Banterer's] fault . . . that all Petersburg, with its glitter and luxury, thunder and rumble, with its infinite types, with its infinite activity, earnest aspirations, with its gentlemen and riff-raff — *clods of dirt,* as Derzhavin says, *gilded* and not gilded, swindlers, scribes, usurers, mesmerists, rogues, peasants and what have you — appears to him as an endless, splendid illustrated almanac, which one may look over only at leisure, out of boredom, after dinner — to yawn over and smile at.[14]

This forced and relatively pedestrian note was not to recur in Dostoevsky's first feuilletons when they appeared only two years later ("The Banterer" was banned by the censorship before it ever appeared, on the strength of Dostoevsky's announcement, the censor taking exception to one phrase in which Dostoevsky declared, " 'The Banterer' will laugh at everything that is worthy of laughter"). In the meantime, he could escape Belinsky's reproach that he was profaning himself by collaborating in such a publication and, for the time being, honor the vow he reported to his brother earlier in that year "never to write to order." [15] Between the collapse of Nekrasov's project and the writing of the four feuilletons that make up his "Petersburg Chronicle" of 1847, he produced *The Double,* "Mr. Prokharchin," and several slighter pieces, some of them unpublished.

The Double was a substantial failure and shook the young author's reputation; "Mr. Prokharchin" all but destroyed it. Belinsky, who had been one of the architects of Dostoevsky's sudden glory, wrote of this tale that "sparks of talent flash in it, but in such a thick darkness that their light gives nothing to the reader." [16] The fading of his dreams of glory, the creative blind alley in which he found himself, a desperate need for money, all led him to accept the offer of the "Saint Petersburg News" (*Sanktpeterburgskie Vedomosti*) when he was invited to replace that newspaper's feuilletonist, who had died. There is no mention of these points in his letters, but the conversational freedom of the form must have been a particular attraction: up to this time he had never enjoyed it in print ("The Banterer" was to have been a joint enterprise, and his announcement was a quite different affair). The new job got him out on the streets in search of material; it advanced him in the double role of flâneur (a word just then winning its place in Cyrillic spelling) and dreamer; it opened up to him the possibility of experiments with personal confession; and it confronted him directly with the theme of the city. He made the most of all these possibilities, as both the feuilletons themselves and the stories of the next two years show — proving what a French feuilletonist claimed of his work when he wrote that it should be considered the literary equivalent of the sketch in painting.[17] Dostoevsky's

"Petersburg Chronicle" came out in four installments, on April 27, May 11, June 1, and June 15, 1847.

The opening of the chronicle for April 27 is vaguely reminiscent of a sketch by Boz: "Up to quite recently I was utterly unable to imagine the inhabitant of Petersburg otherwise than in his dressing gown, in a nightcap, in a tightly shut-up room, and with an unfailing obligation to take something or other every two hours in a tablespoon." [18] The movement, however, is more capricious; where Boz has his subject to deal with and proceeds in a relatively straight line, Dostoevsky has his space to fill, seems to discover his themes only as he writes, and interweaves them almost musically through paragraphs that are often pages long. "But here at last," he goes on, "the sun is shining, and this news unquestionably outweighs any other." He accompanies his imaginary convalescent to the Nevsky Prospect, where "at last . . . [he] gulps down the new dust. . . . The first Petersburg dust after the flood of mud and something very wet in the air, of course, does not yield in sweetness to the ancient smoke of the native hearths" — and the stroller decides to enjoy the spring so completely that, meeting a friend, he even forgets to ask his usual question, "What's new?" [19]

This utterly hopeless "Petersburg question" leads the writer to the first of his several characterizations of the city. "What is most insulting of all," he finds, is that the question is usually asked by a man "utterly indifferent, an indigenous Petersburger . . . who knows in advance that he will get no answer, that there is nothing new . . . but asks all the same, and seems to take an interest, as if some propriety were forcing him, too, to take part in something social and have public interests." Ironically, he concedes that there are such: "We all fervently love our native land, love our dear Petersburg, love to play a little if given a chance: in a word, there are many public interests. But among us circles are more in use. It is even well known that all Petersburg is nothing but a collection of an enormous number of little circles, each of which has its regulations, its decorum, its law, its logic, and its oracle." [20] This fact, observed also by Gogol but differently interpreted, he explains in terms of the national character, "which is still a little shy of public life and looks homeward. Moreover, for public life art is necessary, it is necessary to prepare so many conditions — in a word, it's better at home. There it is more natural, no art is necessary, it's quieter." [21]

This theme of the circle leads the feuilletonist to his favorite theme of isolation, and on to others that will reappear in his stories:

In a circle one can, in the most serene and delightful way, draw out one's useful life, between yawning and gossip, right up to the time when grippe or a wasting fever [*gnilaya goryachka*] visits your domestic hearth and you take leave of it stoically, indifferently, and in happy ignorance of what things had been like with you up to now, and why they had been so. *You die in the dark, at twilight, on a rainy day without a gleam of light, in full puzzlement.*[22]

Noting that intellectual circles, in the last analysis, fare no better, he returns to express his special vexation with "our patriarchal circle, because in it one gentleman, with a most unbearable quality, is always formed and fashioned."

His name is legion. This is the gentleman who has *a kind heart,* and has nothing besides *a kind heart.* As if it were such a wonder to have a kind heart in our time! This gentleman, who possesses such a sterling quality, steps out into the world in the full certainty that his good heart will quite suffice for him to be eternally content and happy. He is so sure of success that he has neglected any other means in providing himself for the road of life. He, for instance, knows neither curb nor restraint in anything. With him everything is openhearted, everything is frank.[23]

Dostoevsky goes on to picture such a man as egotistical and tiresome. The complaint sounds like that of any Russian romantic against complacent philistinism, though it may, since the writer had just begun to visit Petrashevsky and his revolutionary circle, have a political point as well. In any case, his conclusion about the type has a particular bearing on his own subsequent work:

Yes! Only in isolation, in a corner, and most of all in a circle is this excellent work of nature produced, this *specimen of our raw material,* as the Americans say, on which not a drop of art has been expended, in which all is natural, all raw ore, without curb or restraint. Such a man in his full innocence forgets — in fact does not suspect — that life is a whole art, that to live means to make of oneself a work of art, that only in the presence of generalized interests, in sympathy for the mass of society and for its direct, immediate demands, and not in somnolence, not in indifference, from which the mass is falling apart, not in isolation, can his hidden treasure, his capital, his kind heart, be polished into a valuable, genuine, gleaming diamond! [24]

Impatience with the complacent failure of this type to involve himself in society leads him to an ironic lament for the livelier sort of old-fashioned villainy (and an oblique justification of his own artistic method in distinction to Dickens' and partly to Balzac's):

My God! What has become of the old villains of the old melodramas and novels, gentlemen? How pleasant it was when they lived in the world! And pleasant because just now, right here at hand, was the most virtuous man, who finally defended innocence and punished evil. This villain, this *tirano ingrato,* was born so, a villain, all prepared by some secret and quite incomprehensible predisposition of fate. In him everything was an incarnation of villainy. He was already a villain in his mother's womb; not only that: his ancestors, probably with a foreboding of his appearance in the world, intentionally chose a *surname* fully corresponding to the social position of their future descendant. Already by the name alone you felt that this fellow went around with a knife stabbing people, just like that, not stabbing for a penny, but for God knows what. As if he were a machine for stabbing and burning. That was fine! At least it was understandable! But now, God knows what writers are talking about. Now, suddenly, it somehow turns out that the most virtuous man — and what a one! the most unfitted for villainy — suddenly proves an accomplished villain, and moreover without noticing it himself.[25]

There follows, as an example, a sketch of what he was to publish the following year as "A Christmas Tree and a Wedding."

From sociological generalization, personal confession, literary comment, and a literary sketch, he returns abruptly to his métier: "I was walking through the Haymarket. But I am a feuilletonist, gentlemen, I should be telling you about the news . . . for instance, that *Jenny Lind* is going to London. But what is *Jenny Lind* to the Petersburg reader!" The parody of the old-fashioned type of feuilleton is deliberate but casual. He goes on to a genre sketch, in which a Balzacian personification of the city is brilliantly infused with a rare Dickensian note:

I was, then, walking in the Haymarket, and mulling over what to write. Melancholy gnawed me. It was a raw misty morning. Petersburg had got up ill-tempered and angry, like an irritated society maid turned yellow from spite at last night's ball. He [Petersburg] was angry from head to foot. Whether he had slept badly, whether his bile had flowed in disproportionate quantity during the night, whether he had caught a chill or got a head cold, whether he had lost all his money at cards the night before like a boy, to the point where he had to get up in the morning with utterly empty pockets, with vexation at his foolish spoiled wives, at his lazy oafs of children, at his unshaven stern crowd of menials, at his Yid-creditors, at his scoundrelly advisers, slanderers, and various other informers, is hard to say; only he was so angry that it was depressing to look at his huge damp walls, at his marbles, bas-reliefs, statues, columns, which, as it were, were also angry at the bad weather, at the bare wet granite of the sidewalks which had cracked as if from spite under the feet of pedestrians, and finally at the pedestrians themselves, palely green, stern, looking terribly angry, the better part of them beautifully and carefully shaved and hurrying hither and thither to fulfill their obligations. The whole Petersburg horizon looked so sour, so sour . . . Petersburg sulked. It was evident that he wanted, as happens in such cases with some wrathful gentlemen, to concentrate all his dreary vexation on any outside third person who might turn up, quarrel, fall out with somebody for good, bawl the hell out of somebody, and then run away someplace himself, and not for anything continue to stand in the dismal Ingermanland swamp. Even the very sun . . . on the point of hastening with such a friendly smile . . . to kiss its sick, spoiled offspring, stopped midway, glanced with bewilderment and pity at the discontented grumbler, at the querulous, sickly child, and sunk sadly behind leaden clouds. Only a single ray, bright and joyous, as if with a dispensation to visit people, darted sharply out from the violet haze for an instant, sported along the roofs of houses, flashed along dark damp walls, burst into a thousand sparks in each raindrop, and vanished as if offended at its loneliness — vanished like a sudden enthusiasm which flies inadvertently into the skeptical Slavic soul, and which that Slavic soul immediately takes shame at and will not acknowledge. At the same time, the most dismal twilight spread out over Petersburg. One o'clock in the afternoon tolled, and it seemed that the city chimes themselves could not understand by what right they were compelled to strike such an hour in such a darkness.[26]

This brilliant bit of descriptive animism is the high point of Dostoevsky's first feuilleton. After it he gives a short genre sketch of a passing funeral, summarizes a story from a Moscow magazine (which he praises for its "Dickensian charm"), promises one of his own from Petersburg life, and finishes with an ironic admission that he has forgotten "the main thing" — a concert to benefit the Society for Visiting the Poor and the German Philanthropic Society. But the main thing is clearly the long passage just quoted. From a personification of the generalized "inhabitant of Petersburg" evoked in his opening paragraph, victim of the Petersburg atmosphere in the literal sense, he has come to the personification of the city itself and of its atmosphere in the double sense. Not only has the city a presence and a mood reflected in the aspects of its citizens and its buildings alike: it and they are in consonance with the visionary flâneur who, from the depths of Dostoevsky's self-knowledge, is lengthily analyzed at the end of the series as a "dreamer" (*mechtatel*) and claimed as a peculiar Petersburg type. The themes of the city and the dreamer are inextricably related from here on, both in the feuilletons and in the fiction Dostoevsky will write up to his postexile *Insulted and Injured* — and even, it is arguable, considerably beyond.

In the piece for May 11, he ventures on a different sort of personification of Petersburg. He has mentioned the strollers on the Nevsky Prospect, only to brush the theme aside as worn out ("God! one could write a whole book about encounters on the Nevsky Prospect alone. But you know about all this so well from pleasant experience, gentlemen, that in my opinion it is unnecessary to write the book").[27]

Another idea came to me: namely, the fact that in Petersburg people squander terribly. . . . I don't know whether I'm right, but I have always imagined Petersburg (if I may be permitted the comparison) as the younger, indulged son of a respected papa, a man of the old time, rich, open-handed, sober-minded, and very good-natured. Papa has finally retired from affairs, settled in the country, and is delighted that he can, in his backwater, wear his nankeen frock-coat without a breach of decorum. But sonny has been sent into the world, sonny must learn all the sciences, sonny must be a young European, and papa, although he has only heard about enlightenment by rumor, wants his son without fail to be the most enlightened of young men. Sonny immediately gets a smattering of knowledge, starts living, acquires a European set of clothes, acquires a moustache, a little pointed beard, and papa, not noticing at all that sonny at the same time is acquiring a head, is acquiring experience, is acquiring independence, that he, rightly or wrongly wants to live his own life and at the age of twenty has already learned from experience more than papa, living in the ancestral habits, has learned in his own life, seeing in horror the little pointed beard alone, seeing that sonny without counting is raking it in from the wide parental pocket, having noticed at length that sonny is a bit of a schismatic and has his own mind — grumbles, gets angry, accuses both enlightenment and the West, and is vexed chiefly that "her own eggs are starting to teach the chicken." But sonny needs to live, and he has rushed so that one begins involuntarily to reflect at his youthful verve. Of course he squanders unstintingly.[28]

What follows makes it clear that the personification here is not of the essential Petersburg (or of the essentially Dostoevskian Petersburg), but only of its wealthier classes — the very ones to whom Dostoevsky remained contemptuously indifferent all his life. Of all the possible poverties, he says, "the vilest, most disgusting, ignoble, low, and filthy poverty is the fashionable kind," which, though it is rare, preserves its haughtiness and, while scrupling to ask for charity, does not scruple to take it "in the most insolent and conscienceless way." [29]

The real, significant Petersburg yields to study — and, in the more sociological piece for June 1, there is even a flash of the Northern Palmyra in the feuilletonist's regret that the distracted citizen hardly has time "to scrutinize Petersburg more attentively, to study its physiognomy and read the history of the city and of our whole epoch in this mass of stones, in these magnificent buildings, palaces, monuments." The study of the city, he notes, "is really not a useless thing." [30] What it yields to him is an enormous contemporary significance, and his tone for the first time becomes free of any hint of affectation as he gives us a full statement of a view he was to disown in his last period — but never, perhaps, completely abandon:

Here [in Petersburg] one cannot take a step without seeing, hearing, and feeling the contemporary moment and the idea of the present moment. It may be that in a certain regard everything here is a chaos, everything is a mixture; many things can be food for caricature: but on the other hand, everything is life and movement. *Petersburg is both the head and heart of Russia.* We began by speaking about the architecture of the city. Even all this diversity testifies to a unity of thought and a unity of movement. This row of buildings of Dutch architecture recalls the time of Peter the Great. This building in the style of Rastrelli recalls the century of Catherine; this one, in the Greek and Roman style, the latest time; but all together recalls the history of the European life of Petersburg and of all Russia. Even up to the present Petersburg is in dust and rubble; it is still being created, still becoming. Its future is still in an idea; but this idea belongs to Peter I; it is being embodied, growing and taking root with each day, not alone in the Petersburg marsh but in all Russia, all of which lives by Petersburg alone. . . . Everything — industry, trade, the sciences, literature, education, the principle [*nachalo*] and structure of public life — everything lives and is supported by Petersburg alone.[31]

To put it more precisely, what Dostoevsky later disowned was the faith he shows here in the promise of Peter's westernizing ideas, in a national development based on Europeanization. As his views of such a development changed and darkened, so too did his image of the city. But he never wavered in considering Petersburg a symbol — historical, social, even metaphysical — and if his later, well-known references to it as the most fantastic and unnatural city in the world are made literal in the novels, it is ultimately in the service of this view.

Among these sketches for a myth of the city, then, Dostoevsky has here touched on one of his basic ideas. In the last feuilleton, for June 15, the visionary once more supplants the ideologue, to take up the twin themes of the city and the dreamer. He begins with an extraordinary and characteristic image:

June, heat; the city is empty; everybody is at his summer place and living on impressions, enjoying nature. There is something unutterably naive, even something touching in our Petersburg nature when it suddenly, as it were unexpectedly, displays all its might, all its force, puts on green, becomes covered with young leaves, dresses up, turns motley with flowers . . . I don't know why it reminds me of that young girl, sickly and ailing, on whom you sometimes look with pity, sometimes with compassionate love, and sometimes don't even notice, but who suddenly, in one instant and somehow unexpectedly, becomes marvellously, unutterably beautiful, and you, astounded, involuntarily wonder: what force has made these perpetually sad and thoughtful eyes shine with such a light, what has drawn the blood into these pale cheeks, what has infused these tender features with passion and yearning, why does this breast heave, what so suddenly called forth the force, the vitality, and the beauty to the face of this woman and made it shine with such a smile, become animated with such flashing, sparkling laughter? You look around you, you seek something, you conjecture . . . But the moment passes, and perhaps on the next day you will meet again that same sadly thoughtful glance, that same pale face, that same perpetual submissiveness and timidity in her movements — fatigue, weakness, dull melancholy, and even the traces of some useless, numbing annoyance at the momentary enthusiasm.[32]

This elaborate figure offers a valuable key to a whole aspect of Dostoevsky's later art. What we see is another sort of symbolism — that symbolism by which the artist can merge his themes, so that the qualities of one and another partake of a peculiarly close harmony and seem the product of some larger mystery (here a very special kind of *élan vital*). The subject — "our Petersburg nature" — is mentioned only briefly at the beginning; the girl has no role or meaning apart from her symbolic function; there is no question of cause or effect. And yet how inextricably they are mixed, how much human pathos informs the nonhuman subject. Here the pathos takes on the color of a lament for transient beauty; later, in the great novels, it will take on the hues of the gloomy city. What is here crystallized into one outstanding image will there be diffused throughout pages of description, and rarely will the connection be so openly indicated ("I don't know why it reminds me . . ."). Yet the process is essentially the same, and it will call for further discussion in connection with the novels.

Meanwhile, there is one more abiding feature of Dostoevsky's art suggested in this passage — a special attitude toward nature, which he attributes to the whole Petersburger genus a few lines later in the same feuilleton, remarking that "we are in part not arranged right to enjoy Nature; and our Nature, moreover, as if knowing *our* nature, forgot to arrange itself for the best." [33] Nature, in the romantic sense, had little attraction for Dostoevsky, who invokes it rarely and then always with a special purpose.[34] His themes inhere rather in the man-made world of the city; his landscapes are predominantly urban. So it is no accident that the idea of "our Petersburg nature" calls forth the image of a sickly child: the image recurs throughout his work, from *Netochka Nezvanova* to the Marmeladov children of *Crime and Punishment*.

The theme of the Petersburger's alleged insensitivity to nature (Dostoevsky characterizes him as unable to drop his trivial preoccupations, even when he is vacationing away from the city) leads to the question: "Why is it that one most unpleasant habit is so strongly developed in us . . . [the habit] of always, without need, just so, from custom, trusting and already too exactly weighing our impressions, weighing sometimes only an impending, future enjoyment which is still unrealized, [the habit] of valuing it and taking satisfaction in it beforehand, in dreams, of taking satisfaction in fantasy, and naturally of being then unfitted for the business at hand?" [35] This dreaming is made, by implication, a mark of the urban routine, and it underlies the necessity "if only for these few days in the whole year . . . [to] quench our eternal unsated thirst for direct, natural life." For how, he asks, can one help tiring from "eternally chasing after impressions as if after a rhyme for a bad verse, tormented by a thirst for external, direct activity and frightened to the point of illness, finally, by one's own illusions, one's own mental chimeras, one's own reverie and all those auxiliary means by which people try in our time to fill up somehow the dull emptiness of everyday colorless life." [36]

What follows, disguised as a national characteristic, is plainly a personal confession. The habit of dreaming (*mechtatelnost*) arises in the Russian, according to Dostoevsky, not from simple laziness, as critics charge, but almost from its opposite. "The thirst for activity among us reaches a certain feverish, irrepressible impatience" to find some worthy and useful employment, but a way is not offered: the social machine rolls on in its inertia, and no appeal is made to the available reserves of idealistic energy.[37] The result is "a Petersburg nightmare":

Then in characters eager for activity, eager for spontaneous life, eager for reality — but weak, effeminate, gentle — there arises little by little what is called reverie, and a man becomes at length not a man but some strange creature of an intermediate sort — *a dreamer*. Do you know what a dreamer is, gentlemen? It is a Petersburg nightmare, it is a sin personified, it is a tragedy, mute, mysterious, gloomy, savage, with all the furious horrors, with all the catastrophes, peripeties, plots, and denouements — and we say this by no means in jest. Sometimes you meet a man, distracted, with a vague, lackluster look, a pale, rumpled face, who seems always to be occupied with something terribly distressing, some most puzzling business, sometimes exhausted as if from heavy labors, but as a matter of fact producing absolutely nothing: such is the dreamer, seen from the outside. The dreamer is always difficult because he is uneven to an extreme: now he is too gay, now he is too gloomy, now a boor, now attentive and tender, now an egoist, now capable of the noblest feelings. At work these gentlemen are good for absolutely nothing, and though they work . . . they only drag out their jobs . . . They settle for the most part in profound isolation, in inaccessible corners, as if hiding in them from people and from the world [or "from the light": the Russian *svet* means both], and in general there is even something melodramatic that strikes you at first sight of them. They are morose and taciturn with those at home and absorbed in themselves, but they are very fond of everything lazy, light, contemplative, everything that acts tenderly on the emotions or stimulates their sensations. They like to read, and to read all sorts of books — even serious, specialized ones — but usually drop their reading after the second or third page, for they have satisfied themselves fully. Their fantasy, mobile, volatile, light, is already aroused, their impression is already attuned, and a whole world of dreams, with joys, with griefs, with hell and heaven, with captivating women, with heroic feats, with noble activity, always with some titanic struggle, with crimes and all sorts of horrors, suddenly takes possession of the dreamer's whole being. The room vanishes, as does space; time stops or flies so fast that an hour seems a minute. Sometimes whole nights pass in indescribable delights; often in a few hours one lives through a paradise of love or a whole enormous life, gigantic, unheard-of, marvelous as a dream, grandly beautiful. By some unknown whim the pulse speeds up, tears spurt, the pale moist cheeks burn with a feverish fire, and when the dawn with its rosy light flashes in the window of the dreamer, he is pale, sick, tormented, and happy. He throws himself onto the bed almost unconscious, and, falling asleep, still feels for a long time a sickly sweet, physical sensation in his heart . . . The minutes of sobering-up are terrible: the unfortunate cannot bear them, and immediately takes his poison in new, increased doses. Again a book, a musical motif, some ancient recollection, an old one, from real life — in a word, one of a thousand of the most trivial reasons — and the poison is ready, and his fantasy unfolds brightly and luxuriously anew . . . On the street he walks with his head hung low, paying little attention to those around him, sometimes even here forgetting reality; but if he notices anything, then even the most ordinary everyday trifle, *the most empty routine matter, immediately assumes for him a fantastic coloring. His glance is already attuned so as to see the fantastic in everything.* Closed shutters amid broad daylight, a twisted old woman, the gentleman coming toward him waving his arms and talking aloud to himself (the sort, incidentally, of which you meet so many), a family picture in the window of a poor little wooden house — all these are already almost adventures.[38]

Fantasy replaces life for the dreamer, Dostoevsky says, until "he loses completely that moral sensitivity by which a man is able to value all the beauty of the present." [39] "And is not such a life a tragedy!" he concludes: "Is it not a sin and a horror! Is it not a caricature! And aren't we all more or less dreamers!" This is why summer life out of town is so "extremely useful for sick, strange, and gloomy Petersburg, in which youth perishes so quickly, hopes wither so quickly, health so quickly deteriorates, and the whole man is so quickly worked out." [40] Here is the first characterization of a type and a theme that were to occupy the novelist throughout his long career; an enormous list of Dostoevskian characters, from Ordynov in "The Landlady" to Arkady Dolgoruky in *A Raw Youth* could serve as a gloss on this passage by the twenty-seven-year-old author.

On this impassioned note Dostoevsky ends the last of the feuilletons that make up his "Petersburg Chronicle." No documents have survived to tell us why he wrote no more, but it is clear that, as an artist, he had gotten from them what he needed; they are his creative workshop, just as his *Diary of a Writer* was to be in the 1870s. The very shifts in tone are instructive: if the first and second pieces show a kind of aggressive cleverness, and a literary self-consciousness from which the shadow of Lucien de Rubempré may not have been absent, the last are more directly personal and reveal Dostoevsky himself exorcising the demon of reverie, and so anticipating the new approaches that would inform his work up to his exile and, with modifications, long after. The more fanciful personifications of Petersburg in the first feuilletons (the convalescent gentleman and the spoiled son) are significant in their failure: it needed a Gogolian fancy to build such figures, and the realist in Dostoevsky was too strong. Not that the realist, even at this early date, was of the usual sort: it was not a curiosity about the kinds of life lived in the city that impelled the young author, but rather the effect of the city on life itself — understanding life to mean first of all those psychological and moral notions that an ambitious and bookish youth might glean from Schiller, Shakespeare, Balzac, Dickens, Corneille, Racine, Fourier, and his own experience, in which dream and reality were themselves inextricably mixed. The fusion of psychological and moral values appears throughout, most pointedly in the long passage last quoted. As for the city itself, the author's mixture of hatred and admiration is shown held in a larger attitude — fascination. These feuilletons were written when he had exhausted the neo-Gogolian vein of the so-called natural school. That vein had given him *Poor Folk, The Double,* and "Mr. Prokharchin," in all of which the role of the city had been one of background and atmosphere, more implicit than explicit. The new approaches we have seen him experimenting with were to enlarge its role and to deepen its tonality. As he says in the feuilleton for May 11: "One hears how through the colorless motif of our everyday life there sounds another, piercingly vital and melancholy, as in the ball of the Capulets in Berlioz." [41]

Between 1847 and 1873, when he took up his *Diary of a Writer,* Dostoevsky produced a considerable body of journalism, most of it polemical, but only one feuilleton. This was his "Petersburg Visions in Verse and Prose," which appeared without signature in the first of his ill-fated editorial ventures, the magazine "Time" (*Vremya*), for January 1861.[42] The job had originally been consigned to one D. D. Minayev, but Dostoevsky was for some reason dissatisfied with the copy he submitted and hastily wrote a substitute for it, keeping only Minayev's verses.[43] One American critic terms this piece "a wistful recapitulation of his [pre-exile] literary stock-in-trade" and suggests that with it "he seems to be cautiously inquiring" whether the public would still buy his old themes."[44] Even on what little evidence we have, such a conjecture seems quite wrong: why should Dostoevsky have commissioned Minayev to do the piece in the first place, only to replace it with a hastily concocted "cautious" inquiry? In fact, there are signs neither of caution nor of wistfulness in the piece, and it is oriented as much ahead to his new work as backward to the old. It *is* something of a summing-up of his experience as a feuilletonist, but the fact takes on a new significance when we consider that *The Insulted and Injured,* the first Petersburg novel of his postexile period, began appearing in the same issue of "Time" and was, in its author's own words, "a roman-feuilleton." There is thus a particular timeliness and relevance in his remark in "Petersburg Visions" that "the feuilleton in our age is . . . almost the main thing" and in his further statement that "If I were not a casual feuilletonist but a regular, daily one, it seems to me that I should wish to turn to Eugène Sue in order to describe the mysteries of Petersburg." [45]

These "mysteries of Petersburg" are his main subject. Most of the central passage comes virtually verbatim from "A Weak Heart," a work published thirteen years beforc. But its transposition to a personal context lends it new meaning:

I remember once on a wintry January evening I was hurrying home from the Vyborg side. I was still very young then. When I reached the Neva, I stopped for a minute and threw a piercing glance along the river into the smoky, frostily dim distance, which had suddenly turned crimson with the last purple of a sunset that was dying out on the hazy horizon. Night lay over the city, and the whole immense plain of the Neva, swollen with frozen snow, under the last gleam of the sun, was strewn with infinite myriads of sparks of spindly hoar-frost. There was a twenty-degree frost . . . Frozen steam poured from tired horses, from running people. The taut air quivered at the slightest sound, and columns of smoke like giants rose from all the roofs on both embankments and rushed upward through the cold sky, twining and untwining on the way, so that it seemed new buildings were rising above the old ones, a new city was forming in the air . . . It seemed, finally, that this whole world with all its inhabitants, strong and weak, with all their domiciles, the shelters of the poor or gilded mansions, resembled at this twilight hour a fantastic, magic vision, a dream which would in its turn vanish immediately and rise up as steam toward the dark-blue sky. Some strange thought suddenly stirred in me. I shuddered, and my heart was as if flooded with a hot rush of blood that boiled up suddenly from the surge of a powerful but hitherto unknown sensation. I seemed to have understood something in that minute which had till then only been stirring in me, but was still uninterpreted; it was as if my eyes had been opened to something new, to a completely new world, unfamiliar to me and known only by certain obscure rumors, by certain mysterious signs. I suppose that my existence began from just that minute . . .[46]

This epiphany, so curiously reminiscent of Custine's and Gogol's, evidently represents Dostoevsky's discovery of the fantastic city. "From that time," he goes on, "from that very vision (I call my sensation on the Neva a vision), there began to happen to me such strange things" — the strange things being "golden and fervent day-dreams, as if from opium." "There have been no minutes in my life," he concludes, "more full, more sacred, and more pure."[47]

The whole tone of this piece suggests, nevertheless, that the writer has outlived the dreams he is nostalgically recalling — as indeed he had. *The Insulted and Injured,* in which a dreamer for the first time confronts evil and proves powerless against it, is his farewell to the type. In the meantime, as he says ironically of his imprisonment, he had "traveled to the moon." Yet something remains: "I am utterly unable to renounce a fantastic mood. Back in the forties they used to tease me and call me a visionary. . . . Now, of course, there is gray hair, life experience, etc., etc., but meanwhile I have, all the same, remained a visionary."[48]

These confessions are, for present purposes, the heart of the matter. For the rest, his anecdotes and reflections add little to what we have already seen in the earlier feuilletons or to what we shall see in the fiction. Aside from the obvious importance of their matter, however, all of these neglected pieces have a stylistic importance that deserves mention: they show Dostoevsky consciously experimenting with the creation of a narrative stance, a quasi-fictional "I." This is a problem that occupied him continually in the period of his great novels, and only in *Crime and Punishment* — which he originally conceived in the first person — are signs of a personalized narrator completely absent. The Russian word *zapiski* (notes) appears not only in the title of *Notes from Underground* and *Notes from the House of the Dead,* but in the subtitles of *The Insulted and Injured, The Gambler,* and *A Raw Youth.* A vaguely personalized chronicler perplexingly appears and vanishes in *The Possessed* and in *The Brothers Karamazov,* and even for a moment in *The Idiot* (at the beginning of Part II). The technical influence of the feuilleton is not, of course, the whole explanation for these features, but neither is it wholly unrelated to them, and a stylistic study of Dostoevsky's early journalism, together with its continuation in the *Diary of a Writer,* might contribute some interesting sidelights to the understanding of that truly "new word," his style in the novels.[49]

The more serious form of the feuilleton as it developed in France in the 1830s and in Russia in the 1840s is, in sum, a kind of romantic realism. We are warranted in applying a term of literary criticism to journalism in this case not only by the fact that both forms were pursuing similar concerns — the highly personal discovery of the strange in the familiar, of lyrical resonances in the urban "elements of prose" — but also by the fact that the two forms in this period were tending toward each other, to meet in the new form of the roman-feuilleton. Dostoevsky's early journalism shows him most immediately under the influence of romantic realism, and fashioning his image of the city under its aegis. His novels and stories show a different process: the adaptation and evolution of that image as material for art.

6

Evolution of the Myth: From *Poor Folk* to *Notes from Underground*

DOSTOEVSKY'S first published effort was a translation of *Eugénie Grandet* in 1844, but his real literary debut came a year later, with the circulation of *Poor Folk*. It was a prepublication success. Nekrasov, who had intended to read only ten pages of the manuscript, ended by staying up most of the night with it and passed it on to Belinsky with the announcement that "a new Gogol has appeared!" [1] The alleged consanguinity obviously concerned the Gogol of "The Overcoat," for though Russian literature was suffering from an avalanche of stories about poor civil servants, Gogol still stood out as the one writer of genius to have treated the theme. The implication that another major writer had picked up where Gogol left off is clear — and true — enough. (In fact, the restless young Dostoevsky, after handing over his manuscript to Nekrasov, spent that evening reading Gogol aloud with friends.) But one major writer seldom continues the work of another without at the same time quarreling with it; if *Poor Folk* is a continuation of Gogol's "Overcoat," it is also a polemic against it.

A NEW GOGOL

The most striking difference is the way the young newcomer humanizes all that is mechanical and lifeless in Gogol's story. So the symbolic overcoat, which was to Akaky Akakievich the equivalent of a female companion, is replaced by an actual female companion in the person of Varvara Dobroselova. The very names of the protagonists reflect this change: where Gogol's hero bears the ludicrous surname of Bashmachkin (from *bashmak,* shoe), Dostoevsky's is called Devushkin (from *devushka,* girl, maiden). The similarity of his situation to Akaky's only underlines their essential differences. "Can you really have spent your whole life this way," Varvara writes him, "in solitude, amid privations, without joy, without a friendly word, in corners rented from strangers?" [2] And he acknowledges that "[though] I have no polish or style . . . all the same I am a man, in heart and mind I am a man" (August 21). So, where Gogol's hero reads nothing but official documents, Dostoevsky's has literary interests and even literary pretensions. In a central incident, he reads "The Overcoat" and rejects it indignantly, precisely because he recognizes himself caricatured in it: "If a man sets out to describe something, he ought to know all about it" (July 8). Devushkin admits the truth of many of the details, but objects to the tone and to the ending: "But it would have been best of all not to let him die, poor fellow, but to have the overcoat found, to have . . . that general, learning in more detail about his good qualities, ask him into his office again, give him a raise in rank and a good salary . . . I should have done it that way, for instance" (July 8). With consummate irony Dostoevsky does this: at the depth of his degradation, Devushkin is called in by his chief, who speaks sympathetically to him, gives him a hundred rubles of his own money, and shakes his hand. Reporting his good fortune, Devushkin is made to echo Gogol's famous ending to the story of the two Ivans ("It is dreary in this world, gentlemen!"): "It is good to live in this world, Varenka! Especially in Petersburg!" (September 11). But in the world of poverty, as Dostoevsky shows repeatedly in this book, good fortune is always illusory, unable to do anything except underline the bedrock tragedy.

In *Poor Folk* Dostoevsky is staking out his field. The title alone indicates this in a way that the English translation may not quite match, even if we replace the quaint word "folk" with the more accurate "people." The adjective "poor" in Russian (*bedny*) suggests not only poverty but misfortune; it is related to "trouble" (*beda*) and "calamity" (*bedstvie*). The poor man, as Devushkin says, "looks at God's world differently"; he can "get no respect from anyone" (August 1). Through the form of an epistolary novel, Dostoevsky contrives to set forth this different view in all its immediacy, and he manages further — considering the limitations of the form — to ring remarkable variations on his theme. We see, besides the desperate poverty of the two leading characters, that of Devushkin's neighbors, the Gorshkov family, and of Varvara's former neighbor, the "student" Pokrovsky; we have, in Devushkin's report, the "literary" circle of his fellow clerk, Ratazyayev, and with him we visit the moneylender Markov. Dominating Varvara's story are the figures of the procuress, Anna Fyodorovna, and the seducer, Bykov. Every character is either well-to-do or poor, either a victimizer or a victim, so that, as Mochulsky notes, the psychological tale takes on the character of a social novel. It was, in fact, this side of the work that Belinsky singled out for special praise, calling it the first Russian social novel.

The themes are characteristic Petersburg ones. Belinsky himself, in "Petersburg and Moscow," pointed out that the civil servant (*chinovnik*) was "the native, the true citizen of Petersburg" and, regarding the conditions of life in the city: "It is well known that in no other city in the world are there so many young, elderly, and old homeless people as in Petersburg." [3] Habitations, in these circumstances, take on a special emblematic role (and one they will keep clear through Dostoevsky's later novels). In his opening letter, Devushkin describes at some length the "hole" he has landed in — noisy, dark, dirty, where each room is rented separately and houses two or three people. Devushkin himself lives in the kitchen; he has "a little corner" behind a partition; it is a way station — and not the last — on his downward journey. Nor is his situation the worst in the house:

There is a whole family of paupers renting a room from our landlady, only not alongside the other rooms, but on the other side, in the corner, apart. . . . He is a clerk without a job, expelled from the service about seven years ago for something. His name is Gorshkov; such a gray little fellow, he goes about in such a greasy, ragged coat that it's painful to look at him — much worse than mine! Such a pitiful, puny fellow . . . timid, afraid of everybody . . . I am shy at times, but this one is even worse. His family consists of a wife and three children. The oldest, a boy, is just like his father, and just as sickly. The wife was once quite good-looking; you can see it even now. She goes around, poor woman, in such pitiful tatters. . . . It's always quiet and still in their room, as if no one were living there. (April 12)

Gorshkov represents the end of the same road Devushkin himself is traveling, as he clearly realizes. For both, happiness is brief and illusory. Gorshkov is finally vindicated by the court, "so that his circumstances were greatly improved and his honor cleansed of all stain, and everything was better — in a word, he got everything he could have desired" (September 18). Unable to bear the excitement of his good fortune, he dies. This same double reversal takes place just after Devushkin has received the providential hundred rubles from His Excellency, when he is full of elation, and when his own greatest calamity is in preparation: Varvara's departure with Bykov.

Outdoor Petersburg proves no less sordid than the rented rooms in which these obscure tragedies are played out. Devushkin goes for a walk — to freshen his spirits — along the Fontanka (the actual and symbolic majesty of the Neva is not for these people and they seldom approach it, keeping instead to the lesser rivers and canals that crisscross the city):

> The evening was so dark and damp. . . . It wasn't raining, but it might as well have been for the mist. Storm clouds were passing in long, broad strips across the sky. Masses of people were walking along the embankment, and as ill luck would have it, they all had such horrible depressing faces — drunken peasants, snub-nosed Finnish women in boots and bareheaded, workmen, cabbies, people like me on some errand, boys, some metalsmith's apprentice in a striped gown, haggard and sickly looking, with a face bathed in dirty oil and a lock in his hand, a discharged soldier seven feet tall — that's the sort of crowd it was; it was evidently the kind of hour when there could be no other. . . . On the bridges there are women sitting with wet gingerbread and rotten apples, and all of them so dirty, so drenched. It's dreary to walk along the Fontanka! The wet granite under your feet, on either side tall, black, sooty buildings; fog underfoot, fog overhead. How melancholy and dark an evening it was. (September 5)

Even a walk down Gorokhovaya Street ("It's a rich street!") cannot distract the poor man from his preoccupations. The richly appointed carriages and the elegant women he sees there engage his curiosity only until the glitter of this alien world reminds him, by contrast, of his own: "Why, Varenka, are you so unfortunate? My angel, in what way are you worse than any of them?" (September 5). He dwells on the virtues of an organ grinder he has met, but his revolt at social injustice quickly subsides. As he confesses, "I started to talk about that organ grinder, my dear, because I had occasion to feel my poverty twice as much today." A long description then follows of a ten-year-old beggar boy.

Elsewhere, a Balzacian note appears in Devushkin's speculations on the waking town — but the angle of vision already shows what will remain the characteristic Dostoevskian modification:

> Hurrying to work early in the morning, I sometimes take a look at the city, to see how it wakes, gets up, starts to smoke, to fill with life and noise — and *sometimes you feel so small before such a spectacle* that it's as though somebody had given you a flip on your inquisitive nose, and you plod on quieter than water, humbler than grass, and shrug! Now have a look at what's going on in those big, black, sooty buildings . . . There, in some smoky corner, in some damp hole which out of necessity passes for a lodging, some workman has awoken from his sleep; and all night he has been dreaming of the boots, for instance, which he had inadvertently slit the day before, as though it were that kind of rubbish that a man ought to dream! But he's an artisan, he's a shoemaker; it's excusable for him to be thinking only of his subject. His children are crying and his wife is hungry; and it's not only shoemakers who sometimes get up in the morning like that, my darling — that would be nothing and wouldn't be worth writing about, but this is the point, my dear: right here in the same house, one story higher or lower, in gilded chambers, a very wealthy man may have dreamed at night of those same boots — that is, boots in a different manner, boots in a different fashion, but still boots, for in the sense I mean, my darling, each of us is something of a shoemaker; and that wouldn't matter, only it's wrong that there should be no one at that wealthy person's side, no one who could whisper in his ear: "Enough thinking about such things, enough thinking of nothing but yourself, enough living only for yourself. Your children are healthy, your wife is not begging for food. Look around: can't you see some object to worry about more noble than your boots?" (September 5; my italics)

Poverty, as Mochulsky has pointed out, is not only described here: it is analyzed as a special spiritual state.[4] It shapes the book because we see no other. The victims remain always and forever victims — as Dostoevsky suggests by a minor but probably conscious parallel to the situation of *Le Père Goriot*. In his walk down Gorokhovaya Street, Devushkin imagines Varenka living richly, dressed in gold and courted by generals: he would then "be happy simply to glance in at you from the street through the brightly lighted windows; simply to see your shadow. Just from the thought that you were happy and gay, my pretty little bird, I, too, would be gay" (September 5). His dream is very close to Goriot's actual situation. Goriot, too, was a victim — though his daughters at least seemed to be less so; they had at least their vanity, their amours, their worldly satisfactions. But when Varenka is leaving at the end to marry the wealthy Bykov, his generosity to her evaporates before our very eyes, so that even prior to the marriage it is clear that she faces a lifetime of victimization: there will be no Balzacian glitter to contrast with this quasi-paternal misery. Devushkin's misery is unshakable, and it leaves no room for any joy that will not become false ("I meant to describe my grief to you half in joke, Varenka, only it seems that it does not come off with me, joking" [August 5]).

Dostoevsky's perspective allows for undertones of ironic humor, but there is not the psychological distance that would permit the Gogolian grotesque laughter. In scenes that are clearly ludicrous, Dostoevsky extracts a grotesque pathos from the tension between the ridiculousness of the situation and its symbolic seriousness. This use of the grotesque is essentially a theatrical one — a redirection of the devices of traditional stage comedy — and it marks the two unforgettable *scenes* that punctuate this novel in letters.

The first is reported in Varenka's diary. It follows the death of young Pokrovsky and deals with his awkward, worshipful, self-effacing wreck of an alcoholic father — an early sketch for Marmeladov in *Crime and Punishment:*

Anna Fyodorovna [the procuress from whom young Pokrovsky rented a room] herself made the arrangements for the funeral. The simplest sort of coffin was bought and a carter hired. As security for these expenses Anna Fyodorovna seized all the books and all the belongings of the deceased. The old man argued with her, kicked up a row, took away all the books he could from her, stuffed his pockets full of them, put them in his hat, wherever he could, rushed around with them the whole three days, and refused to part with them even when he had to go to church. . . . At last the coffin was closed, nailed shut, put in the cart and taken away. . . . The coachman drove at a trot. The old man ran after him, weeping loudly, his cries quivering and broken from running. The poor man lost his hat and didn't stop to pick it up. His head was drenched from the rain and the wind was rising; the sleet lashed and stung his face. The old man seemed not to feel all this and ran weeping from one side of the cart to the other. The skirts of his threadbare coat fluttered in the wind like wings. Books were sticking out from all his pockets; in his hands was some huge book which he held tightly. Passers-by took off their caps and crossed themselves. Some stopped and gazed at the poor old man in wonder. Books kept falling out of his pockets into the mud. People stopped him and pointed to what he had lost, he picked them up and again raced off in pursuit of the coffin. (July 1)

The second grotesque scene is Devushkin's appearance before His Excellency for having left out a line in copying a document. He is summoned, fresh from being teased by his colleagues: "I stood before him! I can give you no clear account of what I was thinking then. . . . It seems I didn't bow; I forgot. I was so flustered that my lips were trembling, my legs were trembling. And with reason, my dear. In the first place, I was ashamed; I had glanced into the mirror on the right and what I saw there was enough to send a man out of his mind. And in the second place, I had always behaved as if there were no such person as me in the world. So that His Excellency could hardly have been aware of my existence." Hardly has the dressing-down begun when it is interrupted by catastrophe:

My button — the devil take it — the button that had been hanging on by a thread — suddenly broke off, skittered away, gave a little hop (I must have touched it accidentally), and rolled ringing straight, but straight, the damned thing, to His Excellency's feet, and that amid total silence! . . . The consequences were terrible. His Excellency at once turned his attention to my appearance and my costume. I remembered what I had seen in the mirror; I flew to catch the button! Some madness came over me! I bent over, I tried to pick up the button — it was rolling and spinning; I couldn't catch it. In short, with respect to nimbleness, I distinguished myself. Then I felt that my last faculties were deserting me, that everything, everything was by now lost. My whole reputation was lost, the whole man was lost! And then, apropos of nothing, I heard the voices of Teresa and Faldoni [servants of his landlady's], and my ears began to ring. At last I picked up the button, got up and stood erect, and being a fool I might at least have stood quietly at attention! But no: I began trying to put the button back on the torn threads as though sheer effort might make it stay. What's more, I could not keep a smile off my face. (September 9)

As Shklovsky says of this scene, a whole life is over: it has been rendered senseless.

We might rephrase the remark to say that in scenes like this all that is senseless in a given life is crystallized at a moment of extreme tension — often one of public humiliation — and usually only after careful artistic preparation, so that the reader's awareness of all that is involved precludes any catharsis by laughter. So will the grotesque perspective serve the ends of the fantastic realism of the later works. In *Poor Folk* it serves merely to heighten the tonality of the whole piece, as a distillation of the gray moral atmosphere of Petersburg life. That atmosphere darkens appreciably in Dostoevsky's second work (and second polemic with Gogol), the work he called "A Petersburg Poem."

The Double came out two weeks after *Poor Folk,* on February 1, 1846, destined — so its author thought — to raise him to new heights of success. "It will be my chef-d'oeuvre," he wrote his brother; he thought it "ten times better than *Poor Folk.*" [5] In the opinion of the critics and the public, it was nothing of the sort. Konstantin Aksakov saw, and unjustly exaggerated, the tie with Gogol's work: "We simply do not understand how this tale could have appeared. All Russia knows Gogol, knows him almost by heart — and here, in the face of all, Dostoevsky alters and wholly repeats Gogol's phrases." [6] But Belinsky was righter when he emphasized not the borrowings but the tedium of the work: "If the author of *The Double* put a pen into our hands with the absolute right to exclude from the manuscript of his *Double* everything that seemed to us drawn out and superfluous — we would not raise our hand to a single separate place, because each separate place in this novel is a summit of perfection. But the point is that there are far too many such wonderful places in *The Double,* and the same thing over and over again, however wonderful it may be, wearies and bores." [7] With time, Dostoevsky himself admitted the failure of the work, making some changes fifteen years later and planning more, yet as late as 1877 maintained that the idea had been "happy [*svetlaya*] enough" and that he had never expressed a more serious one in his writing.[8]

Critics have generally taken this statement at face value, traced the idea of the double through all of the later fiction, and neglected the work itself.[9] The provocation to treat it this way is real, and Belinsky has summarized it well. There remains, nevertheless, a particular truth in Dostoevsky's principled attachment to this book

— a truth he himself underlined twenty years after its first publication when he changed its subtitle from "The Adventures of Mr. Golyadkin" to "A Petersburg Poem." The book — as the change suggests — has a particular place and significance in the elaboration of the Dostoevskian myth of Petersburg. The mock-picaresque emphasis yields to the mock-epic.[10]

It is, however, an uneasy mockery — without either the high spirits or clear intention of *Dead Souls,* whose subtitle it pointedly echoes, as if what Gogol had done for the Russian province Dostoevsky would now do for the capital. And in fact the whole book is written under the sign of Gogol. The theme of the clerk in love with his chief's daughter and gradually losing his mind comes straight from "Notes of a Madman." The theme of the impostor, the usurping double, comes from "The Nose." Incidents, names, and stylistic turns come from these works and from *Dead Souls.* This is, in fact, Dostoevsky's second and last important polemic with Gogol; the young author is here appropriating all the fantastic Gogolian coloring and rationalizing it — just as he had taken all the pathetic Gogolian material of "The Overcoat" and humanized it in *Poor Folk.* The process of psychological breakdown is traced step by step; all that is bizarre is traced to its source in the poor clerk's consciousness; and the Gogolian elements of style (which hardly survive translation) represent the narrator's attempt to approximate the flavor, as it were, of what is happening. The story of Mr. Golyadkin is told from a Golyadkin-like point of view. This conveys an element of realistic strangeness admirably at times, but it wears badly and eventually muddles the perspective to produce a kind of unintentional grotesquerie, like that of a joke in bad taste that goes on and on. Dostoevsky compels a sympathy with which he is forever tampering.

At the very beginning, the boundaries of dream and wakefulness are called into question. Mr. Golyadkin lies motionless in bed, "like a man not yet quite sure whether he is awake or still sleeping, whether everything going on around him is real and actual, or a continuation of his disordered dreams." But the "dirtyish-green, sooty, dusty walls of his little room," with its cheap and depressing furniture, reassure him, and the indoor Petersburg merges with the outdoor: "At last the gray autumn day, dull and dirty, peeped into his room through the dingy windowpane so angrily and with such a sour grimace that Mr. Golyadkin could no longer possibly doubt that he was not in some remote realm, but in the city of Petersburg, in the capital, in his own flat on the fourth floor of a very large apartment building on Shestilavochnaya Street. Having made such an important discovery, Mr. Golyadkin closed his eyes convulsively, as though regretting his recent dream and wishing to bring it back for a moment." Even when he wakes from a nightmare later in the book, Mr. Golyadkin feels that his waking state is "hardly more cheerful." [11]

Dostoevsky had written while at work on this book that Petersburg and his future life there "seemed so terrible, solitary, joyless" that, at one time, he would have welcomed sudden death with joy.[12] *The Double* is saturated with this mood. The atmosphere of Petersburg is that of a bad dream — and Golyadkin himself is, in Mochulsky's phrase, "an outgrowth of the putrid Petersburg fog, a phantom living in a phantom city." [13] This is most clearly underlined in the pivotal fifth chapter when Golyadkin, fleeing from the scandal he has caused at his chief's party, rushes out onto the Fontanka embankment, "beside himself," to meet his double just as midnight is striking from all the clock towers in Petersburg. Water — the element on which the city is built and constant symbol of chaos — dominates the scene:

It was a terrible November night — wet, foggy, rainy, snowy, fraught with swollen cheeks, head colds, fevers, quinsys, inflammations of every sort and kind — fraught, in short, with all the gifts of a Petersburg November. The wind howled in the deserted streets, lifting up the black water of the Fontanka above the rings, and friskily tapping the lean lanterns on the embankment, which, for their part, chimed in with the howling in a thin, shrill creak, thus producing the endless squeaky, jangling concert so familiar to every inhabitant of Petersburg. It was snowing and raining at the same time. Whipped up by the wind, streams of rainwater spurted almost horizontally, as though from a fire hose, pricking and stinging the face of the unfortunate Mr. Golyadkin like so many pins and needles. Amid the stillness of the night, broken only by the distant rumble of carriages, the howl of the wind, and the creaking of the lanterns, there was the dismal sound of the beating and gurgling of water, streaming from every roof, porch, gutter, and cornice, onto the granite of the pavement. There was not a soul, near or far, and it seemed, in fact, that there could not be at such an hour and in such weather. (ch. 1)

Against such a background, leaning on a railing and gazing into the black depths of the river, the shaken Mr. Golyadkin first feels the approach of his double.

This is more than weather: it is a state of mind or, rather, it is a consonance between the two. Toward the end of the book, the wet snow abates, the starry sky becomes visible, and everything improves to the point where it is "only wet, muddy, damp, and stifling." We have to go back to the Dickens of *Oliver Twist* to find any parallel to the magical somberness of this atmosphere that breeds such monstrous visions. The comparison is just valid enough to be instructive. In both cases the heart of the city is evil (which is why Oliver must go to the country to convalesce), and in both cases the evil is social. But the products of evil are characteristically different. The twenty-five-year-old Dickens sees them as lurid and criminal, where the twenty-five-year-old Dostoevsky sees them as vulgar and empty. Golyadkin is physically a zero: when he looks at himself, "the sleepy, weak-sighted, and rather bald figure reflected in the mirror [is] of such an insignificant character that at first glance it would have attracted absolutely no one's particular attention" (1). The same is true of his spiritual qualities: Dobrolyubov was the first to point out that in his double Golyadkin projected all the petty baseness and mean skills that he associated with "success."

Here is not even Gogolian *poshlost,* but nothingness, raised by the quality of attention it receives to a higher power, where it becomes terror — quintessential "prose" irradiated with a grotesque poetry. It is this that fatigues in a story almost without events. The attempt to tell it from a point of view close to Golyadkin's own (and in language very close to his) blurs detail and precludes variety: the city will never again in Dostoevsky's work be as purely phantasmal, nor will a character: this is his only "poem."

With one other piece — the short story, "Mr. Prokharchin," also published in 1846 — Dostoevsky ends his first Petersburg period, the one that may be said to have passed under the sign of Gogol. This is, once more, a story of isolation and the fear of reality. The title character is an elderly petty civil servant; he lives behind screens "in the darkest and humblest corner" of his landlady's apartment, paying a minimal rent, half starving himself, avoiding the company of his neighbors, looking "less like a rational being than like the shadow of a rational being." "Both his old fellow lodgers lived exactly as he did: both of them, too, were somehow mysterious people and had spent fifteen years lying behind their screens." When his landlady moves to larger quarters and takes on more lodgers, younger and noisier fellow workers of his, a disrupting element enters, and what had looked like a psychological sketch of life in one of the "Petersburg corners" takes on ethical overtones.

The younger lodgers begin to tease Prokharchin and, by way of a practical joke, tell him that his department is to be abolished. This starts in him a process of panic, mixed with an obscure guilt, that ends in madness and death. The guilt is for the money he has been hoarding secretly all these years, under the pretext of sacrificing for a nonexistent sister-in-law. He dreams of a colleague to whom he has not spoken for twenty years, feels unaccountably responsible for his having seven hungry children, fears robbery. The pathos of isolation takes a new form here; because it is self-imposed, it merges with pathology.

The narration, it must be noted, is mannered to the point of obscurity, and the confusion about just what is happening clears up only at the end, where Dostoevsky gives us another of his scandal scenes (which may well be a part of the Gogolian inheritance) and a memorable example of his early realistic grotesque. During Prokharchin's delirium, two "friends" are keeping a vigil; the household is asleep, when "a shout that would have roused the dead" rouses it, followed by "yelling, cursing, and fighting." The friends have quarreled, apparently in searching Prokharchin's things. Meanwhile, the invalid himself is found "lying under the bed . . . so that only the bare, tattered, greasy mattress remained on the bed (there had never been a sheet)." They stretch him out on this greasy mattress while he goes through his last convulsions. The company then sets to examining his wretched effects, which are quickly and depressingly itemized, when suddenly a packet of coins falls from the mattress. In the light — Dostoevsky's favorite — of a single guttering candle there ensues "a scene that would have been extremely curious to a spectator." The lodgers, sleepy, unwashed, and feverish, attack the mattress with scissors, jostling the corpse until it "suddenly and quite unexpectedly plunge[s] head downward, leaving in view only two bony, thin, blue legs," jutting up "like two branches of a charred tree." Grotesquerie passes into farce as the lodgers dive under the bed, thinking that the corpse may be pointing out some new treasure to them, only to bump heads. The scene and the story end in this vein.

None of the great novels, and few of the minor works, will be without such a scandalous scene, in which decorum is almost farcically outraged. The funeral dinner for Marmeladov in *Crime and Punishment* comes immediately to mind as one of the most powerful. In the early works, Dostoevsky's sketches for such scenes are, of course, much less complex, and they differ from their mature counterparts in their relative poverty of dialogue. The scene just quoted, like the earlier interview between Devushkin and His Excellency and like Mr. Golyadkin's two intrusions into parties at the home of his office chief, is one of action; the later ones, involving more articulate characters, will be largely verbal encounters. But in all these cases, the effect tends to be the same — theatrical, grotesque, and suddenly illuminating — a device borrowed from the comic stage and invested with a new function, in which comic force, locked in a context that denies laughter, explodes into pathos and sometimes into tragedy.

After "Mr. Prokharchin," Dostoevsky turns away from the manner of Gogol and the so-called natural school. His direct debt to Gogol and his challenge to the Gogolian method have not been detailed here because they belong more properly in the more specialized context of Russian literary history — where, in fact, substantial researches already exist.[14] The main lines of his debt, however, can be briefly summarized.

Contemporaries were right to find echoes of Gogol on almost every page of Dostoevsky's first works; had they been able to read the letters Dostoevsky was writing at the same time, they could have found the same echoes. Gogol was the lion in the path of Russian letters who had to be reckoned with by any newcomer in those years. And his presence was above all a stylistic one. This is a fact all but impossible to perceive in translation: English has no equivalents for the numerous prefixes, suffixes, and infixes on which the Gogolian effect depends; nor for the particles that can give a sentence phonetic bulk while leaving it semantically weightless; nor even for many of the expressions themselves. Yet the fact remains that, for a Russian, Gogol impresses himself first of all on the ear. Pushkin's prose had given the example of a limpid, rectilinear, classical economy. Gogol's was the first to base itself on "low" colloquial speech (though not only on that).

It is from his "waxy mass of words" that Gogol fashioned his figures — and it is this basic Gogolian material that Dostoevsky was playing upon both in his early works and in his early letters, as the strikingly long lists of parallel passages compiled by scholars indicate. "Influence" here is a fact, but the word may be misleading, and, as Tynyanov argues, "stylization" is probably a more accurate one. Stylization, he notes, is close to parody: both are dualistic instruments, depending for their effect on the implicit presence of the object stylized or parodied. If the stylization is comically motivated, it becomes parody.[15] Dostoevsky in the early works is clearly not making fun of Gogol, but stylizing him.

The end is ultimately polemic, though for a beginning writer this method also proves valuable for testing the possibilities of a given style. In other words, one way to deal with a commanding presence is to use its own arms against it; one way to prove originality is to use old instruments for new ends. This is in general what Dostoevsky did, and Belinsky caught it immediately.[16] Even as he was learning from the Gogolian manner, he was perceiving the Gogolian tales themselves as unfinished business, because their creator had not penetrated to their tragic basis. He indicates this in an article of 1861: "All his life he [Gogol] laughed both at himself and at us, and we all laughed at him, laughed to the point where we finally began to weep from our laughter."[17] So Akaky Akakievich is expanded and humanized into Makar Devushkin, Poprishchin into Yakov Petrovich Golyadkin, and Major Kovalyov's nose into Mr. Golyadkin Junior.

Gogol's image of Petersburg is thus modified. The image of the fantastic city is as strong as before, but it is newly founded, newly rationalized. The supernatural is banished, and, if its semblance at times seems to remain, it remains as the perception of real people, not marionettes. As a result, the city becomes really fantastic in its action on the people who live in it. Gogol had been praised as a realist for picturing social relationships — though his embodiment of them was anything but realistic. Dostoevsky takes these relationships and puts them on a realistic base; for all the differences in style, his strategy is Balzacian, and his early work, as the feuilletons show, uses the formulas of romantic realism. If one term predominates, it is the second, as with Gogol it is the first.

With the failure of "Mr. Prokharchin," Dostoevsky seeks a new direction for his romantic realism, one less immediately connected with Gogol's work. He writes the "Petersburg Chronicle," discovers the possibilities of veiled confession, and turns to the theme of reverie.

THE DREAMER'S CITY

The dreamer's city is the Petersburg that attracts, forms, and tests the artist's consciousness. Three stories — "The Landlady," "A Weak Heart," and "White Nights" — examine the process.

"The Landlady" opens, characteristically, at the end of a period of isolation. For two years the young scholar Ordynov has lived a life of almost savage loneliness; now, forced to look for a new apartment, he wanders the streets, gazing "like a flâneur" at the life he has hitherto only guessed at "with the instinct of an artist" (I.1). "The crowd and the street life, the noise, the movement, the novelty of objects, the novelty of the situation — all this trivial life and everyday flotsam with which the businesslike and busy Petersburg man is so long since fed up . . . all this vulgar *prose* and tedium aroused in him, on the contrary, a certain quietly joyful, bright sensation." He reads in the picture that opens before him "as between the lines in a book." But the life of the city intimidates him, too: "It suddenly occurred to him that all his life he had been lonely, that no one had loved him and that he himself had succeeded in loving no one. Some of the passers-by with whom he entered casually into conversation at the beginning of his walk looked at him rudely and strangely. He saw that they took him for a madman, or for a most original eccentric — which, however, was quite just."

The role of the city is limited essentially to this function, the measuring of Ordynov's isolation. The actual plot of this melodramatic story is set in an industrial suburb, where he undergoes a delirium of love for a beautiful half-mad girl who speaks in the idiom of folk poetry, only to be bested by her epileptic husband (and perhaps father), who wields over her a mysterious absolute power. At the end, Ordynov, more solitary than ever, wanders the streets long and aimlessly, choosing "chiefly the twilight hour" and "places out of the way, remote, rarely visited by people." He is inclined to see the failure of his love in the girl's being "a weak heart," tyrannized by her strange companion. But of course the weakness is also his. Ordynov, as Bem first pointed out in an important article on "The Landlady," already contains the germ of the future tragedy of that frightening urban phenomenon, the underground man — the difference being that, "in distinction to the 'underground man,' the 'dreamer' still has not understood himself, has not created his philosophy of the underground, and is therefore helpless in the face of reality." [18]

"A Weak Heart" (in the Garnett translation, "A Faint Heart") harks back in externals to the stories of two years before. Here once again is a poor clerk who goes out of his mind. But the return to an earlier setting is less important than the new element: the clerk, Vasya Shumkov, is young, good-hearted, beloved, and betrothed. A dreamer sui generis, he goes out of his mind from happiness — and from the guilt that happiness engenders in his own susceptible heart. Alarmed at Vasya's growing oddness, his friend Arkady puts it to him:

> You see I understand you; I know what's going on inside you . . . You are such a kind, gentle fellow, but weak, unpardonably weak. . . . Besides, you're a dreamer, and that's bad, too; you could go off the rails, my friend. Listen, I know what you'd like! . . . You'd like there to be nobody on earth unhappy when you're getting married . . . Yes, brother, admit that you'd like me, for instance, your best friend, to come into a hundred thousand or so all of a sudden; that you'd like all the enemies in the world, for no rhyme or reason, to be reconciled at a stroke, so that they might all joyfully embrace one another in the middle of the street, and then, perhaps, come here to call on you. My dear friend, I'm not laughing; it's true; that's just about what you've been saying to me for a long time now, in one way or another. Because you are happy you want everybody, absolutely everybody, to become happy at once. It hurts you and troubles you to be happy alone.

Ordynov, the passionate dreamer, could neither resist his passion nor win its object; Vasya, the generous dreamer, cannot stand the anomalous burden of happiness in an imperfect world. The analysis of Vasya relates, as Mochulsky observes, to Dostoevsky himself, whose dream of universal harmony never left him. (One might even see Vasya, on a simpler level, prefiguring Ivan Karamazov's intellectual rejection of his ticket to a world founded on the sufferings of children.) And it is this personal element that gives a key to an otherwise puzzling passage on the last page of the story. Arkady, returning home across the Neva, has a vision of the city; it is given in words that Dostoevsky uses thirteen years later in his "Petersburg Visions" and has been quoted in the last chapter (p. 149f, up to the phrase "dark-blue sky"). In the story, too, the vision brings "a strange thought" to Arkady — a sudden insight, which explains his friend's fate and kills all his own gaiety, leaving him dull and morose. In both contexts, the vision is mystical. Its essence seems to lie in the intuition of a new dimension to the city — a discovery that explains to Arkady why his friend has gone mad and plunges him into gloom; for the young Dostoevsky it marks his birth as a writer. The weak heart is overwhelmed to discover that life is more terribly strange than fiction, but to the writer that discovery is the foundation of his art. The city is a microcosm; it is "this whole world with all its inhabitants, strong and weak." Its life, by any ordinary standards, is a dream — just as literally and just as tragically as the romantic critics saw it portrayed in Calderón's play, *La vida es sueño*.

These first two stories are told in the third person and seek to portray the tragedy of the dreamer; the last, "White Nights," is subtitled "A Sentimental Novel from the Memoirs of a Dreamer" and recounts instead the rare charms of such a state. It is a direct outgrowth of Dostoevsky's "Petersburg Chronicle" and takes from it the summer setting of the fourth piece in that series, as well as the lyrical comparison of the Petersburg spring to a suddenly blossoming young girl. The young narrator is, of course, isolated; he confesses that he has lived eight years in the city yet has hardly a single acquaintance: "But what did I need acquaintances for? I was acquainted with all Petersburg as it was." He is a flâneur. From his walks he knows many of the Petersburgers by sight, and he knows the buildings. He relates how, whimsically personified, they even speak to him: "So now you understand, reader, in what sense I am acquainted with all Petersburg" ("First Night"). The dreamer-flâneur does not study the city, but he is wonderfully impressionable, alive to the qualities he himself incarnates, to the life that is "a mixture of something purely fantastic, fervently ideal, and at the same time . . . dingily prosaic and ordinary, not to say incredibly vulgar" ("Second Night").

Of what does he dream? "Of the role of the poet, at first unrecognized, then crowned with success; of friendship with Hoffmann, St. Bartholomew's night, Diana Vernon; of participating heroically in Ivan Vasilievich's capture of Kazan; of Clara Mowbray, Effie Deans, the Council of the Prelates and Huss before them, of the rising of the dead in *Robert le Diable* . . . of Minna and Brenda, of the battle of Berezina, of the reading of a poem at the Countess V.D.'s, of Danton, of Cleopatra *ei* [sic] *suoi amanti,* of a little house in Kolomna" ("Second Night"). These are literary dreams, the mark of the Quixotic situation, and they are clearly Dostoevsky's own. They portray the dreamer in the most sympathetic of lights: here is none of the passionate condemnation of reverie that went into the "Chronicle." The moment is envisaged when the dreamer might repent and wish to trade all his years of fantasy for one day of real life — "but so far that threatening time has not arrived," and "he desires nothing, because he is above desire, because he has everything, because he is satiated, because he is the artist of his own life" ("Second Night").

These sketches of the dreamer and his city are, like the feuilletons to which they are so closely related, experiments, and the fact that they are unsuccessful ones (except for "White Nights") only underlines their importance in the evolution of Dostoevsky's urban themes. Together they represent a new idea and a new point of view, a suitable form for which still eluded the writer. Petersburg in a sense becomes even more insubstantial. Here are no descriptions of Gorokhovaya Street or the spectral embankments, but mystical overviews, generalized descriptions, or isolated details seen through an impressionistic haze. The theme of the dreamer — that "half-sick citydweller," as the narrator of "White Nights" calls himself — with his hair-trigger susceptibilities, his generous youthful enthusiasms, and his incapacity for practical life, does not succeed in the first two stories, for the conflict between dream and reality is too unevenly, and too fantastically, matched. Petersburg, Belinsky had written, "is the touchstone of a man: whoever, living in it, has not been carried away by the whirlpool of phantom life, has managed to keep both heart and soul but not at the expense of common sense, to preserve his human dignity without falling into quixotism — to him can you boldly extend your hand as to a man." [19] This is the balance that Dostoevsky was trying to achieve, and the Petersburg that Belinsky called the touchstone of a man was for him the touchstone of the artist.

Each stage is thus an experiment in reconciling the visionary with the realist, and each stage is dominated by themes that change and limit the forms of reconciliation. The background remains the same, and will, though the light in which it is seen changes continually. In his unfinished novel, *Netochka Nezvanova* (1849), Dostoevsky seems to have found a new formula: "In a word," says the heroine, "although my story was a very unusual one and in it the larger role was played by fate in various . . . even mysterious ways, and though in general there was much that was interesting, inexplicable, even fantastic — still I myself emerged, as if to spite all this melodramatic ambience, the most ordinary child" (ch. 4). In the same work, as Mochulsky points out, some of the same themes explored in "The Landlady" are embodied in a situation stripped of all romantic trappings,[20] and even those elements of the grotesque that figure in the early episodes do so on the level of "the most ordinary."

Netochka Nezvanova was interrupted by the catastrophe of the writer's arrest and exile. For ten years he was far from Petersburg. When he returned, deeply changed, he cast a retrospective look over his old properties in "Petersburg Visions" and produced in fiction *The Insulted and Injured,* which was a sort of epilogue to them. His next important work was *Notes from Underground,* the introduction to the cycle of his major work. Together they form a watershed in the evolution of the myth and of Dostoevsky's art.

EPILOGUE AND INTRODUCTION

On December 22, 1849, just returned from the terrible farce of the mock-execution, Dostoevsky wrote his brother: "The head that created, lived the higher life of art, that had recognized and become accustomed to the higher demands of the spirit — that head is already severed from my shoulders. Memory, together with the figures created and not yet incarnated by me, remains." [21] Twelve years later, his hastily composed feuilleton exercised that memory — and so, at the same time, did the no less hastily composed *Insulted and Injured*. Essaying in this, his first full-length Petersburg novel, the form of the roman-feuilleton, Dostoevsky used it as he had the journalism to recall much of his own early career in the capital. The first-person narrator is himself a writer, whose first work was "about a little downtrodden and even rather foolish clerk, with buttons missing from his uniform." Belinsky is alluded to with sympathy, and the revolutionary Petrashevsky circle, to which Dostoevsky had belonged, more satirically.

But the reminiscence is set in a new perspective, stressed in the original subtitle: "From the Notes of an Unsuccessful Writer." These notes are, among other things, Dostoevsky's literary stock-taking, in which old themes are tested against new pressures: we have here the first villain in his work (though a very melodramatic one), the first crimes (though committed offstage), and the first detective (though he figures only episodically). In short, the novel is a striking mixture of old and new, and within it we can see the writer's metamorphosis into the creator of the major works.

His discovery of the form is no small element in this metamorphosis. Four years before he had announced that he would write "a novel of Petersburg moeurs [*byt*], like *Poor Folk* (but the idea is still better than *Poor Folk*)." [22] As it turned out, the Petersburg moeurs were there, but the scale of the exposition robs the comparison with his first work of much value: in that work, he had managed skillfully to introduce several stories into the confines of an epistolary novel, but they were sketchy when they were not simply flashbacks. Here he manages to keep more than one plot going at the same time by acting on his own recommendation "to turn to Eugène Sue in order to describe the mysteries of Petersburg." As a result, not only is the atmosphere of the city stressed, but its size and social variety. The narrator moves from the crowded downtown streets to a pauper's cubicle, from suburban taverns to a fashionable restaurant; he has to do with an abandoned child, a procuress, a detective, aristocrats. There is a new breadth to his vision, as this characterization of just one of his plot strands may indicate:

> It was a fearful story. It was the story of a woman abandoned, who had outlived her happiness, sick, worn out, and forsaken by everyone, rejected by the last human being on whom she could rely — her father, once injured by her and crazed by intolerable sufferings and humiliations. It was the story of a woman driven to despair, walking the cold, filthy streets of Petersburg and begging alms with the daughter she still considered an infant; of a woman who lay dying for months in a damp cellar, whose father refused her forgiveness up until the last moment of her life, and only at the last moment relented, came running to forgive her — only to find a cold corpse instead of the woman he loved more than everything on earth. It was a strange story of the mysterious, scarcely comprehensible relations of the crazy old man with his little granddaughter, who already understood him, who already, despite her age, understood many things to which some men do not attain in long years of their smooth and secure lives. It was a gloomy story, one of those gloomy and poignant stories that are so frequently played out, unnoticed, almost mysterious, under the heavy sky of Petersburg, in the dark secret corners of the vast city, amid the seething mass of life, dull egoism, clashing interests, gloomy vice, in that deepest hell of senseless and abnormal life . . . (II.11)

There are, nonetheless, familiar elements within the new perspective, as the opening two sentences of the book indicate — the first signaling the roman-feuilleton form, the second recalling a frequent motif of the early stories: "Last year, on the evening of March 22, a very strange thing happened to me. All that day I had been walking around the city in search of a lodging." The constant attention to lodgings in Dostoevsky's work is far from accidental. It is, on one level, a "realistic" concern insofar as Petersburg life was characterized by a severe housing shortage in these years; beyond this, it reflects a technique common to the romantic realists (Balzac, Dickens, and Gogol all use it), whereby a man's surroundings are expressive of some important character trait. But the very frequency of this attention suggests another level of meaning, where the social merges with the metaphysical, to show how Dostoevsky's Petersburgers have no place that is assuredly theirs: they tend to be shelterless not only physically but morally, and they tend to be rootless.

The narrator, Ivan Petrovich, made by chance a witness of old Smith's death, even before he inherits his family secrets and his grand-daughter Nellie, inherits Smith's apartment "on the fifth floor right under the roof . . . consisting of one small entry and one large, very low-ceilinged room, with three slits that passed for windows" (I.1). As another character describes it, it is "a trunk, and not an apartment." Characteristically, no one in this "Noah's ark" of a building knows anything about the man who lived in it for four months. Similarly, when the heroine runs away from home to become the mistress of young Prince Alyosha Valkovsky, she lives with him briefly "in a very nice flat, small, but pretty and convenient, on the third floor of a house in Liteiny." His money soon runs out, however, and they are forced to move to the fourth floor of a "dirty block of buildings [*kapitalny dom*]" on the Fontanka. The change of floor is as indicative as the change of neighborhood — third floors are quite respectable, fourth floors (where a large number of Dostoevskian heroes live) indicate poverty, and fifth floors, when they exist, represent an extreme of poverty. As if to emphasize the isolation of these places, Dostoevsky dwells, in all his works, on the dark and labyrinthine approaches to them — their tenuous connection to the everyday life of the city. One could, in fact, deduce a whole "poetics of the staircase" from his work. These tortuous, dirty, dangerous places have a natural mystery about them, which Dostoevsky was quick to exploit. So Golyadkin's terror at the appearance of his double reaches a crescendo when the double races without difficulty around the turnings where "tenants had left heaps of all sorts of trash, so that a stranger who found himself on these stairs in the dark had to spend half an hour negotiating them, in danger of breaking his legs and cursing the stairs together with the friends who lived in such an inconvenient place" (5). So, too, in *The Insulted and Injured,* the stairway ("narrow, filthy, steep, and never lighted") to the apartment of Natasha and the prince unmasks the elder Prince Valkovsky: by the third floor he is swearing like a cabman, so that the narrator, following behind, can hardly believe that it is he.

By comparison with the previous work, however, these cells are part of a wider picture — "the vast city," the city of the roman-feuilleton. Connecting the several plots, racing with what will become the characteristic feverishness of the later novels from one location to another, is the figure of the narrator. It is he who characterizes the city directly, speaking at the beginning of the charm of the transient March sun in Petersburg, as he does at the end of the "somber, gloomy city, with its crushing, stupefying atmosphere, its infected air, its rich mansions, always begrimed with dirt; with its dingy, weak sun, and its evil, half-crazy people" (Epilogue). If at such times his manner resembles that of the feuilletonist, at others it recalls Dickens.

Quite aside from the figure of Nellie, so obviously reminiscent of Little Nell, from her grandfather with the unlikely name of Smith, from the detective Masloboyev who is drawn with a drollness not unlike that investing Inspector Bucket — aside from all the specific and minor instances of what might be called borrowing, there is a Dickensian element in the book, which inheres in the style and the point of view. Thus in the beginning, old Smith appears, moving "as though he had been wound up with a key" and accompanied by a dog that "seemed as if it, too, were eighty." "When they both walked down the street, the master in front and the dog following, its nose touched the hem of his coat as though glued to it" (I.1). The epilogue likewise provides scenes of happy domesticity, which are as rare in Dostoevsky as they are common in Dickens:

> Nellie was the idol of everyone in the house. Natasha had grown tremendously fond of her, and Nellie returned the affection with all her heart. Poor child! She had never expected to find such people, such love for herself, and I saw with joy how her embittered heart had softened, and how her soul had opened to us all. . . . In the evenings, when we were all together . . . Nellie was carried in her easy chair out to our round table. The door to the balcony was opened. The green garden, lit up by the setting sun, was in full view. From it came the scent of the fresh leaves and the newly opened lilac. Nellie sat in her easy chair, watched us all affectionately, and listened to our talk. (Epilogue)

Here, as Gissing saw, was a striking "spiritual kindred." [23] But the kinship is confined to the theme of Nellie alone and to the atmospheric mystery that surrounds it. For the rest, the novel does what Dickens could never bring himself to do (though he may have been approaching it in *Our Mutual Friend*): with a gentle sympathy, which may have been nostalgia, it shows the utter failure of the good, the kind, and the enthusiastic — in a word, of the "Schilleresque" romantic. Natasha, the attractive and impulsive heroine, loses the object of her intense if masochistic love, Prince Alyosha, and with him the possibility of a future with Ivan Petrovich. Alyosha himself, well-intentioned though utterly without character, at the end loses even a fictive control of his own destiny. Natasha's kind and simple parents lose a large sum on money in the lawsuit trumped up against them by the amoral Valkovsky. Before the story opens, old Smith has lost a fortune and a daughter who herself had lost everything — reputation, love, livelihood, and health. But most striking of all is the case of Ivan Petrovich. Apparently the hero, he is in fact only a shadow, an instrument of the intrigue and of the intriguers. Nor is this — as it might seem in view of his obvious identification with the Dostoevsky of the forties — a failure of artistic conception. The debacle is clearly deliberate: its lesson is that the hero of the forties is only a parody of a hero.[24] He represents the head that on the eve of his exile Dostoevsky said had already fallen from his shoulders. With all his feverish activity, he loses everything that is dear to him, and we learn early in the book that he is writing these memoirs "lying alone on a hospital bed, forsaken by all whom I loved so much and so intensely" (IV.2).

Again and again the antiromantic theme is taken up. Natasha declares sadly in the closing lines that the whole story was a dream. "Vanya," she asks, "why did I destroy your happiness?" — and in her eyes he reads, "We might have been happy together forever." Their story in a sense had been prefigured by the related one of Nellie's mother, whose case elicits from the genial detective Masloboyev a concise diagnosis of a kind of misfortune in which all the good-hearted principals share:

> The point is that this woman was the craziest, the most foolish woman in the world. An unusual woman she was without question; just consider all

the circumstances. Why, this is romanticism, all this is exalted nonsense on the wildest and most insane scale. Take one point: from the very beginning she dreamed only of something like a heaven on earth, of angels; she fell in love with all her heart, trusting utterly, and I'm convinced that she went mad afterwards not because he [Valkovsky] stopped loving her and left her, but because she had been deceived in him, because he was *capable* of deceiving her and abandoning her, because her angel had turned into clay, had spat upon her, and humiliated her. Her romantic and irrational soul could not bear this transformation. (Epilogue)

Failure had always been Dostoevsky's theme; what constitutes the novelty of this treatment of it is the presence of one character — Valkovsky — who is the architect of all the personal failures in the book, the single exponent of a ruthless immoralism before which no sentimental goodness can stand. For all his melodramatic affinities, he has a core of philosophic toughness that lends enormous meaning to his presence in the novel. In a scene that is the first sketch in Dostoevsky's work for all the great ideological dialogues, he characterizes Ivan Petrovich's weakness, playing with him, as the latter notes, like a cat with a mouse: "But what surprises me is your willingness to play a secondary part. . . . Alyosha has taken away your fiancée — I know that — and you, like some Schiller [the name appears here for the first time as a term of abuse], are crucifying yourself for them. . . . It's shameful!" (III.10). The justness of the observation is all the more forceful because it is voiced by an obnoxious cynic who confesses that "one of my most piquant enjoyments has always been to put on that manner myself, to take on that tone, to be kind to some eternally young Schiller, encourage him, and then, suddenly, all at once, disconcert him by suddenly taking off the mask, changing my ecstatic expression to a grimace, and putting out my tongue at him just when he is least expecting such a surprise" (III.10).

The scene of this confrontation is long, and, though it prefigures much that will recur in the later novels, enough is clear from what has been quoted to establish its general meaning. In substance, it heralds an end to Dostoevsky's own Schillerism and the appearance in his work of the problem of evil — which is to say the problem of freedom, of the proposition that "all is permitted." In form, it marks Dostoevsky's first incursion, as a novelist, into philosophical dialectics — as it does his first attempt to draw a character who represents an idea. The latter attempt was pronounced unsuccessful by Dostoevsky's friend and collaborator, Apollon Grigoriev, who called the characters puppets and walking books, at the same time criticizing publicly the writer's late brother as the one responsible for this, because he "drove the high talent of F. Dostoevsky like a post horse." To this Dostoevsky responded with rare candor:

> If I wrote a roman-feuilleton (which I fully acknowledge), then I and only I am responsible for this. So have I written all my life; so I wrote everything I have created, except the tale *Poor Folk* and some chapters from *The House of the Dead.* It has happened very often in my literary life that the beginning of a novel or tale would be already at the printer's and in galley, and the ending would be still sitting in my head, though it had to be written without fail by the morrow. Having grown accustomed to working this way, I proceeded exactly so with *The Insulted and Injured,* but forced by no one this time, and by my own choice. The journal we were beginning [*Vremya*], whose success was dearer to me than anything else, needed a novel, and I offered a novel in four parts. I myself assured my brother that the whole plan had been long since formed (which it hadn't), that it would be easy for me to write, that the first part was already written, etc. I acted in this not because of money. I fully acknowledge that in my novel are exhibited many dolls, and not people, that there are walking books in it, and not characters who have taken on artistic form (which in fact required time and the carrying out of ideas in the mind and heart). At the time I was actually writing, in the heat of work, I of course did not realize this, but only perhaps had a presentiment. But here is what I did know for certain as I began to write: (1) that although the novel would not succeed, still there would be poetry in it; (2) that there would be two or three ardent and strong places; (3) that the most serious characters would be depicted quite truly and even artistically. This certainty was enough for me. The work came out wild, but there are half a hundred pages in it of which I am proud.[25]

If some of the characters in this pioneer effort are walking books, it is a weakness that is already overcome — brilliantly and for good — in *Notes from Underground,* which appeared three years later.

Notes from Underground is generally considered to inaugurate Dostoevsky's second and major period; but it does so by bringing to an end his first period. If the antihero (as he calls himself) marks by his incandescent self-consciousness "an abrupt change in Dostoevsky's approach to characterization," [26] he also represents a projection into the grotesque of some of his literary predecessors' main traits. He is, as the author notes carefully on his first page, "one of the characters of the recent past" whom "I wanted to expose to public view more clearly than is usually done." The means to this exposure are magnification and concentration (one would like to say hyperbole, but the character is too uncomfortably plausible for that): "I have, after all, only carried to an extreme in my life what you have not dared to carry even halfway," the narrator declares to his imaginary interlocutors (II.10). What, exactly, does he represent of the recent past, and what has he carried to an extreme?

He represents the evolution of the dreamer of the forties, condemned (as the hero of "White Nights" foresaw at the end of his adventure with Nastenka) by the fervor of his dreams to an ever deepening solitude, and discovering that solitude may be at the same time an unavoidable and an untenable way of life, that the appetites it encloses do not wither but only turn inward, consuming the ego and issuing in masochism and "dark, subterranean, loathsome — not vice, but petty vice" (II.1). He is tormented by dreams he can neither disavow nor realize and drawn intermittently to a reality he cannot embrace: "I was never able to take more than three months of dreaming at a time without beginning to feel an irresistible need to plunge into society" (II.2). So when reality intrudes to show up the dreams, he must ridicule them, for he is too intelligent to ignore reality. Yet the dreams — which are of what life should be — are too far superior to that reality to be relinquished. He is condemned to a perpetual vacillation, a perpetual, impotent imbalance:

> But how much love, oh Lord, how much love I would feel in those dreams of mine, in those "escapes into the sublime and the beautiful." Though it was fantastic love, though it was never in fact applied to anything human, still there was so much of it, of this love, that afterward one did not even feel the need to apply it in practice: that would have been a superfluous luxury. Everything, however, always ended happily by a lazy and rapturous transition into the realm of art; that is, into beautiful forms of existence which were stolen, ready made, from poets and novelists and adapted to all sorts of functions and needs. I, for instance, am triumphant over everyone; everyone, of course, lies in the dust and is forced to recognize all my perfections voluntarily, while I forgive them all. I, a famous poet and courtier, fall in love; I receive countless millions and immediately donate them to humanity, and at the same time I confess before all the people my shameful deeds — which, of course, are not simply shameful, but contain an extraordinary amount of "the sublime and the beautiful," something in the Manfred

style. Everyone weeps and kisses me . . . while I go off barefoot and hungry to preach new ideas and smash the reactionaries at Austerlitz. Then a march is played, an amnesty is declared, the Pope agrees to leave Rome for Brazil; then there is a ball for the whole of Italy at the Villa Borghese on the shores of Lake Como — Lake Como having been moved to Rome for the occasion; then comes a scene in the bushes, and so on and so forth — know what I mean? [27]

The dream is progressively caricatured and finally ridiculed, but its context leaves the main emphasis on the opening cry from the heart. The same emphasis appears in the final scene with the prostitute Liza when, after he has tried intentionally to humiliate her by confessing the duplicity of his "fine words" in the brothel, she responds by opening her arms in a gesture of profound sympathy, to which he can only sob out: "They won't let me — I can't be — good!" (II.9).

This is his main ethical impulse — to be good, but impossibly, loftily, romantically good. The "they" who will not let him are a complex lot: his own dreamer's conditions, bound to be disappointed; his neurotic craving to bring on a humiliation he regards as inevitable; and, concretely, those few vulgar acquaintances whom, as a young man, he could neither live with nor without. The end of the scene at the Hotel de Paris is thus painfully typical. He has provoked a scandal, and now his dreamer's impulse tears from him a sudden apology:

"I ask for your friendship, Zverkov; I insulted you, but — "

"Insulted? You-u insulted me-e-e! Allow me to inform you, sir, that under no circumstances could you ever insult *me*." (II.4)

The impulse no sooner appears than it is frustrated.

The underground man is clearly not to be explained by the circumstances of his childhood alone; yet these circumstances, as much as we know of them, are significant. He was an orphan, sent by distant and indifferent relations to a school where, "lonely, already crushed by their reproaches, already brooding and silent, looking savagely at everything around him," hating and envying the vulgarity of his schoolfellows, he endured their jibes in almost total isolation (II.3). In Petersburg he is a clerk and a dreamer, like so many early Dostoevsky heroes. His situation sounds, in fact, like a composite summary of all their situations: "My life was even then gloomy, disorderly, and solitary to the point of savagery. I associated with no one, even avoided talking, and hid in my corner more and more. On the job, in the office I even tried not to look at anyone, and I was very well aware that my co-workers considered me . . . an eccentric" (II.1). The incident of his borrowing money to buy a beaver collar so that he might assert his dignity in public against the anonymous officer on the Nevsky is a grotesque variation on the situation of Makar Devushkin, as well as on that of his predecessor, Akaky Akakievich. A Soviet critic's characterization of the typical Dostoevsky hero of the 1840s fits him perfectly:

Dostoevsky's hero is thrown into the world lonely and orphaned. Alone he stands against a threatening, elusive, and implacable order of things [*zakonomernost*]. He is unable to get close to people; the wicked trample him; the benevolence of others provides neither salvation nor relief. He is an isolated monad, everything is against him; he perishes or is saved by flight into seclusion; he shrinks into himself, but even there the implacable hand of "fate" reaches him.[28]

But the underground man is writing in the 1860s, and this description can comprehend neither the psychological complexity that twenty years of aloneness have refined nor the new perspective that a different epoch in the life of the nation (as in the life of the author himself) was to lend. He is the first of Dostoevsky's obsessed talkers, and his "notes" are the first of many confessions. The men of the forties, Dostoevsky included, assumed that they knew what human nature was. But the underground man, speaking for the later Dostoevsky, challenges all these assumptions, in part I by argument and in part II simply by being. While Chernyshevsky with his doctrines of rational self-interest was simplifying the nature of man, Dostoevsky, through this extreme spokesman, was complicating it; while Chernyshevsky was reducing psychology to a scheme, Dostoevsky was proclaiming it an irreducible chaos. In each case, the contention served a further end. Chernyshevsky's novel, *What Is To Be Done?* (which Dostoevsky plainly had in mind when he wrote the *Notes*), pointed a political lesson, showed a way to social change through its pictures of the "new men." Dostoevsky's had rather an antipolitical point: it sought to show the hopelessness of social or political change without a prior regeneration of each individual. The man who had written Russia's first social novel in the forties now renounced the social as an independent category, and he did the same thing for the psychological: both were to be understood, both were to be completed and transcended by religion. The censor, with his legendary stupidity, deleted the passage in which the underground man said as much — and so made absolutely vicious a circle that Dostoevsky had made only relatively so. It would take us too far afield to speculate why Dostoevsky made no attempts in later editions to restore this cut. What is important here is to note that, while others were seeking to adapt the political utopianism of the forties and make it more practical, the former utopian socialist Dostoevsky was trying to show the impossibility of any such adaptation.

The tragedy of the underground man, then, does grow out of the pathos of the earlier works, from whose world he has survived, improbably, "like a mouse in its hole." His is not a Petersburg story only because his notes are not a story — as he himself insists:

> Wouldn't it be better to end my "Notes" here? It seems to me that it was a mistake to start writing them. . . . After all, to tell long stories, for example, about how I have ruined my life through moral disintegration in my corner, through lack of human contact, through loss of touch with everything vital, and vain spite in my underground world, is really not interesting; a novel needs a hero, and all the traits of an antihero have been *deliberately* brought together here, and what is most important, all this will produce an extremely unpleasant impression, because we have lost touch with life, we are all cripples, every one of us, more or less. (II.10)

But his existence is a Petersburg existence, as he himself is aware. In the period of his affair with Liza, he lived in an apartment that was "my privacy, my shell, my case, in which I hid from all mankind" (II.8), wrapped up in that anonymity and isolation from "living life" which is one of the main marks of the metropolis and one of the main themes in Dostoevsky's evocation of it. When he would venture out on the Nevsky Prospect, it was "a martyrdom, a constant, intolerable humiliation at the thought, which turned into a constant and direct sensation, that I was a fly in the eyes of this whole world, a vile, obscene fly — more intelligent than all of them, more cultured, more noble, of course, but a fly that was constantly yielding to everyone, insulted and injured by everyone" (II.1). The later, final stage of such an existence is his living, at the time of writing, in a wretched room on the outskirts of the city. "I am told that the Petersburg climate is getting to be bad for me, and that with my poor means it is very expensive to live in Petersburg. I know all that, I know it better than all these experienced and sage counselors. But I am staying in Petersburg; I won't leave Petersburg! I won't leave because . . . Bah, after all it makes absolutely no difference whether I leave or don't leave" (I.1). The reason, though unexpressed, is clearly implied when he speaks a few lines later of "the particular misfortune of inhabiting Petersburg, the most abstract and intentional city in the whole world" (I.2). It is, simply, that he belongs there, in this city formed unnaturally ("There are," he notes, "intentional and unintentional cities") by the will of a man, on inhospitable ground, *in the service of an idea.* There is an ontological consonance between the "anti-city" built in violation of the natural laws of growth and this anti-hero divorced from life — perhaps even a case of cause and effect. The narrator of *The Insulted and Injured* had referred pointedly to the abnormal life of the capital; here Dostoevsky, in a signed note, states on the first page that "such persons as the [imaginary] writer of these notes not only may, but must exist in our society, when you consider the circumstances under which our society was in general formed." The qualification ("in general") signals a major change of emphasis, a philosophical bias that will henceforth be dominant. Once a theater for social-psychological dramas, Dostoevsky's Petersburg now takes on a broader metaphysical dimension, which envelops the psychological, much as the underground man's speculations envelop his psychological nature while not ceasing to depend on it. As for the social, it remains, but ambiguously: vividly illustrative, it can "explain" only so much. It is almost a decoy, a bait for shallow understandings.

We shall see the implications of this change in Dostoevsky's next novel. What we have in the *Notes* is a brilliant experimental sketch. Its narrator is an extreme representative of the newly seen city, but one who loses none of his representativeness for all that. "As for me," the narrator concludes, "I have, after all, only carried to an extreme in my life what you have not dared to carry even halfway, and what's more, you have taken your cowardice for prudence, and found comfort in that self-deception" (II.10). So we get the image of the underground — an image, incidentally, that problems of translation and usage have tended to obscure. The Russian word, *podpolie,* suggests the space under the floorboards of a house, a sense the narrator plays upon when he compares himself to a mouse and when he tells his imaginary audience, "For forty years I have been there listening to these words of yours through a crack" (I.11).

The man of the 1840s still exists in the 1860s, but he has long since reached an impasse, which his reason is able to comprehend but not to resolve. Two years later, Dostoevsky was to place a new hero — a young man of the sixties — in a similar isolation, there to mature theories quite different but comparable in their extremity, and then to test them in action by transgressing against "living life." Psychologically and ideologically, *Notes from Underground* prepares *Crime and Punishment* — the most finished embodiment of Dostoevsky's myth of Petersburg.

7

Apogee: Crime and Punishment

Dismal, foul, and stinking summertime Petersburg suits my mood and might even give me some false inspiration for the novel.

Dostoevsky, letter of 1865

CRIME AND PUNISHMENT is the first — and arguably the greatest — product of that special realism toward which Dostoevsky had been groping for twenty years; it is unquestionably his greatest Petersburg work. *The Insulted and Injured* had given him the secret of uniting several plots into a single entity, and *Notes from Underground* the secret of transmuting his new ideological concerns into the stuff of fiction. The result, like *Hamlet,* is a metaphysical thriller, a point that critics writing in English cannot be accused of neglecting. What they have tended to neglect is the fact that this is also the first great Russian novel to deal with the life of the one city in Russia that could be compared to the capital cities of the West. A brief historical excursus will show how this is so.

The novel was originally conceived in terms that suggest Zola. Projected under the title of "The Drunkards," it was to deal "with the present question of drunkenness . . . [in] all its ramifications, especially the picture of a family and the bringing up of children in these circumstances, etc., etc." [1] Once Dostoevsky conceived Raskolnikov and his crime, of course, this theme became auxiliary, centering in the story of the Marmeladov family. But even apart from them, it runs like a red thread through the novel. Marmeladov is the first and most important, but hardly the last, of the drunkards Raskolnikov meets, and he himself is taken for one more than once. The sympathetic Razumikhin meets his friend's mother and sister in a state of intoxication; Porfiry pointedly remarks that he does not drink; Raskolnikov's fateful interviews with Zametov and Svidrigailov take place in taverns. The reason for the prevalence of this motif is not far to seek: it was, like so much else in the novel, a particularly acute social problem of the day. In 1860 the government had projected a new system of excise taxes, hoping to control the consumption of alcohol more effectively. Its hopes proved illusory, but they were shared at the time by Dostoevsky's own journal, *Vremya* (Time), which in 1861 devoted a long article to drunkenness in France and particularly to the family side of the question. Again in 1865, when Dostoevsky was beginning work on the novel, the government set up a commission to review the whole question of the "excessive use" of alcohol among the people, provoking a whole series of journalistic comments. As Leonid Grossman has noted, "against the background of these numerous articles disclosing the connection of alcoholism with prostitution, tuberculosis, unemployment, destitution, abandoned children, and the physical dying-out of whole families, the main lines of the story of the Marmeladovs emerge with full clarity." [2] Grossman goes on to say that, in contrast to the Falstaffian tradition of treating this theme in literature, Dostoevsky introduces for perhaps the first time its tragic side; in this, he parallels the innovation of his revered Pushkin, who similarly reversed a comic tradition in his "Covetous Knight," where he turned a tragic light on the figure of the miser (some three years before the appearance of Balzac's Grandet).

The theme of prostitution is closely connected with that of drunkenness, not only in the figure of Sonya but in a number of incidental figures — the seduced girl whom Raskolnikov rescues from her lecherous pursuer, the girl who attempts suicide in the canal, the procuress Louisa Ivanovna, the attractive Duclida. Here, too, he was exploiting an issue of immediate public concern. His own journal had printed in 1862 an article by one M. Rodevich entitled "Our Social Morality," which bespoke sympathy for "fallen women," tracing hunger and poverty as among the chief causes of prostitution and noting, "not infrequently even a mother will sell her daughter into vice because of oppressive poverty." [3] The writer argues that one cannot condemn these daughters "of civil servants who are retired or have large families, or of rich men who have squandered their money": these are women "who have nothing to eat, who are consumed by need, pricked by the needle which provides a pitiful maintenance of pennies for laborious work." [4] One recalls Marmeladov's pathetic account of Sonya's efforts to live as a seamstress. Equally striking in its pertinence to the novel is the point of another article in the same journal, entitled "Remarks on the Question of Social Morality" and signed only "P. S." Here the author goes beyond the question of sympathy for the prostitute. "The external manifestations of vice," he finds, "differ essentially from the internal, and one cannot combine them in one unbroken link. One can meet in a single evening a hundred prostitutes on any fine, brightly lighted street, and nevertheless have not the slightest notion of the state of their morality. To get this notion, it would be necessary to be transported into their internal world, and look at their behavior from there, from the new standpoint." The author sees this as a major literary problem and calls upon contemporary writers to produce "five or six stories of the life of prostitutes, honestly told with all the details and with psychological indications." [5] Dostoevsky, whether deliberately or not, did answer this call: after Liza in *Notes from Underground* came Sonya; and after her the kept women, Nastasya Filippovna and Grushenka.

As it was with alcoholism and prostitution, so with the theme of crime. In the story of Raskolnikov, a number of impulses from the concerns of the day converge. There is, first of all, the fact that at this time Russian juridical thought, and especially criminology, was undergoing a renewal. Grossman thinks it likely that Dostoevsky himself was responsible for the editorial commentaries on a host of articles in his journals dealing with murder, robbery, and the efficacy of legal punishment. Besides theoretical pieces, moreover, he printed a long series entitled, "From the Criminal Affairs of France," which he commended as being "more engrossing than any possible novels because they [the trial accounts] illuminate such dark sides of the human soul, which art is not fond of touching on — so that if it does touch on them, it does so only in passing, in the form of episodes." [6] Included in the series was the case of Lacenaire, whom Dostoevsky characterized in an editorial note as "a phenomenal, enigmatic, fearful, and interesting figure." [7] What is more striking is a whole set of parallels between Lacenaire, as described in

Vremya, and Raskolnikov. The young Frenchman is pictured as having features that were "fine and not without nobility. On his ironical lip there trembled constantly a ready sarcasm." He wanted to devote himself to the study of law and afterwards referred to himself, falsely, as a "student of law." Jailed in 1829 for killing Benjamin Constant's nephew in a duel, he dabbled in literature and on his release, along with a former fellow prisoner, used a three-edged rasp to kill one Chardon and his elderly mother. After the robbery — like Raskolnikov — he found two visitors asking for Chardon at the unlocked door, and with minor differences of detail he avoided being recognized in much the same way.[8]

Finally, one more topical item, closer to home, may have contributed to the writing of *Crime and Punishment.* In the spring of 1865, just when Dostoevsky was forming the idea of his novel, the Petersburg newspapers were filled with detailed stenographic accounts of the trial of Gerasim Chistov, who had killed two old women with a short-handled ax and robbed them of over eleven thousand rubles.[9]

The very theme of money, moreover, struck so forcibly at the beginning and throughout the novel, was of particular pertinence just at this moment. It is true, of course, that Dostoevsky had always made the effects of money, or its absence, a key factor in his fiction, as the title of his first work indicates. But money plays a different role here — a role related as much to the world of *Le Père Goriot* as to that of *Poor Folk.* For the first time the figure of the predator becomes important (Alyona Ivanovna, Luzhin), and the temptation to quick riches immediate and compelling. As Paris and London had done some decades before, Petersburg was becoming a capitalist city, like them subject to new and severe financial crises. One such crisis was acute in the early sixties, and Dostoevsky's *Vremya,* along with the rest of the press, was full of articles about it; one of 1863 was entitled "Where Has Our Money Gone?" and discussed "the commercial, industrial, and financial crisis hanging over us." [10] The situation reached its peak in 1865, the year Dostoevsky began *Crime and Punishment.* He felt the pinch himself, for he had to liquidate his publishing business, making for catastrophic losses in subscriptions. As Grossman sums it up: "Journals were closing down, general credit was falling improbably, the government was issuing loan after loan, the money market was overflowing with paper tokens, the government exchequer was 'oppressed' with a deficit. Such was the year when compassionate passers-by held out a penny on the street to the student Raskolnikov, and the titular councillor Marmeladov created his variation on the folk saying: 'Poverty is not a vice, but destitution, sir, destitution is a vice, sir.' " [11]

Balzac had referred repeatedly to Rastignac as "one of those young men who . . ." — and Dostoevsky evidently intended Raskolnikov also to represent a trend. He was one of the "new men." Half a year before Dostoevsky began work on *Crime and Punishment,* his journal, *Epokha,* printed an article by Strakhov which claimed as the most striking feature of the time the fact that "Russian literature is troubled by the thought of the new men." [12] Turgenev's Bazarov had been the first such, but many others followed. One expression of the trend that particularly exercised Dostoevsky was Chernyshevsky's *What Is To Be Done?* (which bore the subtitle, "From Stories about the New Men"). *Notes from Underground* had been an open argument with it, and *Crime and Punishment* only continued the polemic, incarnating the tragedy of nihilism in Raskolnikov and caricaturing it in Lebezyatnikov and, partially, in Luzhin. Dostoevsky's coworker Strakhov was quick to observe that the new novel was the first to show an unhappy nihilist, in whom life was struggling with theory — and the observation takes particular point against the contention of Chernyshevsky's hero Lopukhov that "a theory should be in its nature cold" and that "the mind should judge about things coldly." [13] The story of Raskolnikov is Dostoevsky's answer by extrapolation to this notion.

Theory entered by another door as well. One of the calligraphic exercises in Dostoevsky's notebooks for *Crime and Punishment* consists of three carefully traced names: "Napoleon, Julius Caesar, Rachel." Whatever the last may mean, the first two are traceable to one of the sensations of early 1865, a book propounding the question of the role and rights of "extraordinary natures" that was widely discussed in the Western and Russian press — Louis Napoleon's *Histoire de Jules César.* It appeared in Paris in March and was already known from numerous reviews when it came out in Russian translation a month later. "When extraordinary deeds testify to a high genius," we read in the preface, "what can be more repulsive to common sense than to attribute to this genius all the passions and all the thoughts of an ordinary man? What can be more false than not to recognize the superiority of these exceptional beings, who appear in history from time to time like flashing beacons, dispelling the darkness of their times and lighting up the future?" [14] In the widespread discussion attending this book, critics were quick to see that the defense of Caesarism was a defense of Napoleonism, that the book was not a history but a veiled self-justification. What is relevant to present concerns is the theory on which that self-justification was made to hinge, the theory that superior natures are beyond the morality that binds the mediocre mass of people. One passage from an article in "The Contemporary" (*Sovremennik*) setting out this theory has been found by a Soviet critic to match the summary Porfiry gives of Raskolnikov's own theory.[15] "Borrowing" here is not in question; rather, we see once more the close correspondence between the concerns of Dostoevsky's novel and those of the day — indicative of a timeliness that must have struck contemporary readers and intensified the impact of the book with myriad relevancies now lost to us.

One last such relevancy — a literary one — calls for mention. The early sixties saw a flood of literature, sketches and feuilletons as well as stories and novels, devoted to the city. This literature was related, of course, to the "physiological sketches" of the forties, but its orientation and tone were already different. Here was no quest for an attitude toward the city, but the expression of one; and here one finds less the personal stylistic note than a concern with reportage. The new literature was a social literature, designed to record the facts of urban poverty, disease, and misery. These works bore titles like "Hell," "Silence," "A Ruined but Sweet Creature," "The Homeless," "The First Lodging," "In the Hospital and in the Cold," "A Day on a Barge, A Night in Lodgings (From the Notes of a Hungry Man)," "The Poor Lodgers (A Physiological Sketch)," *Petersburg Slums,* and so on.[16] One popular subgenre was the description of city streets. In Krestovsky's *Petersburg Slums* a litterateur asks: "Have you read my 'Alley'? . . . Read it; it is really a Dickensian thing. Everyone is wild about it." [17] Other popular subgenres were descriptions of taverns and the dwellings of the poor. Dostoevsky himself published a number of these works in his journals; of the sketch by Gorsky, entitled "In the Hospital and in the Cold," he wrote his brother: "This is not literature at all, and it would be stupid to regard it from that standpoint; it is simply *facts,* and useful ones." [18]

In short, the whole social fabric of *Crime and Punishment,* many of its concerns and many of its figures and themes, attach to the immediate social and literary background of the middle sixties. Even the figure of Porfiry — like that of Dickens' Inspector Bucket — is directly connected with recent reforms in police administration and theory; even the title of the novel matches the title of an article by one V. Popov, published by Dostoevsky in his *Vremya* in 1863: "Crime and Punishment (Sketches from the History of Criminal Law)." [19] All these elements, of course, are either transmuted in the novel or made auxiliary to the main drama; they acquire a predominantly psychological significance and are used to point questions of personal rather than social morality. Yet their background should not be overlooked: it gives the work added weight of reference precisely because so much of the reference was familiar to Dostoevsky's readers and could be taken for granted by the writer, so that a simple allusion might conjure up a whole social context. Dostoevsky's novel was a topical one, and the very evidence of topicality suggests how solid was the realistic ballast he put into it.

In the light of all this, the transition from the original plan of "The Drunkards" to the final version of *Crime and Punishment* becomes clearer. Dostoevsky did not completely abandon the idea of a social novel, but evolved it. In fact, the seeds of that evolution are implicit in his idea of a social novel. Soon after its appearance, he had praised Victor Hugo's *Les Misérables* as an outstanding treatment of the great theme of nineteenth-century literature: the resurrection of the fallen man. This he found a "Christian and highly moral" theme, and in it, right up to the end of his life, he saw also the principal greatness of his favorites, Dickens and George Sand.[20] A social novel, in other words, was unthinkable for him except as it touched on moral resurrection: resurrection was the rationale, the rest important but subsidiary. So the story of the Marmeladovs comes to counterpoint that of Raskolnikov, and the social — which is to say, the urban — background is used to lend perspective and immediacy to these individual dramas. The question must now be confronted more precisely: Just what is the role of the city in Dostoevsky's novel?

ROLE OF THE CITY

Crime and Punishment is, as a recent Soviet critic has said, the first great Russian novel "in which the climactic moments of the action are played out in dirty taverns, on the street, in the sordid back rooms of the poor." [21] What is true of the climactic moments is true of a strikingly high proportion of the others as well. Add the police stations and the shabby hotel where Svidrigailov spends his last night, and you have almost all the set changes this drama requires. Where Balzac, for contrast, alternates the scenes of *Le Père Goriot* between the Maison Vauquer and the various haunts of the aristocracy, Dostoevsky achieves a grimmer and equally effective contrast by alternating his scenes between stifling rooms and the often no less stifling streets. So the book opens with Raskolnikov hurrying downstairs from his fifth-floor cubicle, "which he rented from lodgers," out onto the street, where the July heat and "the closeness, the crush, and the plaster, scaffolding, bricks, and dust everywhere, along with that peculiar summer stench, so familiar to every Petersburger" all irritate his already overworked nerves. "The truly intolerable stench from the saloons, which are particularly numerous in that part of town, and the drunks he kept running into, although it was a weekday, gave a finishing touch to the repulsive and melancholy atmosphere of the picture" (I.1). The neighborhood is carefully specified, in order to explain why Raskolnikov's extreme shabbiness goes unremarked: "Because of the proximity of the Haymarket, the abundance of a certain kind of establishment, and the preponderance of the artisan and working-class population crowded in these streets and alleys of central Petersburg, the general panorama was sometimes enlivened with such types that it was hardly possible to imagine the sort of figure that might cause surprise" (I.1).

Here, then, assailing the nose, eyes, and nerves, is the general scene of the action, carefully and closely observed in innumerable details. If Dostoevsky has been sometimes thought to slight this background, it is because, unlike Balzac, he tends to avoid bald exposition whenever possible; instead of a preliminary scene setting, he begins with action, and the reality of the scene is built in passing, by a host of details called forth in the order of their relevance to what is going on. The setting is a function of the action. To collect these details here would be a pedestrian task, and an unnecessary one: an attentive reading even of the first few pages suffices to discover them. But we may note that distances, too, are indicated with revealing exactitude: Raskolnikov has an even seven hundred and thirty paces from the gate of his building to the huge house fronting on the canal where Alyona Ivanovna, the pawnbroker, lives; seeing Marmeladov home from the tavern where he first meets him is a matter of two or three hundred paces. These distances set up a unity of place that is not artificial. Here is the heart of Petersburg, a neighborhood that is also a microcosm. Its compactness facilitates and rationalizes coincidence, as well as the swift accumulation of the action, just as its social nature underlines the irony of Marmeladov's reference to "this capital, magnificent and adorned with innumerable monuments" (I.2).

There is nothing monumental about these teeming streets and alleys except the quantity of life they contain. Raskolnikov wonders in a moment of reverie "why in all great cities men are not just impelled by necessity, but somehow peculiarly inclined to live and settle in just those parts of the city where there are no gardens or fountains, where there is most dirt and stench and all sorts of filth" (I.6). Yet he himself is drawn to them, as if by an instinctive and obscure fellow-feeling that is a refutation of his intellectual theory about himself. Here, for all its squalor, is quintessential urban life, and its forms, as Dostoevsky had shown in *Notes from Underground,* are liable to be sordid. "I love to hear singing to a street organ," Raskolnikov confesses to an alarmed stranger, "on a cold, dark, damp autumn evening — it must be damp — when all the passers-by have pale green, sickly faces, or better still when wet snow is falling, straight down, when there's no wind — you know what I mean? and the street lamps are shining through it."

Chapter six of part II, from which the above incident is taken, is a fair specimen of the world of the streets as this novel presents it. Raskolnikov slips down from his room at sunset and "greedily" drinks in "the stinking, dusty, city-infected air." From habit he walks toward the Haymarket. He passes the organ-grinder with his fifteen-year-old singer, "dressed up like a lady in a crinolinc, gloves, and a straw hat with a flame-colored feather in it, all old and shabby," and makes inquiry of "a young fellow in a red shirt who stood yawning at the entrance to a corn chandler's shop." Dostoevsky's account is crammed with the sort of detail that makes it a physiological sketch par excellence:

Now he entered the alley, thinking of nothing. At that point there is a long building, entirely occupied by saloons and other establishments for eating and drinking; women kept running in and out of them every minute, bare-headed and without coats. In two or three places they crowded the sidewalk in groups, chiefly around the ground-floor entrances, where one could walk down two steps into various houses of pleasure. From one of them at that moment there came a racket that filled the whole street — the strumming of a guitar, voices singing, great merriment. A large group of women were crowded around the door; some sat on the steps, others on the sidewalk; still others were standing and talking. Alongside, in the street, a drunken soldier with a cigarette was swearing loudly; he seemed to want to go in somewhere, but to have forgotten where. One beggar was quarreling with another, and a man, dead drunk, was lying right across the road. Raskolnikov stopped by the throng of women. They were talking in husky voices; all of them were bareheaded and wearing cotton dresses and goatskin shoes. Some were over forty, but there were others not more than seventeen; almost all had black eyes.

It is here that he meets the good-looking prostitute Duclida, to whom he gives fifteen kopecks for a drink, observing at the same time her "quiet and earnest" coworker, "a pock-marked wench of thirty, covered with bruises." "Only to live," he reflects, "to live and live! Whatever sort of life — only life! . . . Man is a scoundrel! . . . And a scoundrel is the man who calls him one for that." In the tavern called the Crystal Palace he has his fateful conversation with Zametov in which he all but confesses to the murders, runs into Razumikhin, then goes out to stand on the X — Bridge to witness the attempted suicide of the drunken woman. The sordidness of his earlier encounters had reflected his own spiritual state; this one anticipates an impulse to suicide. He feels disgust at the ignobility of what he has witnessed: "No, that's loathsome . . . water . . . not that," he mutters. He goes back to the scene of his crime, again all but confesses, and returns once more to the street — where he will find Marmeladov, crushed by a carriage and dying.

The streets are Raskolnikov's contact with life; it may seem tautological to add, with urban life, but his walk to the islands gives the addition a special point. Here is Nature and, as might be expected, "the greenness and freshness were at first pleasing to his tired eyes, accustomed to the dust of the city and the huge houses that hemmed him in and oppressed him. Here there were no taverns, no closeness, no stench. But soon even these new, pleasant sensations turned morbid and irritating" (I.5). The world of nature offers no lasting solace and no way out because Raskolnikov's whole world is the man-made one of the city; there and there alone his drama arises, and there it must be played out. Theories, like cities, are made by men and their creators must come to terms with them; escape cannot remove the problem of reconciling "living life" with the conditions of city life. So even amid the sickly life of the streets, Raskolnikov finds a kind of tentative community. His own is a tragedy of the garret, and it is kept significantly apart from his experience out of doors. There his generosity comes instinctively into play, in his quixotic attempt to save the seduced and drunken girl from her pursuer, in his disinterested gift of money to Duclida, in his helping the injured Marmeladov and lavishness to his family; and there, too, if a coachman whips him for getting in the way, a passer-by will slip him a small charity "for Christ's sake."

The real city, in short, rendered with a striking concreteness, is also a city of the mind in the way that its atmosphere answers Raskolnikov's spiritual condition and almost symbolizes it. It is crowded, stifling, and parched. All the more significant, then, is the single contrasting "spiritual landscape" evoked in describing Svidrigailov's last night. Svidrigailov's element is absurdity and chaos. After the abandonment of his designs on Dunya, he wanders through a series of taverns to wind up in a "pleasure garden" whose claim to the title is "one skinny three-year-old spruce tree and three little bushes," accompanied by "two little clerks" who attract him because they both have "crooked noses, one slanting to the right and the other to the left" (VI.6). Even the tentative communication Raskolnikov finds possible in public places is impossible here. Svidrigailov is chosen to decide a dispute, but though he listens to them for a quarter of an hour, "they were shouting so that there wasn't the slightest possibility of understanding anything." As his suicidal intention ripens, the rain begins: "The water fell not in drops, but beat on the ground in streams. Lightning flashed every minute and one could count to five in the space of each flash." Drenched to the skin, he goes about settling his affairs and exactly at midnight, in a roaring wind, crosses the river and wanders in a bleak and "endless" street in search of the shabby Hotel Adrianople. There, in a cramped and filthy room, he watches a sordid argument through a crack in the wall and undergoes his nightmares. He hears (or dreams he hears) the cannon shots signaling a flood — the primal chaos, the revolt of element on which the city stands.[22] Raskolnikov's symbol is aridity; Svidrigailov's is water. The landscapes in which they make their fateful moves reflect this. Svidrigailov goes out to kill himself (as Dostoevsky had originally planned for Raskolnikov to do). In a thick mist, he walks along a "slippery dirty wooden sidewalk," "picturing the waters . . . which had risen high during the night, Petrovsky Island, the wet paths, the wet grass, the wet trees and bushes and at last the very bush [under which he plans to kill himself]." The streets are empty (Raskolnikov never encounters empty streets); the houses look "despondent and dirty." "A dirty, shivering dog" crosses his path "with its tail between its legs." In such a setting, he chooses a sour-faced Jewish doorman wearing an incongruous "Achilles helmet" as witness of his suicide, and with him he holds his last, absurd human conversation. They stare at each other for a long moment. Then "Achilles" breaks the silence with his caricatured Russian:

"Vot you vont here?" . . .
"Nothing at all, my friend," replied Svidrigailov. "Good morning!"
"Dis ain't no place."
"I'm leaving for foreign parts, my friend."
"Foreign parts?"
"To America."
"To America?"

Svidrigailov took out the revolver and cocked it. Achilles raised his eyebrows.
"Vot's diss? Dese chokes (jokes) ain't no place here."
"And why not, pray?"

"Chust becoss it ain't de place."

"Well, friend, it makes no difference to me. The place is good enough. If they ask you about it, tell them he said he'd gone to America."

He put the revolver to his right temple.

"You kent here, dis ain't de place!" Achilles gave a start, his pupils growing bigger and bigger.

Svidrigailov pulled the trigger. (VI.6)

Svidrigailov's last hours are spent on the outskirts of the city, in symbolically different weather, yet the "atmosphere" here, for all its difference from that of Raskolnikov's heart of Petersburg, is one with it in emotional tonality: it is, in Svidrigailov's own characterization, "gloomy, harsh, and queer."

The atmosphere of the interiors is no less so. From the anonymity of the labyrinthine alleyways to the secrecy of the labyrinthine stairways is only a step. Scenes of a comparable intensity are played out on them — most often of flight and evasion. The book opens with a description of Raskolnikov's creeping down the stairs of his own building "like a cat" to avoid a humiliating meeting with his landlady. On the pawnbroker's "back staircase, dark and narrow," he suffers agonies of fear as he tries to leave the scene of his crime. Staircases are (despite the confusion of directions) a kind of entrance to the underworld, linking the public with the private. They are, as it were, the tendrils of the city, half-public, half-private, uniting into great and artificial groups the various closed worlds of rented rooms and apartments. Already enclosed, they inspire a kind of claustrophobia, but the rooms do this to an even greater extent.

At the beginning of chapter three (part I), Raskolnikov awakens and looks about with hatred at "a tiny hencoop of a room about six paces in length" with "dusty yellowish paper peeling off the walls" and "so low-ceilinged that a man of more than average height would feel uneasy in it and seem at every moment to be about to bump his head on the ceiling." And the room is in keeping with his state of mind: "He had positively withdrawn from everyone, like a tortoise in its shell, and even the face of the servant girl who was obliged to serve him and sometimes looked into his room provoked him to irritation and convulsions." Here is the extreme of isolation and the fitting birthplace of his theory. His mother notices immediately when she enters. "What a terrible room you have, Rodya, it's just like a coffin," she remarks; "I'm sure it's half from your room that you've become such a melancholic." And Raskolnikov, thinking of the murder he has just committed, takes up the point. "Yes," he answers, "the room had a lot to do with it . . . I thought of that, too . . . If you only knew, though, what a strange thing you said just now, mother" (III.3). Later, in his confession to Sonya, he repeats: "I hid in my corner like a spider. You've been in that hole, you've seen it. . . . And do you know, Sonya, that low ceilings and tiny rooms cramp the soul and the mind?" (V.4). What is worse, they take on an attraction of their own: "Ah, how I hated that garret! And yet I wouldn't go out of it! I purposely wouldn't" (V.4). Like all of Dostoevsky's dreamers, from Ordynov through the underground man, Raskolnikov "preferred lying still and thinking" (V.4). The difference is that his dreams are rational dreams — not a substitute for the world but a plan for mastering it. "You don't suppose," he asks Sonya, "that I went into it headlong like a fool? I went into it like a wise man, and that was my downfall" (V.4). For such wisdom his airless and sordid little cubicle is a telling symbol.

The only other room in the book comparable to this in its extremity is the room taken by Raskolnikov's quasi-double, Svidrigailov, in the Adrianople. The parallels are striking: "It was a little cell with one window, so low-ceilinged that even Svidrigailov could barely stand up in it; a very dirty bed, together with a plain painted chair and table, took up almost all the space. The walls, which seemed to consist of a few planks knocked together, were covered with worn paper, so dusty and tattered that the pattern was indistinguishable, though one could still divine the color (yellow). One part of the wall and ceiling was angled, as is customary in attics, though in this case it was a stairway that went over the sloping portion" (VI.6). For the rest, the apartment of the Marmeladovs, the room into which Luzhin first puts Dunya and Raskolnikov's mother, Razumikhin's room, and those of the pawnbroker all share a depressing poverty, depressingly itemized, and function on the social and realistic, rather than on the personal and symbolic, level. The single exception is Sonya's, "a large but extremely low-ceilinged room . . . [that] looked like a barn; it was a very irregular quadrangle and this added a grotesque note. A wall with three windows opening on to the canal ran aslant so that one corner, forming a very acute angle, was a deep recess, hard to descry in the weak light; the angle of the other corner was monstrously obtuse. In all of this large room there was hardly any furniture" (IV.4). The room of the sacrificial prostitute, like that of the murderer, is low and poor: but though irregular, it is spacious. His is like a coffin; hers, Dostoevsky reports, is like a desert: but even in a desert life is possible. And where his has a single window facing inward, on the courtyard, hers has three windows, looking out on to the canal. Sonya's room, like its mistress, is oriented toward austerity, but outward — toward life.

Of these streets and rooms is the Petersburg of *Crime and Punishment* made up. It is the city of unrelieved poverty. The wealthy are depraved and futile, like Svidrigailov, or silly and obnoxious, like Luzhin. Magnificence has no place in it, because magnificence is external, formal, abstract, cold. The striking scene where Raskolnikov, returning home from his visit to Razumikhin, pauses to take in the majestic panorama along the river, suggests this: "When he was attending the university, he had stopped at this same spot, perhaps a hundred times, to gaze at this truly magnificent spectacle and almost always to wonder at the vague and elusive impression it produced in him. This magnificent panorama always seemed to exude an inexplicable coldness: this splendid picture was for him the embodiment of some blank and dead spirit. He wondered every time at his somber and enigmatic impression, and, mistrusting himself, put off seeking an explanation" (II.2). In its mysterious intensity, this recalls the sunset vision on the Neva of "A Weak Heart" and "Petersburg Visions." But where, in the earlier context, the city seemed to be invested with magic, here it is divested even of life.[23] This beauty is rare, as is the sunlight itself. The real city lies not along the majestic river but by the narrow canals, and it is closer to Svidrigailov's characterization: "This is a city of half-crazy people. If we were a scientific people, doctors, lawyers and philosophers could make the most valuable investigations in Petersburg, each in his own field. There are few places where you'll find so many gloomy, harsh and strange influences on the soul of man as in Petersburg. Consider the influence of the climate alone" (VI.3). The real city is here, where for all its distortion there is life — which means people and suffering. Raskolnikov had bowed to Sonya, saying that he was bowing "to all the suffering in the world"; at the end he kneels in the middle of the Haymarket, "bow[s] down to the earth, and kiss[es] that filthy earth with joy and rapture" (VI.8). "He's bowing down to all the world and kissing the great city of St. Petersburg and its pavement," a drunken workman comments. The pavement is as holy as the earth; it, too, in its terrible way, bears life.

In this scene, a magnificent touch follows the workman's comment: "Quite a young fellow, too!" another bystander remarks.

> "And a gentleman," someone observed in a sober voice.
> "These days there's no telling who's a gentleman and who isn't."

Here to the exalted emotional reality is added a reminder of the mundane social reality — its constant foil in this work. The role of "the great city of St. Petersburg" as it existed, concretely and socially, in the middle of the 1860s, is fundamental in *Crime and Punishment.* Only once this is recognized can the significance of that role be fully and truly assessed.

SIGNIFICANCE OF THE CITY

If much of Dostoevsky's social detail can be called naturalistic, his point of view cannot. There is, in the last analysis, small interest shown in the determining role of social forces, and no description of the city that betrays any quasi-scientific interest in how its life is lived. By quasi-scientific I mean a detached interest in the phenomenon as such. Detachment in this sense was foreign to the premises of Dostoevsky's art, and Vyacheslav Ivanov's remark about his attitude toward nature is equally true of his attitude toward the city: "It is as though he had taken an oath never to become what the lyrical poet Fet calls 'an idle spectator of Nature.' "[24] The static surface of things leaves him as cold as the panorama on the Neva leaves Raskolnikov: for him, significant action is all, and the significance of any action inevitably establishes the relevant point of view. In a notebook passage planned for the narrator of *The Possessed,* he makes clear his general policy:

> I do not describe the city, the setting, the customs [*byt*], the people, the occupations, the relations and curious fluctuations in those relations, of the strictly private . . . life of our city. . . . I have no time to occupy myself directly with a picture of our parts. I consider myself the chronicler of a single private and curious event, which took place among us suddenly and unexpectedly of late, and struck us all with astonishment. It goes without saying that since the thing happened not in the sky but among us, it is impossible for me not to touch sometimes on the purely pictorial and customary side of our . . . life; but I forewarn [the reader] that I shall do this only to the exact extent that the most unavoidable necessity requires. I shall not concern myself specially with the descriptive part of our contemporary ways.[25]

These words, designed for a different book and a different locale, still fit the narration of *Crime and Punishment* — in fact, all of Dostoevsky's Petersburg works. Here the "single private and curious event" is, of course, the murder: this is what determines the relevance of everything else in the novel. The fact that Dostoevsky was able to make good his stated intention to "re-explore [*pereryt*] all questions" in the book only demonstrates his skill in using this sort of concentration.

His notebooks make clear the enormous difficulty he had in deciding on a point of view. Originally this was to be a retrospective confession, by Raskolnikov himself, but the plan was dropped as too constricting. What we have instead is a compromise of genius: third-person narration, which allows the inclusion of scenes (like Svidrigailov's suicide) otherwise impossible, and yet is so close to Raskolnikov's point of view as to approach interior monologue.[26] The only perspective on Raskolnikov comes from his own actions, his own words, and those he inspires in the other characters. His is the only mind into which we penetrate, his the only thoughts we read — and his the guiding perception of the city.

The last may be new in degree, but not in kind. It is a perception based on isolation, that isolation which comes finally to define so much of Dostoevsky's myth of Petersburg. It is first of all symbolized by the tiny and sordidly furnished rooms and apartments: Raskolnikov's "coffin," Alyona's spotless and characterless den, the crowded pigsty of the Marmeladovs — and before them the underground man's "mouse hole," the cubicle Ivan Petrovich takes over from old Smith, the room of the narrator of "White Nights," "into which a different sun shines," Golyadkin's refuge, and Devushkin's side of the kitchen. Located often at the top of dark and dirty stairways, in huge blocks of apartment buildings, these are the discrete cells of which the city is made, and their trapped inhabitants are a product or outgrowth of the fantastic city.

It is possible to dream in such places, but hardly to live, as the physical and spiritual health of Dostoevsky's characters plainly testifies. (In *Crime and Punishment,* Razumikhin and Dunya alone among the principal characters are conspicuously healthy, and their lives alone survive Raskolnikov's tragedy unchanged.) Dostoevsky's characters so regularly suffer from some unnamed fever — the product of poverty and climate, as well as the emblem of their spiritual states — that this becomes a feature in its own right of the fantastic city. Disease for Dostoevsky, as for the romantics, "represented the negation of the ordinary, the normal, the reasonable and contained the dualism of life and death, nature and non-nature, continuance and dissolution, which dominated their whole conception of life." [27] Added to isolation, it creates fear. "Petersburg is hell for me," Dostoevsky had written his brother Mikhail at the very beginning of his career: "It is so miserable, so miserable to live here. And my health, it appears, is worse. Moreover, I am terribly afraid." [28]

Crime and Punishment is unusual among Dostoevsky's novels in that it is set entirely in the summer. Twenty years before, in the fourth installment of his "Petersburg Chronicle," he had spoken of the need to get away from the city in the summer, to "quench with the variety of natural phenomena our eternal unsated thirst for direct, natural life." Here we see the alternative. From the stultifying closeness of his room Raskolnikov, ill and weak, is driven into the stinking, no less stifling streets. There is, of course, an obvious symbolism in the state of airlessness that surrounds him — but, as will be shown, his situation is only an extreme form of the general Petersburg condition. After reading his mother's letter, Raskolnikov feels "stifled and cramped in that little yellow room that was like a cupboard or trunk." His eyes and mind "seek space" and he hurries down to the street, where he walks, "as usual, without noticing his way, whispering and even speaking aloud to himself" (I.3). This walk — and the others like it — can be plotted in detail on a map: Dostoevsky's directions are precise. Yet the city through which he walks fades and reappears as his attention rests on it or takes flight. And since the narration adheres so closely to his point of view, something of a sporadic solipsism results, creating a city that is fantastic in its evanescence and showing that the streets, far from dispelling isolation, only underline it. Nor do they offer relief from oppression. Raskolnikov's love for them is a perverse one: "I like it," he says, "when all the passers-by have pale, green, sickly faces"; he goes out "to feel even more nauseated." He is in this respect, as in others, like the underground man, who liked to walk along some of the same crowded streets "at dusk just when they become more crowded with people of all sorts, merchants and artisans going home from their day's work, with faces worried to the point of looking malicious"; what attracts him is "just that cheap bustle, that blatant prosaic quality" (II.8). (So too will Arkady Dolgoruky, the narrator of *A Raw Youth,* find fascinating "the faces of poor people hurrying back home to their corners from work and trade," each with "his own sullen anxiety in his face" — and "perhaps not one common uniting thought in the crowd." [29]) This is a petty, masochistic pleasure, the paradoxical community one atom of the city can feel at observing the separateness of the other atoms.

Individuals, then, are the basic units of Dostoevsky's myth of the city — not, as in the case of Balzac's professed intention and Dickens' practice, families. By and large, Dostoevsky's families tend to be parodies of what is usually understood by that word. Marmeladov is the head of his family in an ironic sense only, and Katerina Ivanovna shows her motherliness by goading her stepdaughter into prostitution and, in her madness at the end, making grotesque street performers of her children. Raskolnikov's family is without a father. It may be taken as a general rule that, when families do appear in Dostoevsky's fiction, they tend to be shown in process of dissolution. The city, sociologically speaking, is largely responsible for this dissolution; and so, for literary purposes, it makes the ideal background for dramas of isolation. In this respect, Dickens' treatment is exceptional, for he still follows tradition — the double tradition here being the sentimental one (exemplified in *The Vicar of Wakefield*) and, even more important, the comic one that finds its happy ending par excellence in a wedding. Tolstoy, the more thoroughgoing realist, knew better, noting in his plans for *War and Peace* that marriage seemed to him a starting point, rather than a denouement.[30] And in his novels of Paris, despite his programmatic statement that he regarded the family as the essential unit of society, Balzac also either omitted it or showed its disintegration.

Dostoevsky's novels from *Crime and Punishment* on show an increasing concern with the family as a theme — but always in the light indicated above. He is most explicit on the subject in *A Raw Youth,* in which he goes into the theme of "accidental families" (*sluchaynye semyi*) — a term whose significance is obscured by Constance Garnett's translation, "exceptional families." In his *Diary of a Writer,* Dostoevsky takes issue with Tolstoy precisely on this point:

> Never has the Russian family been more shaken, disintegrated, unsorted, and formless than at present. Where will you find today "Childhoods and Boyhoods" that could be represented in such clear and harmonious fashion as that, for example, of Count Leo Tolstoy, in his depiction of *his own* epoch and his own family, or in his *War and Peace*? All these creations are now *no more than historical pictures of the distant past.* . . . The contemporary Russian family is becoming more and more an *accidental* family. Precisely *accidental* — there you have the definition of the contemporary Russian family. (July-August 1877, ch. 1)

In a similar sense, the city is accidental — not in its founding, but in the "abstract" results of that intentional founding. Petersburg becomes "the most fantastic city, with the most fantastic history of all the cities of the earth" [31] in terms of the abnormality of the life that is lived there. The absence of roots, frequent changes of apartment, precariousness of employment — these are further signs. And so, of course, is the absence of nature: the only vegetation in the city of *Crime and Punishment* are the pathetic geraniums in Raskolnikov's room and the pitiful young spruce tree and two bushes of the "pleasure garden." Even the climate is inimical to normal life, producing those "pale, green, sickly faces" that Raskolnikov professes to love and provoking a kind of reciprocal action in coloring the Petersburgers' own perception of their city: it can be seen as early as *Poor Folk* and *The Double*. This reciprocity very often issues in action that is hallucinatory, or seems to be.

Preceding the doubt about what is or is not hallucination, and giving it foundation, are actual illness and fever. The illness is often — as with Raskolnikov — unspecified, apparently a generally run-down condition that leaves the body weak and the mind dangerously active. This is the natural state of the dreamer, his physical debility reflecting his alienation from "normal life," his feverish mental freedom representing both a contributing cause and a compensation. The fever is the badge of alienation, poverty, malnutrition — the mark of the Petersburg hero or antihero in Dostoevsky's heroically antiheroic Petersburg. Dreams are born of it, which represent themselves as spiritual illness, and they move the dreamer "to see the fantastic in everything." [32] The earliest essays in this direction are the most extreme: *The Double* deals, confusingly, with the psychopathology of hallucination, as does, less obviously, "The Landlady." Bem, in fact, has explained the latter as an experiment in "the dramatization of delirium." [33] Neither of them was fully appreciated until the twentieth century — though it is only fair to add that this latter-day appreciation was prompted by a desire unknown to earlier critics, the desire to see their place in the process that led to the later works. In any event, *Crime and Punishment* is the supreme example of this technique. Where the actual goings-on of the earlier work were too obscure, here they are made clear. Through the filter of Raskolnikov's fever and distraction, objective time, place, and situation shine through; their color is that of the filter, but the outlines are their own.

Thus Raskolnikov's movements at the scene of the murder are described as mechanical, and afterwards he moves about the pawnbroker's apartment in a state "of blankness, even dreaminess." Returned home, he spends the night on his sofa, *seeming* to wake up from time to time. Walking the streets, he falls into meditation, talking to himself, noticing only what obtrudes upon his reverie or what catches his attention in the brief pauses between meditation. The scene on K — Boulevard where he tries to rescue the drunken and seduced young girl from her pursuer is an excellent case in point. He has not yet committed murder; he is still contemplating it, spurred on by the knowledge of his sister's imminent self-sacrifice on his behalf. When the subject recurs to him, he feels "a hammering in his head, and there [is] a darkness before his eyes." Looking for a place to sit, he notices a woman walking in front of him, and his attention fastens on her, "at first reluctantly and, as it were, with annoyance, and then more and more intently" (I.4). From a scrutiny of her dress and manner, Raskolnikov reconstructs the circumstances of her seduction and even imagines the scene of her return home. The incident is a telling one, not only for what it indicates about Raskolnikov, and not only as an incident characteristic of the Petersburg of this book, but because it also exemplifies the general manner in which the city is seen. What, after all, do we know of this girl's affecting story? The answer is, only what Raskolnikov observes and imagines. His deductions are certainly plausible, given the objective facts (which a policeman confirms). But we shall never know if his version is true. We have the girl's situation, but only Raskolnikov's notion of its meaning, only Raskolnikov's projection of its pathos.

Of the characters most intimately involved in Raskolnikov's fate, something similar is true. Sonya, for instance, is seen only in his company, only in reaction to him and through his reaction to her. And Svidrigailov, of whom this cannot be said, nevertheless appears so abruptly in Raskolnikov's room that the latter wonders pointedly and repeatedly whether he is only a continuation of his dream. (Svidrigailov himself — as befits the double of Raskolnikov — is subject to the same doubts about what is real and what is hallucination; these terrible doubts are the substance of his last night at the Adrianople.) This centrality of Raskolnikov's point of view extends even to Porfiry the detective, whose intimate probings of Raskolnikov's conscience (in the double French sense) entitle us to say of him, as Voltaire said of God, that if Porfiry did not exist it would have been necessary for Raskolnikov to invent him. And, in a special sense, the suspicion is permissible that he did.

That sense is not a literal one, of course. R. P. Blackmur, who first made this point in print, offers no convincing justification for slighting the detective as "that thirty-five-year-old roly-poly of the disengaged intellect called Porfiry," but he is right in insisting that "he is a fancy of the pursuing intellect whom Raskolnikov must have invented had he not turned up of his own accord" and in pointing out further:

As Svidrigailov and Sonya between them represent the under-part, and the conflict in the under-part, of Raskolnikov's secret self, so Polfiry represents the maximum possible perfection of the artificial, intellectual self under whose ministrations Raskolnikov *reasons* himself into committing his crime, and who therefore is the appropriate instrument for driving him to the point of confessing it. It is Porfiry . . . who whenever he comes to sack Raskolnikov leaves him in a state of collapse, just as it is either Svidrigailov or Sonya who gives him strength.[34]

What Blackmur does not credit is the full force of Raskolnikov's attraction to Porfiry, which — despite his resistance, by turns fierce and weary — represents an attraction to confession; before he ever meets Porfiry he displays this in his talk with Zametov in the tavern. The police stand for the retribution Raskolnikov yearns for and resists at the same time. They too — almost as an institution — represent an impulse of Raskolnikov's own fevered psyche.

In what could well be an epigraph to the whole novel, Dostoevsky writes: "In a morbid state, dreams are often distinguished by an unusual vividness and clarity, and by an extraordinary resemblance to reality. Sometimes a monstrous picture will take shape, but the setting and the whole process of presentation are nevertheless so plausible and contain details so subtle, unexpected, yet artistically consonant with everything else in it, that the dreamer could never have invented them while awake, were he even such an artist as Pushkin or Turgenev" (I.5). In the light of this statement, and reinforced by many clear hints, the fact is unmistakable: this whole novel is like a bad dream, and the social and physical Petersburg in which the action takes place is no less so.

Poverty also seems like a bad dream in the extremity of its depiction in the Marmeladov family. Is not having "nowhere to go" the mark of the most terrifying nightmares? Dostoevsky, as Arnold Hauser has noted, is "one of the few genuine writers on poverty, for he writes not merely out of sympathy with the poor, like George Sand or Eugène Sue, or as a result of vague memories, like Dickens, but as one who has spent most of his time in need and has literally starved from time to time."[35] But this valid observation needs to be taken a step further, for otherwise it might appear to leave Dostoevsky among the humanitarian novelists, the fighters for social justice — as, from his early work, he was judged to be. The fact is that from *Poor Folk* on, he is developing a special and different theme of his own — the revolt of the poor man — which is based on the protest of an individual against an unjust fate. Poverty is thus considered as the destruction of the right of individuality, as the suppression of its potentialities.[36]

The result of all the factors discussed so far — isolation, fever, dreaming, rootlessness, the unnatural city, poverty — is crime. This is by no means to say that Raskolnikov's crime is the socially determined effect of these abstract causes. Dostoevsky had a streak of the naturalist in him, but it was always subsidiary to other conceptions. What can be said, rather, is that all these factors furnish together *the perfect theater* for Raskolnikov's crime, at once providing the opportunity and feeding the impulse. Berdyaev justly points out that Dostoevsky "shows the ontological consequences of crime," but he overstates his case in claiming that "this spiritual nature [refuses] to explain evil and wickedness by reference to social environment." [37] It would be truer to say that he refuses to explain these things by reference to social environment alone, for Dostoevsky's notebooks make clear his own increasing uncertainty about the real motive for Raskolnikov's crime[38] — as does the final text of the novel. In the last analysis, the motives are plural, just as the causes are antecedent to motive.

With the story of Raskolnikov, crime enters Dostoevsky's world, and none of the novels that follow will be without its murder (or, in the case of *A Raw Youth,* its near-murder). This fact alone is important. It is not crime in general that interests Dostoevsky, but only crime against life: how negligible are questions of property can be seen from Raskolnikov's characteristic neglect of what he has stolen. As a result, there can be no correspondence between Dostoevsky's myth of the criminal and Balzac's, for the glamor that suffuses the Balzacian criminal is essentially a military glamor: his brilliance is the brilliance of a strategist at war with society, a sui generis pursuer of *la carrière ouverte aux talents.* In prison Dostoevsky had met criminals, and in his report of those years he treats his fellow convicts by and large in the traditional Russian way, as "unfortunates." What they have done anyone, in principle, might do; their crimes are frequently crimes of passion; their common humanity is only too evident. There is, however, another class of criminal that fascinated him, represented by one Orlov, "a criminal such as there are few, who had murdered old people and children in cold blood":

This was not at all an ordinary man. . . . I can positively assert that never in my life have I met a man of such strength, of so iron a will as he. . . . His was literally a full victory over the flesh. It was evident that the man's power of control was limitless, that he despised every kind of torture and punishment, and feared nothing in the world. We saw in him only infinite energy, a thirst for action, a thirst for vengeance, a thirst to achieve his chosen end. Among other things I was struck by his strange haughtiness. He looked down on everything with incredible disdain, but without any effort to raise himself above others — just, somehow, naturally. . . . He was very sharp-witted, and somehow strangely open, though by no means talkative. (*The House of the Dead,* I.4)

Orlov is a healthy and spontaneous specimen of what Raskolnikov would make himself through will and intellection. Dostoevsky shows an awed fascination for him. But he goes no further than this and never really takes the "exceptional nature" as a problem to investigate. In the major novels, the problem that occupies him is that of the man who is not quite exceptional but seeks to be, who spurns the obscure promptings of his real nature to follow a theory, to act on an idea. The Russian word for crime means "transgression" or "overstepping" — and one of Dostoevsky's main themes, from *Crime and Punishment* onward, becomes the tragedy of overstepping the proper bounds of intellect by taking it alone as a sanction for action. Raskolnikov's intellect sanctions his crime (just as Ivan Karamazov's intellect will sanction Smerdyakov's crime); his punishment and his hopes for salvation come through the discovery that intellect is insufficient, that it cannot prevent moral suffering, that the holiness of life is a fact impermeable to reason. Dickens' late realization that the criminal does not struggle away from his crime but toward it is the essence of Dostoevsky's practice. His criminals are all amateurs — a fact that underscores their similarity to Everyman. This is why we cannot feel the excitement of the detached spectator in reading *Crime and Punishment,* as we do in reading *Le Père Goriot*. "All of us without exception," as Blackmur comments, are "deeply implicated in the nature of the Crime." [39]

We are in the same way implicated in the moral crime of Sonya's enforced prostitution, and this robs her profession of any vestige of the excitement that a Balzac might find in it. Here again the sense is plain in which Dostoevsky can be called the inheritor of romantic realism. Alone among the major Russian writers of his time, he deals in large measure with the themes of romantic realism — and consistently he reinterprets them, gives them a new sense and a quite new drama by detypifying them, removing them from social categories, and returning them to the undifferentiated fund of common humanity whose mark is, above all, suffering. In his notebooks, this is spelled out:

THE IDEA OF THE NOVEL. The Orthodox view[;] in what does Orthodoxy consist. There is no happiness in comfort; happiness is purchased by suffering. Man is not born for happiness. Man earns his happiness, and always with suffering. There is no injustice here, for the title and consciousness of life (i.e., directly sensible by the body and the spirit, i.e., by the whole vital process) is acquired by experience *pro* and *contra,* which one must take upon oneself.[40]

The burden of suffering, then, is to be assumed by experience *pro* and *contra* — which means, in Raskolnikov's case, experience of the intellect and the contrary experience of the spirit. The form is that of a debate. The experience pits the deepest irrational sources in him against the highest refinements of dialectical skill. Here again Dostoevsky the inheritor shows his innovation; it is, as Arnold Hauser formulates it, "the fact that he is a romantic in the world of thought, and the movement of thought has the same motive power and the same emotional, not to say pathological, impetus in him as the flood and stress of the feelings had in the romantics." [41] This can already be seen in the morbid dialectics of the man from underground, and it persists throughout the subsequent novels: this, more than anything else, separates his early period from his late. His novels are, as the Soviet critic Bakhtin has shown, "polyphonic," in the sense that they are peopled with incarnate points of view which the author allows full and independent play, and which he neither complements nor resolves as do traditional omniscient narrators.[42] Viewpoints clash in the open, as it were, outside of any governing moral convention or *parti pris*.

The polyphonic novel, Bakhtin says, was possible only in the period of capitalism — a statement equally true of the romantic realism of Balzac and Dickens. But he goes on to suggest that the development of capitalism in Russia (and especially in Petersburg) peculiarly favored this new literary mutation, because capitalism had come suddenly "and caught intact a variety of social worlds and groups which had not, as in the West, begun to lose their distinct apartness." (Compare Balzac's lament about the disappearance of social distinctions in his time.) For aristocratic writers with their roots in the relatively changeless countryside, a stable and inclusive point of view might still be possible; but in the cities, the contradictions of a time of transition were "bound to manifest themselves especially sharply, while at the same time the individuality of those worlds that had been thrown off their ideological balance and into collision was bound to be especially full and clear." In this way, Bakhtin argues, "the objective preconditions were created for the essential multilevel and multivoice structure of the polyphonic novel." [43] It remains only to add that this historical picture lent a symbolic plausibility (if not an actual one) to the way in which Dostoevsky managed to bring characters from different social classes into contact with one another on a footing of essential equality. It is not that he erases class barriers; what he does is to concentrate on certain déclassé aristocrats whose fortunes or tastes have led them out of their conventional circles and into the arena of free-floating atoms, the heart of Dostoevsky's mythical city where a common rootlessness does make for a common human destiny — and where the very absence of conventional norms can suggest to a mortally sick Katerina Ivanovna and a dangerously isolated Raskolnikov that all, indeed, is permitted.

In Bakhtin's analysis, then, we have the particularization of Lewis Mumford's general observation: "Perhaps the best definition of the city in its higher aspects is to say that it is a place designed to offer the widest facilities for significant conversation." "The dialogue," he goes on, "is one of the ultimate expressions of life in the city: the delicate flower of its long vegetative growth," and he adds: "Not by accident, then, has more than one historic city reached its climax in a dialogue that sums up its total experience of life. In the Book of Job, one beholds Jerusalem; in Plato, Sophocles, and Euripides, Athens; in Shakespeare and Marlowe, Dekker and Webster, Elizabethan London. In a sense the dramatic dialogue is both the fullest symbol and the final justification of the city's life." [44] Mumford's list of literary monuments to particular cities, if extended in time, would have to include Balzac's Paris, Dickens' London, and Dostoevsky's Petersburg. All of them, most notably the last, fit and illustrate his definition.

We are in a position to see now why it is that Dostoevsky's myth of the city — the third great one in the nineteenth century — has about it such an unrivaled sense of modernity in the mid-twentieth century. Is it not, in the first place, because his myth divests the city of any facile glamor, removes from it the happy ending of "success," informs it with a spirit of searching and anguish? He presented for the first time the life of the city in all its sordidness — not simply to show what these conditions automatically did to people, as the naturalists would show, but to raise the problem of how, within them, sentient human beings might pursue the quest for dignity. And on a less literal level, he raised the chaotic city to the position of a symbol of the chaotic moral world of man, so that the contradictions of the second find their counterpart in the contrasts of the first.[45] He showed, without abstraction, bare human consciousness striving in a world where there were few of the usual categories of normality, striving with a terrible and unsought freedom, isolated and rootless, together without community, to rediscover the conditions for "living life." The nature of the struggle is ultimately intellectual, the seductions ideological, the goal a new or an old morality — something to fill the void. With two devastating world wars behind us and a last one threatening in the offing, with a displacement of persons unparalleled in modern times, amid a technological revolution that makes tradition more an object of nostalgia than something that can be lived, with nations acting on principles that are Raskolnikov's raised to the nth power, it is Dostoevsky's city and his alone that prefigures our dilemma. In any present-day metropolis can be found pieces from

Dickens' myth or from Balzac's. But our private and collective fears and uncertainties, our besetting struggles with what the existentialists term absurdity, are engaged only by the myth of "the most abstract" and "the gloomiest city in the world," whose heroes are forever wandering the streets, aimless and distracted.

Crime and Punishment introduces the great themes that fill the later books — questions of transgression, guilt, and suffering, of freedom and authority, of "new men," positivism, socialism, the difficulties of belief and the tragedy of unbelief. In Raskolnikov's story we see Dostoevsky not only discovering these themes, but refining his myth of Petersburg to accommodate them. The city, here and henceforth, is "gloomy, harsh, and queer" in ways quite absent from the earlier works; he had regarded it from the very beginning as a symbol, but only here does the symbol take on its full freight, with all the implications of its abstract origins explored in the contemporary cultural context. This new fullness of his use of the city contains a kind of transcendence: when "The Drunkards" had metamorphosed into *Crime and Punishment,* the artist, too, had metamorphosed, "found himself," as we say retrospectively. And it was precisely his developing myth of the city that had led him to the discovery.

After this, the possibilities of the city no longer called for the same exploration. Among the remaining novels of his major period, only *A Raw Youth* re-creates the essentially Dostoevskian Petersburg — and then, significantly, the result is a potpourri of familiar motifs and an engaging failure. In the others, the symbolic presence of Petersburg is of fundamental importance, but it operates as a fixed quantity. This is most strikingly seen in *The Possessed* and *The Brothers Karamazov,* where theories related to Raskolnikov's and matured, like his, in the Petersburg ambience, result in murder. Stavrogin and the young Verkhovensky were both educated in the capital and tasted their first corruption there; Ivan Karamazov is the Petersburg intellectual par excellence.

There is, finally, another sense in which *Crime and Punishment* inaugurates Dostoevsky's major period. This fullest treatment of the Dostoevskian city, this first presentation of the major themes, is also the first full example of the peculiar realism associated with his name. In *Crime and Punishment* Dostoevsky brought a technique to maturity, and the great novels all reflect the poetics we have seen him fashioning through his Petersburg works.[46] One might speak with full justice in this connection of a Dostoevskian "poetics of the city."

8

Poetics of the City

The new reality, created by the artist of genius, is *real,* because it reveals the very essence of existence, but it is *not realistic,* because it does not reproduce our reality. . . . Dostoevsky's world grew slowly over the course of twenty years, from *Poor Folk* to *Crime and Punishment.* Only in the latter novel did it coalesce definitively, as a *particular spiritual* reality.

K. Mochulsky

Taking into account the positivistic mood of his time, he managed, as an artist, by way of very complex techniques and combinations, to keep within the bounds of the really permissible and empirically possible, at the same time introducing into his work all those elements of the fantastic to which his own tendencies of innate mysticism, and the romanticism of his literary upbringing, constantly inclined him.

Leonid Grossman

An aristocratic reviewer of Dostoevsky's first large novel of the city complained in 1861: "Unnaturalness of situation can never be artistic! In all the kinds of art, the epochs of artistic decline are always distinguished by unnaturalness; this can be observed in painting, in architecture, even in music: all the more so in literature. And unnaturalness of situation is here (in the novel) at every step." [1] His last observation, at least, is right. The literal unnaturalness of Dostoevsky's situations corresponds to the unnaturalness of city life, his new artistic conventions to the new social conventions and intellectual currents he found there. This — as so much else in his art — becomes especially clear by contrast with Tolstoy, whose notes for *War and Peace* contain the admission that "the life of civil servants, of merchants, of seminarists and peasants is uninteresting and half incomprehensible to me, [whereas] the life of the aristocrats of that time [the period of 1812] . . . is comprehensible, interesting, and dear." [2] The aristocratic life Tolstoy shows is measured on the epic scale, subject to the slow changes of the seasons and the years, as is the life of the land. "We Russians," he writes, "do not in general know how to write novels in the sense in which they understand this kind of composition in Europe, and the work offered here is not a tale: in it no single thought is advanced, nothing is proved, no single event of any kind is described; still less can it be called a novel, with a starting point, constantly complicated interest, and a happy or unhappy denouement with which the interest of the narration ends." "I cannot call my composition a tale," he adds, "because I do not know how to make my characters act only for the sake of proving or clarifying any one idea or series of ideas." [3]

REALISM IN A HIGHER SENSE

Dostoevsky does just what Tolstoy says he cannot do. He concentrates his novel around a single key event, and he makes his characters act in demonstration or clarification of a series of ideas. This is his "new word," the fruit of his study of European literature, the alternative to what he called a "landowners' literature." It is, in short, his "realism in a higher sense." One of his notes reads: "With full realism, to find the man [or the human] in a man [*Pri polnom realizme nayti v cheloveke cheloveka*]. This is primarily a Russian trait, and in this sense I am of course of the people [*naroden*] (for my direction flows out of the depth of the Christian spirit of the people) — though I am unknown to the Russian people of the present, I shall be known to those of the future. They call me a psychologist: not true: I am only a realist in a higher sense, i.e., I depict all the depths of the human soul." [4] That "only" in the last sentence seems a curious gesture of modesty, as if to practice this realism were somehow less ambitious than to deal in psychology. What it may well indicate is his struggle against the numerous outcries that his work was "unnatural," "impossible," "subjective" — accusations all the more forceful given the utilitarian bias of his time.[5]

For it was his time that Dostoevsky was seeking to portray. Did they say he exaggerated? Dostoevsky's answer was one he said all portraitists know: "All art consists in a certain portion of exaggeration, provided . . . one does not exceed certain bounds." [6] There were difficulties, however, in knowing both the time and the permissible limits of exaggeration — difficulties that seemed insuperable to the diametrically opposite talent of Goncharov. In a letter to Dostoevsky, he finds a character from one of his minor sketches "improbable." For a realist like Goncharov, the mere fact that a character may *seem* improbable already constitutes an artistic fault: "You say yourself that 'such a type is arising'; forgive me if I let myself note a contradiction here. If it is arising, then it is not yet a *type*. . . . Creative work (I mean the creative work of an objective artist, like you, for example) is only possible, in my opinion, when life has taken fixed form; it does not accommodate the life that is new and in process of formation." [7]

Dostoevsky's answer is not recorded, but his whole work makes clear what it must have been. Already six years before, in 1868, he had anticipated such an argument:

> I have completely different concepts of reality and of realism [he wrote Maykov] than do our realists and critics. My idealism is more real than theirs. Lord! To rehearse clearly what all we Russians have lived through in the last ten years in our spiritual development — but wouldn't the realists cry that this is fantasy! Nevertheless, it is primordial, true realism! This really is realism, only deeper, while they stay on the surface [*a u nikh melko plavaet*]. . . . With their realism you won't explain one hundredth of the real, actually occurring facts. But we, with our idealism, even prophesy facts. It has happened.[8]

The reference to prophecy concerns the fact that a student, out of a nihilist belief that any means to the rectification of the social order was permissible, had killed and robbed a moneylender just at the time the installment of *Crime and Punishment* describing Raskolnikov's crime came out.[9] The coincidence evidently made a great impression on Dostoevsky, as a vindication of his attempts to follow "life in process of formation." But equally noteworthy is his emphasis on the spiritual development of the Russians. He knew that the surface of things changes slowly and imperceptibly: his search was beneath the surface. For this he found the eye of the ordinary observer — with whom he equated the realist — insufficient. To Balzac's claim that where the public sees red, the real artist sees blue, and to Dickens' parallel claim that "what is exaggeration to one class of minds and perceptions is plain truth to another," Dostoevsky adds his own: the important thing "is not in the object, but in the eye: if you have an eye, the object will be found; if you don't have an eye, if you are blind — you won't find anything in any object." [10]

Such an eye could see, for instance, in certain filthy taverns a spectacle "so vulgar and prosaic that it borders almost on the fantastic" (*A Raw Youth,* II.5.2). This is the Gogolian gift. But the same eye could also perceive the broad significance in what sometimes masquerades as eccentricity. He states this most clearly in his foreword to *The Brothers Karamazov:* "Not only is an eccentric 'not always' a particularity and a being apart, but, on the contrary, it may well be that such a person sometimes carries within himself the very heart of the whole, while the rest of the men of his epoch have for some reason been temporarily torn from it, as if by a gust of wind." The realist in a higher sense, in other words, is looking for the adumbration of just those types Goncharov claims do not yet exist — looking not for the statistical average, or the recognizably universal, but rather for the statistical exception and the new guise of the universal that is just coming to birth.

In the statement quoted above, Dostoevsky's reference to the epoch is not accidental. Preparing to write this novel, he stated in a letter his "irrefutable conclusion" that a writer should know, besides his craft, "the reality he is portraying, historical and current, down to the finest points. . . . That is why, preparing to write a very large novel, I thought to immerse myself specially in the study — not of reality, properly speaking: I am familiar with it without that — but of the details of the present." [11] A double purpose, then, impelled him to scan the present: on the one hand, he needed typical details, on the other those exceptional facts that might illustrate what one could term "typicality in a higher sense." This search led him, as it had led Balzac and Dickens before him (Gogol felt no such need), to the newspapers of the day. He was an avid follower of the *faits divers* — and nowhere, it may be noted in passing, are things so diverse as in a large urban center.

So we find him asking a correspondent in 1867: "Do you receive any newspapers? Read them, for God's sake; nowadays it is impossible to do otherwise — not in the interests of fashion, but in order that the visible connection of all matters, public and private, may become constantly stronger and clearer." [12] This is the quest for a pattern — a quest any conventional realist might approve. But it is not all, as a later letter makes clear:

> I have my own special view of reality (in art), and what the majority call almost fantastic and exceptional sometimes constitutes the very essence of reality for me. In my opinion, the commonness of some occurrences and the conventional view of them are not realism at all, but even the contrary. In every issue of the newspapers you find accounts of the most real and oddest facts. For our writers they are fantastic; they don't even attend to them: nevertheless they are reality, because they are *facts*.[13]

For this reliance on his special "eye," Dostoevsky's sometime friend and biographer Strakhov termed him "the most subjective of novelists," claiming justly and obtusely that "he almost always created characters in his own image and likeness." Condescendingly he reports the writer's frequent assertion "that he considered himself a complete realist, that those crimes, suicides, and all sorts of mental distortions which constitute the usual theme of his novels were essentially a constant and usual phenomenon in reality and that we only let them pass without attention." [14] But what Strakhov goes on to treat as a useful if mistaken conviction went far deeper than he apparently suspected: it had roots in both literary tactics and literary strategy.

The tactical application has to do with a word that has no precise English equivalent, *zanimatelnost*. It means the quality of compelling attention, of engrossing; it is that essence which continental critics termed "l'intéressant." In 1870, Dostoevsky wrote a correspondent that he had reached the point where he placed this quality "above artistry" [15] — a telling exaggeration, but exaggeration all the same. What it may remind us of is the fact that Dostoevsky was, as he called himself, a proletarian writer, one dependent on the advances of often rapacious publishers and ultimately on the favor of a public quite unprepared for the concerns that most exercised him. This abject condition, which made him so envy the financial independence of writers like Turgenev and Tolstoy, may actually have been his making, as it was arguably the making of Balzac. In any case, he wrote, like Shakespeare, for a motley audience, and to do so he took lessons not only from the author of *Hamlet* but from the contemporary practitioners of the "sensation novel" in England and the roman-feuilleton in France. He cursed his bondage to deadlines, but he also admitted their bracing effect on his work.[16]

The strategic side of his predilection for extremities raised him above the level of his Western confrères, who made the same arguments but could not produce the same vindications of them. It is aptly summarized in Merezhkovsky's epigram that "a novel of Dostoevsky's is not a tranquil, smoothly developing epos, but a collection of the fifth acts of many tragedies." [17] The sort of plot that Tolstoy could not use, Dostoevsky could — and use it, moreover, in what may be the only exception in nineteenth-century European literature to the recently enunciated principle that the importance of plot in the novel is in inverse proportion to that of character.[18] Dostoevsky at his best raises melodramatic unlikelihood (however accidentally based in fact) to the level of tragic inevitability. Not for him was the superficial view of things (why doesn't Hamlet just *kill* Claudius?); the eye that scanned the city and found its vulgarities luminous and fantastic was concerned, beyond fact, with potentiality.

Haunted by a dream of the golden age, he perceived in the fallen world a latent criminality in all men, even the most apparently healthy. Alyosha Karamazov was to admit as much, and Freud to generalize the admission. This perception led naturally to an awareness of that thin experiential line which divides fantasy from reality and impulse from accomplished fact, and it led Dostoevsky to illuminate as had never been done before the twilight zone of dreams and hallucination, the link between inner and outer reality. His poetics is in many ways an instrument for the exploration of potentiality.

His treatment of character shows this, and one critic would have us drop the term in favor of "individuality" (*lichnost*), on the grounds that "character" is too conventional, a catchall made up of current convictions, customary feelings, habitual patterns of action and reaction.[19] The suggestion is fair, if not expedient. Dostoevsky's people *are* characters, but to say that they *have* character is beside the point. The customary adjectives will not stick. "With many," we read in *A Raw Youth,* "a logical conclusion sometimes turns into a very strong feeling, which takes hold of the entire being." Usually we meet Dostoevsky's heroes after this has happened, to witness, as Evnin has put it, "not the changes of the hero but his incessant, ever more intense oscillations between the same polar extremities which he combines within himself — which arise from his 'idea-feeling' [*ideya-chuvstvo*]." [20] He does not so much develop as progressively express this self-division and so advance to meet his tragic fate.

Dreams play a great role here, as the fullest expressions of potentiality. Raskolnikov underlines this in his reaction to the fearful dream of the mare beating. The ostensible subject of his dream has been an incident from childhood, but he is quick to seize its real meaning. "My God!" he cries, "can it really be, can it really be, that I will actually take an ax, strike her on the head, smash her skull . . . that I will slip in the sticky warm blood, break the lock, steal and tremble, hide, all spattered in the blood . . . with the ax . . . My God, can it be?" (I.5). The process is shown with equal clarity in *A Raw Youth,* where the narrator reports his erotic dream of Katerina Nikolayevna's surrender to him — as payment for a blackmail he protests he has no conscious intention of ever using. After reporting the dream in detail, he cries:

> Oh, away with that base memory! Accursed dream! I swear that until that loathsome dream nothing like that shameful thought had entered my mind. There had never even been any unconscious dream of the sort (though I had kept the [incriminating] "document" sewn up in my pocket, and I sometimes gripped the pocket with a strange smile). How could all this have presented itself to me so ready-made? It was because I had the soul of a spider! In other words, all this had long ago been conceived and lying there in my corrupt heart, lying there in *desire,* but my waking heart was still ashamed, and my mind did not yet dare to picture anything of the sort consciously. But in sleep the soul presented and laid bare everything that was in my heart, with utter accuracy, in a complete picture, and — in prophetic form. (III.2.5)

Dreams, then, serve often to reveal the potentialities of a character and in general to show up "that faculty in man (and in the Russian . . . more especially) of cherishing in his soul the loftiest ideal side by side with the most abject baseness, and all quite sincerely" (*A Raw Youth,* III.2.5). This bifurcation within the Dostoevskian hero is dramatized by the much-discussed device of the double, in which the divided character gives illusory birth to one of his conflicting sides: so Mr. Golyadkin in the early story produces Mr. Golyadkin Junior, and Ivan Karamazov in the last novel produces his petty-bourgeois devil. Hallucinations of this kind are well within the bounds of realism — or can be accepted as such by the rational-minded — because they can be accounted for by natural processes (unless, of course, one entertains Svidrigailov's hypothesis that preternatural visitations may really occur, but only to diseased minds — who do not produce them, but are uniquely receptive to them). Where probability is clearly forced beyond the limits of conventional realism is in the author's use of *objectified* doubles. Svidrigailov is one of these. He appears to Raskolnikov at first as a continuation of his dream, and, as he says, a particular affinity does exist between them. On one level, of course, he is Raskolnikov's cynicism personified, so his suicide has a particular significance: in an early plan, Raskolnikov was to end by shooting himself.[21] The way that other characters are made to symbolize the potentialities of a Dostoevskian hero is succinctly indicated by a four-line note in the plans for *Crime and Punishment:*

> Svidrigailov — despair, the most cynical.
> Sonya — hope, the most unrealizable.
> (Raskolnikov should express this himself.)
> He has become passionately attached to them both.[22]

Such an extreme insistence that we are all parts one of another evidently allows an observation of the classical unities very rare in the novel. The restricted neighborhood in which the action of *Crime and Punishment* takes place — the handful of streets and the rooms so near to each other — is typical of Dostoevsky's practice in all his novels, as is the related device of large group scenes that bring all the important characters together in one place for the development of some crucial piece of action. And to this unity of place he adds a striking unity of time. *Crime and Punishment,* exclusive of the epilogue, deals with the events of only two weeks. Only his first novel, *Poor Folk,* covered a period of months (from April to September), and the young writer apparently found even this expanse too great, for his second novel already showed the characteristic Dostoevskian compression: the action of *The Double* covers only four days. The whole list of Dostoevsky's works shows the same thing: *A Raw Youth* covers seven days, the main action of *The Brothers Karamazov,* six.[23] This swiftness of action represents an attempt to seize a complicated set of interrelations at a given moment, by something like what Joyce called an epiphany. The perception behind it may be due in part to features of the writer's own biography — the moment of radiant clarity before an epileptic seizure ("Mahomet's second"), and perhaps the moment before the firing squad, after the command, "Aim!" had been given. In any case, the axiom holds as stated in an early work: "There are minutes in which one lives, mentally, much more than in whole years." [24] Or, as the notebooks for *Crime and Punishment* put it more philosophically: "What is time? Times does not exist; time is numbers, time is the relation of being to nonbeing." [25]

Clearly, the novelist who proceeds on such premises must deliberately violate the canons of "normative" Flaubertian realism, to achieve the concentration and unity demanded by his notion of realism in a higher sense, and to deny him the right to do this in the name of "truth to life" is to confuse artistic conventions — a confusion that the practitioners of art are less likely to make than the critics who follow in their wake. (Maupassant, for instance, in defining his realism, was at pains to emphasize that there were as many valid ways of writing a novel as there were genuine talents.) It is all the more regrettable, then, to find Simmons in his *Dostoevsky: The Making of a Novelist* so far failing to understand the method his subject professed as to call the device of coincidence simply a "trap for weary novelists" and to find the coincidences in *Crime and Punishment* "perhaps the principal artistic blemish in the work." "In real life," he writes, "coincidental happenings do not violate the laws of probability, and in fiction our credibility is forfeited if coincidence is overworked." [26] After the discussions of this matter in connection with Balzac and Dickens, there should be no need to establish again the artistic legitimacy of coincidence, particularly since the tragic vision has always relied on this device.

What is actually more remarkable here is the degree to which Dostoevsky, who defines existence romantically in terms of heightened moments, manages nevertheless to embrace the contrary poetics of realism. There is a reminder of this in his expressed admiration for Poe, who, he noted, "almost always takes the most exceptional reality, puts his hero in the most exceptional external or psychological position, and tells — with what power of penetration, with what amazing fidelity! — about the state of that man's soul." And further:

> In his faculty of imagination, there is a feature we do not meet in anyone else: this is the power of detail. Try yourself, for example, to imagine something quite extraordinary or even something not to be met with in reality and only possible; the image which is traced before you will always include certain more or less general traits of a whole picture, or will be built on some particularity, some detail of it. But in Poe's stories, you see sharply all the details of the image or event he is presenting to such a degree that, finally, you as it were convince yourself of its possibility, of its reality — whereas this event is either completely impossible or has never yet happened on earth.[27]

Poe's technique, he seems to be suggesting, is fundamentally the same as his own — with the difference that Dostoevsky took special pains to keep within the bounds of the empirically possible, the outer limits of literary realism.

Within these bounds, however, he tended to be a serious emotional hyperbolist, as Gogol had been a comic one. He is free with the adverb "very"; among his most frequent words are "frenzy" (*isstuplenie*), "rapture" (*upoenie*), "suddenly" (*vdrug*), "even" (*dazhe*). His style is fitful and often jerky in its movement, to match the intensity and eccentricity of the action; it abounds in superlatives, not, as a Soviet critic has shown, just in adjectives but in nouns and verbs (which are in Russian susceptible to intensification in a way that defies translation) and even in pronouns.[28] The juxtaposition of these forms produces, of course, the sharpest sort of contrast — and contrast is a key principle in his work, as in the work of Balzac and Dickens. Not for him are the carefully nuanced parallelisms by which Tolstoy defines characters and relations. In

Dostoevsky frontal opposition is much more common. It can be seen in the very paradox of the phrase he used to designate his method, "fantastic realism." It can be seen in the note for *Crime and Punishment* quoted above, where Svidrigailov and Sonya are contrasted with each other, the one representing "the most cynical" despair as the other represents "the most unrealizable" hope, with Raskolnikov in the middle, "passionately" attached to them both. This organizational principle of contrast finds expression on every level of his art, from the phrase through the alternation of scenes to the realm of conception — this last appearing in *Crime and Punishment* in the way that the framework of a detective novel is filled with characters whose nature contrasts with it: here the conventional murderer, prostitute, and detective are replaced, respectively, by the rebel, the saint, and the sage.[29] So a passage from the notebooks reads: "Svidrigailov and Dunya (scene of violence)[.] Did not succeed. The night in debauch. On the next day he shot himself. *Contrasts*. Descriptions of the hemorrhoidal[?] Petersburg dens[?] (more poetical[ly?])." [30]

To the principle of potentiality, then, we should add that of extremity. Dostoevsky is the poet of extremes, a calling he considered to be eminently national. In *Diary of a Writer* he speaks of

> the urge for negation in a man . . . negation of everything, of the most sacred thing in his heart, of his highest ideal, of all that his people hold most sacred — which he has always revered, but which has suddenly become, as it were, an insupportable burden for him. Particularly striking is that haste, that impetuosity, with which the Russian sometimes hurries to reveal himself in certain significant moments of his own life or the nation's — to reveal himself whether it be in good or evil. Sometimes there is simply no restraint in this. Whether it be love, or liquor, debauch, egotism, envy — to one of these the Russian will give himself up wholeheartedly . . . The kindest man may suddenly somehow turn into a loathsome debauchee and criminal; it is only a matter of his getting caught up in this whirlwind, in the fatal whirl of convulsive and momentary self-negation and self-destruction, so peculiar to the Russian national character at certain crucial moments. (1873, "Vlas")

Extremity wedded to contrast produces the peculiar Dostoevskian effects of lighting, of chiaroscuro; in description, salient features jut almost symbolically out of the surrounding dark. Raskolnikov, on his first visit to the pawnbroker, rings the bell: "A moment later, the door was opened a tiny crack: the old woman was looking over her visitor with evident distrust through the crack, and all that could be seen were her little eyes, glittering out of the darkness" (I.1). In his first visit to Sonya's room, we read: "The candle end had long since started to flicker out in the crooked candlestick, dimly lighting up in the poverty-stricken room the murderer and the harlot who had so strangely been reading together the eternal book" (IV.4). A similar Rembrandt-like illumination informs the scene where the truth about Raskolnikov dawns on his friend Razumikhin:

> It was dark in the corridor; they were standing by the lamp. For a minute they looked at one another in silence. Razumikhin remembered that minute all his life. Raskolnikov's burning and steady look seemed to grow more intense every moment, piercing into his soul, into his consciousness. Suddenly Razumikhin shuddered. Something strange, as it were, passed between them . . . Some idea, some hint, as it were, slipped, something awful, hideous, and suddenly understood on both sides. . . . Razumikhin turned pale as a corpse.
>
> "Do you understand now?" Raskolnikov said suddenly, his face twitching nervously. (IV.3)

Almost any one of his scenes will bear out the statement in *Diary of a Writer* that "lighting could be made interesting." The phrase comes from a remarkable illustration of his visual imagination at work, too long to quote here except to note that, in this detailed suggestion for a genre painting of "a poor Jewess in childbed" by the light of a candle, he goes on to justify some pitiful details with the parenthetical assertion: "There is such poverty, gentlemen, I swear there is; this is the purest realism — realism, so to speak, reaching to the fantastic" (March 1877, 3.2).

By this distaste for bright daylight and preference for dimly lighted nocturnal scenes, Dostoevsky converts his backgrounds into a marvelous and mysterious space, out of which visions are momentarily born and into which they threaten momentarily to return. Alone among the great Russian novelists of his time, he rejected the clarity of the daylight background of nature. But then he was alone among the great Russian novelists of his time in taking the city as his subject. That the connection between the manner and the milieu is not fortuitous is made explicit in one of the stories where the narrator, walking the steaming night streets of Petersburg, confesses: "It suddenly occurred to me that if the gaslights were extinguished everywhere it would be more cheerful, that the heart is sadder when they are burning just because they shed a light on everything." [31]

From the foregoing, the nature of Dostoevsky's descriptions (which drew Tolstoy's praise[32]) becomes clear. The city evoked with such economy is perfectly real, but it is no more seen in an open and even light than anything or anyone in these books. This was well put more than half a century ago by Merezhkovsky, who found that "the author of *Crime and Punishment* understands the poetry of the city" and explained: "In forests, on the seashore, under the open sky, everybody saw the mystery, everybody felt the abysses of nature, but in our dismal prosaic cities no one, except Dostoevsky, felt so deeply *the mysteries of human life*." [33] So with his descriptions of people, a momentary notation establishes all that is important, the expressive physical correlative of personality. Raskolnikov is "remarkably handsome, with beautiful dark eyes, dark hair, taller than average, slim and well built" (I.1). Sonya, in her everyday clothes, is "a modestly and even poorly dressed girl, still very young, almost like a child, with a modest and seemly manner, with a candid but somewhat frightened face" (III.4). Description in Dostoevsky is usually based in some character's point of view — a device which tends to charge it, however casual it may be, with multiple significance. The opening description of Marmeladov in the tavern is exceptional only in its length. He and Raskolnikov have been scrutinizing each other:

> He was a man over fifty, of medium height and solid build, grizzled and balding, his face yellow, even greenish from constant drinking, his eyelids swollen, and out of them gleaming two reddish eyes, tiny as chinks, but lively. Yet there was something very strange about him; his eyes shone as though with exaltation — perhaps there were even sense and intelligence there — but at the same time there gleamed something like madness. He was dressed in an old, completely ragged black dress coat, with the buttons missing. Only one still held on somehow, and that one he buttoned, evidently wishing to preserve a semblance of respectability. A crumpled, stained, and bespattered shirtfront stuck out from his nankeen waistcoat. His face had been clean-shaven, like a clerk's, but evidently not recently, so that a thick grey stubble covered it. And there was something respectable and clerk-

like in his manner, too. But he was uneasy; he kept ruffling up his hair and sometimes, in misery, would prop up his head with both hands, resting his ragged elbows on the stained and sticky table. (I.2)

Intuition here alternates with an exact observation that is never idle: in view of all that has preceded it, that last phrase about Marmeladov's "ragged elbows on the stained and sticky table" takes on an enormous force of implication. And the whole passage may remind us that Dostoevsky's most intense (one might almost say, most loving) descriptions are lavished on objects that are physically sordid; descriptions of conventional beauty tend to be unemotional, like the cold panorama of the Neva cited earlier, or unconvincing — and, in any case, they are rare. The reason is that here as elsewhere Dostoevsky sees not a simple, conventional unity but a complex union of opposites. Beauty for him is not truth, nor truth beauty: both are ambiguous. The fullest statement on the subject is put into the mouth of Dmitri Karamazov:

Beauty is a terrible and awful thing! It is terrible because it is indefinable, and it cannot be defined because God has given us nothing but riddles. Here the shores come together; here all contradictions live side by side. I'm very uneducated . . . but I have thought a great deal about this. There are a terrible lot of mysteries! . . . Beauty! I can't endure the thought that a man of lofty mind and heart begins with the ideal of the Madonna and ends with the ideal of Sodom. Even more terrible: a man with the ideal of Sodom in his soul does not renounce the ideal of the Madonna, and his heart truly burns, truly burns — just as in his youthful, innocent days. No, man is broad, even too broad: I'd have him narrower. The devil only knows what it's all about! What the mind regards as shame is sheer beauty to the heart. Is there beauty in Sodom? Believe me, it is exactly in Sodom that it resides for the great majority of people — did you know that secret? It's awful that beauty should be mysterious as well as terrible. God and the devil are fighting there and the battlefield is the hearts of men.[34]

A similar observation can be made about his working conceptions of tragedy and comedy. Neither is conventionally pure in his hands. Vyacheslav Ivanov has written that "true tragedy, like true mysticism, is possible only on the soil of a deeply realistic view of the world," adding that "the tragic struggle must be fought out between the actual and the effective realities." [35] Translated into terms of character, this axiom raises problems for the tragic novelist who also acknowledges an allegiance to realism. Dostoevsky puts this concisely in a letter to Pobedonostsev in which he discusses his troubles with the figure of Father Zossima in *The Brothers Karamazov;* will his design, he wonders, be intelligible to the public? "And here, besides, there are the obligations of artistry: there was a need to present a figure modest and majestic — while life is full of the comic and only majestic in its inner sense, so that willy-nilly, out of artistic requirements, I was obliged in the biography of my monk to touch on even the most vulgar sides, in order not to damage artistic realism." [36] The truly comic is just as unstable in the major novels. We have it pure in the naive expression of the letter Raskolnikov receives from his mother and in Razumikhin's immediate and ludicrous reverence for Dunya — but the one immediately induces an acute anxiety and feeds a desperate resolve in Raskolnikov, while his teasing Razumikhin immediately precedes his tense first interview with Porfiry.[37] True humor and gaiety are possible only for the naive characters and serve in their rarity to emphasize by contrast the grimmer realities and issues of Dostoevsky's world. What is much more common is the sour joke, the joke in deliberate bad taste, like Svidrigailov's suicide. Here the comic is frozen half metamorphosed into its opposite; the result is a concept occupying a central place in Dostoevsky's poetics — the grotesque — and constituting, in his new treatment, not the least of his claims to greatness.

THE GROTESQUE

The grotesque, like the romantic realism to which it is so closely connected in the nineteenth century, has received little attention in its own right. Both concepts have seemed marginal to critics and literary historians. Thus the romantic realists tend most often to be considered as realists *tout court* — as great but imperfect links in the chain of evolution that culminated in such figures as Flaubert and Tolstoy. This is as fair as calling the finest rosé d'Anjou a respectable though weak and imperfect sort of claret — but we have until recently been living in the age of literary claret. By the same token, the modern grotesque has been studied chiefly in its relation to romanticism, as one of the several forms of that movement's reaction against the neoclassical notion of ancient art; and in this view it has tended to be equated with the monstrous, the supernatural, and the quasi-human. It is therefore fitting but (for present purposes) regrettable that the only recent study of the subject — Wolfgang Kayser's *The Grotesque in Art and Literature* — follows this line, modernizing it somewhat to include Kafka and the surrealists, but rather extending the traditional notion than revising it. Kayser centers his discussion on the German tradition, treats Gogol superficially — he is, after all, closest to this tradition — and Balzac, Dickens, and Dostoevsky not at all. "The grotesque," he finds, "is a structure. Its nature could be summed up in [the] phrase . . . *The grotesque is the estranged world. . . .* It is our world, which has been transformed." In his final formulation, the grotesque is "an attempt to invoke and subdue the demonic aspects of the world." [38] Such an approach could accommodate Dostoevsky only occasionally, in scenes like that of Ivan Karamazov and the devil, in the reports of Svidrigailov's haunting, or in an early piece like "The Landlady" — and even then only uneasily.

On the other hand, Victor Hugo's manifesto of 1827, by its very nature, opens more promising perspectives, according a new and sustained importance to the idea of the grotesque, though it persistently skirts a definition. In what is perhaps his most meaningful statement he insists that "it is from the fruitful union of the grotesque with the sublime, that the modern spirit is born — so complex, so various in its forms, so inexhaustible in its creations, and quite opposed, in so being, to the uniform simplicity of the classical spirit." [39] If it was Hugo's genius to have seen this union, he can hardly be blamed for failing to foresee its nature as other writers would develop it. Relying on tradition, he finds the essence of the grotesque to be comic, and its function that of a foil (as in Shakespearian tragicomedy): "Alongside the sublime, as a means of contrast, the grotesque is . . . the richest source that nature can open up to art." Sublimity unrelieved, he finds, denies an audience's natural need to rest a little, "even from beauty"; hence the value of the grotesque as "a pause, a term of comparison, a point of departure from which one rises toward the beautiful with fresher and keener perception." [40] Hugo's argument is oriented toward the future, but it is based necessarily on the literature and aesthetics of the past. So the grotesque remains for him comic (albeit a higher form), and beauty a unitary term, a still pure ideal.

Thirty years after the manifesto, literary fact had superseded this theory. Just as realism had outgrown its own comic heritage to achieve a protean independence, so the grotesque outgrew its comic heritage, with similar results. The first process was completed a little earlier, but both are products of the century — the second, if anything, even more so. Already in the second decade, the grotesque had been made to invade the real, the seriously real, in Hoffmann's tales; but it is only with Gogol that we see a major attempt to *identify* it with the real, symbolically, in the Petersburg tales. (The significance of this innovation is clear if we compare these stories with the Ukrainian tales he wrote before them, where a conventional — which is to say, purely supernatural — grotesque is exploited strictly on a folk basis.) Then, two years after the Petersburg tales were collected, Dostoevsky began his own writing career.

He began it, as we have seen, by attempting to imitate Gogol in this respect, notably in *The Double,* with its mechanical images, baroque narrative style, and the rest. His reasons for abandoning the Gogolian form of grotesque are instructive. In the first place, he found the comic angle of vision inadequate to the truth he was after: "In belles lettres there are types and real people, i.e., the sober and maximally full truth about a man . . . In Manilov and Sobakevich we do not see real people . . . A type is very often a half-truth, and a half-truth is very often a lie. Oh, it is not to belittle such a genius as Gogol that I say this. In satire full truth is downright impossible."[41] The comic eye sees too narrowly; equally important, however, was the insufficiency of the recording instrument, as far as Dostoevsky was concerned. For the Gogolian vision was clothed in a style from which it was inseparable: his people were literally made of words, their idiosyncrasies being less psychological than lexical, their vitality a borrowing from that of their ever-present creator. Gogol's stories, like poetry, could not be paraphrased and retain their force; Dostoevsky's, by and large, could — and this is one measure of their essential realism. Gogol's grotesque, in short, inhered in style, where Dostoevsky's own would inhere in situation, as a quality of experience. Where Gogol created a grotesque world, Dostoevsky discovered one.

Once more, the eye was central. The eye, however, is controlled by the mind's categories of meaning. Thus the grotesque — any deviation from a conventional ("natural") norm so sharp as to seem monstrous, but not so sharp as to obscure the norm itself — can always appear comic if the perceiver is emotionally detached enough.[42] Such detachment, easy for Gogol, was almost impossible for Dostoevsky, who saw always, underlying the greatest comic works of Cervantes, Voltaire, Griboyedov, and Gogol himself, a pure and moving tragedy.[43] In this, of course, he was at one not only with the romantic view of Don Quixote, but with the whole anticomic temper of romanticism. This is made explicit enough in a letter of 1868, where he observes that "of all the good [*prekrasnye*] characters in Christian literature, Don Quixote stands as the most finished of all. But he is good solely because he is ludicrous at the same time. Dickens' Pickwick (an idea infinitely weaker than Don Quixote; but enormous all the same) is also ludicrous and that is just his appeal. There is compassion for the good man who is laughed at and who does not know his own value — and so there appears sympathy in the reader too. This arousing of compassion is the secret of humor." [44]

So in his own writing, Dostoevsky frequently inverts the standard comic practice by taking a grotesque situation and depriving the reader of any possible emotional detachment, while at the same time he intensifies the aberration. It is a technique that produces a powerful and ambiguous effect, like a conversation with an intelligent madman. Here, by invalidating old responses and compelling new ones, was one secret of his "new word" in literature. The effect is seen most consistently in *Notes from Underground,* and its mechanism is formulated most succinctly by the underground narrator when he refers, in a telling juxtaposition, to "those filthiest, most ludicrous, and most terrible moments of my life" (II.4). Here is signalized a new discovery of the disgusting and disquieting as material for an art that is neither comic nor sensational: a new advance for realism in its reclaiming of territory from the comic. Thus does Dostoevsky force his way past our conventional responses. The resulting experience is an acutely painful one for the reader, difficult to define and difficult to resolve, just because the presentation involves him in the most serious and the most real problems — makes him feel, in Marmeladov's phrase, all the impossibility of having nowhere to go. Such a direct, almost hypnotic hold on the reader's consciousness is truly realism in a higher sense.[45]

The fact constitutes a large part of Dostoevsky's enormous contribution to the novel, for he differs from Hugo in refusing to see the grotesque as an adjunct or foil to beauty. Coming midway in the century-long process of the revaluation of beauty, after the romantic discovery of "horrible beauty" and before the Yeatsian notion of "terrible beauty," he sees the grotesque rather as a necessary avenue to spiritual beauty in art, in the same way that he claimed suffering as the necessary way to happiness in life. Whatever these terms may mean to Dostoevsky, they contain not the slightest hint of their conventional meanings: the one has nothing to do with decoration or passivity, just as the other has nothing to do with placid contentment. In fact, despite his constant references to them as ends ("happiness is *bought with* suffering"), it is doubtful on the evidence of the novels that either occupies more than a nominal place in his universe. He could never have written a piece like *Family Happiness* or a scene like the famous encounter of Prince Andrey with the oak tree, because the world of nature tended in his myth to be less a fact of life than a religious symbol.[46] One comes in reading him to the eventual realization that the grotesque defines the very atmosphere of his world. The seventeen-year-old writer, saturated in romanticism, had already taken such a position. On 9 August 1838 he wrote his brother: "One condition alone is given to the lot of man: the atmosphere of his soul consists of a merging of heaven with earth. What an unlawful child, then, is man. The law of spiritual nature is broken. . . . It seems to me that our world is a purgatory of heavenly spirits obscured by sinful thought. It seems to me that the world has taken on a negative sense, and that out of a lofty, refined spirituality has emerged a satire." [47] In such a fallen world (of which the city is a symbol, just as the life of nature is the symbol of redemption), people are stripped down to their basic humanity, much as they are in the writing of the French existentialists; the difference is that Dostoevsky's grotesque world is linked to a traditional, Christian source of meaning by the slender thread of aspiration, whereas his spiritual descendants, breaking that thread, are left not with the aberrant (since there is nothing to aberr from), but with "the absurd."

This is not to say that the absurd is absent from Dostoevsky's universe, but only to point out that it is marginal, serving in its extremity as a foil for the dominant grotesque. In *Crime and Punishment,* absurdity centers on the figure of Svidrigailov. His suicide, for example, is described in comic terms, and the purity of comic effect is preserved by closing the scene with the pulling of the trigger: we do not hear the shot or see the body fall; his death is no more meaningful or real than his life; he can, as it were, vanish but not die. In other words, this figure, inaccessible to any hope of spiritual redemption, is presented as also inaccessible to any large degree of sympathy from the reader — in accordance with the demands of the comic. The way this is managed can be seen in the pleasure-garden scene preceding the suicide. Here, as in Svidrigailov's final dialogue with "Achilles," there is a striking change in narrative style; Dostoevsky comes closer to Gogol in his conscious manipulation of our reactions. The point of view is approximately Svidrigailov's, as the point of view throughout the rest of the novel is approximately Raskolnikov's, and it is as permeated with meaninglessness as the other is pregnant with fateful implication.

An equally notable stylistic manipulation, but one less forced and serving a different end, introduces Sonya in Marmeladov's deathbed scene. Here is the long central sentence, translated as literally as possible to preserve the effect of the original:

> Sonya stopped in the hall at the very threshold, but did not cross over the threshold and gazed like one lost, conscious, it seemed, of nothing, having forgotten about her bought-at-fourth-hand, silk, indecent-here, colored dress with a very long and ludicrous train, and [about] her immense crinoline, which filled up the whole doorway, and about her light-colored shoes, and about the parasol, useless at night, but which she had taken with her, and about the ridiculous round straw hat with a bright flame-colored feather. Under this put-on-at-a-boyish-tilt hat there looked out a thin, pale, and frightened little face with opened mouth and motionless-from-horror eyes. (II.7)

The ludicrous — because incongruous — element that Dostoevsky is at pains to underline here is not absurd but charged with meaning; pre-established sympathy freezes any comic effect and invests a clownish costume with high seriousness by locking it into a new context. This is the work of the true Dostoevskian grotesque.

Throughout the novel the Marmeladov family will furnish the most constant and extreme example of the grotesque, as if the writer were underlining his insistence that such people do exist. Sonya's whole situation, caught above in a kind of verbal icon, is grotesque, though it is less insisted upon probably because her professional life is so extraneous to her saintly function in the book as the exponent of a realized redemption. Besides, she is less realistically presented, hardly a creature of flesh and blood at all.

Her father is already a different story. He is, after all, the cause of her fall, rendering it sacrificial where his own is utterly without redemption. If she promises to surmount hers, he is the acquiescent victim, as he is the creator, of his own: "Why am I to be pitied, you say? Yes! there's nothing to pity me for! I ought to be crucified, crucified on a cross, not pitied! But crucify, O Judge, crucify and when it is done, have pity. And then I myself will go to be crucified, for it's not merriment I thirst for, but tears and affliction" (I.2). His story, told to Raskolnikov and to the tavern at large, is accompanied by the most chilling laughter:

> "I was at Sonya's today; I went to ask her for a pick-me-up! Heh, heh, heh!"
>
> "Surely she didn't give it to you?" cried one of the newcomers, and began to roar with laughter.

A student of the subject has noted that Dostoevsky's heroes "rarely laugh a good, gay, innocent laugh." [48] Yet laughter is frequent in his novels, of the kind just quoted. Marmeladov's giggle is a pathetic sign of self-abasement; the newcomer's guffaw is no less inappropriate. Both, though differently motivated, serve as counterpoint, as instruments of the grotesque.

A parallel function is served by Marmeladov's stylized, highfalutin bureaucratic speech, at once a reminder of his past calling and the last remnant of his doomed aspirations to dignity. The contrast is deliberate between his ragged appearance and the language with which he accosts Raskolnikov: "May I take the liberty, my dear sir, of engaging you in polite conversation? For although your exterior is not prepossessing, my experience descries in you an educated man and one unaccustomed to drink" (I.2). The comic possibilities of such a contrast — which Dostoevsky forgoes or, more specifically, turns to other uses — can be seen in his revered colleague, Dickens. Mr. Micawber is a kind of literary cousin to Marmeladov. He bears a similarly ludicrous name and speaks in a similarly ludicrous style, but in his case the adage that the style is the man bears a very different significance. It is not just that Micawber's speech provides an emotional outlet in amusement, but that it is made an aesthetic justification of his personal failings: art in him atones for nature. For Marmeladov's situation there is no issue except death, and all the art of Dostoevsky's presentation only underlines this hopeless truth. The comic, inverted, takes on a tragic force.

The same grotesque inversion can be seen in Dostoevsky's handling of the comic device of the public scandal. It is a traditional device canonized in the *romans gais* of which Dostoevsky was so fond,[49] and of course in Gogol's classic *Inspector General;* it persists in our own day as the basis of the Marx Brothers' farce. Man, as individual, enjoys the violation of those constricting social conventions that purport to define him. He also enjoys the unmasking of a villain, and in *Crime and Punishment* there is one petty villain whose unmasking caps the first of the two great scandal scenes. At the end of Marmeladov's wake, Luzhin, the pompous and malevolent suitor for Dunya's hand — who has, incidentally a verbal tag ("very, very" [*vesma i vesma*]), just as Uriah Heep has his " 'umble" — receives his comeuppance on the combined testimony of Lebezyatnikov and Raskolnikov, who convict him of trying to make Sonya appear a thief. The satisfaction one feels at this discomfiture is on a par with that produced by Micawber's great accusation: "You Heep of infamy!" Even here, however, the context mitigates the comic effect: "Sonya, timid by nature, had known before this that she could be destroyed more easily than anyone, and that anyone could insult her with impunity. Yet, all the same, up to that moment it had seemed to her that trouble might be avoided somehow by care, meekness and submissiveness . . . [Now] in spite of her triumph and her justification . . . a feeling of helplessness and injury made her heart contract. She began to weep hysterically"

(V.3). In this incident, pathos alternates with comedy; in the rest of the long scene, they are inextricably mixed.

The very conception of this "senseless" funeral dinner is ominous; Marmeladov's unhinged widow puts into it the last of her little money — perhaps, as the narrator conjectures, out of that peculiar poor man's pride that seeks to keep up appearances at all costs. Her helper in the arrangements is "a pitiful little Pole" who is living ("God knows why") in the building; the absurdity of his situation and behavior is mentioned only in passing, but it is indicative of the tone of the whole affair. Discord underlies the apparent harmony of the preparations: it is symbolized in the table appointments, lent by the various lodgers and "of all styles and sizes." When the landlady, Amalia Ivanovna, dresses up suitably for the occasion, Marmeladov's widow suspects her of preening and condescension, and resolves to "bring her up short and remind her of her proper place." When the party first assembles, it consists of

> the little Pole; one miserable clerk in a greasy coat, with a pimply face, a repulsive smell about him, and nothing at all to say; and a deaf and almost totally blind old man who had once worked in some post office and whom someone, for reasons unknown, had maintained since time immemorial at Amalia Ivanovna's. There also appeared one drunken retired lieutenant, essentially a quartermaster clerk, with the loudest and most indecent laugh, and — just imagine — without a waistcoat! One of the visitors sat straight down to the table without even greeting Katerina Ivanovna; and, finally, one individual for lack of a suit was about to present himself in his bathrobe — but this was so unseemly that Amalia Ivanovna and the little Pole managed between them to get him out of there. The Pole, however, had brought with him two other Poles who had never lived at Amalia Ivanovna's and whom no one had seen on the premises before. All this irritated Katerina Ivanovna extremely. For whom, then, had all these preparations been made? Even the children, to save space, had not been seated at the table . . . [Instead, they were] set up in a back corner on a trunk. Both of the little ones had been placed on a bench, while Polenka as a big girl had to look after them, feed them, and keep their little noses wiped like well-bred children's. (V.2)

It is necessary to quote all these details because, by their oppressive accumulation, they establish the tonality of the scene. The same contrast operates here that operated in Raskolnikov's first meeting with Marmeladov — except that in this case it is the presence of death and madness that diverts any comic force into grotesquerie. Soon after the company is assembled, scandal breaks into the open. Katerina Ivanovna, in a stage whisper, pours out to Raskolnikov "all her suppressed feelings and her righteous indignation at the failure of the dinner — her indignation, however, frequently yielding place to the liveliest and most uncontrollable laughter at the expense of the guests there assembled, and most of all at the expense of her landlady." Her laughter, as chilling as Marmeladov's earlier, turns continually into fits of coughing. She shows Raskolnikov her bloodstained handkerchief. She continues to insult her guests and they, sniggering with delight, encourage the quartermaster clerk to make a scene. The landlady tells a pointless story in absurd broken Russian; Katerina Ivanovna moves her to frenzy with open insults. Bedlam breaks loose:

> Amalia Ivanovna started to run about the room, shouting at the top of her voice, that she was mistress of the house and that Katerina Ivanovna must "away from her rooms go this minute"; then she rushed for some reason to collect the silver spoons from the table. A great racket and uproar arose; the children burst into tears. Sonya ran to try to restrain Katerina Ivanovna, but when Amalia Ivanovna shouted something about "the yellow ticket," Katerina Ivanovna pushed Sonya aside and rushed at Amalia Ivanovna.

But this is not the end. The sudden appearance of Luzhin brings a momentary respite, until it appears that he has come to lodge his trumped-up accusation of theft against Sonya. For a while he has the company with him, and new outcries arise. Then Lebezyatnikov comes forward with his confounding testimony, which Raskolnikov supports, and Luzhin beats a crestfallen retreat, the outcries of the disorderly company now against him. The quartermaster clerk is moved to hurl a glass after him, but it strikes Amalia Ivanovna: "She screamed, and the clerk, who had lost his balance in throwing, fell heavily under the table" (V.3). The farcical tempo accelerates — Amalia Ivanovna takes Katerina Ivanovna for the cause of this (amid loud laughter) and orders her out of the house immediately: "And with these words she began to grab everything she could lay her hands on that belonged to Katerina Ivanovna, and throw it on the floor. Half dead already, almost fainting, gasping for breath and pale, Katerina Ivanovna jumped up from the bed where she had sunk in exhaustion and hurled herself at Amalia Ivanovna." After a brief and unequal struggle, she runs out into the street, "with the vague purpose of going somewhere now, immediately, and at whatever cost, to find justice." The energy and the gestures of farce now move to a climax, but so do the ever-present tragic motifs:

Polenka, terrified, had taken refuge with the children on their trunk in the corner, and there, her arms around the two little ones, all atremble, she set about waiting for her mother to come back. Amalia Ivanovna dashed raging about the room, screaming, wailing, and hurling to the floor everything she could lay her hands on. The lodgers were yelling incoherently; some were commenting as best they could on what had happened; others quarreled and swore; still others struck up a song . . .

"Now it's time for me to go," thought Raskolnikov. "Well, Sofya Semyonovna, let's see what you'll say now [to his confession]!"

And he set off for Sonya's room. (V. 3)

For sheer grotesque power this scene comes close to rivaling the scene of Lear on the heath. Throughout his career Dostoevsky developed the device of scandal, and he deployed it widely;[50] it had appeared in simpler form as early as *The Double* and plays a major role in each of the great novels, beginning with the prologue to the series, *Notes from Underground* (the scene at the Hotel de Paris). It serves admirably his tendency to observe the unities of time and place, since it brings together a host of important characters and allows an explosive forward movement of the action, fed by complex and intense collisions. In addition, it serves the twin functions of confession and exposure — and, in some of its variations, the confrontation in action of opposing ideologies. The device is a sensational one, deriving now from farce, now from melodrama; that Dostoevsky can make it produce so different an effect precisely because of its "low" derivation is yet another example of the way his work tends, as Vinogradov noted, "toward a syncretism of genres." [51]

In the scene of the funeral dinner, madness is only one of several themes or motives contributing to the grotesque effect. But in the scene on the street a little later, where Katerina Ivanovna forces her terrified children, bizarrely costumed, to become streetsingers, it alone is operative. In this companion piece to the earlier scandal — played now before the whole city — is the foreseen end of the elder Marmeladov's tragedy, for it is also Katerina Ivanovna's death scene. "Ah, let us sing in French, 'Cinq Sous,' " she cries, for "seeing that it is in French, people will know at once that you are children of good family, and that will be much more touching" (V.4). Here the subject of madness, which the romantics had rescued from the area of comedy, can be seen rescued in turn from all romantic exaltation. The picture, while hardly usual, is distressingly real — and even Katerina Ivanovna's ravings contain enough desperate truth to make it clear that the grotesquerie of madness is only one extreme of a continuum on which all human experience has a place. She was once a governor's daughter, as she is forever insisting; and Marmeladov had been an honest and provident husband and father. If we are seeing the fifth act of their double tragedy, we are at least aware of the preceding ones, with their beginnings in "normality."

The point is important because it reminds us of a peculiarity of Dostoevsky's grotesque already implicit in his criticism of Gogol's characters (quoted above). For him the grotesque is most often a quality of situation or of behavior and not — as with Gogol and Dickens — a quality of character, except insofar as a situation may have left its permanent impress on a character. The Marmeladovs are explained in terms of their situation and their history, which cannot be said of any Gogolian character: humors have no past. Henry James made the same point about the grotesque characters of Dickens; they add nothing to our understanding of human character. Just the opposite is true of Dostoevsky's, and for exactly the reason James went on to formulate so well: for the truly great novelist "there are no oddities, for him there is nothing outside of humanity." [52] By compelling us to revise our usual responses to apparent oddity, Dostoevsky at once ennobled the grotesque and made it a powerful instrument for enlarging the province of realism. It is not just that the realistic (or naturalistic) is freighted with symbolism, but rather — as Renato Poggioli put it — that "the naturalistic and the symbolic are interchangeable in the world of Dostoevski." [53]

It will be obvious that neither the nature nor the extent of the Dostoevskian grotesque is exhausted in the examples here cited; further examples, and further variations, could be traced easily and at length. Such a tracing, however, would not serve the present purpose — which is less to elaborate a system than to describe in its main features a neglected but central element in Dostoevsky's art. "Tragedy," he once wrote, "consists in the consciousness of monstrosity" (*Tragediya sostoit v soznanii urodlivosti*).[54] So, in a certain sense, did beauty for him. He saw both as hallmarks of modern reality and chose to express his vision in terms of the grotesque city. Here, taking "modern" in a narrower sense than Hugo intended it — and so converting his retrospect into a prophecy — was the modern spirit born of the fruitful union of the grotesque with the sublime. In this respect as in others, romantic realism underwent a mutation in Dostoevsky, gained a new direction, and so a new lease on life. For his is no longer a romantic realism, though it exists at a similar tangent to the direction of Flaubert or Tolstoy. Many names have been suggested for it, and we might call it "symbolic realism" to emphasize its difference from what came before or "mythical realism" to emphasize the continuity.[55] It is in any case the instrument whereby he achieved his myth of Petersburg — the fantastic city that symbolizes and contains lives as rootless, as abstract, as grotesque, as drab, and as incandescent as its own.

Conclusion

To ask now how Dostoevsky is related to the romantic realists is to raise a formidable series of questions about his art, about theirs, and about the terms of the whole discussion so far. Are not these terms, it may be asked, rather arbitrary and narrow? Why limit romantic realism to Balzac, Dickens, and Gogol — to the questionable exclusion of writers like Stendhal, Hugo, even Flaubert? Is there really only one realism? And why, among a field that strikingly includes all manner of popular writers like Paul de Kock, Dumas, Sue — all of whom also inspired Dostoevsky's enthusiasm and clearly influenced his art — pick only these three for consideration?

Moreover, what exactly is the nature of this consideration? Is it a question of influence or of accidentally parallel work? Is there any intention to imply a historical movement and, if so, to imply that it existed chiefly to prepare the advent of Dostoevsky? All these questions concern critical limits; there are still others that concern historical limits. Did romantic realism simply turn into realism, and, if so, where does Dostoevsky fit into the picture? Or, if the tradition somehow continued, what happened to it during the rest of the nineteenth century and in our own? Trying to meet these questions offers a final chance to qualify — and in qualifying to clarify — what has been said in the preceding chapters.

CONNECTIONS

First of all, romantic realism itself.

The very fact that literary historians and critics have been able to argue for a plurality of romanticisms and a plurality of realisms makes any arbitrary limitation of the hybrid term doubly impossible. Romantic realism is possible in countless varieties, in infinitely variable proportions. Indeed, considering the difficulty of marshaling wide consent for a definition of either of its components, it is likely that a zealous application of the terms could be made to cover almost any novelist of the last century: this is particularly true if we take them to be generic rather than historical. Have we not been told that the novel form is in itself realistically oriented — and that every work of literature was in its day romantic? But even on a historical footing, one must admit many writers not considered here. Stendhal, for all his eighteenth-century inheritance, produced work — most notably in *Le Rouge et le noir* — that was highly realistic precisely because it was highly romantic: indeed, a point-by-point demonstration of the realistic propensities inherent in French romanticism could find no better text. Hugo, in *Notre Dame de Paris* and even more in *Les Misérables,* shows a different combination of the two; they seem more distinguishable, the romantic lyrical note obviously primary, the romantic intention allowing or disallowing realistic presentation from chapter to chapter, admitting the wonderful chapter on Parisian argot but obstructing any view of Jean Valjean as a fully human being. Hugo the novelist is a romantic realist in whom the adjective heavily outweighs the noun — a fact, incidentally, that makes all the more striking the prophetic clairvoyance of Hugo the critic, who not only foresaw the new importance of the grotesque, but at the age of twenty-one called for a new type of novel, the dramatic novel, which might imitate the movement of life, might speak to the eye by descriptions and to the intelligence by the way the characters "could represent, by their several and repeated collisions, all the forms of the work." [1] Here, even more than in *Les Misérables,* is adumbrated the Parisian novel of Balzac and the "polyphonic" novel of Dostoevsky.

The preponderance of "romantic" in the romantic realism of Hugo's novels finds its opposite in the practice of Flaubert. Charles Lalo was not the first critic to observe that he was "a passionate romantic," though he "strayed into realism" and though he was the official "apostle of the impersonality of art." [2] The extent of Flaubert's willed victory over an inherent romanticism in *Madame Bovary* and *L'Education sentimentale,* however, shows him in the role no longer of romantic realist, but of antiromantic realist, the unsurpassed exemplar of a new poetics that drew on previous work only to challenge it.

But what — to take one final example — are we to make of a writer like Conrad, who confessed:

The romantic feeling of reality was in me an inborn faculty. This in itself may be a curse but when disciplined by a sense of personal responsibility and a recognition of the hard facts of existence shared with the rest of mankind becomes but a point of view from which the very shadows of life appear endowed with an internal glow. And such romanticism is not a sin. It is none the worse for the knowledge of truth. It only tries to make the best of it, hard as it may be; and in this hardness discovers a certain aspect of beauty.[3]

His preface to *The Secret Agent* reads quite like the program of a latter-day Balzac or Dostoevsky when he says: "Then the vision of an enormous town presented itself, of a monstrous town more populous than some continents and in its man-made might as if indifferent to heaven's frowns and smiles; a cruel devourer of the world's light. There was room enough there to place any story, depth enough there for any passion, variety enough there for any setting, darkness enough to bury five millions of lives." It would seem that these statements, to the extent they represent his actual work, must mark Conrad, too, as a romantic realist.

Yet these admissions not only do not affect the canonical status of Balzac and Dickens; they actually underline it. For they all refer to isolated works, and not to a sustained achievement, to a gradually built corpus whose very diversity and volume allows a rivalry not so much with the *état civil* as with the *état naturel* itself. Thus they remind us, by way of forcible contrast, of what Stefan Zweig claimed for the trio of Balzac, Dickens, and Dostoevsky when he set them apart from all the rest of their nineteenth-century colleagues as novelists "in the higher sense," each endowed with an encyclopedic genius, each "a universal artist who constructs a cosmos, peopling it with types of his own making, giving it laws of gravitation that apply to it alone. . . . Each figure, each happening in such a world will be so impressed with the author's personality, that they not only become typical for him but for us likewise . . . a vision of a new kind of world." [4] That is, they were mythmakers, and this condition was one to which more self-consciously "artistic" writers, concerned with the maximum refinement of each single work, could not attain. This is acknowledged in Flaubert's criticism of Balzac: "What a man Balzac would have been if he had known how to write! But he lacked only that. An artist, after all, would not have accomplished so much, would not have had that amplitude." [5] What allows their work this amplitude, while at the same time serving it as a unifying focus, is the inexhaustible theme of the city — in all the ways we have seen.

But what, one might well ask, about those other and equally industrious mythifiers of the city, the popular novelists, Dumas and Sue, Reade and Collins, Butkov and Krestovsky, purveyors of *la littérature industrielle?* Did they not do at least as much to create a myth of the city — and did not the first pair at least influence Dostoevsky as much as any greater writer? Are not in fact many of the techniques here ascribed to romantic realism ascribable as well to them? Just as there is a *bas romantisme,* is there not a *bas romantisme réaliste?* There is, and it did influence Dostoevsky — as, indeed, it influenced Balzac and Dickens.[6] This last fact is already a reason for excluding them from consideration here: what was least perishable in their work has survived in the work of others, allied to a more serious myth. The myth of the popular novelists, as the most brilliant of their students has shown, represented not radical discovery but conservative reassurance. In it figured only the very rich and the very poor — and in such a way, moreover, that the poor readers of these works might conclude that the miseries of the rich were no different from their own, their lot, in the last analysis, no better.[7] The popular myth was serious in its effect, but not in its conception. Nor, as time has shown, can the forms it took be called literature in any lasting sense.

The work of Balzac and Dickens was all that these other works were not, and it was, moreover, popular itself; the romantic realists were perhaps the last great novelists (in the West, at least) to escape the situation and the effects of alienation. They wrote just at the time when a tremendous new audience was forming, and they took advantage (at a price) of the means that came into being to satisfy the new market. Sainte-Beuve had said that French literature in the third decade of the century was becoming "industrial," and the same could be said of English and Russian, with the result that Balzac, Dickens, and Dostoevsky could and did call themselves proletarian writers, working against deadlines, writing in installments for magazines and newspapers — forced, even when a political censorship was absent, to submit to the practical censorship of audience and publisher alike.

That they could do so and still achieve greatness is a mystery that must be set down finally to genius, though the ability of genius to work within these limitations may have something to do with one further similarity among them. Each had a literary education based to a significant extent on second-rate literature or worse. Balzac formed his tastes on Pigault-Lebrun and Ducray-Duminil, on the *roman gai,* the *roman noir,* and the melodrama; Dickens, who shared a liking for Paul de Kock, devoured indiscriminately popular works and eighteenth-century classics while still a child; Gogol, besides the usual schoolboy smattering, had chiefly the Ukrainian folk and puppet tradition to draw on. While each felt the high calling of art, each had roots in a rather different tradition. What is more, though all three had achieved a substantial measure of fame by the middle of the 1840s, they seemed almost completely unaware of each other's work.

Dostoevsky is the exception here. Not only was his literary education incomparably wider than any of the others', but it included them all, and if we can find relics of his youthful enthusiasm for all the transient *succès d'estime* or *de scandale* in his early letters, the later ones testify to an abiding admiration for precisely these three.[8] In this persistence of attention to Balzac, Dickens, and Gogol one can see him the inheritor of romantic realism. And, in seeing, one must confront the question of influence.

"It is difficult," Grossman began an article over half a century ago, "to find in world literature a second example of such an astonishing kinship between two writers of different countries and generations as is displayed by Balzac and Dostoevsky." [9] The statement appears exaggerated only until one actually takes up its challenge or unless second-rate writers are admitted to the comparison. For Dostoevsky's work over the entire length of his career bears witness to this kinship. He made his literary debut in 1844 with a somewhat romanticized translation of *Eugénie Grandet,* and we have seen how he consciously embarked on literary journalism three years later under the sign of Lucien de Rubempré. By the same token, in his last published piece, the Pushkin speech of 1880, he was to cite Rousseau's famous Mandarin passage — not from the original, but in its Balzacian context in *Le Père Goriot*. In the years between, Balzac's presence can be felt constantly. Trying to give his brother an idea of the length of *Poor Folk,* he specified that "its bulk [was] that of *Eugénie Grandet*"; his friend Grigorovich reports that in the forties, "Balzac was our favorite writer; I say 'our' because we were equally engrossed in him, considering him immeasurably above all the French writers." [10] The next decade was spent in imprisonment and exile, with little opportunity for reading; but when, in the sixties, Dostoevsky renewed his literary work, he managed as well to renew his acquaintance with Balzac. Late in that decade, while finishing *The Idiot* in Florence, pressed by deadlines and harassed by creditors, he found the works of Balzac in a local library and spent days there, unable to tear himself away.[11] Moreover, when in the same years he undertook the literary education of his second wife, Anna Grigorievna, the first book he gave her was *Le Père Goriot,* the second, *Les Parents pauvres.*[12]

Testimony is thus abundant that Dostoevsky never lost the enthusiasm he had expressed to his brother as early as 1838. He had read, he wrote, "almost all of Balzac," adding parenthetically, "Balzac is great! His characters are works of the mind of the universe! Not the spirit of the time, but whole millennia prepared by their travail such an issue in the soul of man." [13] The statement is a key one because it suggests better than any other the nature of Balzac's impact on the young Dostoevsky: how, after all, can one be "influenced" by the mind of the universe? What he seems to have appreciated in Balzac from the beginning is exactly the ability — which Balzac himself had seen as a rivalry with God — to create, people, and order a new universe. What Balzac did for him, in short, was to show just how large a scope might be successfully allowed to a novelist's ambition.

For this reason it is idle to search out parallel passages; the presence of Balzac was too large and too diffuse to compel the kind of point-by-point polemic in which we have seen Dostoevsky engaging with Gogol. The fact that Svidrigailov uses Vautrin's favorite expression, "assez causé," or that the description of Rogozhin's house parallels Balzac's description of the Grandet house, proves no more than that Dostoevsky had read Balzac. The situational parallels that have been discovered between *Gambara* and *Netochka Nezvanova, Eugénie Grandet* and "Mr. Prokharchin," *L'Enfant maudit* and "The Landlady," *Le Curé de village* and *The Brothers Karamazov,* or *Ferragus* and *Crime and Punishment* tell no more —if indeed they are not merely fortuitous.[14] Had Balzac been a demonstrable influence, we should see many more signs of it in the early work, where the young Dostoevsky was finding his own manner; what we see there instead are signs of Hoffmann's influence and Gogol's. From them he developed his tools; from Balzac, he developed an orientation.

To all this there is one apparent, and complex, exception. That is the case of *Crime and Punishment* vis-à-vis *Le Père Goriot.* Some of the complexities are historical: did Dostoevsky, for instance, embark on his cycle of great novels by means of a conscious reworking of Balzac's novel? The most assiduous student of the subject intimated that he did — but on a textual basis that has recently been proved erroneous. In his influential study, *Biblioteka Dostoevskogo* (Dostoevsky's Library; 1919), Leonid Grossman cited the ending of Balzac's novel as it had appeared in an 1835 Russian translation in the "Library for Reading":

> He [Rastignac] cast a glance over this buzzing hive, from which it seemed he wished in advance to suck all the honey, and uttered this fateful exclamation:
>
> — Now it's war between us!
>
> He went down into Paris. On the way he still hesitated whether to direct his steps toward the handsome apartment on the Rue d'Artois or to his former dirty apartment at Madame Vauquer's — and woke up before the doors of M. Taillefer. The shade of Vautrin had drawn him to this house and placed his hand on its lock. He closed his eyes fast so as not to see it. He sought an honest pretext in his heart and in his destitution. Victorine loved her father so tenderly! Rastignac asked for Madame Couture. Now he is a millionaire, and proud as a baron.[15]

Grossman assumed that this ending, actually the invention of the translator (and by no means the least of his outrages), was that of Balzac's original — which would have made Rastignac an important precursor of Raskolnikov in his surrender to Vautrin's theories and would have made *Crime and Punishment* in its turn a deliberate response to a picture of triumphant amorality. The fact, however, that the "Library for Reading" version was a distortion of the original does not settle the problem; for the possibility persists that the impressionable young Dostoevsky may in fact have read this version and meditated its lesson for the thirty years until, as is known, he reread the book in French. Or he could have read a truer translation in 1835 in "The Telescope." We shall probably never know.[16]

Whichever *Goriot* he read, it is quite likely that he did read the translation of Janin's review of the book that the "Library for Reading" published in 1835. It included this paragraph:

> It was an amusing mixture of everything on earth — opinions, annoyances, sympathies, pity, despair, ignorance, learning; and over this whole repulsive chaos destitution ruled. The house in which they live as boarders represents the absence of all family ties; such a house is a sort of cross between a jail and a poorhouse. Here everything in the world is a continuous object of calculation — your hunger, your cold, your sickness, and your health. . . . Here M. Balzac has found an excellent opening.[17]

What makes the passage worth quoting, whether or not Dostoevsky ever read it, is the striking way it characterizes his own work, especially *Crime and Punishment*. If Balzac's fiction was regarded as a mixture of everything on earth, Dostoevsky's has been seen as similarly fashioning a new unity out of the most disparate elements — philosophical dialogues, religious confessions, criminal proceedings, low comedy, news of the day, personal prejudices, and private passions.[18] If the Maison Vauquer could be seen as a cross between a jail and poorhouse, so could the houses of Raskolnikov, Razumikhin, and the Marmeladovs.

The point might be almost infinitely extended, and it is the main one to make about Dostoevsky's relation to Balzac. In *Crime and Punishment* he confronts what Henry James called "the lesson of Balzac" and shows that he has mastered it by the originality of his gloss on the Balzacian text: "If he were well depicted in his struggle with Paris, the poor student would furnish one of the most dramatic subjects of our modern civilization." [19] The more specific parallels that have been pointed out so often — the fact that Rastignac and Raskolnikov are both from the provinces, both supported by the sacrifice of mother and sisters, both poised between an angel and a devil, both daunted by the cul-de-sac of poverty and so tempted to immorality — all show Alphonse Karr's celebrated maxim in reverse: *plus c'est la même chose, plus ça change.* The use of contrast as a key device, the enormous role of the city as such, the heightened dramatic element, the serious grotesque — all the items of a shared poetics only go to make the same point, as does the tragic view of the intellect common to both writers.

In short, despite the fact that Balzac was enormously popular in Russia (especially in the forties around the time of his visit there), and despite the fact that Tolstoy, for instance, read him a great deal, Dostoevsky remains the only Russian writer whose work as a whole shows deep affinities with his. The supporter of orthodoxy and autocracy who devised the legend of the Grand Inquisitor was spiritually akin to the Catholic monarchist who reported in his notebooks the "hours of melancholy joy, of laughter and reflection" inspired by "imagining Jesus Christ meeting Julius II or even Leo X." [20] To say this is not to minimize their differences; the consanguinity rests on them, in fact. A young woman who met Dostoevsky during the year before his death reports that he urged her to read without fail *Le Père Goriot, Les Parents pauvres,* and *Un Grand Homme de province à Paris* (it is significant that he should recommend only the Parisian section of *Illusions perdues*). She goes on to record the following conversation:

> "Well, and whom would you rank higher, Balzac or yourself?"
> Dostoevsky did not grin at my simplicity, and after reflecting a second, said:
> "Each of us is valuable only to the extent that he has brought to literature something of his own, something original. That is the whole affair. To compare us is something I cannot do. I think that each has his merits."

Ideas, he added, outlast human beings, and one had to think that, consciously or unconsciously, "one generation continues the work of another." [21] The process, conscious *and* unconscious, is what his own career shows.

To discuss Dostoevsky and Dickens is to enter upon different ground. Here there can be no question of inheritance, for they were substantially of the same generation; less than a decade separates

Dickens' birth in 1812 from Dostoevsky's in 1821. This means that, aside from *Pickwick,* Dostoevsky could have read none of his English colleague's most important work during his formative years; and though it is on record that in the prison hospital at Omsk the only reading he would accept consisted of *Pickwick* and *David Copperfield,* there is no record that he ever knew at firsthand the last three great novels (except, perhaps, for *Bleak House*), in which the Dickensian scope most nearly approached his own.[22] The index to his *Letters* shows that he mentions by name only five works of Dickens — *Pickwick, The Old Curiosity Shop, Dombey and Son, David Copperfield,* and *A Christmas Carol* — as against twenty of Balzac's. Moreover, he was compelled to read them in translation, so that the enormous impact of Dickens' style must have been largely lost to him, despite his rather suspect declaration that "we understand Dickens in Russian translation . . . almost as well as the English, even, perhaps, with all the nuances." [23] Even more clearly than in the case of Balzac, we are dealing with spiritual affinities, rather than influence.

The readiest proof of this is a negative one, available to anyone who is willing to go through the critical literature devoted to the subject of influence.[24] What is most tangible, he will find, is most trivial — as in a Soviet critic's enumeration of no less than twenty-two specific parallels between *Pickwick* and Dostoevsky's minor burlesque, *A Friend of the Family*[25] — or else egregiously wrong, as in Lionel Trilling's pronouncement that "the influence of Dickens upon Dostoevsky is perhaps nowhere exhibited in a more detailed way than in the similarities between Blandois [from *Little Dorrit,* a book Dostoevsky almost certainly did not read] and the shabby-genteel devil of *The Brothers Karamazov* and also Smerdyakov of the same novel." [26] On the other hand, the temptation is sound to find features of the one strongly reminiscent of the other, as the nineteenth-century critic Druzhinin did in their portrayals of children; as Mario Praz does, noting that General Ivolgin in *The Idiot* "recalls Micawber with one or two of the characteristics of William Dorrit";[27] or as Miller does in likening Little Dorrit to Myshkin.[28] It is sound because it can remind us of the considerable extent to which the two writers worked in similar conventions and favored similar themes. Not only did they extend the romantic concern with children to encompass crimes against the young; they both pursued the psychology of crime itself. No longer a willed attitude, as in Balzac, it became the issue of deep self-division and the ground for strange relationships. Edgar Johnson has observed that "the uneasy slumbers of Jonas and Montague [in *Martin Chuzzlewit*] and their dark dreams are subtly revelatory; the tormented nightmares of Raskolnikov . . . are not more steeped in coagulated horror than these fevered visions that link murderer and victim in a hideous awareness of each other coiling even below the level of consciousness." [29] The Dostoevskian theme of the double appears in Dickens' *Great Expectations* (Magwich) and *Our Mutual Friend* (Harmon), as well as in others of his novels; so, notably, do dreams and madness.

Moreover, just as more than one Dickens novel might have been called *The Insulted and Injured,* so might more than one Dostoevsky novel take as an epigraph Dickens' idea of "representing London — or Paris, or any other great place — in the light of being actually unknown to all the people in the story, and only taking the color of their fears and fancies and opinions." The one suggests the mutual tendency to a subjective realism, just as the other suggests the shared theme of sympathy for the poor and downtrodden. And it is noteworthy that this last point is what Dostoevsky chose to emphasize when, late in his career, he referred to the "humble people, righteous but yielding, religious fanatics and downtrodden folks, such as appear in almost every novel of the great Christian — Dickens." [30]

From saying all this it is but one dangerous step to considering Dickens, with his retreats into comedy and happy endings, as a kind of Dostoevsky *manqué.* And this is a tendency that has been marked among the intellectuals of the English-speaking world ever since Dostoevsky's appearance in Constance Garnett's translations. In fact, even now that it has begun to be reversed by a new generation of critics, the lines of that reversal sometimes tend to plead only that he was not so *manqué* after all. The reasons for such injustices have their roots in changing literary fashion — and not only that aspect of it which makes Dostoevsky seem so contemporary today. They inhere as well in Dickens' tenacious reputation as a jolly humorist, and in the reaction against it that began with

Carlyle's obituary observation that beneath his "sparkling, clear, and sunny utterance," beneath his "bright and joyful sympathy with everything around him . . . deeper than all, if one has the eye to see deep enough, [were] dark, fateful, silent elements, tragical to look upon, and hiding amid dazzling radiances as of the sun, the elements of death itself." [31] For to recognize precisely the hidden nature of these elements is to recognize, with Gissing, how much of Dostoevsky's achievement "is beyond Dickens, as we know him" — a fact that "would not have been so but for the defects of education and the social prejudices which forbade his tragic gift to develop." [32]

The final corrective — not to such a view in itself, but to many of its implications — is to admit, as Gissing does, that "a master's general conception of the human tragedy or comedy must be accepted as that without which his work could not take form." [33] We must, in other words, respect Dickens' absolute right to his myth in the same way that we respect any other great writer's, for otherwise we could be drawn into the equally plausible absurdity of calling Dostoevsky a Dickens *manqué* and criticizing him for his inability to achieve the generous and humane perspective of his less narrowly obsessed English confrère. Following the wiser course, moreover, yields a picture of Dickens as the creator of a unique form of romantic realism, one in which a frequently tragic myth of the city is locked into a comic frame, the two elements intermingling to produce a vision whose grotesqueness leans to the comic as Dostoevsky's does to the tragic, but no less complexly and no less seriously.

The case of Gogol has been treated fully enough in earlier chapters and needs less specific attention here. There is no question that he did influence Dostoevsky perceptibly in the early work; his position in Russian letters at the time could not be ignored. But a Russian critic has named the relationship well in calling it "influence by repulsion." [34] Dostoevsky, he says, in a succinct statement of what I have detailed earlier,

> perceived with unusual force the tragic nature of Gogol's plots. But the means of treating these plots was unacceptable to him. The gruesome world of the Gogolian mascarade — whose participants were not real people but masks, behind which their genial author stood, setting them in motion

somewhere behind the scenes with a puzzling impassivity — did not evoke laughter from Dostoevsky, but demanded an immediate reaction, called forth the need to breathe life into these simulacra of human beings, to humanize the Gogolian mirages with feelings of love and compassion.[35]

Indeed, the punishment for considering people as dead souls is the whole burden of Raskolnikov's story. What Dostoevsky took over from Gogol was a new characterization of the city of Petersburg in all its strangeness and mystery.[36] And, though he must have found it in Balzac and Dickens too, his tremendous achievements in the handling of the grotesque are traceable primarily to Gogol, insofar as they are traceable to any outside source. For Gogol is a supreme master of the comic grotesque, and, when he provoked Dostoevsky to humanize his work, he provoked him to quarrel not with the noun, the thing, but only with the means of treatment, the adjective. Hence Dostoevsky's discovery of the tragic grotesque. He alone had the eye to make it, but Gogol, more than any other writer, helped to attune, train, and direct that eye.

Dostoevsky, then, is the inheritor of romantic realism in the sense that he knew the work of Balzac, Dickens, and Gogol and gauged the novelty of his own "new word" in terms of theirs. Yet the identifiable instances of specific influence, except in the case of Gogol (a different case because he was in the native tradition), are uniformly disappointing to a critic in search of a deepened understanding of Dostoevsky. This is so, I would suggest, because of the very concept of "influence" — a conception that has always appealed more to the cataloguing than to the critical mind. It is a dead-end notion, for it can do no more than hold up to view paired findings. A more fruitful approach is implicit in Victor Shklovsky's metaphor: "Books are not the world, but windows on the world. The windows of various houses can open a view on one and the same landscape; this landscape is one and the same, although it is variously seen. The likeness of the landscape, at the same time, is not a borrowing from one window by another." [37] If, at this point, a further argument for such a view is required, one is ready to hand, in a case where there is not the slightest trace of influence or even of direct personal knowledge. That is the astonishing parallel between Dostoevsky and Baudelaire.[38]

Both born in 1821, they were members of the same literary generation, and what their work shows above all is a strikingly similar series of reactions to the romantic tradition. Nor need the difference of the genres in which they worked be a stumbling block here. Dostoevsky in his letters was fond of emphasizing the poetic nature of his novels, and this confession in a letter of 1870 sounds a characteristic note: "Being more a poet than an artist [*khudozhnik*], I have eternally taken up themes beyond my strength." [39] And, as if approving both the Dostoevskian intention and the forms that embody it, Baudelaire writes: "In matters of art, I confess that I do not dislike extremes; moderation has never seemed to me the sign of a vigorous artistic nature." [40]

Both took the city as subject, and both saw it as evil:

> Le coeur content, je suis monté sur la montagne
> D'où l'on peut contempler la ville en son ampleur,
> Hôpital, lupanar, purgatoire, enfer, bagne,
> Où toute énormité fleurit comme une fleur.
>
> Epilogue to *Le Spleen de Paris*

It was, moreover, fantastic for both:

> Fourmillante cité, cité pleine de rêves,
> Où toute énormité fleurit comme une fleur.
> Les mystères partout coulent comme des sèves
> Dans les canaux étroits du colosse puissant.
>
> . . . . .
>
> Exaspéré comme un ivrogne qui voit double,
> Je rentrai, je fermai ma porte, épouvanté,
> Malade et morfondu, l'esprit fiévreux et trouble,
> Blessé par le mystère et par l'absurdité.
>
> "Les Sept Vieillards"

And it was fantastic because both could see the hidden luminosity in the most ordinary things or events: "In certain, almost supernatural spiritual states, the profundity of life reveals itself entire in the spectacle, however ordinary it may be, that one sees before him. That spectacle becomes its symbol." [41] As a result, Dostoevsky might have addressed Petersburg with Baudelaire's very words: "You gave me your mud, and I have turned it into gold."

Dostoevsky's concentration on the city, as we have seen, involved a relative indifference to the world of nature and to the traditional beauties it contained. The rationale of such an attitude is stated succinctly by the young Baudelaire, in his *Salon de 1846*: "The first job of an artist is to substitute man for Nature — and to protest against her." In this way, the notion of beauty is made a purely human thing, inherent in man's moral nature and, like it, ambivalent. So we find Baudelaire apostrophizing Beauty in terms that strikingly prefigure Dmitri Karamazov's speech about the coexistence of the ideas of Sodom and the Madonna:

> Viens-tu du ciel profond ou sors-tu de l'abîme,
> O Beauté? ton regard, infernal et divin,
> Verse confusément le bienfait et le crime,
> Et l'on peut pour cela te comparer au vin.
> "Hymme à la Beauté"

Moreover, the more specific view of feminine beauty in Dostoevsky — of a Nastasya Fillipovna or a Grushenka — finds its counterpart in "Allégorie:"

> Elle croit, elle sait, cette vierge inféconde
> Et pourtant nécessaire à la marche du monde,
> Que la beauté du corps est un sublime don
> Qui de toute infamie arrache le pardon.
> Elle ignore l'Enfer comme le Purgatoire,
> Et quand l'heure viendra d'entrer dans la Nuit noire,
> Elle regardera la face de la Mort,
> Ainsi qu'un nouveau-né — sans haine et sans remord.

It is a natural step from such a conception of beauty to the conclusion that "the Beautiful is always bizarre" [42] — and hence to a new valuation of the grotesque: "The mixture of the grotesque and the tragic is agreeable to the spirit, as discordance is to blasé ears." [43] Moreover, the view of the grotesque as consisting of deeply ambiguous comic elements underlies Baudelaire's thinking on the subject, as it does Dostoevsky's practice:

> The Sage laughs only with trembling. . . . Human laughter is intimately tied to the accident of an ancient fall, of a degradation both physical and moral. . . . Laughter is satanic — and therefore profoundly human. . . . Laughter is essentially contradictory, which is to say that it is at the same time the sign of an infinite greatness and an infinite wretchedness — infinite wretchedness relative to the absolute Being of Whom he has a conception, infinite greatness relative to the animal world. It is from the per-

petual collision of these two infinitudes that laughter is released. . . . The comic is, from the point of view of art, an imitation; the grotesque is a creation.[44]

These lines, like all the others quoted from Baudelaire, point to a fundamental dualism in his thinking, a notion of man as the contradictory animal. "There are in every man," he wrote in *Mon coeur mis à nu,* "at every moment, two simultaneous tendencies — the one toward God, the other toward Satan." [45] The statement would be unremarkable were it not for the emphasis on simultaneity, an emphasis we have seen shared by Dostoevsky's underground man and one that opened up for both writers enormous possibilities of psychological exploration. One such possibility is the innate human faculty for perversity, for self-punishment and self-contradiction. Mario Praz has called attention to a long passage that Baudelaire translated from Poe's "The Black Cat" and introduced with the words, "This passage deserves quotation." The core of the passage is the following:

And then came, as if to my final and irrevocable overthrow, the spirit of *Perverseness.* Of this spirit philosophy takes no account. Yet I am not more sure that my soul lives, than I am that perverseness is one of the primitive impulses of the human heart — one of the indivisible primary faculties, or sentiments, which give direction to the character of Man. Who has not, a hundred times, found himself committing a vile or a silly action, for no other reason than because he knows he should *not?* Have we not a perpetual inclination, in the teeth of our best judgment, to violate that which is Law, merely because we understand it to be such? This spirit of perverseness, I say, came to my final overthrow. It was [an] unfathomable longing of the soul to *vex itself.*" [46]

Indeed, with all the shades of perversity in the works of Dostoevsky, they probably do not exceed the number disclosed by a reading of Baudelaire. In his prose poem, "Le Mauvais Vitrier," Baudelaire's narrator cites the Stavrogin-like behavior of a friend who tempted death "to play the gambler, to experience the pleasures of anxiety, for no reason at all, out of caprice, out of idleness"; and the main incident of the piece is a study in a similarly motivated sadism. Or consider this item from *Fusées,* which might as well have come from Dostoevsky's own notebooks: "A man goes to a shooting gallery, accompanied by his wife. He aims at a clay doll and says to his wife, 'I am imagining that it's you.' He closes his eyes and hits the doll. Then he says, kissing the hand of his companion: 'My angel, how I thank you for my skill!' "[47]

Such psychological explorations are in both cases, of course, the issue of a deep personal unrest. What Dostoevsky and Baudelaire knew — to extend Eliot's remark about the latter alone — they found out for themselves. Both struggled toward a religious belief they could never grasp securely; Dostoevsky confesses as much in a letter in which he calls himself inescapably a child of the century of disbelief, and Baudelaire (after Pascal) enters in his notebooks a series of propositions entitled "Calcul en faveur de Dieu." [48] Elsewhere, in a formulation to which Dostoevsky would have subscribed wholeheartedly, he notes: "Theory of true civilization. It is not in gaslighting, or in steam, or in levitation. It is in the diminution of the traces of original sin." [49] If neither was very clear about the means of achieving such a diminution, both at least called attention to the problem in a way that led Charles Lalo to group them together in a subchapter entitled: "Deux pénitents émérites: Baudelaire et Dostoiewsky à confesse." [50] The point is capable of lengthy elaboration; suffice it to note here that both Baudelaire and Dostoevsky did use literature extensively as a means of veiled or objectified confession. Freud's observation about Dostoevsky, in the passage beginning, "A man who alternately sins and then in his remorse erects high moral standards lays himself open to the reproach that he has made things too easy for himself," [51] is almost a gloss to Baudelaire's lines in "Au Lecteur:" "Et nous alimentons nos aimables remords, / Comme les mendiants nourissent leur vermine / . . . Croyant par de vils pleurs laver toutes nos taches."

There is, in short, no European writer who displays a more striking thematic affinity with the mature Dostoevsky than Baudelaire — of whom he remained, apparently, in total ignorance. It is true that a link can be found between them in the person of Balzac, whom both praised extravagantly at a time when his reputation was in relative eclipse; but the fact of this admiration cannot explain all the specific points of coincidence. In fact, there is no way to explain them fully — but their problematic existence may remind us at least that influence is not the only or even the most important way of relating the work of different artists: there is also the whole question of the possibilities open to any given literary generation. In the case of

Baudelaire and Dostoevsky, these possibilities were determined largely by a romanticism that could neither be used nor rejected in the forms in which they found it as young men. Both "cruel talents," they both were its inheritors and its transmuters.

If Dostoevsky in his maturity, however, ignored Baudelaire and the whole contemporary European cultural situation out of the conviction that Europe was decadent and doomed,[52] the same cannot be said of Tolstoy, and it is curious to note that in his *What Is Art?* he has only ridicule for Baudelaire, but takes Dostoevsky into his very select pantheon. One explanation may be that, in Tolstoy's terms, Dostoevsky is redeemed by his *myth,* which is based on compassion and the will to believe. Here the difference in genre comes to the fore because myth, as Ivanov says, requires more than symbols or even the vision that creates them: it requires action, story, pattern — such as are possible only in the novel, heir to the classical epic and drama. In this sense, though a lyric poet may have a system, he cannot have a myth. And it is myth that finally joins Dostoevsky to romantic realism.

THE COMMUNITY OF MYTH

Conscious creation of myth is, in the strictly literary terms used so far, the distinguishing mark of the romantic realists. Yet helpful as literary terms and literary history may be in explaining how it happened that writers so separate could echo one another in so many key ways, often without knowing it, we need to go beyond them to see the full significance of romantic realism — to see that the four writers discussed here were, each in his own way, discovering a common fund of specifically "modern" experience: the experience of the great city. We can better appreciate their importance if we realize how new their enterprise was — not only because changes in the city had made it almost a new sociological entity, but also because previous literary attempts to deal directly with it had been limited to cataloguing and description, at best to a patient assembly of facts — picturesque, edifying, or touching. Their problem, then, was to find a form for what was formless, a way to express their vision of the new urban alienation, of the struggle for existence in the jungle of cities. In meeting this problem, the reporter's eye was essential but insufficient; it took as well that "second sight" we have seen each of them claiming, that sensitivity for "the poetry of fact" and the "luminosity" of prosaic scenes. The solution of the problem turned out to be implicit in the very faculty that let them see it in the first place. That is to say, the very moral sensitivities that let them see the sickness of their cities (the real, social *mal du siècle*) led them to depict their cities ultimately in moral terms — taking moral here to mean a concern with the quality and possibilities of life. It is these terms that shape the myth of each, and each writer's investigation of the city must be seen equally as a quest for myth.

Such an investigation, obviously, could not be the work of a single year or a single book. The outlines of a myth are finally disengaged from the work of each of these writers only in the light of the whole body of his works — a point made by Balzac when he planned the edifice of his *Comédie humaine,* of which each separate work would be only "a fragment"; a point made of Dickens by Chesterton when he called the novels "simply lengths cut from the flowing and mixed substance called Dickens"; and a point detectible in Dostoevsky by his variation on the Balzacian *retour des personnages,* to be discussed later. Even Gogol, who dealt with Petersburg on so much smaller a scale, nevertheless achieved his myth by the same process of theme and repeated variations.

Thus the nature of the new city life ("community" would be too strong a word) is investigated by the device of bringing an isolated hero to confront the hostile city, frequently after a childhood spent elsewhere — this last, incidentally, is a feature taken in each case from the writer's own biography. Coming to the city, these characters all tend to find themselves in the position of the Dickensian hero, who is, in J. Hillis Miller's summary,

> alienated from the human community. He has no familial tie. He is an orphan, or illegitimate, or both. He has no status in the community, no inherited role which he can accept with dignity. He is characterized by desire, rather than by possession. His spiritual state is one of an expectation founded on a present consciousness of lack, of deprivation. He is, in Wallace Stevens' phrase, "an emptiness that would be filled." [53]

Equally characteristic for all is "the fundamental question of all Dickens' novels" as Miller puts it: "How is a person who cannot withdraw going to avoid being destroyed by the evil forces in the world? How is someone who begins as an outcast going to discover anything which will be a support for his identity and source of a coherent life?" [54] For isolation confronts all these characters with evil on a variety of levels. There is, in the first place, the unreality of social life, which judges a man's worth by the cut of his trousers or his overcoat, the aristocratic particle in his name or his house on Harley Street; only Dostoevsky is an exception here because he alone managed so largely to eschew the transient social distinctions of his day. There is, beyond this, another element of evil, more intimately tied with tragedy because more inherent in the urban man who lives divorced from the natural rhythms of life: this is what Balzac called the tragedy of thought, the ravages that dedication to thought wreak on a man. Dickens must be found wanting here, but Gogol approaches it in his portrayals of artists — and Dostoevsky, as Gide pointed out, returns time and time again to the theme of the demonic nature of intellect. We have seen his contrasts between the misused dialectic skill of the underground man and Raskolnikov and what he called with vague but portentous emphasis, "living life." (It is surely significant that, for all four writers, "living life" — the sound alternative to the unhealthy life of the city — turns out to be a vague, unattainable, and ultimately anachronistic quasi-pastoral ideal, a kind of secular ideal of life before the Fall. In fact, it is not too much to infer that each has updated the biblical myth by supposing that the path from Eden led not to the wilderness but to the city. So Balzac shows the mechanism of corruption at its tragic work; while Dickens, in surveying the terrible forms of alienation, tries at the same time to speak for humane values, not only through the narration of his stories but through his depictions of pure virtue within them. For Gogol no such attempt is possible, and the extremity of unnatural life he found in Petersburg is reflected in the extremity of alienation in his point of view. His anguished discovery, however, became his successor's premise: Dostoevsky could take the worst for granted, the urban alienation as a fait accompli.)

Both the unreal conditions of social life and the equally unreal conditions of intellectual activity are involved in a form of evil at once social and personal: crime. Balzac in his Parisian novels saw it largely in terms of the former and invested it with an infernal glamor in the person of Vautrin, whose personal genius so predominates that he is able to turn from the professional enemy to the professional protector of society. Aside from the ambiguous example of *Oliver Twist,* Dickens rather tended to combine a social impetus to crime with considerations of a more psychological sort, so that his treatment appears to point more toward Dostoevsky than toward Balzac — specifically, toward the blurring of that line which separates the criminal and the extraordinary from the ordinary and normal. In so doing, he came, as did Dostoevsky, to relate murder (the favorite crime of both) by a network of devious ties to the whole death-oriented direction of the modern city. In this, as writers from Ruskin to Lewis Mumford have emphasized, there is a profound historical insight. What Ruskin observed about *Bleak House* could be extended, by way of the Marmeladovs and the whole crowd of miscellaneous drunkards and prostitutes, to *Crime and Punishment* as well:

> In the single novel of *Bleak House* there are nine deaths . . . carefully wrought out or worked up to: one by assassination, Mr. Tulkinghorn; one by starvation with phtisis, Jo; one by chagrin, Richard; one by spontaneous combustion, Mr. Krook; one by sorrow, Lady Dedlock's lover; one by remorse, Lady Dedlock; one by insanity, Miss Flite; one by paralysis, Sir Leicester. It is the fact that all these deaths, but one, are of inoffensive, or at least, in the world's estimate, respectable persons; and that they are all grotesquely either violent or miserable, purporting thus to illustrate the modern theory that the appointed destiny of a large average of our population is to die like rats in a drain, either by trap or poison.[55]

All such investigations of evil, crime, and death, treated sensationally by the popular novelists of the same period, in the hands of these writers become part of a more serious search for meaning and possibilities of meaning in the chaos of the city. The same may be said of the terms they used to set forth these investigations. The extravagant, the bizarre, the grotesque, which others could use to produce a crude or factitious sense of novelty, became for these writers the basis of their claim to realism, the outward sign of the newness of the social patterns they were describing. Each emphasized the solidity of his physical city, to set off the unreality of the life lived in it. And by so doing each was admonishing his readers, in effect: "The old assumptions, the old categories, are no longer valid; we must try to see afresh." The comfortable certainty of Fielding, for instance, that he could take as his subject "human nature" and simply illustrate it, amusingly or otherwise, was no longer available to them. Theirs was not the familiar daylight world; Apollo did not reign there, and beauty itself was dethroned.

It was not, of course, only that cities were becoming ugly — though that is true and duly recorded by these writers. Far more important, the *ideal* of beauty was becoming less and less relevant to the facts of contemporary life, for beauty was a classical notion and bound to share the fate of the whole classical (and neoclassical) world view. In its narrowly aesthetic sense, it was giving way to a notion that allowed for more passion and more irregularity — that of the sublime[56] — and when the union of the sublime with the grotesque, which Hugo championed, was effected by the romantic realists, it spelled a major aesthetic revolution. Lear had been democratized: his tragic province had been appropriated by the writers of novels and peopled with Goriots, Poprishchins, Marmeladovs.

As a result of this revolution, social position no longer had any necessary connection with the possibilities of tragedy: any individual might contain the requisite magnitude. (Since the grotesque has been seen here as a particular kind of tragicomedy, it is interesting to note parenthetically how in the century 1750–1850 the locus of comedy underwent a parallel shift, from the social to the individual, from a censorious to an amiable view of idiosyncrasy.[57]) The individual, in short, was as much terra incognita as the city he inhabited — as full of contradictions, eccentricities, even monstrosities.

As we have seen, the radical newness of all this created problems of form. One answer these writers found may be seen in the polarized traditional figures of the devil and the angel, which preside over the search of each and over the myth of each. For the quests and the myths of the romantic realists, though their materials are profane, are themselves essentially religious in nature. In Balzac, Dickens, and Gogol, the devil symbolically haunts the city of which he appears in the last analysis to be the patron; and in the first two at least, the road to salvation is usually indicated by the angelic figure of some self-sacrificing young woman. Dostoevsky, while he uses this scheme, transforms it by internalizing the devil, just as in general he tends to remove so many features of the romantic realists' myths to a psychological level. As Berdyaev points out: "All Dostoevsky's 'divided' people have a devil, though less clearly visible than Ivan's is to him." [58]

This observation leads us to one of the most significant indications of myth in the romantic realists, one that Dostoevsky carried to the furthest possible refinements consonant with realism. This is the deeply *organic* nature of his fictional city — and theirs — by which everything becomes implicated in everything else;[59] and it is this that permits us to speak of the unique created universe of each. Influenced perhaps by the comic tradition, all four writers make a person's habitation as deeply revelatory of character as his face; houses, apartments, and rooms are all charged with meaning. Related to this is the treatment of names: with the partial exception of Balzac, these writers all incline to credit the dictum *nomen, omen* and to assign surnames that are themselves suggestive. "Must one not recognize with Sterne," Balzac asks in *Ursule Mirouet,* "the occult power of names, which sometimes mock and sometimes define characters?" [60] And in fact each of these writers has a whole gamut, from the openly emblematic (Veneering, Bashmachkin, Raskolnikov [from *raskolnik,* dissenter, schismatic]) to the more vaguely suggestive (Jarndyce, Poprishchin, Lebezyatnikov).[61] Coincidence serves the same function — emphasizing the interrelatedness of all — and not infrequently indicating the tragic necessity that presides over these various worlds. The weather too, of course, reflects human moods and situations. "The rain," Dickens writes in *Little Dorrit,* "fell heavily on the roof, and pattered on the ground, and dripped among the evergreens and the leafless branches of the trees. The rain fell heavily, drearily. It was a night of tears." Except for that last explicit sentence, the passage might have come from Gogol or Dostoevsky; even without it, the implication would have been the same.

These mythical, or mythified, worlds display another sort of atmosphere besides. It was to this that Henry James referred when he found in Balzac "an absolutely greater quantity of 'atmosphere' than we shall find prevailing within the compass of any other suspended frame." [62] If the primacy of Balzac is debatable, his typicality is not: James's claim might as plausibly be urged for any of the other writers discussed here. What the word "atmosphere" at once suggests and derives from is the sense of mystery in things; the love of all these writers for effects of chiaroscuro is emblematic of the way things can only really be glimpsed in their moments of salience from an encompassing secret. Here is the meaning of the fondness of the romantic realists for masks, labyrinthine streets and dark staircases, nocturnal scenes. Here also is the rationale of their predilection for the plot of the detective novel with its sensational secrets and sudden revelations: the mythified city, like the people it contains, can only be understood if its strangeness is acknowledged first; the separate myths themselves are voyages of discovery.

What Dostoevsky does, however, is to incorporate all these features and take them one step further by making the individual personality the ultimate repository of mystery, the nucleus, as it were, of all these concentric circles. His characters, as I have noted, are not describable in the straightforward terms that usually suffice to describe the characters in Balzac, Dickens, or Gogol. They are compounded of contradictions, always in flux, always liable to realize in action some potentiality hitherto dormant. As Shklovsky observes, in Dostoevsky's later novels "a double and often even a triple motivation is given for an action; at first an event is narrated and a first clue [*razgadka*] given for the motives of the hero's action; then the motivation is subjected to discussion and replaced. The relations among the heroes are presented at once on several levels; the quarrels of the heroes among themselves and the internal division [*razlad*] of the heroes give a peculiar scintillation to the motives of the action." [63] The result, to readers accustomed by modern psychology and modern events to think of human beings in terms of their contradictions and unconscious impulses, appears more lifelike, more "realistic" than older, more conventional depictions. But at the same time its tendency is to destroy the notion of character altogether. Who, for instance, is Raskolnikov? He is an ungraspable bundle of contradictions, to which each of the characters he meets possesses a clue: but the clues all together are not susceptible of any final synthesis. He is organically tied, we know, to Svidrigailov, who is his double, an extreme version of one group of his tendencies. And yet, though Svidrigailov may illustrate a great deal about Raskolnikov, he does not help us very much to grasp his individuality, his character. Nor, for that matter, does Sonya, his good angel and something of a double herself. Dostoevsky's notebooks for *Crime and Punishment* bear out this point by detailing the fact that, as the novel progressed, he found himself increasingly uncertain about his hero's motives in killing the two women. He moved, that is, from a more or less conventional notion of motive to a recognition, based on intuition, that there is no such thing as a single motive, or even a clearly dominant one. At the heart of human action he found darkness, a mystery.

This is just what allows us to talk about the way his myth is established through a slow accumulation. Over the course of many novels, a unity is built up by means that Grossman has seen as a unique variation on the Balzacian technique of the *retour des personnages:*

> Recurrent images and repeated situations — these form the basis of his narrative art. Characters with related qualities and similar fates run through his portrait gallery, lending his work a striking unity. Balzac would lead one character — Rastignac or Vautrin — through a whole series of novels that went into the *Human Comedy*. Dostoevsky developed a single character in a host of figures over the whole cycle of his works, without ceasing to vary, to strengthen, and to enrich his basic theme-image [*tema-obraz*]. What interests him is not the separate expressive figure but the problem incarnate [*chelovek-problema*], the drama incarnate [*chelovek-drama*]. The solution of such a problem knows no end, and the action of such a conflict envisages no finale. It is always continuing and lives without ceasing to evoke endless new variants in the creative experiments of the great artist. Let us arrange these pivotal images of the novelist according to the chief headings of his image system.
>
> Dostoevsky's leading types are many and various. They are the thinkers and dreamers, the abused girls [*porugannye devushki*], the sensualists, the voluntary buffoons, the doubles, the underground men, the Russian broad nature ("the impetuous ones"), the pure in heart, the righteous ("the most wise teachers of life"), the outcasts, the shady dealers, the virtuosi of investigation and the court, the nihilists, the proud and meek women, the impressionable children and meditative adolescents.[64]

The key observation here is that Dostoevsky is more concerned with the "problem incarnate" than with any separate figure — and while this is not so true of a Mitya Karamazov or a Marmeladov, it is unquestionably true of Raskolnikov, Myshkin, Stavrogin, and numerous others.

It is this open-ended notion of character that Ortega y Gasset in his stimulating essay called "Notes on the Novel" both praises and seems to misunderstand. Making an absolute distinction between action and character, he finds the first quite superfluous, the second all. "When we are fascinated by a novel," he writes, "it is not because of its subject, not because we are curious to know what happened to Mr. So-and-so. The subject of any novel can be told in a few words and in this form holds no interest." [65] "We are fascinated by Don Quixote and Sancho," he says, "not by what is happening to them. In principle, a *Don Quixote* as great as the original is conceivable in which the knight and his servant go through entirely different experiences. And the same holds for Julien Sorel or David Copperfield." [66] Confining the discussion for the moment to the last-named example, it would not be hard to show that Ortega is palpably wrong, for the notion of a David Copperfield apart from the whole apparatus of the Dickensian myth is inconceivable. We are told that David is a novelist, but who can for a moment believe it, who can find the slightest concrete warrant for supposing him to have the artist's gift or range? Is he imaginable apart from the particularly Dickensian world in which he functions, apart from the very cadences of the Dickensian prose? The argument of this whole study, insofar as it is valid, tends to suggest a negative answer. And the same sort of argument, adjusted to the originality of Dostoevsky's practice, would have to qualify Ortega's conclusion that "the novel must now revolve around the superior interest emanating from the inner mechanism of the personages. Not in the invention of plots but in the invention of interesting characters lies the best hope of the novel." [67] For Dostoevsky, whom he praises, gives us in figures like Raskolnikov not characters but problems incarnate, which are discoverable *only* in action, *only* in the particular situations and under the particular pressures of the plot, only in their relation to the whole myth in which they participate organically. One might still meet and recognize a Vronsky on any street today; a Raskolnikov could be met and recognized only in Dostoevsky's Petersburg, could only breathe its air.

Another way of approaching this problem is to see that Dostoevsky, along with the other mythographers of romantic realism, gives us a world compounded in part not only of elements of romanticism, but of romance as well. Henry James's celebrated definition of romance in his preface to *The American* would be apposite here. Its source, however, is in Hawthorne, who wrote in the preface to *The House of the Seven Gables:*

> When a writer calls his work a Romance, it need hardly be observed that he wishes to claim a certain latitude, both as to its fashion and material, which he would not have felt himself entitled to assume had he professed to be writing a Novel. The latter form of composition is presumed to aim at a very minute fidelity, not merely to the possible, but to the probable and ordinary course of man's experience. The former — while, as a work of art, it must rigidly subject itself to laws, and while it sins unpardonably so far as it may swerve aside from the truth of the human heart — has fairly a right to present that truth under circumstances, to a great extent, of the writer's own choosing or creation. If he think fit, also, he may so arrange his atmospherical medium as to bring out or mellow the lights and deepen and enrich the shadows of the picture. He will be wise, no doubt, to make a very moderate use of the privileges here stated, and, especially, to mingle the Marvellous rather as a slight, delicate, and evanescent flavor, than as any portion of the actual substance of the dish offered to the public.

The "certain latitude" of which Hawthorne speaks differs in degree and kind in our four novelists, but not in function: all use this liberty not to escape historical fact, but to render it more truly. All of them took liberties with probability in order to discover the often unsuspected realities of a given time and place, and in piecing together their discoveries they pieced together what we can only call a myth, the premises of the investigation finding expression as the laws of their mythical worlds, the discoveries themselves emerging only slowly and tentatively from the repeated operation of those laws in work after work.

The very scope of such achievements suggests the need to revise some still-too-common assumptions. Because romantic realism did historically precede (and, in good part, provoke) "normative" mid-century realism, it is often assumed to be a crude form of what came later; the realists themselves were the first to propagate such a view. The fallacy in this, however, should be doubly plain to us by now, since the recent history of aesthetics shows how clearly changing styles reflect not "progress," but only changing ways of looking at the world, each unchallengeable within its own terms. The notion of progress in art is always a glorification of the current style, always invidious, judging earlier works by standards quite foreign to their makers. Now that realism seems largely to have spent itself, it should be easier for us to see how easily one might reverse the usual positions and regard postromantic realism as a dwindling of the previous method, the triumph — since it confined itself so closely to the normal and the everyday — of a narrower ideal. The argument (and Balzac, Dickens, Dostoevsky all made it) is fruitless, but where arguments on this level are conducted, it has at least a corrective plausibility.

After romantic realism, in any case, there did come a new bifurcation in the novel. The romantic elements turned into fin-de-siècle symbolism, the realist ones into the aesthetic of Flaubert and Tolstoy, with their principled rejection of myth, and so on into the naturalism of Zola and others. By the early years of this century, these currents of symbolism and naturalism were meeting again, in new monuments to the city: Joyce in this way immortalized his Dublin in *Ulysses,* and Proust his Paris in *A la Recherche du temps perdu*. But all that is another story.

SELECTED BIBLIOGRAPHY
NOTES
INDEX

Selected Bibliography

Abraham, Pierre. *Créatures chez Balzac.* Paris, 1931.

Alain [pseud.]. "Avec Balzac," in *Les Arts et les dieux.* Paris, 1958.

——— *En lisant Dickens,* in *Les Arts et les dieux.* Paris, 1958.

Annenkov, P[avel] V[asilievich]. *Literaturnye vospominaniya.* Leningrad, 1928.

Annensky, Innokenty Fyodorovich. *Kniga otrazhenii.* St. Petersburg, 1906.

Antsiferov, N. P. *Byl i mif Peterburga.* Petersburg, 1924.

——— *Dusha Peterburga.* Petersburg, 1922.

——— *Peterburg Dostoevskogo.* Petersburg, 1923.

Auerbach, Erich. *Mimesis,* trans. Willard Trask. Princeton, 1953.

Bakhtin, M. M. *Problemy tvorchestva Dostoevskogo.* Leningrad, 1929.

Baldensperger, Fernand. *Orientations étrangères chez Honoré de Balzac.* Paris, 1927.

Balzac, Honoré de. *L'Oeuvre de Balzac,* ed. Albert Béguin. 16 vols. Paris; Formes et Reflets, 1949–1953.

Bardèche, Maurice. *Balzac romancier.* Paris, 1940.

Baudelaire, Charles. *Oeuvres complètes.* Paris: Bibliothèque de la Pléiade, 1956.

Becker, George J. "Realism: An Essay in Definition," *Modern Language Quarterly,* X (June 1949), 184–197.

——— ed. *Documents of Modern Literary Realism.* Princeton, 1963.

Béguin, Albert. *Balzac visionnaire.* Paris, 1946.

Belinsky, V. G. "Peterburg i Moskva," in his *Sobranie sochinenii v tryokh tomakh,* vol. II. Moscow, 1948. Pages 763–791.

Bely, Andrey. *Masterstvo Gogolya.* Moscow-Leningrad, 1934.

Bem, A. L. "Gogol i Pushkin v tvorchestve Dostoevskogo," *Slavia,* VII (1929), 62–86, VIII (1930), 82–100, 297–311.

——— "Hugo i Dostoevsky," *Slavia* (Prague), XV (1937–38), 73–86.

——— "Lichnye imena u Dostoevskogo," in *Sbornik v chest na Prof. L. Miletich.* Sofia, 1933. Pages 409–434.

——— ed. *O Dostoevskom.* 3 vols. Prague, 1929, 1933, 1936.

——— "Pervye shagi Dostoevskogo (genesis romana *Bednye lyudi*)," *Slavia,* XII (1933), 134–161.

——— " 'Shinel' Gogolya i *Bednye lyudi* Dostoevskogo," *Zapiski russkago istoricheskago obshchestva v Prage,* I (1927), 47–56.

——— "Sumerki geroya (etyud k rabote: otrazheniya 'Pikovoy damy' v tvorchestve Dostoevskogo)," *Nauchnye trudy russkago narodnago universiteta v Prage,* IV (1931), 158–172.

——— "Tayna lichnosti Dostoevskogo," in V. V. Zenkovsky, ed., *Pravoslavie i kultura.* Berlin, 1923.

Berdyaev, Nicholas. *Dostoevsky,* trans. Donald Attwater. New York, 1934.

Beuchat, Charles. *Histoire du naturalisme français.* Paris, 1949.

Bitsilli, Pyotr Mikhaylovich. "K voprosu o vnutrenney forme romana Dotoevskogo," Sofia University, *Godishnik,* XLII (1945–46), 1–71.

——— "Problema Cheloveka u Gogolya," Sofia University, *Godishnik,* XLIV (1947–48), iv, 3–31.

Blackmur, R. P. "*Crime and Punishment:* A Study of Dostoevsky's Novel," *The Chimera,* I (1943), 7–28.

Blinoff, Marthe. "Dostoievski et Balzac," *Comparative Literature,* III (1951), 342–355.

Borgerhoff, E. B. O. "*Réalisme* and Kindred Words," *PMLA,* LIII (1938), 837–843.

Bowman, H. E. "The Nose," *Slavonic and East European Review,* XXXI (1952), 204–211.

Butt, John, and Kathleen Tillotson. *Dickens at Work.* London, 1957.

Caillois, Roger. "Balzac et le mythe de Paris," in Albert Béguin, ed., *L'Oeuvre de Balzac,* vol. IV. Paris, 1950. Pages i–xvii.

Castex, P. G. "Baudelaire et Balzac," *Orbis Litterarum,* XII (1957), iii–iv, 179–192.

Chesterton, G. K. *Charles Dickens: A Critical Study.* New York, 1906.

Churchill, R. C. "Dickens, Drama, and Tradition," in Eric Bentley, ed., *The Importance of Scrutiny.* New York, 1948. Pages 182–202.

Cizevsky, Dmitry. "Neizvestny Gogol," *Novy zhurnal,* no. 27 (1951), pp. 126–158.

——— "O 'Shineli' Gogolya," *Sovremennye zapiski,* LXVII (1938), 172–195.

——— "The Unknown Gogol," *Slavonic and East European Review,* XXX (June 1952), 476–493.

Curtius, Ernst-Robert. *Balzac.* Paris, 1933.

Delattre, Floris. *Dickens et la France.* Paris, 1927.

De Quincey, Thomas. *Collected Writings,* vol. III, ed. David Masson. London, 1897.

Dolinin, A. S., ed. *F. M. Dostoevsky, statyi i materialy.* 2 vols. Petersburg, 1922. Leningrad, 1925.

Dostoevsky, F. M. *Pisma,* ed. A. S. Dolinin. 4 vols. Moscow-Leningrad, 1928, 1930, 1934, 1959.

——— *Sobranie sochinenii,* ed. L. P. Grossman et al. 10 vols. Moscow, 1956.

——— *Polnoye sobranie knudozhestvennykh sochinenii,* vol. XIII (*Statyi za 1845–1878 gody*), ed. B. Tomashevsky and K. Khalabayev. Moscow-Leningrad, 1930.

Dupee, F. W., ed. *The Selected Letters of Charles Dickens.* New York, 1960.

Duron, Jacques-Robert, et al. *Balzac: Le Livre du centenaire.* Paris, 1952.

Eikhenbaum, Boris. "Kak sdelana 'Shinel' Gogolya," in his *Skvoz literaturu.* Leningrad, 1924.

Eng, Johannes van der. *Dostoevskij romancier.* The Hague, 1957.

Engel, Monroe. *The Maturity of Dickens.* Cambridge, Mass., 1959.

Erlich, Victor. "Gogol and Kafka: Note on 'Realism' and 'Surrealism,'" in Morris Halle et al., eds., *For Roman Jakobson.* The Hague, 1956.

Evnin, F. I. "Roman *Prestuplenie i nakazanie,*" in N. L. Stepanov, ed.,

Tvorchestvo F. M. Dostoevskogo. Moscow, 1959. Pages 128–172.

Faguet, Emile. Introduction to vols. VII and VIII, of Petit de Juleville, *Histoire de la langue et de la littérature française*. Paris, 1899.

Fairchild, Hoxie Neale. *The Romantic Quest*. New York, 1931.

Fielding, Kenneth J. *Charles Dickens: A Critical Introduction*. London, 1958.

Ford, George Harry. *Dickens and His Readers: Aspects of Novel-Criticism since 1836*. Princeton, 1955.

Forster, John. *The Life of Charles Dickens*. 2 vols. London: Everyman's Library, 1927.

Freud, Sigmund. "Dostoevsky and Parricide," in William Phillips, ed., *Art and Psychoanalysis*. New York, 1957. Pages 3–21.

Futrell, Michael H. "Dostoyevsky and Dickens," *English Miscellany*, VII (1956), 41–89.

——— "Gogol and Dickens," *Slavonic Review*, XXXIV (1956), 443–459.

Galich, L. "Realizm Dostoevskogo," *Novy zhurnal*, XIII (1946), 188–198.

Gautier, Théophile. *Les Jeunes-France: Romans goguenards*. Paris, 1873.

Gibian, George. "The Grotesque in Dostoevsky," *Modern Fiction Studies*, IV, 3 (1958), 262–270.

Ginisty, Paul. *Le Mélodrame*. Paris, 1910.

Gippius, Vasily. *Gogol*. Leningrad, 1924.

——— ed. *N. V. Gogol v pismakh i vospominaniyakh*. Moscow, 1931.

Gissing, George. *Charles Dickens: A Critical Study*. New York, 1904.

——— *Critical Studies of the Works of Charles Dickens*. New York, 1924.

Glivenko, I. I., ed. *Iz arkhiva F. M. Dostoevskogo: Prestuplenie i nakazanie, neizdannye materialy*. Moscow-Leningrad, 1931.

Gogol, N. V. *Sobranie sochinenii v shesti tomakh*. Moscow, 1952–53.

Grossman, Leonid Petrovich. *Balzac en Russie*. Paris, 1946.

——— "Balzak i Dostoevsky," *Russkaya mysl*, no. 1 (1914), pp. 44–55.

——— *Biblioteka Dostoevskogo*. Odessa, 1919.

——— "Dostoevsky i Evropa," *Russkaya mysl*, no. 11(1915), pp. 54-93.

——— "Dostoevsky-Khudozhnik," in N. L. Stepanov, ed., *Tvorchestvo F. M. Dostoevskogo*. Moscow, 1959. Pages 330–416.

——— "Gofman, Balzak i Dostoevsky," *Sofiya*, V (1914), 87–96.

——— "Gogol — Urbanist," in N. V. Gogol, *Povesti*. Moscow, 1935. Pages 7–36.

——— "Gorod i lyudi *Prestupleniya i nakazaniya*," in F. M. Dostoevsky, *Prestuplenie i nakazanie*. Moscow, 1935. Pages 5–52.

——— "Kompozitsiya v romane Dostoevskogo," *Vestnik Evropy*, no. 9 (1916), pp. 121–156.

——— "Problema realizma u Dostoevskogo," *Vestnik Evropy*, no. 2 (1917), pp. 65–100.

——— *Poetika Dostoevskogo*. Moscow, 1925.

——— *Seminary po Dostoevskomu*. Moscow-Petrograd. 1922.

——— ed. *Tvorchestvo Dostoevskogo, 1821–1881–1921*. Odessa, 1921.

——— *Tvorchestvo Dostoevskogo*. Moscow, 1928.

——— *Zhizn i trudy F. M. Dostoevskogo: Biografiya v datakh i dokumentakh*. Moscow, 1935.

Gukovsky, G. A. *Realizm Gogolya*. Moscow, 1959.

Hauser, Arnold. *The Social History of Art,* vol. II. New York, 1952.

Hill, T. W. "Books That Dickens Read," *The Dickensian,* XLV (1949), 81–90, 201–207.

House, Humphry. *The Dickens World.* London, 1942.

Hugo, Victor. *Préface de Cromwell,* ed. Maurice Souriau. Paris, 1936 [?].

Hunt, Herbert J. *Balzac's Comédie Humaine.* London, 1959.

Hunt, Joel. "Balzac and Dostoevskij: Ethics and Eschatology," *Slavic and East European Journal,* XVI, 4 (1958), 307–323.

Ivanov, Vyacheslav. *Freedom and the Tragic Life: A Study in Dostoevsky,* trans. Norman Cameron. New York, 1957.

Ivask, Yury. "Bodler i Dostoevsky," *Novy zhurnal,* no. 60 (1960), pp. 138–152.

Jakobson, R. "O khudozhestvennom realizme," *Michigan Slavic Materials,* II (1962), 29–36.

James, Henry. "Honoré de Balzac," in his *French Poets and Novelists.* London, 1919.

——— "The Lesson of Balzac," in Leon Edel, ed., *The House of Fiction: Essays on the Novel of Henry James.* London, 1957.

Janin, Jules. *La Confession.* Paris, 1861.

Jennings, Lee Byron. *The Ludicrous Demon: Aspects of the Grotesque in German Post-Romantic Prose.* Berkeley and Los Angeles, 1963.

Johnson, Edgar. *Charles Dickens: His Tragedy and Triumph.* 2 vols. New York, 1952.

Kaufmann, Pierre. "Le Pathétique de Dostoiewski," *Confluences,* III (1943), 401–409.

Kayser, Wolfgang. *The Grotesque in Art and Literature,* trans. Ulrich Weisstein. Bloomington, 1963.

Kettle, Arnold. "Dickens: *Oliver Twist,*" in his *Introduction to the English Novel,* vol. I. London, 1951. Pages 123–138.

Khodasevich, Vladislav. "Peterburgskie povesti Pushkina," in his *Statyi o russkoy poezii.* Petersburg, 1922. Pages 58–96.

Komarovich, V. " 'Mirovaya garmoniya' Dostoevskogo," *Ateney,* no. 1–2 (1924), pp. 112–142.

——— "Peterburgskie feletony Dostoevskogo," in Yu. Oksman, ed., *Feletony sorokovykh godov.* Moscow-Leningrad, 1930. Pages 89–126.

Le Breton, André. *Balzac, l'homme et l'oeuvre.* Paris, 1905.

——— *Le Roman français au XIXe siècle avant Balzac.* Paris, n. d.

Lednicki, Waclaw. *Russia, Poland and the West.* New York, 1953.

Leroy, Maxime. *Histoire des idées sociales en France,* vol. III. Paris, 1954.

Levin, Harry. *The Gates of Horn.* New York, 1963.

——— "Some Meanings of Myth," *Daedalus,* LXXXVIII (Spring 1959), 223–231.

Lindsay, Jack. *Charles Dickens: A Biographical and Critical Study.* London, 1950.

Lukacs, George. *Der Russische Realismus in der Weltliteratur.* Berlin, 1952.

——— *Studies in European Realism,* trans. Edith Bone. London, 1950.

Marceau, Félicien. *Balzac et son monde.* Paris, 1955.

Marsan, Jules. "Le Mélodrame et Guilbert de Pixérécourt," *Revue d'histoire littéraire de la France,* 1900, pp. 196-220.

Martino, Pierre. *Le Roman réaliste sous le Second Empire*. Paris, 1913.

Matoré, G. "En marge de Th. Gautier: 'Grotesque,'" in *Etudes romanes dédiées à Mario Roques*. Paris, 1946. Pages 217–225.

Maupassant, Guy de. "Le Roman," preface to *Pierre et Jean*. Paris, 1909.

Maynial, Edouard. *L'Epoque réaliste*. Paris, 1931.

Messac, Régis. *Le "Detective Novel" et l'influence de la pensée scientifique*. Paris, 1929.

Mikulich, V. [pseud.] *Vstrechi s pisatelyami*. Leningrad, 1929.

Miller, J. Hillis. *Charles Dickens: The World of His Novels*. Cambridge, Mass., 1958.

Mochulsky, K. *Dostoevsky: Zhizn i tvorchestvo*. Paris, 1947.

Monod, Sylvère. *Dickens romancier*. Paris, 1953.

Moser, Françoise. "Balzac et la vie galante de son temps," *Mercure de France*, 15 August 1937, pp. 59–83.

Mumford, Lewis. *The City in History*. New York, 1961.

——— *The Culture of Cities*. New York, 1938.

Nilsson, Nils Ake. *Gogol et Pétersbourg*. Stockholm, 1954.

Oksman, Yu., ed. *Feletony sorokovykh godov*. Moscow-Leningrad, 1930.

Ortega y Gasset, José. *The Dehumanization of Art and Other Writings on Art and Culture*. New York, 1956.

Passage, Charles E. *Dostoevski the Adapter*. Chapel Hill, 1954.

Pellissier, Georges. *Le Réalisme du romantisme*. Paris, 1912.

Pereverzev, V. *Tvorchestvo Dostovskogo*. Moscow, 1922.

Phillips, Walter C. *Dickens, Reade and Collins: Sensation Novelists*. New York, 1919.

Picon, Gaëtan. "Balzac et Dieu," *Cahiers du Sud*, XLII (1955), 276–284.

Pletnev, R. "Preobrazhenie mira (priroda v tvorchestve Dostoevskogo)," *Novy zhurnal*, no. 43 (1955), pp. 63–80.

Poggioli, Renato. *The Phoenix and the Spider*. Cambridge, Mass., 1957.

——— "Kafka and Dostoevski," in Angel Flores, ed. *The Kafka Problem*. New York, 1946. Pages 97–116.

Pradalié, G. *Balzac historien*. Paris, 1955.

Praz, Mario. *The Romantic Agony*. New York, 1956.

Rahv, Philip. "Notes on the Decline of Naturalism," in John W. Aldridge, ed., *Critiques and Essays on Modern Fiction*. New York, 1952. Pages 415–423.

Reizov, B. G. "K istorii romanticheskogo urbanizma: 'Ispoved' Zhyulya Zhanina i 'Otets Gorio' Balzaka, in S. V. Kastorsky, ed., *Iz istorii russkikh literaturnykh otnoshenii XVIII–XX vekov*. Moscow-Leningrad, 1959. Pages 132–140.

Remizov, Aleksey. *Ogon veshchey*. Paris, 1954.

Reynier, Gustave. *Les Origines du roman réaliste*. Paris, 1912.

Rodzevich, S. "K istorii russkogo romantizma (E. T. Gofman i 30–40 gg. v nashey literature)," *Russky filologichesky vestnik*, LXXVII (1917), 194–237.

Rozanov, V. V. *Legenda o velikom inkvizitore F. M. Dostoevskogo*. St. Petersburg, 1906.

Salvan, Albert J. "L'Essence du réalisme français," *Comparative Literature*, III (1951), 218–233.

Seduro, Vladimir. *Dostoyevski in Russian Literary Criticism, 1846–1956.* New York, 1957.

Seillière, Ernest. *Le Romantisme des réalistes: Gustave Flaubert.* Paris, 1914.

Shklovsky, Victor. *Za i protiv: Zametki o Dostoevskom.* Moscow, 1957.

Simmons, Ernest J. *Dostoevsky: The Making of a Novelist.* London, 1950.

Skaftymov, A. "*Zapiski iz polpolya* sredi publitsistiki Dostoevskogo," *Slavia,* VIII (1929), 101–117, 312–339.

Slonimsky, A. *Tekhnika komicheskogo u Gogolya.* Petersburg, 1923.

Stepanov, N. L., ed. *Tvorchestvo F. M. Dostoevskogo.* Moscow, 1959.

Strakhov, N. N. *Biografiya, pisma i zametki iz zapisnoy knizhki F. M. Dostoevskogo.* St. Petersburg, 1883.

Taine, Hippolyte. "Balzac," in *Nouveaux Essais de critique et d'histoire.* Paris, 1901. Pages 1–94.

Thibaudet, Albert. *Le Liseur de romans.* Paris, 1925.

——— *Réflexions sur le roman.* Paris, 1938.

Tortel, J. "Esquisse d'un univers tragique ou le drame de la toute-puissance," *Cahiers du Sud,* no. 310 (1951), pp. 367–381.

Trubetskoy, N. S. "O dvukh romanakh Dostoevskogo," *Novy zhurnal,* no. 60 (1960), pp. 116–137.

——— "Ranii Dostoevsky," *Novy zhurnal,* no. 61 (1960), pp. 124–146.

Tynyanov, Yury. "Dostoevsky i Gogol (k teorii parodii)," in his *Arkhaisty i novatory.* Leningrad, 1929. Pages 412–455.

Van Ghent, Dorothy. "The Dickens World: A View from Todgers's," *Sewanee Review,* LVIII (1950), 419–438.

Vengerov, Semyon Afanasievich. *Pisatel-Grazhdanin: Gogol.* St. Petersburg, 1913. (Vol. II of his *Sobranie sochinenii.*)

Veresayev, V. *Gogol v zhizni.* Moscow-Leningrad, 1933.

Vinogradov, V. V. *Evolyutsiya russkogo naturalizma.* Leningrad, 1929.

Voloshin, G. "Vremya i prostor u Dostoevskogo," *Slavia,* XII (1933), 162–172.

Watt, Ian. *The Rise of the Novel.* London, 1957.

Weidlé, Wladimir. "La Place de Balzac dans l'histoire des lettres," in UNESCO, *Hommage à Balzac.* Paris, 1950. Pages 412–452.

——— "Mysli o Dostoevskom," *Sovremennye zapiski,* LXII (1936), 401–408.

——— *Zadacha Rossii.* New York, 1956.

Weinberg, Bernard. *French Realism: The Critical Reaction, 1830–1870.* New York, 1937.

Wellek, René. "The Concept of Realism in Literary Scholarship," in his *Concepts of Criticism* (New Haven, 1963), pp. 222–255.

Wilson, Edmund. "Dickens: The Two Scrooges," in his *The Wound and the Bow.* Boston, 1941. Pages 1–104.

Z. E. and R. Sh. "Grotesk," in *Literaturnaya entsiklopediya,* vol. III. Moscow, 1930. Cols. 28–37.

Zamotin, I. I. *F. M. Dostoevsky v russkoy kritike. Chast pervaya, 1846–1881.* Warsaw, 1913.

Zelinsky, V., ed. *Kritichesky kommentary k sochineniyam F. M. Dostoevkogo.* 3 vols. Moscow, 1901.

——— ed. *Russkaya kriticheskaya literatura o proizvedeniyakh N. V. Gogolya.* 3 vols. Moscow, 1900.

Zenkovsky, V. V. "Problema krasoty v mirosozertsanii Dostoevskogo," *Put* (1933), II, 36–60.

Zola, Emile. *Les Romanciers naturalistes.* Paris, 1881.

Zweig, Stefan. *Three Masters: Balzac, Dickens, Dostoeffsky.* New York, 1930.

Notes

1. Realism, Pure and Romantic

1. Edouard Maynial, *L'Epoque réaliste* (Paris, 1931), p. 11.

2. Lane Cooper in his book, *An Aristotelian Theory of Comedy* (New York, 1922), cites Cicero: "Comedy is an imitation of life, a mirror of custom, an image of truth" (p. 91). See his translation from the *Tractatus Coislinianus,* which he calls the best ancient treatise on comedy: "The diction of comedy is the common, popular language" (p. 226). See also his quotation of John Tzetzes (c. 1110–1180): "Tragedy differs from comedy in that tragedy has a story and a report of things [or "deeds"] that are past, although it represents them as taking place in the present, but comedy embraces fictions of the affairs of everyday life" (p. 86).

3. Pierre Martino, *Le Roman réaliste sous le Second Empire* (Paris, 1913), p. 35.

4. *Ibid.,* pp. 74–75.

5. *Ibid.*

6. Preface to *The Nigger of the Narcissus,* in Morton Zabel, ed., *The Portable Conrad* (New York, 1954), p. 708.

7. Ian Watt, *The Rise of the Novel* (London, 1957), p. 28; and see pp. 29ff for an excellent critical summary of this problem.

8. George J. Becker, "Realism: An Essay in Definition," *Modern Language Quarterly,* X (June 1949), 185.

9. Maynial, p. 8. Harry Levin brilliantly shows the role of parody in this process, beginning with Cervantes; see "The Example of Cervantes," in his *Contexts of Criticism* (Cambridge, Mass., 1957).

10. *The Gates of Horn* (New York, 1963), p. 85. Cf. Irving Babbitt: "At the bottom of much so-called realism . . . is a special type of satire, a satire that is the product of violent emotional disillusion." *Rousseau and Romanticism* (New York, 1919), p. 104.

11. See A. W. Schlegel: "The comic must always be founded not only in national, but also in contemporary manners." *Lectures on Dramatic Art and Literature* (London, 1883), p. 438.

12. D. H. Lawrence, "John Galsworthy," in Edward D. McDonald, ed., *Phoenix: The Posthumous Papers of D. H. Lawrence* (New York, 1936), pp. 540ff.

13. Cf. George Lukacs: "Realism is the recognition of the fact that a work of literature can rest neither on a lifeless average, as the naturalists suppose, nor on an individual principle which dissolves its own self into nothingness. The central category and criterion of realist literature is the type, a peculiar synthesis which organically binds together the general and the particular both in characters and situations. What makes a type a type is not its average quality, nor its mere individual being, however profoundly conceived; what

makes it a type is that in it all the humanly and socially essential determinants are present on their highest level of development, in the ultimate unfolding of the possibilities latent in them, in extreme presentation of their extremes, rendering concrete the peaks and limits of men and epochs." *Studies in European Realism,* trans. Edith Bone (London, 1950), p. 6.

14. Albert Thibaudet, *Réflexions sur le roman* (Paris, 1938), pp. 32–33.

15. Letter to N. N. Strakhov, 23 and 26 April 1876; *Polnoye sobranie sochinenii,* LXII (Moscow, 1953), 268.

16. *Oeuvres complètes* (Paris: Bibliothèque de la Pléiade, 1956), p. 780.

17. Maupassant, "Le Roman," preface to *Pierre et Jean* (Paris, 1909), pp. xiii, xv.

18. See Gautier's remark about Henry Monnier: "His bourgeois characters — and no one has painted them more truly — bore you like actual bourgeois by endless floods of clichés and solemn asininities. This is no longer comedy; it is stenography." Introduction to Henry Monnier, *Paris et la province* (Paris: Garnier Frères, 1866), pp. 5–6. Cf. Jules Janin's conclusion in his preface to *La Confession* that "to imagine nothing is the only resource left to us."

19. See Baudelaire's notes entitled "Puisque réalisme il y a" (*Oeuvres complètes,* p. 991): "[Champfleury] dreamed up a word, a banner, a *hoax,* a watchword or password, to sink the rallying-cry: *Romanticism.* He believed that you always need one of these magic words, whose sense may be quite indeterminate.

"Imposing *what he believes* to be his method (for he is shortsighted as to his own nature) on everybody, he launched his firecracker and made his disturbance.

"As for Courbet, he became the clumsy Machiavelli of this Borgia, in Michelet's historical sense.

"Courbet theorized over an innocent farce with a compromising sterness of conviction. . . .

"Once the hoax was launched, it had to be believed in."

20. Georges Pellissier, *Le Réalisme du romantisme* (Paris, 1912), pp. 6, 78.

21. See Harry Levin, "What Is Realism?" *Comparative Literature,* III (1951), 196.

22. *Letters of William and Dorothy Wordsworth: The Middle Years,* ed. E. de Selincourt (Oxford, 1937), II, 705; letter of 18 January 1816. In context the words refer specifically to *The White Doe.*

23. *Splendeurs et misères des courtisanes,* in *L'Oeuvre de Balzac* (Paris, 1949–1953), V, 589–590. This edition is hereafter abbreviated as *Oeuvre.*

24. "Poetry, Myth, and Reality," in Allen Tate, ed., *The Language of Poetry* (Princeton, 1942), p. 10.

25. Harry Levin, "Some Meanings of Myth," *Daedalus,* Spring 1959, p. 227.

26. "Balzac lu et relu," *Oeuvre,* XVI, viii.

27. "Journal of *The Counterfeiters,*" trans. Justin O'Brien, as appendix to *The Counterfeiters* (New York, 1951), p. 384.

28. *Splendeurs et misères,* p. 248.

29. Emile Zola, *Les Romanciers naturalistes* (Paris, 1881), p. 128.

30. "It is hard not to see what the nineteenth century is seeking: a thirst for strong emotions is its true character." Stendhal, *Histoire de la peinture en Italie,* ch. 184; cited in Louis Maigron, *Le Romantisme et les moeurs* (Paris, 1910), p. 125.

31. Lukacs, p. 83.

32. *The Idea of a Theater* (Princeton, 1949), p. 9.

33. *Selected Essays, 1917–1932* (New York, 1932), pp. 381–382.

34. Paul Ginisty, *Le Mélodrame* (Paris, 1910), p. 11. See also J. Tortel, "Esquisse d'un univers tragique ou le drame de la toute-puissance," *Cahiers du Sud,* no. 310 (1951), *passim.*

35. Larousse, *Grand dictionnaire du XIXe siècle* (Paris, 1874), XII, 393.

36. Jules Marsan, "Le Mélodrame et Guilbert de Pixérécourt," *Revue d'histoire littéraire de la France,* 15 April 1900, p. 218.

37. G. Wilson Knight, "King Lear and the Comedy of the Grotesque," in *The Wheel of Fire* (London, 1949), p. 163.

38. See, e.g., Byron's complaint in *Don Juan,* 13.94–95: "The days of Comedy are gone, alas! / When Congreve's fool could vie with Molière's *bête:* / Society is smooth'd to that excess, / That manners hardly differ more than dress. / Our ridicules are kept in the back ground — / Ridiculous enough, but also dull; / Professions, too, are no more to be found / Professional; and there is nought to cull / Of folly's fruit; for though your fools abound, / They're barren, and not worth the pains to pull. / Society is now one polish'd horde, / Form'd of two mighty tribes, the *Bores* and *Bored.*"

Cf. Hazlitt's remark: "The progress of manners and knowledge has an influence on the stage, and will in time perhaps destroy both tragedy and comedy. Filch's picking pockets in the *Beggar's Opera* is not so good a jest as it used to be: by the force of the police and of philosophy, Lillo's murders and the ghosts in Shakespear will become obsolete. At last there will be nothing left, good nor bad, to be desired or dreaded, in the theatre or in real life" *Characters of Shakespear's Plays,* in P. P. Howe, ed., *The Complete Works of William Hazlitt,* IV (London, 1930), 194. To these statements might be added many others of the same tendency, all resumable in the title of one of Stendhal's articles, *La Comédie est impossible en 1836.*

39. *Splendeurs et misères,* preface to the 1st ed., 1844, in *Oeuvre,* XV, 353–354 (my italics).

40. In the poem, "O Muses, accourez . . ."

41. Hoxie M. Fairchild, *The Romantic Quest* (New York, 1931), p. 251.

42. "Celle-ci et celle-là, "*Les Jeunes-France* (Paris, 1873), pp. 194–197. The significance of such an attitude as it affects the conventional form of the literary hero is traced in Levin, *The Gates of Horn,* pp. 56–63.

43. B. G. Reizov, "K istorii romanticheskogo urbanizma: 'Ispoved' Zhyulya Zhanina i 'Otets Goriot' Balzaka," in Academy of Sciences of the USSR, Institute of Russian Literature, *Iz istorii russkikh literaturnykh otnoshenii XVIII-XX vekov* (Moscow-Leningrad, 1959), pp. 132–140.

44. *La Confession* (Paris, 1861), ch. 42, pp. 217–219.

45. *Tableau de Paris* (Amsterdam, 1782), I, iii–iv, vi. Mercier's ambitions, though not his actual performance, prefigure Balzac in a number of striking ways. The opening paragraph of his preface, for instance, is noteworthy in this regard for its stress on moeurs and for the image of Paris as something

approaching a living thing: "I am going to speak of Paris, and not of its buildings, temples, monuments, curiosities, etc.; enough others have written about them. I shall speak of public and private customs [moeurs], of the dominant ideas, of the present intellectual situation, of everything that has struck me in this bizarre heap of customs that are ever changing, the foolish ones and the reasonable alike. I shall speak further of its limitless grandeur, of its monstrous riches, of its scandalous luxury. It sucks up money and men; it absorbs and devours other cities, *quaerens quem devoret*" (p. iii).

One may even find a curious, if casual, anticipation of Balzac's socio-zoological theory in his preface to the *Comédie humaine,* where Mercier comments that "man is an animal susceptible to the most various and astonishing modifications" (p. xiii) and remarks on the "infinity of forms that literally metamorphose the individual according to place, circumstances, and time" (p. xiv). And Balzac's repeated comparisons of Parisian life to that of the American Indians develop Mercier's observation that "Parisian life is perhaps, in the order of nature, like the wandering life of the Savages of Africa and America" (pp. xiii–xiv).

46. *L'Hermite de la Chaussée-d'Antin ou observations sur les moeurs et les usages français au commencement du XIXe siècle par M. de Jouy* (7th ed., Paris, 1815), III, 292ff; quoted in Nils Ake Nilsson, *Gogol et Pétersbourg* (Stockholm, 1954), p. 20.

47. *Ibid.* (my italics).

48. *Oeuvre,* II, 387, 389.

49. *Oeuvre,* XV, 89–90.

50. "De l'Héroïsme de la vie moderne," *Oeuvres* (Paris: Bibliothèque de la Pléiade, 1956), pp. 679–680.

51. Albert Thibaudet, *Le Liseur de romans* (Paris, 1925), p. 215.

2. Balzac

1. Balzac, *Oeuvre,* XIV, 819.

2. Baudelaire, *Oeuvres complètes* (Paris, 1956), pp. 956, 1037.

3. Maxime Leroy, *Histoire des idées sociales en France,* III (Paris, 1954), 177, 179.

4. "Honoré de Balzac," in *French Poets and Novelists* (London, 1919), p. 72.

5. *Oeuvre,* V, xiv.

6. "One of the greatest merits of the *Comédie humaine* is certainly its having expressed the increasing importance of economic life in the last century. But one must add that it slighted the main thing, which was production, and overestimated the accessory — speculation." Charles Lalo, *L'Art et la vie,* III (Paris, 1947), 86.

7. Lukacs, p. 60.

8. The point is taken, along with the quotations from *La Fille aux yeux d'or,* from Gaëtan Picon, *Balzac par lui-même* (Paris, 1956), p. 152.

9. *Oeuvre,* XIV, 444.

10. *Ibid.,* XV, 100.

11. *La Fille aux yeux d'or, Oeuvre,* I, 818.

12. *Ferragus, Oeuvre,* II, 389.
13. *La Fille aux yeux d'or, Oeuvre,* I, 801.
14. *Ibid.,* p. 802.
15. *Oeuvre,* XV, 297.
16. Cf. the comparison of Scott and Cooper in "Lettres sur la littérature," *Oeuvre,* XIV, 1066–1067.
17. *Ibid.,* p. 1225.
18. "Théophile Gautier," in *L'Art romantique, Oeuvres complètes,* p. 1037 (my italics).
19. Introduction to *Romans et contes philosophiques* (1831), *Oeuvre,* XV, 77.
20. *The Gates of Horn,* p. 201.
21. Preface to *L'Histoire des Treize, Oeuvre,* I, 793.
22. Maurice Bardèche, *Balzac romancier* (Paris, 1940), p. 47.
23. Introduction to *Romans et contes philosophiques, Oeuvre,* XV, 77.
24. Preface to 1st ed. of *Ferragus* (1833), *Oeuvre,* XV, 91 (my italics).
25. Preface to *Scènes de la vie de province* (1833), *Oeuvre,* XV, 162.
26. Balzac, speaking through Félix Davin, introduction to *Etudes philosophiques* (1834), *Oeuvre,* XV, 108–110.
27. *Ibid.,* p. 110.
28. *Ibid.* (my italics).
29. "Lettres sur la littérature" (1840), *Oeuvre,* XIV, 1066.
30. "Lettre à M. Hyppolite Castille" (1846), *ibid.,* p. 1225.
31. Albert Béguin, *Balzac visionnaire* (Geneva, 1946), pp. 178–179. See his excellent discussion of the myth of the courtesan, pp. 149–180, to which I am greatly indebted.
32. *Code des gens honnêtes* (1825), *Oeuvre,* XIV, 64–65. Cf. Diderot: "I do not hate great crimes; first of all because beautiful paintings and tragedies are made of them; and then, the fact is that great and sublime actions and great crimes are both characterized by energy." "Salon de 1765," *Oeuvres complètes,* ed. J. Assezat (Paris, 1876), X, 342; cited in Herbert Dieckman, "Diderot's Conception of Genius," *Journal of the History of Ideas,* II (1941), 181.
33. *Splendeurs et misères, Oeuvre,* V, 561.
34. Erich Auerbach, *Mimesis* (Princeton, 1953), pp. 471–472.
35. *Oeuvre,* IV, 21 (my italics). Further page references to *Le Père Goriot* are included in parentheses in the text.
36. *Oeuvre,* XV, 369.
37. Balzac, speaking through Félix Davin, introduction to *Etudes des moeurs au XIXe siècle* (1835), *Oeuvre,* XV, 147.
38. Cf. Bardèche, p. 61.
39. *Splendeurs et misères, Oeuvre,* V, 249.
40. "But if you have a genuine feeling, hide it like a treasure; do not let it ever be suspected: you would be lost." *Oeuvre,* IV, 102.
41. Cf. Tortel, pp. 367–381. Nor was this a feature of literature alone, as the career of Vidocq, the model for Vautrin, shows.
42. Félicien Marceau, *Balzac et son monde* (Paris, 1955), p. 279.
43. "Lettre à M. Hyppolite Castille" (1846), *Oeuvre,* XIV, 1225, and *passim.*

44. *Ibid.*, p. 1220.
45. *Béatrix*, preface to the 1st ed. (1839), *Oeuvre*, XV, 319.
46. *Illusions perdues* (1837–1843), *Oeuvre*, IV, 1047. Further page references to this work are indicated in parentheses in the text.
47. "In [Balzac] drama, like the glittering light of the sun, dominates everything; it illuminates, warms, animates beings, objects, all the recesses of the scene; its burning rays pierce the thickest foliage, making everything there appear, tremble, sparkle." Balzac, speaking through Félix Davin, introduction to *Etude des moeurs au XIXe siècle, Oeuvre*, XV, 143.
48. *Correspondance de H. de Balzac, 1819–1850* (Paris, 1876), I, 100.
49. *Oeuvre*, V, 333. Further page references to this work are included in parentheses in the text.
50. *Oeuvre*, V, notes, iii. See also R. Messac, *Le "Detective Novel" et l'influence de la pensée scientifique* (Paris, 1929), pp. 301–302.
51. Curtius, *Balzac*, p. 37.
52. *Illusions perdues, Oeuvre*, IV, 1055.
53. *Ibid.*, p. 1062.
54. *Oeuvre*, V, 512.
55. *Ibid.*, p. 513.
56. *Oeuvre*, XV, 354.
57. *La Fausse Maîtresse;* quoted in Pierre Citron, *La Poésie de Paris dans la littérature française de Rousseau à Baudelaire* (Paris, 1961), II, 197.

3. Dickens

1. The phrase serves him as title for an 1867 article in *All the Year Round*.
2. Preface to the Charles Dickens Edition of *Martin Chuzzlewit*.
3. G. K. Chesterton, *Charles Dickens: A Critical Study* (New York, 1906), p. 286.
4. George H. Ford, *Dickens and His Readers* (Princeton, 1955), p. 140.
5. "The Ruffian," in *The Uncommercial Traveller*.
6. *The Gates of Horn*, p. 79.
7. *Eugénie Grandet* (Paris: Garnier Frères, 1955), p. 121.
8. Arnold Kettle, *An Introduction to the English Novel* (London, 1951), I, 126. The reference is specifically to the opening chapters of *Oliver Twist*.
9. John Forster, *The Life of Charles Dickens* (London: Everyman's Library, 1927), II, 279.
10. Quoted in Monroe Engel, *The Maturity of Dickens* (Cambridge, Mass., 1959), p. 9; and Walter C. Phillips, *Dickens, Reade and Collins: Sensation Novelists* (New York, 1919), p. 100.
11. George Gissing, *Charles Dickens: A Critical Study* (New York, 1904), pp. 31–32. See Forster's remark, I, 301: "No one was more intensely fond than Dickens of old nursery tales, and he had a secret delight in feeling that he was here only giving them a higher form. The social and manly virtues he desired to teach, were to him not less the charm of the ghost, the goblin, and the fairy fancies of his childhood; however rudely set forth in those earlier days. What now were to be conquered were the more formidable

dragons and giants that had their places at our own hearths, and the weapons to be used were of a finer than the 'ice-brook's temper.' "

12. Edgar Johnson, *Charles Dickens: His Tragedy and Triumph* (New York, 1952), I, 261. On the *Arabian Nights* and the question of Dickens' reading in general, see also T. W. Hill, "Books that Dickens Read," *The Dickensian,* XLV (1949), 81–90; 201–207. Jack Lindsay notes that while still a parliamentary reporter Dickens, "drawing on his memories of Eastern fable . . . wrote a tale about Howsa Kummauns and the odalisque Reefawm. For the time being, he did not quite know what to do about this new turn in his interests; and he put the sketch aside. Then later, in 1855, he turned it up, found that it expressed what he was still feeling, and remodelled it . . . calling it the Thousand and One Humbugs." *Charles Dickens: A Biographical and Critical Study* (London, 1950), p. 85.

13. The note appears as early as *Pickwick Papers;* in the preface to the first edition, Dickens, speaking of himself in the third person, observes: "If any of his imperfect descriptions, while they afford amusement in the perusal, should induce only one reader to think better of his fellow-men, and to look upon the brighter and more kindly side of human nature, he would indeed be proud and happy to have led to such a result."

14. *Correspondance entre George Sand et Gustave Flaubert* (Paris: Calmann-Lévy, n.d.), p. 436.

15. *Ibid.*, p. 433.

16. See, e.g., Dostoevsky's remarks on Dickens in *Diary of a Writer,* June 1876. See also Floris Delattre who, discussing George Sand as the most authentic representative of French humanitarian romanticism, concludes: "Finally, if you add to this union of reality and romance, or, rather, to this sort of vulgarization of romanticism which G. Sand's novels constitute, that taste for the marvelous and the fantastic which is indicated by the success in France of the Tales of Hoffman, with their mixture of bizarre imagination and exact observation, of the monstrous itself with the burlesque; if you recall, on the other hand, that veritable passion which the people of all countries feel for the combination of the tragic and the grotesque, the horrible and the comic — will you not have reconstituted, in some sense, the very elements of Dickens' genius?" *Dickens et la France* (Paris, 1927), p. 95.

17. *Polnoye sobranie sochinenii,* XXX (Moscow, 1951), 177.

18. *French Poets and Novelists* (London, 1919), p. 147.

19. See "The Streets — Night," esp. the paragraph beginning, "But the streets of London." This point of view was to become a constant one in Dickens. Also, *Oliver Twist,* ch. 23: "Bleak, dark, and piercing cold, it was a night for the well housed and fed to draw round the bright fire and thank God they were at home; and for the homeless starving wretch to lay him down and die. Many hunger-worn outcasts close their eyes in our bare streets, at such times, who, let their crimes have been what they may, can hardly open them in a more bitter world."

20. *Dickens romancier* (Paris, 1953), p. 48.

21. David Masson, ed., *The Collected Writings of Thomas De Quincey* (London, 1896–97), III, 393, 375. See also vol. I (*Autobiography*), p. 182: "No man ever was left to himself for the first time in the streets, as yet

unknown, of London, but he must have been saddened and mortified, perhaps terrified, by the sense of desertion and utter loneliness which belong to his situation. No loneliness can be like that which weighs upon the heart in the centre of faces never-ending, without voice or utterance for him . . . The great length of the streets in many quarters of London . . . and the murky atmosphere which, settling upon the remoter end of every long avenue, wraps its termination in gloom and uncertainty . . . are circumstances aiding that sense of vastness and illimitable proportions which for ever brood over the aspect of London in its interior."

22. I am indebted to Miller, pp. 94ff, for this interpretation of *The Old Curiosity Shop.*

23. Alain, *En lisant Dickens,* in *Les Arts et les dieux* (Paris: Bibliothèque de la Pléiade, 1958), p. 822.

24. Humphry House, *The Dickens World* (London, 1942), p. 205.

25. Ch. 38; quoted and discussed in Miller, p. 102.

26. F. W. Dupee, ed., *The Selected Letters of Charles Dickens* (New York, 1960), p. 209 (10 February 1855).

27. *Our Mutual Friend,* book I, ch. 6. Cf. Dickens in a journalistic piece: "The Seine at Paris is very gloomy, too, at such a time, and is probably the scene of far more crimes and greater wickedness; but this river looks so broad and vast, so murky and silent, seems such an image of death in the midst of the great city's life." ("Down With the Tide," in *Reprinted Pieces*).

28. Engel, pp. 138–144; and A. O. J. Cockshut, *The Imagination of Charles Dickens* (London, 1961), pp. 175–179.

29. Gissing, *Critical Studies,* p. 53.

30. For a reflection of this, see the chapter called "Nurses' Stories," in *The Uncommercial Traveller.* See also Johnson, I, 12ff.

31. James George Frazer, *The Golden Bough* (London, 1957), II, 716.

32. Dorothy Van Ghent, "The Dickens World: A View from Todgers's," *Sewanee Review,* LVIII, 3 (1950), 419–438; and Miller, pp. 116ff.

33. Van Ghent, p. 419.

34. See Miller, p. 154.

35. See, on the question of Dickensian names, the interesting monograph of Elizabeth Hope Gordon, *The Naming of Characters in the Works of Charles Dickens* (Lincoln, Nebraska, 1917), and particularly her discussion of the category she calls "vaguely suggestive names." Dickens' notebook, quoted in Forster's biography, with its long lists of possible names, is of course an important primary document here. On the role of nicknames and epithets, see Monod, p. 277.

36. See Oliver Elton, *A Survey of English Literature, 1780–1880* (New York, 1920), IV, 208.

37. Preface to the Second Series of *Sketches by Boz;* preface to the 1st ed. of *Little Dorrit.* John Butt and Kathleen Tillotson, in their *Dickens at Work* (London, 1957), note an important aspect of Dickens' relation to his public, tied as it was to his choice of publishing novels in instalments: "Through serial publication an author could recover something of the intimate relationship between story-teller and audience which existed in the ages of the sagas and of Chaucer" (p. 16).

38. Dupee, ed., *Selected Letters*, p. 227.

39. R. C. Churchill, "Dickens, Drama, and Tradition," *The Importance of Scrutiny*, ed. Eric Bentley (New York, 1948), p. 189.

40. "Fiction — Fair and Foul — 2," *Nineteenth-Century Opinion*, ed. Michael Goodwin (Penguin Books, 1951), p. 167; the article originally appeared in *The Nineteenth Century*, October 1881.

41. *Oeuvre*, IV, 20.

42. Walter C. Phillips, *Dickens, Reade and Collins: Sensation Novelists* (New York, 1919).

43. Robert Gorham Davis, "The Sense of the Real in English Fiction," *Comparative Literature*, III (1951), 216.

44. See Ford, who makes this point (p. 123) in the course of an excellent discussion of the problem.

45. Forster, I, 59.

46. Lukacs, p. 56.

47. Preface to the 1st ed. of *Nicholas Nickleby*.

48. Forster, II, 278.

49. *Household Words*, I (15 June 1850), 265–266; quoted in Richard Stang, *The Theory of the Novel in England, 1850–1870* (New York, 1959), p. 157.

50. M. M. Bakhtin, *Problemy tvorchestva Dostoevskogo* (Leningrad, 1929).

51. Chesterton, p. 190.

52. Miller, p. 85.

53. *Letters* (Nonesuch), III, 186; quoted in Miller, p. 250.

54. Harry Levin has found the basic Dickensian myth in the way his novels take us back, "recurrently and obsessively, to the old folk tale about the Babes in the Wood. Little Nell, David Copperfield, Esther Summerson, Pip, and his other waifs are pitted against the wicked witches of sullen bureaucracy and greedy industrialism." "Some Meanings of Myth," *Daedalus*, Spring 1959, p. 230.

55. "A world of commonplace affairs," House, p. 58; "marvellous fidelity," Gissing, p. 134.

56. Henry James, "Our Mutual Friend," in *The House of Fiction*, ed. Leon Edel (London, 1957), p. 257.

57. House, p. 222.

58. George Bernard Shaw in *The Bookman*, LXXXXIX (1934), 209; quoted in Ford, pp. 235–236.

4. Gogol

1. The outstanding Dostoevsky scholar, Leonid Grossman, was apparently the first to cast doubt on the statement, noting that it does not appear in any of Dostoevsky's writings. See his introduction, "Urbanizm Gogolya," to N. V. Gogol, *Povesti* (Moscow-Leningrad, 1935), p. 26. Melchior de Vogüé is frequently assumed to have reported the words as Dostoevsky's, when in fact he attributes them only to a Russian "very much involved in

the literary history of the last forty years" — the period 1846–1886; see his *Le Roman russe* (Paris, 1897), p. 96.

2. In 1841, F. I. Buslaev, historian of literature and professor at Moscow University, found Gogol in a coffeeshop in Italy, raptly reading Dickens. See Vasily Gippius, *N. V. Gogol v pismakh i vospominaniyakh* (Moscow, 1931), p. 213.

3. See Nils Ake Nilsson's monograph, *Gogol et Pétersbourg* (Stockholm, 1954), which argues for the decisive influence of both Jouy and Balzac.

4. N. P. Antsiferov, *Dusha Peterburga* (Berlin-Petersburg, 1922), p. 62.

5. "Peterburg," *Polnoye sobranie sochinenii kn. P. A. Vyazemskogo,* III (Petersburg, 1880), 157–58.

6. The translation is Edmund Wilson's, from *The Triple Thinkers* (London, 1952), p. 57.

7. Quoted in Waclaw Lednicki, *Russia, Poland and the West* (New York, 1953), p. 55.

8. N. Gogol, *Sobranie sochinenii v shesti tomakh* (Moscow, 1952–53), VI, 121; this edition hereafter is abbreviated *SS*.

9. Quoted in G. A. Gukovsky, *Realizm Gogolya* (Moscow, 1959), p. 246.

10. *SS,* VI, 13–14.

11. *SS,* VI, 107–108.

12. *SS,* VI, 109–110.

13. *SS,* III, 216. All of the Gogol stories discussed in the present chapter are in this volume; further page references are included in parentheses in the text.

14. See Grossman, "Urbanizm Gogolya," p. 12.

15. See Gukovsky's excellent discussion of this point, pp. 250ff.

16. *Masterstvo Gogolya* (Moscow-Leningrad, 1934), p. 16; a fuller discussion of the Ukrainian influence is available in Vasily Gippius, *Gogol* (Leningrad, 1924).

17. See the chapters entitled "O literaturnoy tsiklizatsii" and "Romantichesky naturalizm: Zhyul Zhanen i Gogol" in V. V. Vinogradov, *Evolyutsiya russkogo naturalizma* (Leningrad, 1929). See also Michel Gorlin, "Hoffmann en Russie," in his *Etudes littéraires et historiques* (Paris, 1957), pp. 189–206.

18. V. V. Rozanov, *Legenda o velikom inkvizitore* (Petersburg, 1906), p. 260.

19. "Notes on the Decline of Naturalism," in John W. Aldridge, ed., *Critiques and Essays on Modern Fiction* (New York, 1952), p. 418.

20. S. A. Vengerov, *Pisatel-Grazhdanin: Gogol* (Petersburg, 1913), p. 19.

21. See the subtle and informed discussion of this in Gukovsky, pp. 252ff and *passim*. Identifying atmosphere ("a definite tonality of exposition, emotional, and evaluating the matter of the exposition *through emotion,* unifying the system of imagery of the exposition and providing a foundation for it") as a practice that first arose in the period of preromanticism, he nevertheless finds Gogol's use of it antiromantic, that is, essentially realistic. Finding that Pushkin uses atmosphere significantly in his prose — though with an important element of subjectivity — he concludes: "Thus Pushkin prepared Gogol in this regard, but he did not provide what we see in

Gogol, in whose mature works the specificity of emotional tonality, the signs of coloring and atmosphere — as distinct from Pushkin — are brought sharply to the fore and color all the elements of the exposition; and in Gogol, they are motivated and based in a new way, not by the character of the individual perceiving reality, but by the character of that reality itself, which is represented, evaluated, and revealed — a reality, moreover, which is chiefly evaluated in its social aspect" (p. 255). What makes it impossible wholly to accept Gukovsky's frequently persuasive argument is his failure to take fully into account all of Gogol's idiosyncrasy. He acknowledges the oddness, but not its extent — which leaves him free to attribute quirks in these tales to Petersburg life, an assumption for which there is some warrant but little convincing proof.

22. From Faddey Bulgarin's review in *Severnaya pchela,* no. 73, 1835; reprinted in V. Zelinsky, *Russkaya kriticheskaya literatura o proizvedeniyakh N. V. Gogolya* (Moscow, 1900), I, 57.

23. Rozanov, p. 262; *SS,* III, 93.

24. Letter of M. Grabovsky to P. A. Kulish, 17 November 1843; reprinted in Zelinsky, III, 66–67.

25. In this, of course, he prefigures Kafka. For a discussion of the parallel, see Victor Erlich, "Gogol and Kafka: Note on 'Realism' and 'Surrealism,' " in Morris Halle et al., eds., *For Roman Jakobson* (The Hague, 1956), pp. 100–108.

26. André Malraux, *Saturne* (Paris, 1951), p. 83. On Gogol and Goya, see S. Shambinago, "Gogol i Goya," in his *Trilogiya romantizma* (Moscow, 1911). One might also apply to Gogol the opening sentence of Baudelaire's essay on Goya, changing only the name of the country: "En Russie, un homme singulier a ouvert dans le comique de nouveaux horizons."

27. See Gippius, *Gogol,* p. 54. (By "later" I mean later in the series of tales as arranged by Gogol for vol. III of the 1843 collected works.)

28. *Ibid.,* p. 51.

29. These examples are taken from Bely's interesting discussion of this point, p. 36.

30. Cizevsky has demonstrated how "even purely realistic details in Gogol are hyperbolic and improbable." See his article, "Neizvestny Gogol," *Novy zhurnal,* XXII (1951), 155–156.

31. Cf. A. Slonimsky, *Tekhnika komicheskogo u Gogolya* (Petersburg, 1923), pp. 28–29: "The view of Gogol as a 'realist' for a long time distorted the perception of Gogol [by the critics] and led to irreconcilable contradictions. As a result of the fact that the serious element in Gogol's humor was observed apart from its connection with comic devices, the significance of these comic devices became incomprehensible."

32. Gippius, *Gogol,* p. 91.

33. "The main hero of almost all the works of Gogol, the hero whom we meet in almost every work, is the Devil." Dmitry Cizevsky, "O 'Shineli' Gogolya," *Sovremennye zapiski,* LXVII (1938), 193.

Bely makes much the same point, punning that in the laughter of the Petersburg stories the devil of *Evenings on a Farm near Dikanka* has become a trait (" 'chort' *Vecherov* stal 'chertoy' "), a mania afflicting a whole range of Gogolian characters (p. 186). He is, furthermore, extremely acute on the central importance of kinlessness in Gogol's apprehension of the city; his observations on this score underline the double significance of alienation — and prepare his conclusion that "The root of Gogol's laughter in the second [Petersburg] phase is laughter from horror" (pp. 194, 51–52, 187–190, and *passim*).

34. Boris Eikhenbaum makes this an essential criterion of the grotesque. "Kak sdelana 'Shinel' Gogolya," in his *Skvoz literaturu* (Leningrad, 1924), p. 191.

35. Cizevsky, "Neizvestny Gogol," p. 154. This observation seems first to have been made by Rozanov; see his *Legenda o velikom inkvizitore,* p. 177.

36. Cizevsky, *ibid.,* pp. 154–155. Cf. Walter Bagehot: "Ornate art, as much as pure art, catches its subject in the best light it can, takes the most developed aspect of it which it can find, and throws upon it the most congruous colors it can use. *But grotesque art does just the contrary.* . . . This art works by contrast. It enables you to see, it makes you see, the perfect type by painting the opposite deviation. It shows you what ought to be by what ought not to be; when complete, it reminds you of the perfect image, by showing you the distorted and imperfect image." "Wordsworth, Tennyson, and Browning or Pure, Ornate and Grotesque Art in English Poetry," in Mrs. Russell Barrington, ed., *The Works and Life of Walter Bagehot,* IV (London, 1915), 301.

In discussing the importance of contrast as a conscious element in Gogol's work, Gippius quotes an article of the young Gogol's on architecture: "True effect lies in *sharp opposition;* beauty is never so sharp and evident as in contrast" (*Gogol,* pp. 81–82).

37. *SS,* IV, 246.

38. The point is far from clear. Gogol himself gave contradictory testimony. Writing to Zhukovsky from Naples on 10 January 1848 (new style), he says of becoming a writer: "Everything happened as though independent of my own volition. I never thought, for example, that it would be my lot to be a satirical writer and make my readers laugh. It is true that while I was still in school I would feel at times a disposition to merriment and would pester my chums with out-of-place jokes. But these were temporary attacks; in general I was rather of a melancholy character and inclined to thoughtfulness. Afterwards illness and the blues were added to this. And just this illness and these blues were the reason for that gaiety which appeared in my first works: in order to divert myself, without a further aim or plan, I thought up heroes and placed them in humorous situations — there you have the origin of my tales!" (Gippius, *N. V. Gogol v pismakh i vospominaniyakh,* p. 372). Elsewhere, however, he offered lofty hindsight interpretations of his work. Nabokov dismisses these as irrelevant (*Nikolai Gogol,* Norfolk, Conn., 1944, p. 57). Cizevsky more subtly observes ("Neizvestny Gogol," p. 136) that Gogol's ideological interests were more obscured than served by the maverick vitality of his literary talent. But the most brilliant formulation of this paradox is Bely's.

Gogol, he says, began with captivating trifles on which the music of the style conferred a unity; he then achieved integrity of style at the expense of such melody: "and [was] suddenly horrified by the narrow tendency in which his style had withered, as a result of which the organism of his work turned out — headless; and the head — remained without a body. Belinsky took hold of the headless body, having discovered in it a tendency of enormous significance, while from the unfinished head of the process he was fashioning, sundered from its body, Gogol scooped out the brain and made — a police helmet, and arrested his own work. But the 'police helmet,' stuck into the *Correspondence* and the *Author's Confession,* could not deflect the current that went through Gogol the creator into the rationally headless [*rassudochno-bezgolovoe*] body of his creations — whose head turned out to be all of Russian literature, which continued to develop Gogol's cause — without Gogol the preacher" (*Masterstvo Gogolya,* p. 27).

5. The Most Fantastic City

1. Berdyaev writes: "The fact is that really to 'get inside' Dostoevsky it is necessary to have a certain sort of soul — one in some way akin to his own — and we had to wait for the spiritual and intellectual movement which marked the beginning of the twentieth century before such souls could be found. The extraordinary interest in Dostoevsky and his work dates from this time." Nicholas Berdyaev, *Dostoevsky,* trans. Donald Attwater (New York, 1934), p. 14; see also pp. 226–227.

A similar conclusion, reached from opposite premises, is stated at the beginning of V. Pereverzev's little-known book; the year, 1922, is especially significant: "It is our lot to meet the hundredth anniversary of Dostoevsky's birth at a moment of great revolutionary change, at the moment of the catastrophic destruction of the outworn old world and the construction of a new. Chronologically, Dostoevsky belongs to the old world. . . . But [though he was] a contemporary of Turgenev, Pisemsky, Saltykov, and Tolstoy, he is a stranger among them. . . . Dostoevsky in style and spirit is close to the most popular writers of the beginning of the twentieth century . . . One can say that all contemporary literature follows in the footsteps of Dostoevsky, as all classical literature followed in the footsteps of Pushkin. Dostoevsky is still a contemporary writer; the present time has still not rendered obsolete the problems that are dealt with in the work of this writer. For us to speak of Dostoevsky still means to speak of the deepest and most burning questions of our current life. Caught in the whirlpool of a great revolution, involved in the problems it has posed, ardently and painfully apprehending all the peripeties of the revolutionary tragedy, we find in Dostoevsky — ourselves. . . . 'The Prophet of the Russian Revolution' — thus Merezhkovsky entitled one of his critical works on Dostoevsky. Prophet or not, it is an incontestable fact that Dostoevsky understood deeply the psychological element of revolution, that even before the revolution he clearly saw in it what many — not only in his time but even at the time of the revolution itself — did not even guess." *Tvorchestvo Dostoevskogo* (Moscow, 1922), pp. 3–4.

2. Pyotr Mikhailovich Bitsilli, "K voprosu o vnutrenney forme romana Dostoevskogo," *Godishnik,* Sofia University, History-Philology Faculty, XLII (1945–46), 23.

3. Of the thirty-five novels, stories, and sketches listed in the index of the 1956 Soviet edition of Dostoevsky's *Collected Works,* twenty-four are set in Petersburg: *Poor Folk, White Nights,* "Bobok," *The Eternal Husband,* "Mr. Prokharchin," *The Double,* "A Christmas Tree and a Wedding," *Notes from Underground, The Idiot,* "The Crocodile," "A Gentle Creature," *Netochka Nezvanova, A Raw Youth,* "Polzunkov," *Crime and Punishment,* "A Novel in Nine Letters," "An Unpleasant Predicament," "A Weak Heart," "The Dream of a Ridiculous Man," "A Centenarian," *The Insulted and Injured,* "The Landlady," "An Honest Thief," "The Wife of Another and the Husband Under the Bed." In addition to these, Petersburg plays some part in *The Possessed.*

4. Quoted in N. P. Antsiferov, *Peterburg Dostoevskogo* (Petrograd, 1923), p. 20.

5. See F. I. Evnin, "Roman *Prestuplenie i nakazanie,*" in N. L. Stepanov, ed., *Tvorchestvo F. M. Dostoevskogo* (Moscow, 1959), pp. 169–70.

6. Antsiferov, p. 31.

7. N. N. Strakhov, *Biografiya, pisma i zametki iz zapisnoy knizhki F. M. Dostoevskogo* (St. Petersburg, 1883), p. 359.

8. Letter to N. N. Strakhov, 18–30 May 1871, in *Pisma,* ed. A. S. Dolinin (Moscow-Leningrad, 1928–59), II (1930), 365.

9. "Peterburg i Moskva," in *Sobranie sochinenii v tryokh tomakh* (Moscow, 1948), II, 767.

10. See V. L. Komarovich, "Peterburgskie feletony Dostoevskogo," in Yu. Oksman, ed., *Feletony sorokovykh godov* (Moscow-Leningrad, 1930), to whom I am indebted for much of what follows. Antsiferov's *Dusha Peterburga* (Petersburg, 1922) is also useful on this subject.

11. Pleshcheyev and Grigoriev were writing feuilletons strikingly like Dostoevsky's in the late forties — so much so that V. S. Nechayeva, a painstaking scholar of Dostoevsky's texts, was led to include in the text of the "Petersburg Chronicle" a piece that was later proved to be Pleshcheyev's (see Komarovich, p. 123). As for Grigoriev, compare this characterization of Petersburg, from a feuilleton of 1847: "In this new world there flashed before me a vein of life completely fantastic; a fearful mystic exhalation [*veyanie*] swept over my moral nature — but, on the other hand, I recognized with the help of its rather dreary scent and its rather dirty color a strangely vulgar world" (quoted in Antsiferov, *Dusha Peterburga,* p. 135).

12. Quoted in Komarovich, p. 97, n. 1.

13. *Pisma,* I, 84.

14. F. M. Dostoevsky, *Statyi za 1845–1868 gody* — vol. XIII of B. Tomashevsky and K. Khalabayev, eds., *Polnoye sobranie khudozhestvennykh sochinenii* (Moscow-Leningrad, 1930), XIII, 5; hereafter referred to as *Poln. sobr.* The announcement appeared in *Otechestvennye zapiski* (National Notes) in November 1845. Here and elsewhere, my translation aims at rendering as scrupulously as possible not only the sense of the Russian original, but its form. Dostoevsky, particularly in the early writings, tends to be wordy, involved, ambiguous, and sometimes downright obscure.

15. *Pisma, I,* 75 (letter of 24 March 1845). In the same letter he repeats, with evident aproval, Beranger's characterization of contemporary French feuilletonists as "a bottle of Chambertin in a bucket of water."

16. Quoted in K. Mochulsky, *Dostoevsky: Zhizn i tvorchestvo* (Paris, 1947), p. 59.

17. Nestor Roqueplan, *Regain: La Vie parisienne* (new ed., Paris, 1869), p. iv.

18. *Poln. sobr.*, XIII, 8.

19. *Ibid.*

20. *Ibid.*, p. 9.

21. *Ibid.*

22. *Ibid.* (my italics).

23. *Ibid.*, p. 10.

24. *Ibid.*, pp. 10–11.

25. *Ibid.*, p. 11.

26. *Ibid.*, pp. 12–13.

27. *Ibid.*, p. 17.

28. *Ibid.*, pp. 17–18.

29. *Ibid.*, p. 18.

30. *Ibid.*, p. 21.

31. *Ibid.*, p. 23 (my italics). Dostoevsky's view of Petersburg architecture was to change radically with the years; see his *Diary of a Writer*, "Little Pictures," I (1873). See also Wladimir Weidlé, *Zadacha Rossii* (New York, 1956), pp. 218–223

32. *Poln. sobr.*, XIII, 26–27.

33. *Ibid.*, p. 27. The capitalization of "Nature" and the italics are not in the original, but have been added to render the difference between the Russian words, *priroda* and *natura.*

34. See R. Pletnev, "Preobrazhenie mira: Priroda v tvorchestve Dostoevskogo," *Novy zhurnal*, no. 43 (1955), pp. 63–80.

35. *Poln. sobr.*, XIII, 27–28.

36. *Ibid.*, p. 28.

37. *Ibid.*, pp. 28–29. These arguments are couched in deliberately vague though emphatic terms; in the Russia of Nicholas I, their political implications could hardly be developed.

38. *Ibid.*, pp. 29–31 (last italics mine).

39. *Ibid.*, p. 31.

40. *Ibid.*, pp. 31–32.

41. *Ibid.*, p. 20.

42. I have rendered as "visions" the Russian word *snovideniya,* which is literally compounded of the words for "dream" and "vision," because "dream-visions" seemed both too cumbersome and misleadingly reminiscent of an obsolete literary form.

43. See Strakhov, p. 213; and *Poln. sobr.*, XIII, 595. Charles E. Passage, *Dostoevski the Adapter* (Chapel Hill, 1954), relates as much as is known of the circumstances; see pp. 113–114.

44. Passage, p. 114.

45. *Poln. sobr.*, XIII, 155–156.

46. *Ibid.*, pp. 156–157.

47. *Ibid.*, p. 157.

48. *Ibid.*, p. 160.

49. Komarovich was the first critic to make these points, in his "Peter-

burgskie feletony Dostoevskogo"; see esp. pp. 116–117. See also Leonid Grossman, "Dostoevskii — Khudozhnik," in N. L. Stepanov, ed., *Tvorchestvo F. M. Dostoevskogo* (Moscow, 1959), pp. 353–354.

6. Evolution of the Myth

1. Dostoevsky recounts the whole story in his *Diary of a Writer,* January 1877, ch. 2.

2. April 8; all references to *Poor Folk* are by date of letter and are indicated hereafter in parentheses in the text.

3. V. G. Belinsky, "Peterburg i Moskva," in *Sobranie sochinenii v tryokh tomakh* (Moscow, 1948), II, 785.

4. Mochulsky, p. 32.

5. *Pisma,* I, 85, 87.

6. Quoted in Mochulsky, p. 41.

7. V. Zelinsky, ed., *Kritichesky kommentary k sochineniyam F. M. Dostoevskogo* (Moscow, 1901), I, 165.

8. *Diary of a Writer,* November 1877, ch. 1.

9. Simmons is the most obvious example of this, basing almost the whole of his book on the theme of the double with a singlemindedness that verges at times on the mechanical. But even Mochulsky, who has written the best single work on Dostoevsky, virtually omits specific comment on the artistic side of the work.

10. Beyond the change of subtitle, this shift in emphasis is reflected in Dostoevsky's removing the elaborate chapter headings that had appeared in the original edition. The first chapter, for instance, had originally been entitled: "How the Titular Councillor Golyadkin Woke Up. How He Accoutred Himself and Set Out for the Place Where his Path Led. How Mr. Golyadkin Justified Himself in his Own Eyes and How Then he Deduced the Rule that it Is Best of All to Act in Bold Fashion and With a Frankness Not Devoid of Nobility. Where Mr. Golyadkin Finally Called." F. M. Dostoevsky, *Sobranie sochinenii v desyati tomakh* (Moscow, 1956), I, 635; the twenty-two subsequent pages contain the other chapter titles, all in the same mock-picaresque vein, together with passages excised in the reworked edition of 1865–66.

11. Ch. 10. References to the Russian edition are by part, chapter, and section — hereafter abbreviated (I.2.1) — or by whatever divisions appear there, arranged in descending order.

12. *Pisma,* I, 79.

13. Mochulsky, p. 42.

14. See A. L. Bem's articles, " 'Shinel' i *Bednye lyudi*" and " 'Nos' i *Dvoinik*" in the collection he edited, *O Dostoevskom,* III (Prague, 1936), 127–166; Yury Tynyanov, "Dostoevsky i Gogol (K teorii parodii)" in *Arkhaisty i novatory* (Leningrad, 1929), pp. 412–455; V. V. Vinogradov, "Shkola sentimentalnogo naturalizma" in his *Evolyutsiya russkogo naturalizma* (Leningrad, 1929); and V. Pereverzev, *Tvorchestvo Dostoevskogo* (Moscow, 1922), *passim.*

15. Tynyanov, pp. 415–416.

16. Reviewing *Poor Folk* and *The Double* in 1846, Belinsky wrote that, for all the obvious echoes of Gogol in these works, they showed so much independence that Gogol's influence "will probably not be prolonged . . . though Gogol will nonetheless remain forever his creative father [*otets po tvorchestvu*]." Zelinsky, I, 34.

17. Quoted in Bem, *O Dostoevskom,* III, 125.

18. Bem, "Dramatizatsiya breda (*Khozyayka* Dostoevskogo)," in *O Dostoevskom,* I, 78.

19. Belinsky, "Peterburg i Moskva," pp. 787–788.

20. Mochulsky, pp. 23–24.

21. *Pisma,* I, 129.

22. *Ibid.,* II, 586.

23. "Not seldom, in reading [Dostoevsky]," Gissing remarks, "one is reminded of Dickens, even of Dickens's peculiarities in humour. The note of his books is sympathy; a compassion so intense as often to seem morbid — which indeed it may have been . . . But read the opening of the story called in its French translation *Humiliés et Offensés;* it is not impossible that Dickens's direct influence worked with the writer in those pages describing the hero's kindness to the poor little waif who comes under his care; in any case, spiritual kindred is manifest. And in how alien a world, regarding all things outward!" *Charles Dickens,* p. 292.

24. The point is made in Mochulsky, p. 170.

25. Dostoevsky's confession and vindication of his brother was first published in *Epokha* in September 1864; it is reprinted in full in Strakhov, *Biografiya,* pp. 208–212, and appears also in *Poln. sobr.* XIII, 350ff.

26. Ernest J. Simmons, *Dostoevsky* (London, 1950), p. 106.

27. Part II, ch. 2. I take this same ambivalence to underlie the underground man's puzzling tirade on Russian romantics, of whom he is clearly one — at least with a half of his nature.

28. V. Ya. Kirpotin, *F. M. Dostoevsky: Tvorchesky put* (*1821–1859*) (Moscow, 1960), p. 373.

7. Apogee: *Crime and Punishment*

1. *Pisma,* I, 408 (letter to A. A. Krayevsky, editor of *Otechestvennye zapiski,* 8 June 1865).

2. Leonid P. Grossman, "Gorod i lyudi *Prestupleniya i nakazaniya,*" introduction to *Prestuplenie i nakazanie* (Moscow, 1935), p. 23. The specific historical background that follows is taken almost entirely from this article, which stands virtually alone in treating the subject.

3. *Ibid.,* pp. 24–25.

4. *Ibid.*

5. *Ibid.,* pp. 25–26.

6. "Protsess Lasenera," *Poln. sobr.* XIII, 521–522.

7. *Ibid.,* p. 522. Besides this introduction, Dostoevsky's hand is perceptible in the article itself, and — testifying to the impression the case made on him — the name of Lacenaire recurs in the manuscripts of *The Idiot* and *A Raw Youth.*

8. Grossman, "Gorod i lyudi," pp. 29–30.

9. *Ibid.*, p. 31.

10. *Vremya,* 1863, III, *Sovremennoye obozrenie* (Contemporary Review); cited in Grossman, p. 10.

11. *Ibid.*

12. *Ibid.*, p. 12.

13. *Ibid.*, p. 16. The story of Sonya also has its role in this polemic with Chernyshevsky. Thus where he has his young intellectual, Kirsanov, rescue Nastenka Kryukova from a life of vice, Dostoevsky has his hero rescued by the prostitute. The theme of the prostitute's moral superiority, of course, first appeared in *Notes from Underground.*

14. Quoted in Evnin, p. 154.

15. See *Ibid.*, p. 156.

16. *Ibid.*, p. 133.

17. Part III, ch. 29; quoted in *ibid.*, p. 134.

18. *Pisma,* I, 352; quoted in *ibid.*, p. 134.

19. Grossman, "Gorod i lyudi," p. 21, n. 1.

20. See his remarks of 1862 on *Les Misérables* and *Notre Dame de Paris* in *Poln. sobr.*, XIII, 525–527.

21. Evnin, p. 139.

22. See Dostoevsky's macabre vision of the water-filled Petersburg cemeteries in "Bobok." See also Antsiferov's observation in his tracing of the development of the myth of Petersburg from the founding of the city: "In the history of Petersburg one phenomenon of nature acquired a special significance that imparts to the Petersburg myth a quite exceptional interest. The periodically recurring inundations, the pressure of an angry sea on the daringly erected city, announced to the city by cannonades in the awful autumn nights, evoked images of the ancient myths. Chaos was seeking to swallow up the created world." *Byl i mif Peterburga* (Petersburg, 1924), p. 57.

23. Mochulsky has pointed out another side of this scene's symbolism: "The soul of Petersburg is the soul of Raskolnikov: in it are the same grandeur and the same coldness. The hero 'wonders at his somber and enigmatic impression and puts off finding its solution.' The novel is dedicated to the solution of the mystery of Raskolnikov-Petersburg-Russia. Petersburg is just as double as the human consciousness to which it has given rise. On the one hand, the majestic Neva, in whose azure water is reflected the golden cupola of St. Isaac's Cathedral . . . on the other hand, the Haymarket, with its alleys and back streets, packed with poverty . . . It is the same with Raskolnikov: 'He is remarkably handsome, with fine dark eyes and dark brown hair, above average in height, slender and well-built' — a dreamer, a romantic, a lofty spirit and a proud, noble and strong personality. But this 'fine man' has his own Haymarket, his own filthy underground: 'the thought' of the murder and the robbery" (p. 238).

24. Vyacheslav Ivanov, *Freedom and the Tragic Life: A Study in Dostoevsky* (New York, 1957), p. 41.

25. L. P. Grossman, ed., *Tvorchestvo Dostoevskogo, 1821–1881–1921* (Odessa, 1921), pp. 25–26.

26. The point is made by Grossman, "Gorod i lyudi," p. 45.

27. Arnold Hauser, *The Social History of Art,* II (New York, 1952), 671.

28. *Pisma,* I, 96 (letter of 7 October 1846). Cf. his confession in "Petersburg Visions" that already in childhood, "almost lost, abandoned in Petersburg, I somehow constantly feared it" (p. 56).

29. Part I, ch. 4, sec. 3. As one might guess from the recurrence of this motif, the observation of just such people was a favorite pastime of Dostoevsky. See "Little Pictures" in his *Diary of a Writer,* 1873, where the creative process is laid bare as we see the writer composing stories to explain the impressions the passing crowd makes on him.

30. *Polnoye sobranie sochinenii,* XIII (Moscow, 1949), 55.

31. *Winter Notes on Summer Impressions,* ch. 3.

32. "Petersburg Chronicle," feuilleton of June 15; see above, Chapter 5.

33. "Dramatizatsiya breda (*Khozyayka* Dostoevskogo)," in Bem, ed., *O Dostoevskom,* I, 77–124.

34. R. P. Blackmur, "*Crime and Punishment,* a Study of Dostoevsky's Novel," *The Chimera,* I (Winter 1943), 26–27.

35. Hauser, II, 852.

36. The argument is made by Bem in *O Dostoevskom,* III, 83.

37. Berdyaev, p. 90.

38. He writes in one notebook, for example: "Without fail put the course of the action on a true footing and destroy the uncertainty; i.e., *one way or another* explain the whole murder, and establish clearly its character and relations." I. I. Glivenko, ed., *Iz arkhiva F. M. Dostoevskogo: Prestuplenie i nakazanie: Neizdannye materialy* (Moscow-Leningrad, 1931), p. 66.

39. Blackmur, p. 27.

40. Glivenko, p. 167.

41. Hauser, II, 856.

42. M. M. Bakhtin, *Problemy tvorchestva Dostoevskogo* (Leningrad, 1929); see also N. S. Trubetskoy's discussion of *Crime and Punishment* from this point of view in his article "O dvukh romanakh Dostoevskogo," *Novy zhurnal,* no. 60 (1960), pp. 116–137.

43. Bakhtin, p. 30.

44. *The City in History* (New York, 1961), pp. 116–117.

45. Cf. Berdyaev, pp. 40–41, 57–58.

46. See George Lukacs' chapter, "Dostojewskij," in his *Der Russische Realismus in der Weltliteratur* (Berlin, 1952), p. 142, where he suggests that Dostoevsky's vision of life in Petersburg shapes his vision of life in all the narratives, regardless of where he situates them.

8. Poetics of the City

1. Count Kushelev-Bezborodko, reviewing *The Insulted and Injured;* reprinted in V. Zelinsky, ed., *Kritichesky kommentary k sockineniyam F. M. Dostoevskogo* (Moscow, 1901), II, 13.

2. *Polnoye sobranie sochinenii,* XIII (Moscow, 1949), 55.

3. *Ibid.,* pp. 54–55.

4. Strakhov, *Biografiya,* "Iz zapisnoy knizhki F. M. Dostoevskogo," p. 373.

5. For a somewhat different interpretation of this remark, see Renato Poggioli, "Dostoevski, or Reality and Myth," in *The Phoenix and the Spider* (Cambridge, Mass., 1957), p. 25. This essay is probably the best English-language treatment to date of Dostoevsky's realism, and my remarks are intended to supplement rather than repeat it.

6. *Poln. sobr.*, XIII, 540.

7. I. A. Goncharov, *Sobranie sochinenii v vosmi tomakh*, VIII (Moscow, 1955), 457 (letter of 11 February 1874).

8. *Pisma*, II, 150–51 (letter to Maykov, 11–23 December 1868).

9. See Strakhov, *Biografiya*, pp. 289–290.

10. S. Balukhaty, ed., *Russkie pisateli o literature*, II (Leningrad, 1939), 198.

11. *Pisma*, III, 206 (letter to Kh. D. Alchevskaya, 9 April 1876).

12. *Ibid.*, II, 43 (letter to S. A. Ivanova, 27 September 1867).

13. *Ibid.*, II, 169 (letter to N. Strakhov, 26 February–10 March 1869).

14. Strakhov, *Biografiya*, p. 226.

15. *Pisma*, II, 297 (letter to S. A. Ivanova, 9–21 October 1870).

16. Ivan Petrovich, the writer-narrator of *The Insulted and Injured*, confesses: "Working under a strain, a certain special nervous irritation builds up in me; I think more clearly, feel more vividly and deeply, and even my style is under full control, so that work done under pressure turns out better" (Epilogue). Dostoevsky's wife, Anna Grigorievna, noted of this passage: "F. M. talked that way of his mood when he had to work under pressure" (Grossman, ed., *Tvorchestvo Dostoevskogo, 1821–1881–1921*, p. 30).

17. Quoted in A. L. Bem, "Tayna lichnosti Dostoevskogo," in V. V. Zenkovsky, ed., *Pravoslavie i kultura* (Berlin, 1923), p. 193.

18. Ian Watt, *The Rise of the Novel* (London, 1957), p. 279.

19. S. Askoldov, "Psikhologiya kharakterov u Dostovskogo," in A. S. Dolinin, ed., *F. M. Dostoevsky: Statyi i materialy*, II (Leningrad, 1925), 5.

20. Evnin, p. 169.

21. Glivenko, p. 216.

22. *Ibid.*

23. For a fuller discussion of this aspect of Dostoevsky's work, see G. Voloshin, "Vremya i prostor u Dostoevskogo," *Slavia*, XII (1933), 162–172.

24. *Netochka Nezvanova*, ch. 3.

25. Glivenko, p. 173.

26. Simmons, *Dostoevsky*, p. 144.

27. *Poln. sobr.*, XIII, 523.

28. A. V. Chicherin, "Poetichesky stroy yazyka v romanakh Dostoevskogo," in Stepanov, ed., *Tvorchestvo Dostoevskogo*, p. 471.

29. The formulation is Yury Tynyanov's, from his *Arkhaisty i novatory* (Leningrad, 1929), p. 427; it concludes an interesting discussion of contrast in Dostoevsky, pp. 426–427. Stimulating observations on structural contrast in the early work can also be found in N. S. Trubetskoy, "Ranii Dostoevsky," *Novy zhurnal*, no. 61 (1960), pp. 124–126.

30. Glivenko, p. 211 (my italics).

31. "The Dream of a Ridiculous Man," ch. 1.

32. See *Polnoye sobranie sochinenii,* LVIII (Moscow-Leningrad, 1934), 117.

33. Quoted in Zelinsky, I, 139.

34. *The Brothers Karamazov,* I.3.3. Similar statements are made by Valkovsky, the underground man, Svidrigailov, Versilov, and others.

35. *Freedom and the Tragic Life,* p. 40.

36. *Pisma,* IV, 109 (letter of 24 August–13 September 1879).

37. Still, these examples of humor tend to bear out Lytton Strachey's observation that humor in general serves Dostoevsky as a "makeweight," balancing the extravagance of his technique and eliminating the risk of unreality. See his *Characters and Commentaries* (New York, 1933), p. 172. Strachey's examples, it must be added, are less happy than his observation.

38. Wolfgang Kayser, *The Grotesque in Art and Literature,* trans. Ulrich Weisstein (Bloomington, 1963), pp. 184, 188; Balzac's name does not appear in the index; Dickens receives passing mention on seven pages, Dostoevsky on one. Lee B. Jennings and Mark Spilka have also recently provided informative and stimulating discussions of the grotesque, though in rather different contexts — tending to confirm the axiom upon which the present discussion rests; namely, that the word may fairly be used to mean a variety of things, so long as its meaning on any given occasion is indicated with sufficient precision to distinguish it from other possible (and equally legitimate) meanings. See Jennings, *The Ludicrous Demon: Aspects of the Grotesque in German Post-Romantic Prose* (Berkeley and Los Angeles, 1963), esp. ch. 1; and Spilka, *Dickens and Kafka: A Mutual Interpretation* (Bloomington, 1963).

39. *Préface de Cromwell,* ed. Maurice Souriau (Paris, n.d.), p. 195.

40. *Ibid.,* p. 203.

41. Quoted by I. I. Lapshin, "Komicheskoye v proizvedeniyakh Dostoevskogo," in Bem, *O Dostoevskom,* II, 45.

42. Cf. Bergson: "Indifference is its [the comic's] natural environment, for laughter has no greater foe than emotion." "Laughter," in Wylie Sypher, ed., *Comedy* (New York: Anchor Books, 1956), p. 63.

43. Lapshin, pp. 33–34.

44. *Pisma,* II, 71 (letter of 1–13 January 1868 to S. A. Ivanova).

45. Bitsilli makes a similar point in comparing Dostoevsky and Gogol. He finds the most striking difference between them the fact that, "in Gogol the disintegration of an individuality is presented as the result of its wretchedness, its obtuseness, its automatism," whereas in Dostoevsky the process appears in terms of a self-analytical search for identity. "Hence," Bitsilli concludes, "the tragic nature of his characters and of their vision of life, which borders . . . on comicality" (p. 44).

46. See Pletnev, pp. 63–80. Dostoevsky, Pletnev notes, "in creating his periodic *iconographically conventional* descriptions of nature, leaned consciously on the ecclesiastical literary tradition" (p. 80).

47. *Pisma,* I, 46.

48. Lapshin, pp. 34–35.

49. See Bardèche, p. 27.

50. For further discussion of this from a somewhat different point of view, see Grossman, "Dostoevsky — Khudozhnik," pp. 344–348.

51. Vinogradov, p. 278.

52. "Our Mutual Friend," in *The House of Fiction,* p. 257. See above, Chapter 3.

53. *The Phoenix and the Spider,* p. 28.

54. Quoted in Mochulsky, p. 407.

55. A modern student of the problem has culled nine principal variants from the critical literature on this subject; he lists mystical realism, realistic symbolism, transcendental or symbolic realism, the realism of an epileptic, demoniac realism, fantastic realism, realism of the nth degree, allegorical realism, and psychological realism. Johannes van der Eng, *Dostoevskij romancier* (The Hague, 1957), pp. 44–45.

Conclusion

1. Quoted in Philippe Van Tieghem, *Petite Histoire des grandes doctrines littéraires en France* (Paris, 1957), p. 198.

2. Lalo, *L'Art et la vie,* I (1946), 13.

3. Conrad, preface to *Within The Tides* (1915); quoted in Miriam Allott, *Novelists on the Novel* (New York, 1959), p. 54.

4. Zweig, *Three Masters* (New York, 1930), pp. ix–x.

5. Flaubert, *Correspondance,* III (Paris, 1927), 68.

6. See Grossman in Stepanov, ed., *Tvorchestvo Dostoevskogo,* pp. 338–339; see also his *Biblioteka Dostoevskogo* (Odessa, 1919).

7. See Tortel, "Esquisse d'un univers tragique ou le drame de la toute-puissance," pp. 367–381.

8. Dostoevsky's lifelong devotion included as well George Sand and Hoffmann, but the nature of his attachment to Sand is essentially that of his attachment to Dickens, just as the nature of his attachment to Hoffmann may be largely associated with his admiration for Balzac.

9. Grossman, "Balzak i Dostoevsky," *Russkaya mysl,* January 1914, p. 44.

10. D. Grigorovich, *Literaturnye vospominaniya* (Moscow-Leningrad, 1928), p. 135.

11. J.-W. Bienstock, "Dostoïevski et Balzac," *Mercure de France,* CLXXVI (1924), 424; Grossman, *Biblioteka Dostoevskogo,* p. 31.

12. Grossman, *Biblioteka Dostoevskogo,* p. 37.

13. *Pisma,* I, 47 (letter of 9 August 1838).

14. See *Pisma,* I, 465–466 (notes).

15. *Biblioteka dlya chteniya* (Library for Reading), 1835, vol. IX, "Inostrannaya slovesnost," p. 106; quoted in B. G. Reizov, *Balzak* (Leningrad, 1960), p. 169.

16. For a full discussion of the problem, see Reizov, pp. 163–172.

17. Quoted in Grossman, *Biblioteka Dostoevskogo,* p. 29.

18. See Grossman, "Iskusstvo romana u Dostoevskogo," *Svitok,* I (Moscow, 1922), esp. p. 82. One might similarly apply to Dostoevsky's style what Taine said of Balzac's: "This style is a gigantic chaos; everything is there: the arts, the sciences, the professions, all of history, philosophies, religions — there is nothing that has not furnished it with terms." "Balzac," in *Nouveaux Essais de critique et d'histoire* (Paris, 1866), p. 111.

19. *Le Père Goriot, Oeuvre,* IV, 147.

20. The remark is from Balzac's notebooks of the 1830s, printed in his *Pensées, sujets, fragments,* ed. J. Crépet (1910), p. 33; and quoted in Curtius, *Balzac,* p. 265.

21. V. Mikulich (pseud. of Lidiya Ivanovna Veselitskaya), *Vstrechi s pisatelyami* (Leningrad, 1929), pp. 155–156; the last quotation, she notes, is approximate, not verbatim.

22. See Grossman, *Biblioteka Dostoevskogo,* pp. 12, 139. His library contained French translations of *Dombey and Son* (1869) and *Bleak House* (1871).

23. *Diary of a Writer,* 1873, "Apropos of the Exhibition."

24. See Dostoevsky, *Pisma* (notes), II, 407; B. G. Reizov "K voprosu o vliyanii Dikkensa na Dostoevskogo," *Yazyk i literatura,* V (Leningrad, 1930), 253–270; I. I. Zamotin, *F. M. Dostoevsky v russkoy kritike,* I (Warsaw, 1913), 29; and Michael H. Futrell, "Dostoyevsky and Dickens," *English Miscellany,* VII (Rome, 1956), 41–89.

25. Reizov, "K voprosu o vlyiyanii Dikkensa na Dostoevskogo."

26. Trilling, *The Opposing Self* (New York, 1955), p. 57.

27. Praz, *The Hero in Eclipse in Victorian Fiction* (London, 1956), p. 388, n. 22.

28. Miller, *Charles Dickens,* pp. 240–243.

29. Johnson, *Charles Dickens,* I, 477. Johnson goes on to suggest a parallel here with the Myshkin-Rogozhin relationship, while Miller finds an equally plausible one with *The Brothers Karamazov* (pp. 128–129).

30. *Diary of a Writer,* January 1876.

31. Quoted in Johnson, II, 1155.

32. Gissing, *Charles Dickens,* pp. 293–294.

33. *Ibid.,* p. 285.

34. A. L. Bem, " 'Shinel' Gogolya i *Bednye lyudi* Dostoevskogo," *Zapiski russkago istoricheskago obshchestva v Prage,* I (1927), 51.

35. A. L. Bem, "Dostoevsky — Genialny chitatel," in *O Dostoevskom,* II, 19.

36. A far-ranging case for the influence of Pushkin, and particularly of his "Queen of Spades," on Dostoevsky's work is developed by Bem in his "Sumerki geroya (Etyud k rabote: Otrazheniya 'Pikovoy damy' v tvorchestve Dostoevskogo)," *Nauchnye trudy russkago narodnago universiteta v Prage,* IV (1931), 158–172.

37. *Za i protiv: Zametki o Dostoevskom* (Moscow, 1957), p. 180.

38. There is one recent treatment of this parallel — Yury Ivask's "Bodler i Dostoevsky," *Novy zhurnal,* no. 60 (1960) — in the course of which the author observes justly that an epigraph could be found in Baudelaire for every chapter of Dostoevsky's novels. In general, however, Ivask's headings or points of comparison are more impressive than the discussion they introduce.

39. *Pisma,* II, 291; quoted in Grossman, "Dostoevsky — Khudozhnik" (1959), p. 338. On this subject, see Grossman's discussion, pp. 336–339.

40. "Richard Wagner et Tannhäuser à Paris," *Oeuvres complètes* (Paris, 1954), p. 1073. In subsequent notes, this edition is abbreviated as *O. C.*

41. *Fusées, O. C.,* p. 1197.

42. "Exposition universelle de 1855," *O. C.*, p. 691.

43. *Fusées, O. C.*, p. 1199.

44. *De l'essence du rire* (Paris, 1925), pp. 23–24, 33, 39. This composite passage is taken from George Gibian's article, "The Grotesque in Dostoevsky," *Modern Fiction Studies*, IV, 3 (1958), 270, which pursues a line very different from the one in this study.

45. *Mon coeur mis à nu, O. C.*, p. 1211.

46. *The Romantic Agony* (New York, 1956), p. 144. Praz quotes Baudelaire's translation; I have substituted Poe's text.

47. *O. C.*, pp. 1198–1199. This is a sketch for his prose poem, "Le Galant Tireur."

48. *Mon coeur mis à nu, O. C.*, pp. 1207–1208.

49. *Ibid.*, p. 1224.

50. Lalo, I, 64–71.

51. "Dostoevsky and Parricide," in William Phillips, ed., *Art and Psychoanalysis* (New York, 1957), p. 3. Cf. Lalo, who refers to Baudelaire as "ce pénitent-né, enclin à 'pécher fortement' pour le plaisir anxieux, mais délicieux, de se repentir de même" (p. 65).

52. See L. P. Grossman, "Dostoevsky i Evropa," *Russkaya mysl*, no. 11 (1915), p. 70.

53. Miller, p. 251. The applicability to Lucien, Oliver Twist, Raskolnikov, and others is obvious enough. Less apparent perhaps is the extent to which such a formula fits Gogol's Petersburg tales — but it has been brilliantly developed by Bely in his *Masterstvo Gogolya*, pp. 51–52 and *passim*.

54. *Ibid.*, p. 35.

55. Ruskin, quoted in Mumford, *The Culture of Cities* (New York, 1938), p. 270.

56. Cf. Wladyslaw Folkierski, *Entre le classicisme et le romantisme* (Cracow-Paris, 1925), pp. 579–580. Folkierski argues that the eighteenth-century critical mentality, impressed with some of the works of pre-romanticism, found it impossible to explain this impressiveness by reference to the traditional *beau classique*, and so tried to get around the difficulty by creating the category of the sublime — a course of action that loosed a whole series of new aesthetic problems.

57. Stuart M. Tave has traced this process in *The Amiable Humorist* (Chicago, 1960); for a summary statement, see his preface, pp. vii–ix.

58. Berdyaev, *Dostoevsky*, p. 110. Cf. Ivanov, *Freedom and the Tragic Life*, part III, ch. I, "Demonology."

59. Cf. Baudelaire's notation in *Fusées:* "Ivresse religieuse des grandes villes. — Panthéisme. Moi, c'est tous; tous, c'est moi" (*O. C.*, p. 1190).

60. Quoted in Fernand Baldensperger, *Orientations etrangères chez Honoré de Balzac* (Paris, 1927), pp. 45–46.

61. On the subject of names in Balzac, see besides Baldensperger, Spoelberch de Lovenjoul, "A propos de la recherche et de la physionomie des noms dans l'oeuvre de H. de Balzac," in his *Causeries d'un chercheur*. For Dickens, see Elizabeth Hope Gordon, *The Naming of Characters in the Works of Charles Dickens* (Lincoln, Nebraska, 1917); and C. A. Bodelsen, "The Physiognomy of the Name," *A Review of English Literature*, II (July 1960), 39–48. For Dostoevsky, see A. L. Bem, "Lichnye imena u Dostoev-

skogo," in *Sbornik v chest na Prof. L. Miletich* (Sofia, 1933), pp. 409–434.

62. James, "The Lesson of Balzac," in *The House of Fiction*, p. 71.

63. Shklovsky, *Za i protiv*, p. 188.

64. Grossman, "Dostoevsky — Khudozhnik" (1959), p. 399.

65. *The Dehumanization of Art and Other Writings on Art and Culture* (New York, 1956), p. 61.

66. *Ibid.*, p. 62.

67. *Ibid.*, p. 95.

Index